HOW TO FILE FOR CHAPTER 11 BUSINESS BANKRUPTCY WITH OR WITHOUT A LAWYER

by
Benji O. Anosike, B.B.A., M.A., Ph.D.

First Edition, January 1983
Second (Fully Revised) Edition, April 1992
Third Revised Edition, March 2004

Library of Congress Cataloging-in-Publication Data

Anosike, Benji O.
  How to file for chapter 11 business bankruptcy with or without a lawyer / by Benji O. Anosike.
    p. cm.
  Includes bibliographical references and index.
  ISBN 0-932704-61-1
   1. Bankruptcy--United States--Popular works. 2. Bankruptcy--United States--Forms. 3. Corporate reorganizations--United States--Popular works. 4. Corporate reorganizations--United States--Forms. I. Title.

KF1544.Z9A56 2004
346.7307'8--dc22

2003070047

D1567642

Printed in the United States of America
ISBN: 0-932704-61-1
Library of Congress Catalog Number:

Published by:

Do-It-Yourself Legal Publishers
60 Park Place
Newark, NJ 07102

Acknowledgements.

We are deeply grateful and indebted to the following persons and/or entities: to Julius Blumberg, Inc., the New York legal forms printer, whose sample forms are reproduced in the text for illustration; to **Matthew Bender and Company, Inc.**, the New York publisher of the authoritative Collier on Bankruptcy volumes, whose forms and documents are extensively used on the pages of this manual for illustrations, courtesy of Matthew Bender; and to Lakewood, Colorado's John H. Williamson, the bankruptcy legal practitioner and authority, author of The Attorney's Handbook on Chapter 11 Bankruptcy and chapter 13, and the publisher, Argyle publishing company, for their excellent volumes and a limited number of select forms and documents reproduced therefrom for our own illustrative purposes on the pages of this text; and many, many others too numerous to mention herein. All of the above named parties have, in one way or the other, by their deeds, pioneering works and/or research in the field – and by their unselfish readiness to share and to disseminate the fruits thereof – made the present undertaking both more purposeful and easier for the author and the present publisher.

THE PUBLISHER'S DISCLAIMER

TABLE OF CONTENTS

Page

FOREWORD: The Publisher's Message . . . . i-vii
PREFACE AND INTRODUCTION TO THIS EDITION 1-7

Chapter

1. SOME PRELIMINARY BACKGROUND INFORMATION
What is Chapter 11 Bankruptcy? 9
What is the Nature of the Reliefs Obtainable From Filing Chapter 11 Bankruptcy? 9
What Could Lead a Company to File For Chapter 11? 11
Should You File For Chapter 11? 13
Some Alternatives to Chapter 11 14
How Does Chapter 11 Basically Work in a Summary Nutshell? 16
How Does Chapter 11 Compare Against Chapter 13 Bankruptcy? 17

**2. LET'S LEARN A FEW THINGS FROM THE CASE HISTORY OF A MAJOR AMERICAN COMPANY
THAT WENT THROUGH CHAPTER 11: THE ITEL CORPORATION** 19-23

**3. THE STEP-BY-STEP PROCEDURES FOR FILING FOR & PROCESSING A
CHAPTER 11 CASE FROM START TO FINISH** 25

Step 1: Determine That You Meet the Eligibility Requirements to File Under Chapter 11 26

Step 2: Gather Necessary Information & Identify The Causes of the Debtor's Financial Problems 27
Step 3: Make Preliminary Assessment of The Case 28
Collect the Information Needed To Prepare the Chapter 11 filing Forms 28
Determine If Preferential or Fraudulent Transfers Were Made 29
Determine If You Should Elect To Be Treated as A "Small Business" 30
Determine Whether & When To Employ An Attorney 30
Step 4: Order the Initial Forms You'll Need To File the Bankruptcy 31
Step 5: Fill Out The Initial Petition Forms 31
Step 6: Properly Sign The Forms & File Them With the Court 68
The Venue, Properly Place/Court District Where To File 68
The Chapter 11 Filing Fees 69
Documents To File 69
Filing an "Emergency" Case Situation 69
Time and Notice requirement 70
Court Notifies Creditors of the Bankruptcy Filing & Its Order of Relief 70
Step 7: Unless You Are a "Small Business," The U.S. Trustee Will Will Probably Appoint The
Committee of Creditors 71
Why Would Additional Committees Be Warranted 72
The Powers and Duties of the Creditors' Committees 72
Step 8: Attend the Meeting Or Meetings of Creditors 76

Step 9: If a Trustee is Appointed, Here's What to Do 79
What's the Significance of a Trustee Being Appointed? 79
Typically, A Trustee Would Probably not be Appointed in Your Case 79
How the Trustee's Appointment Could be Terminated 81
Step 10: If an Examiner is Appointed, Here's What to Do 81
The Conditions Under Which One May be Appointed 81
What a Chapter 11 Examiner Does 81

Step 11: You'll Probably Remain as "Debtor in Possession." Here are Your
Legal Rights, Powers & Duties 82

Step 12: Work on Putting Together a Plan of Reorganization Within the Time Required 84

Step 13: Know the Basic Requirements For an Acceptable Reorganization Plan 85

Step 14: Fulfill the Disclosure Requirements First, Before Making Any
Solicitations For Plan Acceptances From Creditors & Others 89
 The Disclosure Statement & Hearing 89
 The Great Importance of This Statement In Chap. 11 Cases 91
 Coming Up With An Acceptable Disclosure Statement – Providing "Adequate Information"... 91
 What a Good Disclosure Statement Should Contain. 92

Step 15: You May Now Commence Solicitations For Votes of Acceptance For Your
Proposed Plan From Creditors & Others 94
 Procedures For Formal Solicitation of Votes on the Plan 95
 Who Are Eligible to Cast Ballots of Acceptance (or Rejection) on the Plan? 95
 How a Ballot is Counted as an Acceptance or a Rejection 96
 What Constitutes a Binding Acceptance of a Plan? 96
 How Does the Court Compute Whether the Requisite Majorities Have Been Achieved? 97

Step 16: Do You Want to Modify the Plan? Here's How 97

Step 17: Attend the Court Confirmation Hearings on the Proposed Plan 98
 What Are the Procedures in Confirmation Hearings? 100
  Section 1129(a) Confirmation Standards 101
  Section 1129(b) or "Cram Down" Alternative Confirmation Standards 105

Step 18: Carry Out the Provisions of the Court-Confirmed Plan of Reorganization 107

**4. THE LEGAL EFFECT OF COURT CONFIRMATION OF A REORGANIZATION
PLAN FOR THE DEBTOR, CREDITORS, SHAREHOLDERS, & OTHERS** 109-110

**5. HANDLING SOME OF THE PRACTICAL PROBLEMS INVOLVED IN IMPLEMENTING
THE CHAPTER 11 PLAN** 111
The Effects of the Order Of Confirmation 111
Nature of the Chapter 11 Discharge 111
Implementation, Distribution and Consummation of the Plan 112
Post-Confirmation Functions To Be Performed Under The Plan 112
Conditions Precedent To Plan Implementation 113
Actual Implementation of the Plan 113
Modifying Plan After Confirmation 114
Closing The Chapter 11 Case 114

**6. HANDLING SOME COMMON PRACTICAL PROBLEMS YOU MAY ENCOUNTER
AS A DEBTOR IN POSSESSION; THE PROCEDURES INVOLVED** 116
Handling of Automatic Stay Matters 117
Relief From Stay Based on Debtor's Lack of Equity in Property 117
Relief From Stay Based on Cause 118
Operation of the Business By the Debtor In Possession 120
Use, Sale or Lease of Cash Collaterals by Debtor In Possession 123
What Constitutes Cash Collateral? 123
Making Use of Cash Collateral 124
Use, Sale or Lease of Other Estate Property Other than Cash Collateral 125
Handling Claims & Security Interests by Debtor In Possession 126
Duty to Examine Proofs of Claim & File Objections 127
Handling Executory Contracts & Expired Leases 130

APPENDICES

A. OTHER SAMPLE BANKRUPTCY FORMS & REPORTS CITED IN THE MANUAL AND/OR
TYPICALLY USABLE IN CHAPTER 11 CASES (WHERE TO FIND THEM) 133-4

B. THE LEGAL POWERS & RESPONSIBILITIES OF A TRUSTEE 197

C. CLASSIFICATION OF CLAIMS & INTERESTS 199
    Classification Categories For Claims 200
        Nonpriority Prepetition Unsecured Claims 200
        Priority Claims 200
        Secured Claims 200
        Subordinated Claims 200
    Classification Categories for Interests 201
    Principles Governing Classification of Claims & Interests for
        Purpose of Treatment Under the Plan 201
    Priority of Claims & Interests 203
    Classification Categories 203
        Secured Claims 203
        Superpriority Claims 203
        Priority Unsecured Claims 204
        Nonpriority Unsecured Claims 204
        Subordinated & Nonpriority Unsecured Claims 204
        Interests 204

D. THE CONCEPT OF "IMPAIRMENT" OF CLAIMS OR INTERESTS IN CHAPTER 11 CASES . . 205-6

E. U.S. BANKRUPTCY COURT LOCATIONS IN EACH STATE 207-213

F. GLOSSARY OF TERMS & SOME RELEVANT DEFINITIONS 214-224

G. SOME BIBLIOGRAPHY 226

H. ORDERING YOUR BANKRUPTCY FORMS 228

I. LIST OF OTHER PUBLICATIONS FROM DO-IT-YOURSELF LEGAL PUBLISHERS 229

INDEX 230

FOREWORD:

THE PUBLISHER'S MESSAGE

To All Our Dear Readers:

The Unprecedented Rate of Business Bankruptcies Today

Wouldn't you please take even a wild guess at this little "quiz"? **Question:** What one element would you say all these famous American companies have in common—Penn Central Corporation, Continental Steel Corporation (formerly Penn-Dixie Steel Corporation), Toys 'R' Us, Inc. (formerly Interstate Stoves Inc.), Miller-Wohl, and Dynamic Corporation of America? **Answer:** What they have in common is a kind of "new lease on life" in their past history, a rescue from a critical financial crisis in which they had been involved – thanks to Chapter 11 of the Federal Bankruptcy Law, which permits financially distressed companies (as opposed to individuals) to "reorganize" under the protection of this law!

In all likelihood, it would probably be no news to you that the United States—indeed the western industrialized community as a whole—has lately been experiencing a flood of business (as well as non-business) failures, insolvencies and bankruptcies, the like of which has not been seen since the Great Depression!* (See the graph below). *The message? One way it could be summed up is: that as a business executive or operator of any kind in today's climate, you can hardly do any better than adequately familiarize yourself with the basic processes and procedures of the on fundamental source of relief available under the law for a company which somehow finds itself in the midst of serious financial distress—the Chapter 11 reorganization relief.*

Increasingly, a growing number of companies in financial difficulties, big and small, look to one principal arena for protection or relief from their problems: BUSINESS REORGANIZATION UNDER CHAPTER 11 OF THE U.S. BANKRUPTCY CODE.

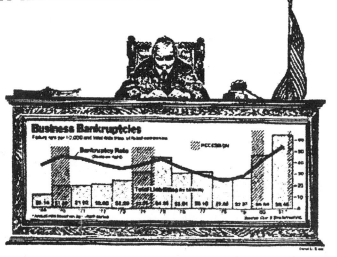

Major Bankruptcies Since January 1981	Total Liabilities At Time of Filing ($ millions)
Itel	$1,700.0
Seatrain Lines	785.5
AM International	510.0
McClouth Steel	322.8
Lionel Corporation	165.3
Sambo's Restaurants	130.3
Bobbie Brooks	62.0
Cooper-Jarrett	28.0
J.W. Mays	20.2
Advent Corporation	14.6
Jartran	n.a.

n.a. Not available.
Securities and Exchange Commission, Office of U.S. Trustee

A Surge of Failures in Europe in 1982

Troubled European Companies		
In millions of dollars, translated at current exchange rates		
Company	Total Debt Outstanding	Business
AEG Telefunken (West Germany)	$2,200	Electrical products
Banco Ambrosiano (Italy)	400	Banks, industrial holdings
Laker Airways (Britain)	359	Airlines
Rollei Werke (West Germany)	300	Cameras
Agache-Willot (France)	217	Textiles
Wienerwald (Switzerland)	111	Restaurants
Van Delden (West Germany)	70	Textiles
DeLorean Motor (Britain)	24	Autos

Why The "New Popularity" of Chapter 11 Among America's Business Executives?

Interestingly, historically, the American corporate executive has been reputed to view the term "bankruptcy" with timidity and in dread. Harvey R. Miller, a New York bankruptcy attorney and expert, once described the traditional image of the average American corporate and business executive this way:

> "...many corporate executives dread [bankruptcy]. To some chief executives, bankruptcy in business means abject failure no less than personal bankruptcy does, with all the associated stigma.... And too often, the delay [by executives to consider the bankruptcy option] results in the unnecessary termination of the business."*

A logical question, then, is: Why? Why this new—and still growing—"romance" of the Chapter 11 bankruptcy by the American business community, or, conversely, this sudden apparent "sex appeal" of bankruptcy to this group? An increasing "street smartness"—a kind of pragmatic sophistication—on the part of the traditional American business operator, perhaps. There are bits of evidence pointing to a slow but steady awakening of the business and financial community to the harsh reality that failure, even delay, in taking a timely advantage of the relief of bankruptcy provided under the law, out of some code of personal morality, is not only bad business, but also one which can turn a bad but still salvageable situation into a disastrous one!**

How & Why Chapter 11 Could Be The Failing Businessman's Ultimate Best Friend

Make no mistake about this. A growing number of businessmen and women, whatever their private moral or philosophical view of bankruptcy, are fast coming to the tortured realization that, in the final analysis, for a company that somehow finds itself in a serious financial crisis today, the Chapter 11 shelter is just about "the only game in town"—the ultimate viable mechanism for relief available to them under the law! In today's business climate of mounting record-level in-

---

*Quoted from "Often It Pays To Go Bankrupt," *The N.Y. Times*, April 18, 1982.

**"After more than 20 years of practicing bankruptcy law," says Harvey R. Miller, "the biggest failure I see is the inability of business to recognize soon enough that they should obtain relief under the [bankruptcy] law.... too often resulting in the unnecessary termination of business."

terest rates, depressed domestic markets, diminished or vanishing foreign markets, ravaging infla-
tion, and great financial distress, generally, the reality has apparently begun to come more and
more clear with each passing day!

*Centrally, only the Chapter 11 mechanism could "buy" you and your company, when in a state
of extreme financial distress, that critical extra margin of time and opportunity you might desper-
ately need to pull yourself together and, probably,put your financial house back into shape; with
the protection the bankruptcy law gives you, you shall have had a much-needed stable, noncrisis
environment in which your management, creditors, and other interested parties may make decisions—deliberately and rationally—on issues of continuation, reorganization, or liquidation of
the company.*

But there's more that the Chapter 11 does for you. A lot more. For one thing, once in Chapter
11, you'll be relieved of the often decisive burden of having to meet accruing interest payments on
most of your debts. The horrendous pressure of hundreds, possibly thousands, of creditors competing with each other to have you into court and obtain judgments against you, or to seize or slap
liens upon your business inventory or assets—all actions of whatever kind that would, in short,
precipitate your liquidation—are automatically halted. The effect of these, in turn, is to provide
your struggling company with a number of welcome opportunities: opportunities to cut losses and
expenses, to effect economies in the company's operations, to renegotiate and reschedule your
debt repayment, and, ultimately, to rescue and rehabilitate the company in one form or another.

Even then, there are safeguards* built into the system which ensure that protection is not one-
sided or wholly slanted in favor of the debtor, but accords equal treatment to all similarly situated
creditors, stockholders, and other interested parties on a nondiscriminatory basis. *The ultimate
result is, in short, a system that winds up being beneficial to both the creditor, the debtor and
stockholder alike, for, as Patrick Murphy, an experienced San Francisco bankruptcy lawyer quite
accurately put it, "It's only rehabilitated debtors who repay debts."*

Consider The Congressional Rationale For Enacting The Law

Consider, for a moment, the facts of why Congress felt it most wise and necessary, even urgent,
to enact the modern business bankruptcy law, in the first place. Indeed, Congress revised the business bankruptcy law only in 1978 and strengthened the unique business reorganization and rehabilitation aspects of the law to make that goal the principal purpose of the system.

The motivating force? The harsh but enduring lessons of the nation's past, specifically of the
Great Depression of the 1930's were not lost on Congress: namely, that there are many cases when
the overall human, national and business interests are best served by protecting a financially distressed company and giving it a chance at getting "a new lease on life," as opposed to merely leaving the company totally to itself to settle its financial scores with its creditors—a path to an almost
certain dismemberment and total shutdown.

The purpose of the law should not be mistaken, however. The real purpose intended by the business bankruptcy system (and its laws) is not to mandate that every financially failing or distressed
company that files for reorganization be necessarily and definitely   kept alive—in every instance. Not at all! **Rather, its underlying principle is to "mandate" that some time and opportunity is allowed to enable all interested parties (the debtor, shareholders, creditors, etc.) to gather the
relevant facts to make the crucial decision as to whether the company should reorganize and stay
alive, on the one hand, or liquidate and die, on the other hand.** The point of the law is that, in matters such as this, the mere act of making that choice alone—the choice between reorganization and
liquidation—invariably has many national and human consequences that extend beyond the purely private interests of the creditors and the investors only.

---

*e.g., the right to petition to place a company under reorganization against its will, and, under certain circumstances, the
opportunity to file their own reorganization plan, the right to "adequate protection" for the company's use of secured collateral while it is under reorganization.

Chapter 11 Has Often Served Well The Higher Interests Of Society At Large

In the recent history of the United States, many major companies* (as well, of course, as smaller ones) have had to take advantage of the protections provided under the bankruptcy law by undergoing reorganizations. As in most things in human situations, not all of these companies fared better even after they had undergone reorganization. Nevertheless, what is more relevant for a businessman seriously in debt, is the encouraging reminder that many many companies that would almost certainly have gone out of business otherwise, have been successfully reorganized and been saved—thanks to Chapter 11. And many—Penn Dixie Corp. (now Continental Steel Corp.), Toys 'R' Us Inc., Penn Central Corporation, Dynamics Corp. of America, W.T. Grant & Company, and others—have emerged from Chapter 11 and gone ahead to attain greater heights in business!

And here's the central point here: In each of these instances where there's been a post-bankruptcy survival and subsequent success by the reorganized company, it has been during—and because of—the bankruptcy reorganization process that the extent of the company's shortcomings were analyzed and the determination made as to whether such shortcomings were serious enough to warrant letting the company die, and if not, what remedial measures to undertake to rehabilitate the company. And those successfully rehabilitated businesses have, of course, benefitted their creditors, as well as the communities of their operation and the nation—by providing employment, income, revival of the communities, etc.

What it all boils down to, then, is that, as Harvey K. Miller sums it up, "There are many instances [in today's highly specialized and technological economy] where capital goods are technologically so specialized that they cannot be used for other manufacturing purposes. Consequently, it is not a realistic alternative to liquidate the business. In such cases, the fact of current losses is not a sufficient reason for halting production and closing down for good. Such businesses may deserve more time and attention in a noncrisis atmosphere while their ills are aired and viability restored."**

What This Manual Is Meant to Do For You: Become "Bankruptcy Literate"!

Take this from us, friends: Whatever your personal wish or preference (wouldn't we all like never to have to say the word 'bankruptcy'!), the high probability in contemporary business climate is that the word "bankruptcy" and all that goes with that are matters about which you are likely to hear more and more of, not less, in the foreseeable months and years ahead. Increasingly, the name of the game for business operators in general, and operators of financially distressed businesses (of which there would continue to be plenty!), in particular, would be this: Are you at least minimally **"bankruptcy literate"**? How much do you know about the basics, at least; some ideas about the elementary financial (and legal) aspects of the Chapter 11 procedures—matters such as whether at all you should file for one or just plain begin to think about or plan for it; what reliefs you would expect from a Chapter 11; at what stage or level of your financial difficulties to file (if at all), or merely begin to contemplate filing, or at least begin calling in some financial professionals to assess the prospects of filing; when you can still get the optimum benefit out of bankruptcy and can still avoid running the risk of running up more debts, losses or further erosion of the value of your assets to the point perhaps where reorganization may even become unprofitable or unwarranted? In short, some ideas of the general procedures in Chapter 11 and your potential role in the procedures, if it should ever become necessary!?

The point here is that, as we at least see it, the realities of the current and foreseeable economic

---

*The list of such recently reorganized companies includes such big names in American business as Penn Central Company, W.T. Grant & Company, Daylin Inc., Korvette's, Equity Funding, Food Fair Inc., Railway Express Agency, Diamond Reo Motors, Penn Dixie Steel Corporation (now the Continental Steel Corporation), Toys 'R' Us Inc., Moller-Wohl, Itel Corporation, Seatrain Lines, AM International, McClouth Steel, Lionel Corporation, Sambo's Restaurants, Bobbie Brooks, Cooper Jarrett, J.W. Mays, Advent Corporation, Jartran, Braniff Airlines International Corporation, Wickes Companies, White Motors, and Manville Corporation—to name just a few.

** "Often It Pays To Go Bankrupt," *The N.Y. Times,* April 18, 1982.

and financial climate are ones that make it increasingly important and relevant, even necessary, that every business executive or operator, or a would-be one, should at least be minimally "bankruptcy literate"—the same way as the average manager would be expected to possess a minimum command of the basics in business finance, accounting, marketing, and the like. And any business operator of today who ignores this "new reality" does so at his own (and his investors' and creditors') peril and competitive disadvantage!

With this present manual-guide and its simplified, step-by-step treatment of the subject readily in hand, never again should the average business owner or operator have a legitimate excuse for going without this crucial business knowledge—and legal protection—of contemporary times!! This is one central purpose this publication is meant to serve you.

Just as purposefully, this manual equally seeks to serve other equally vital purposes and uses to you. The goal is: i) to simplify and de-mystify (for the non-lawyer as well as the lawyer alike) the concept and procedures of business bankruptcy by providing the essential facts and information, as opposed to fairy tales or mythologies; and ii) to promote and commonize, among the nation's business executors and operators, the responsible use, or, at least, consideration of the unique features provided by the business bankruptcy option in a search for solution to an ailing or financially distressed company.

Mass Misconceptions And Ignorance About Business Bankruptcy Abound Among The Public, Lawyers And Non-Lawyers, Alike!

It should, perhaps, come as no surprise to anyone that mythologies, misconceptions, and plain mass ignorance about bankruptcy are grossly widespread among America's business executives. A case in point: In March 1981 the Baptist Medical Center of New York had filed for Chapter 11 with $6 million in debts. The executives of the center were surprised when the stigma and public community disapproval they expected never materialized. "I thought that after going into Chapter 11 bankruptcy there was no tomorrow—that it would be a disgrace and an embarrassment," declared Thomas L. Byram, the executive director of the center. "With the new Federal [bankruptcy] code, we were able to take some of our contracts which were financially killing us, and get revised contracts that were more economically sound for us. Chapter 11 helped us." "Few people understand bankruptcy," explains David P. Michaels, a New Jersey based bankruptcy trustee and consultant to troubled companies who has officiated as trustee for the past eight years.

Nor is such widespread ignorance and misconception about bankruptcy matters limited only to the non-lawyer. Quite to the contrary, the phenomenon is, oddly enough, sadly widespread even among the lawyers themselves. Case in point: When the **Manville Corporation,** the nation's largest asbestos company, filed for Chapter 11 in August 1982, over 50 attorneys representing thousands of persons who had previously filed asbestos-related personal injury suits against Manville descended on a South Carolina island for two days of preliminary strategy planning and briefings on bankruptcy law procedures. At the end of the two days of the South Carolina educational sessions, the lawyers had still not learned enough, and the sessions were moved to New York and continued there by expert bankruptcy lawyers and law professors hired to provide the instructions ("briefings"). Many of the lawyers in attendance candidly admitted their lack of familiarity with bankruptcy laws. "Before this thing, I didn't know how to spell bankruptcy," said one attorney, who was said to be speaking for many of his colleagues. "I think we all know how to do that now."*

That myths should be widely substituted for facts in such "elite" and "smart" echelons of our society, is, by and large, something borne out of the attitude of timidity and sense of repulsion with which the business and legal communities, indeed, the general public, have traditionally approached bankruptcy. By rejecting the bankruptcy option outright and shutting their minds to the system and its procedures, these persons remain ignorant of the real facts, and must consequently rely on myths, (mis)conceptions and (mis)perceptions. **The most tragic thing about this, though, is that it is this kind of psychological disposition that often leads the business executive or the lawyer to neglect bringing a timely use of the bankruptcy option into play until it shall have become virtually too late for the company.***

---

*Account and quotations from "Lawyers Plan Strategy Against Manville," *The N.Y. Times,* Aug. 30, 1982. p. D3

**As Miller sums it up, "In effect, the refusal [of these executives] to consider the relief that Congress has made available often results in the financially distressed business feeding upon itself until there is nothing left to rehabilitate."

For once, then, with the publication of this manual, **business bankruptcy, the double-headed monster and ultra taboo of the business world,** would be taken out of the closet, stripped naked of mythologies and legal and technical mumbo jumbo, and made accessible to the public for the benefit of the layman and the expert alike!

This manual is, to our knowledge, the first and only one of its kind around or ever attempted: A comprehensive, nationally-oriented how-to-do-it publication on this mysterious, often dreaded, but increasingly recurring issue in the business world, written in layman's language for use by the lay business person; one that is written on business (as opposed to personal) bankruptcy and with the expressed purpose of making a kind of 'mini bankruptcy expert' out of the non-lawyer and the lawyer alike with a minimum expenditure of time, effort or money. Yet, in this Publisher's considered view, never in the nation's history has the need and relevance of an instructional manual of this type on the subject been more apparent or urgent than in this epoch of such mounting historic business failures and financial distress in the nation, indeed in the western industrialized world at large!

But one or two words of caution are called for. First, you must read through the manual, every word of every chapter (including the footnotes, especially!), from the beginning to the end, if you are to derive the most benefit from the manual. Do not just glance through or hastily skim around it. *Secondly, the central use and purpose to which this manual should be put should not be mistaken:* Look at this manual -- and use it -- primarily as a source book, a source by which you are to acquire the information, education, appreciation, knowledge, and understanding of the concepts and procedures involved. It is of course only logical to expect that, having acquired such a wealth of knowledge, some readers may want to "put it to work" by way of proceeding to actually drawing up the bankruptcy court papers themselves, and undertaking the filing, processing and prosecution of their cases in court. Or, just as importantly, they may simply prefer to stop at putting such knowledge to work as merely a tool in assessing or planning for the bankruptcy option, or for better advising or understanding the professional they employ who directly undertakes the bankruptcy filing for them.

Newark, New Jersey

Thank you again.

— — DO-IT-YOURSELF LEGAL PUBLISHERS

PREFACE TO THIS EDITION
AND INTRODUCTION

HOW TO GET THE MOST OUT OF THIS MANUAL

Just over two decades Ago, in the early 1980s, when the first edition of this guidebook was published, my Publisher, the Do-It-Yourself Law Publishers, in their FOREWORD to that edition, depicted the prevailing fashion of the time among the nation's financially troubled business operators and executives and pointedly bemoaned the *"attitude of timidity and sense of repulsion with which the business and legal communities, in deed, the general public, have traditionally approached bankruptcy."* The publishers went on, adding:

> "By rejecting the bankruptcy option outright and shutting their minds to the system and its procedures, these persons [i.e., the American business managers and executives] remain ignorant of the facts...and the ultimate tragedy about this is that it is this kind of psychological disposition that often leads the business executive and the lawyer to neglect bringing a timely use of the bankruptcy option into play until it shall have become virtually too late for the company [to be salvaged through bankruptcy]."*

That characterization — the part, particularly, about the average American business manager and executive seeming somewhat intimidated and slow to at least examine or consider the bankruptcy option — was accurate. That is, accurate for that time. Quite accurate. Fortunately, that's not so anymore, though — TODAY!

Dramatic Change in the "stigma" of Bankruptcy in America

Today, as of the time of the research and writing of this revised edition of the manual some nine or ten years later, much has dramatically changed in the American bankruptcy world, in general, and in the world of business bankruptcy and Chapter 11, in particular. Much has changed in varying respects and areas — in the text of the law, in the procedures, and the legal forms used in filing for bankruptcy, in the sheer numbers of bankruptcy filings and the kinds of companies and debtors who file for bankruptcy, etc., etc. But those are comparatively the minor points. BY FAR, THE MOST FUNDAMENTAL AND SWEEPING TRANSFORMATION OF ALL IN THIS REGARD, EXPERTS AND OBSERVERS SAY, HAS BEEN THIS: the dramatic turn around in the public attitude of Americans towards bankruptcy! Experts see this, in a word, as being the most profound change because of what this says or portends, actually or potentially, for the "bankruptcy mentality" of the society at large. In any event, whatever the rationale or reasons for it,* *whether it is a

---

* "Foreword: The Publisher's Message," in *How to File for 'Chapter 11' Bankruptcy Relief From Your Business Debts,* (1983) at p. **vi**

**The current record level in bankruptcy filings in the early 1990's, judged by many experts as one of the all-time highest in United States history, has been largely attributed by experts and analysts to essentially the frenetic corporate (and consumer) borrowings that was indulged in by American businesses, and actively encouraged by banks and credit companies, in the high-flying 'go-go' years of the 1980's. The scenario is given this way: company debt, accumulated by American companies through the 1980's, is far higher today, by any measure, than it was in the eight previous national recessions since World War II, and as industrial production, employment and sales had shrunk and revenue fallen in the current recession — the usual hallmarks of recessions — indebted companies run short of cash to pay loan installments that fall due, forcing many to default and, increasingly, to declare bankruptcy. (See "How Bankruptcy Can Feed Doubt," *New York Times,* Dec. 17, 1990, p. D2.) And for an explanation of the broader, historical underpinnings, see *The Bankruptcy of America,* by Stephen D. Wilson, (Ridge Mills Press: Germantown, TN: 1991).

THE TIDE OF BANKRUPTCY FILINGS OVER THE DECADES

A look at the trends

Twenty years ago, consumers accounted for about 82 percent of all filings, but the percentage has grown dramatically. Last year, it reached 97 percent.

That's because the number of personal filings has ballooned, more than tripling in 20 years, while the number of total business filings has been slowly shrinking.

About five years ago, filings by public companies began to rise. This chart shows a rolling four-year average, in order to more fairly illustrate the trend.

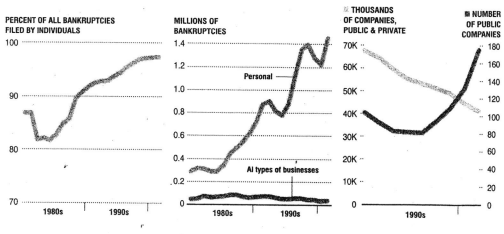

The bigger they are

Seven of the 15 biggest bankruptcies on record have come since the start of 2001. Another six were casualties of the savings and loan crisis of the late '80s and early '90s.

COMPANY	FILING DATE	ASSETS
1. Enron Corp.	12/2/2001	$63.4 billion

The scandal-plagued energy trader is trying to bounce back as a far smaller company.

| 2. Texaco Inc. | 4/12/1987 | $35.9 billion |

The oil industry giant was protecting itself from an $11 billion court judgment it lost in a battle with rival Pennzoil.

| 3. Financial Corp. of America | 9/9/1988 | $33.9 billion |

The biggest victim of the savings & loan debacle, Financial Corp. was the holding company for the American Savings and Loan Association.

| 4. Global Crossing Ltd. | 1/28/2002 | $25.5 billion |

The debt-strapped telecom was the biggest bankruptcy in the industry over the past year.

| 5. Pacific Gas & Electric | 4/6/2001 | $21.5 billion |

California's largest utility sought protection at the height of last year's energy crisis there.

| 6. MCorp | 3/31/1989 | $20.2 billion |

Once Texas' second-largest bank holding company, MCorp took the Federal Reserve all the way to the Supreme Court, claiming the Fed couldn't force it to bail out its failing subsidiaries. MCorp lost.

| 7. Kmart Corp. | 1/22/2002 | $17.0 billion |

January's filing was the biggest ever for a retailer.

| 8. First Executive Corp. | 5/13/1991 | $15.2 billion |

Another casualty of the S&L crisis of the early '90s.

| 9. Gibraltar Financial Corp. | 2/8/1990 | $15.0 billion |

Gibraltar was forced into bankruptcy by Bank of America, which was trustee for holders of nearly $100 million in Gibraltar junk bonds.

| 10. FINOVA Group Inc. | 3/7/2001 | $14.1 billion |

Super-investor Warren Buffett helped bring the lender out of bankruptcy last year.

| 11. HomeFed Corp. | 10/22/1992 | $13.9 billion |

The year before its filing, the savings bank lost more than $800 million.

| 12. Southeast Banking Corp. | 9/20/1991 | $13.4 billion |

Once Florida's largest company and a lender to blue-chip clients, its bankruptcy caused a local scandal. The bank claimed the FDIC seized it to make tens of millions of dollars by selling it to First Union.

| 13. Reliance Group Hldgs. | 6/12/2001 | $12.6 billion |

Once the flagship of investor Saul Steinberg's financial empire, its insurance subsidiary was taken over by the Pennsylvania Insurance Department. One of its largest bondholders was Carl Icahn.

| 14. Imperial Corp. of Amer. | 2/28/1990 | $12.3 billion |

Another S&L casualty, it was the parent of Imperial Savings, which held more than $1.3 billion in junk bonds.

| 15. Federal-Mogul Corp. | 10/1/2001 | $10.2 billion |

One of the world's largest auto parts makers, it filed to help resolve its asbestos claims.

consequence of the long-running frequent national recessions in the country, or in spite of it, what almost everyone completely agrees on is that what has been the historical reluctance on the part of Americans to file for bankruptcy has undergone a drastic erosion in recent months and years, and that the shame and stigma previously associated with insolvency or filing for bankruptcy, is now largely a thing of the past, as large numbers of American companies, big and small, as well as individuals, have trooped to the bankruptcy courts in recent times in search of a remedy for their debt problems in record numbers and at record pace unmatched in the past.*

Suffice it to say, simply, that most experts and observers viewing the present business (and personal) bankruptcy scene even today in the early 21st century when there is an all-time record bankruptcy filings by personal and business debtors alike, would probably agree with the expert assessment made by Dr. Stanley Fisher, a Livingston, New Jersey counseling psychologist and official of the New Jersey Psychological Association, that *"There's no question that the stigma as we usually know it has been removed from bankruptcy [among Americans]. There's a whole group of people [today] who see it as a good business maneuver."**

And, as another public debt expert, **Segal Togut**, a New York City bankruptcy lawyer and Chapter 11 specialist put it, *"Nowadays, [especially with many large corporations filing for Chapter 11, the practice has now] gained respectability. The public's perception is that they don't care whether a company is in bankruptcy or not."***

Alright. So we have it! That's the world we've come to today; the "real world" we have to function in today, like it or not. But, given that fact, *HERE'S THE BIG QUESTION:* how do you and others like you, business owners, operators and managers of today (or of the foreseeable future) operating in today's bankruptcy-colored business environment, begin to acquire those tools of "bankruptcy literacy" which experts now acknowledge being so vital, even indispensable, in these current unsettling economic times? And, just as well, how do you do this AFFORDABLY, in a READILY ACCESSIBLE WAY?

This is exactly the critical question to which the manual provides the businessman and woman with an answer — a straightforward, practical, and above all, affordable but effective answer.

The purpose and mission of this manual remains, for this author, the same as in the past. It's simple: to simplify and demystify, for the average business manager out there in the "real world," the basic procedures and processes involved in business bankruptcy and thereby reduce the need for the manager to resort to mythologies and misconceptions in such matters; and to foster, even promote and commonize, among American business managers and executives the RESPONSIBLE use and consideration of the unique remedies offered by the Chapter 11 option for a company confronted with

---

*In 1990, for example, more than 1300 companies were filing for bankruptcy each week, a pace rarely matched in the past, according to Dun & Bradstreet Corporation, the national authority which tracks such data nationwide. More than 55,000 companies declared bankruptcy in the 11 months from January to November 1990, listing $64.1 billion in debts they cannot pay, a sum which is equal to 1.1 percent of the gross national product and whose comparative historical magnitude can be measured by realizing that not since the Depression has the level even approached 1 percent of G.N.P. Since 1978 (to 1992), more than 6 million companies and individuals have marched into the nation's bankruptcy courts — a number equal to more than all the filings up to that point combined since the turn of the present century. In the New York City region, for example, one of the hardest hit areas by the current national recession, from September 1989, the beginning of the recession in the city, through December 1991, in the Southern District of New York (comprising Manhattan, the Bronx, Westchester, and five other counties), there were 3,602 Chapter 11 filings, which even gets more revealing when you take account of how the filings escalated year after year: 789 in 1989, 951 in 1990, and 1,283 in 1991, more than three times the number in 1987. In the month of January 1992, the last figure available just before this revised edition of the manual was to go to press, 212 companies — which included Macy's and TWA — filed Chapter 11, a one-month courthouse all-time record! (See, for example, "How Bankruptcy Can Feed Doubt;" *New York Times,* Dec. 17, 1990, p. D2, and "The Unkindest Cuts of All: How Recession Did a Job on Jobs," *New York Daily News,* Feb. 25, 1992, p. 45).

**Cited from "Bankruptcies Increase Sharply as the Stigma of Filing Fades," *The New York Times,* Sunday, Nov. 24, 1991, Section 12, at p. 10. Another expert, Dr. Robert W. Johnson, senior researcher at the Purdue University business school's Credit Research Center in West Lafayette, Indiana, makes a similar point: "The shame of bankruptcy does not seem to be as great as it once was." ("Americans Confront the Debt the House Built," *New York Times,* Sunday, Aug. 11, 1991, Section 4 at p. 7.)

The Biggest Chapter 11 Business Bankruptcies In American History

Going Chapter 11

United has joined the list of top bankruptcies in the United States.

	DATE	ESTIMATED PREBANKRUPTCY ASSETS IN BILLIONS
WorldCom	July '02	$103.9
Enron	Dec. '01	63.4
Texaco	April '87	35.9
Financial Corp. of America	Sept. '88	33.9
Global Crossing	Jan. '02	25.5
Adelphia Communications	June '02	24.4
United Airlines	Dec. '02	22.7
Pacific Gas and Electric	April '01	21.5
MCorp	March '89	20.2
Kmart	Jan. '02	17.0

Source: BankruptcyData.Com; Bloomberg Finanical Markets

The New York Times

United Airlines at a Glance

CHIEF EXECUTIVE: Glenn F. Tilton	2001 REVENUE: $16.1 billion
HEADQUARTERS: Elk Grove Township, Ill.	2001 NET LOSS: $2.1 billion
EMPLOYEES: 81,000	AIRPLANES: 566*

Top Domestic Routes *2002, through June*	UNITED AIRLINES' PASSENGER SHARE	UNITED AIRLINES' AVERAGE PASSENGERS PER DAY
Chicago/New York	33.7%	2,333
New York/San Francisco	42.0	1,727
Los Angeles/San Francisco	72.9	1,561
Chicago/Washington, D.C.	59.8	1,518
Los Angeles/New York	21.7	1,403
Chicago/Los Angeles	35.3	1,360
Chicago/San Francisco	54.7	1,345
Chicago/Denver	51.4	1,207
Denver/New York	47.1	1,175
Denver/San Francisco	70.0	1,009

*Owns 45 percent of its aircraft.

Sources: Company reports; Merrill Lynch. Airline Industry Quarterly Review

The New York Times

serious debt problems. And, not the least of all, to provide at long last the smaller, less well-to-do, undercapitalized, often marginal business concerns, a more affordable and readily accessible avenue of gaining some "bankruptcy literacy". For, contrary to the experience among the smaller companies who have traditionally underutilized the Chapter 11 remedy, the bigger corporations, on the other hand, and elite crop of wealthier and more financially sophisticated companies, with the advantage of superior legal and financial advice from expert "gurus", have generally recognized the useful purposes and value of the Chapter 11 option, and have historically used it to their best advantage whenever they had to.

You can put this manual to a fruitful use in one of two ways. You may chose to use it to actually draw up the bankruptcy papers YOURSELF, and do the filing and processing of your Chapter 11 case all by yourself. Or, you may choose simply to use the manual as a reference guide and resource material for bankruptcy planning and education on the basics of Chapter 11 as preparatory background that would all too likely serve you well in consulting or working with the legal professional you engage to actually do the bankruptcy filing for you or your company. Either way, the value it serves you will be just as invaluable.

The Changes in This Revised Edition

The scope and contents of the materials have not only been revised but expanded in this edition (the entire Chapter 5, for example, parts of Chapter 1, and a new Appendix A packed with an array of fully illustrated legal forms, are newly added) to make the volume still more self-sufficient, while the pertinent major changes that have occurred in the laws, rules and procedures are also incorporated herein as of 1992. Probably the most substantive practical changes to come along in the rules and procedures since the original edition of this manual — the most important, perhaps, from the standpoint of the practical needs of the reader or user of the manual — is in the bankruptcy forms and papers officially used in filing for bankruptcy. This revised edition fully reflects those changes, incorporating the newly prescribed bankruptcy forms which went into use effective August 1, 1991, the effective date of a new set of revised bankruptcy rules as well. With the use of these new revised bankruptcy forms and rules, formal bankruptcy filings are simplified under the current procedures, and the reader will probably find that there are fewer forms to complete or to file and that the present forms have more precise specificity, and more clearly indicate where to fill in different pieces of information required.

Contents of the Different Chapters

The first two chapters, **Chapters 1 and 2**, titled "Some Preliminary Background Information," and "Let's Learn a Few Things from the Case History of a Major American Company That Went Through Chapter 11: The Itel Corporation," respectively, attempt to provide an overview impression and background information preparatory for the book's main objective of giving the how-to of actually filing for bankruptcy. Chapter One covers matters ranging from a summary of the Chapter 11 procedure, to discussion of the typical filers and why people or companies file for Chapter 11, the bankruptcy and non-bankruptcy alternatives available to financially-troubled businesses, the basic benefits and protections (as well as pitfalls) of filing for Chapter 11 and a comparison of the advantages and disadvantages of filing under Chapter 11 with filing under Chapter 13 of the Bankruptcy Code. And Chapter TWO undertakes a brief case history of the Itel Corporation, a major American company whose practical experiences in successfully going through a Chapter 11 reorganization, demonstrates, primarily as an illustrative point, the processes, procedures, and salutary results of Chapter 11 reorganization for a business.

Chapter 3, by and large probably the most relevant and significant chapter in the entire text — from the standpoint of a debtor anxious either to get the actual Chapter 11 filing behind him or to at least get into the actual mechanics involved in filing for one — constitutes, you might say, the functional equivalence of the "meat" and "beef" of the manual.

It deals with the actual preparation and filing of a voluntary Chapter 11 case, providing the filer a fully-illustrated, systematic, step by step, simple-to-follow set of facts and procedures for undertaking the Chapter 11 filing — from completing the initial "petition" legal forms, to filing them with the court, processing the case and going through the proceedings from start to finish, including the working out of acceptable Chapter 11 Debt Payment Plan.

Chapter 4, deals with the legal effects and implications of the bankruptcy court confirming (i.e., approving) a Chapter 11 plan of reorganization — what it means for the debtor company, the creditors, shareholders, etc., and the obligations and responsibilities it imposes on the debtor company.

Chapter 5, addresses the handling of the administration of a Chapter 11 case following the initial filing of the case, with the precise mechanics and procedures involved in the practical handling of such common administrative and legal issues typically confronted by the debtor already in Chapter 11, fully discussed. Specific topics discussed include the operation of the debtor's business while the company is in Chapter 11, procedures for fighting off creditors when they attempt (as they often do) to have the court lift the "automatic stay" protection enjoyed by the debtor to allow them to sell off certain vital debtor assets in the bankruptcy estate, securing proper court authorization for use, sale or lease of cash collaterals or other estate property by the debtor company, the handling of claims by creditors, and of the unexpired leases and contractual obligations held by the debtor.

Chapter 6, addresses essentially the same issues as **Chapter 5**, but in somewhat great details.

In summary, in this era especially of the essentiality of familiarity with bankruptcy procedures, this manual should competently serve as a general or specific guide and reference for the educational and practical needs of the general public at large, and the small and medium-size business operators and managers, in particular, in gaining the all-important Chapter 11 "bankruptcy literacy." Indeed, it should also serve the same useful purpose for the average lawyers not specializing in bankruptcy, who so often have typically been grossly ignorant themselves on the subject, as well as serve the needs of other professionals with a related interest in the subject, such as accountants, financial analysts and operatives, and the like. Finally, with the present (revised) edition in hand, you can at least be certain, among other things, that you are working with the latest and most up-to-date information at hand on the law and procedures — *painstakingly updated to work for YOU in the* early 21st century, *as the early edition had worked for you (and others like you) in the 1980's and 90's!*

Here it is. I humbly commend it to YOU, the small and medium-size business operators and managers of America (and others) whether or not you have serious debt problems at the moment. Enjoy it. Utilize it!

Thank you.
Benji Anosike, the author.

How Chapter 11 Works

The parent of the department store Barneys New York filed for Chapter 11 bankruptcy protection in order to force a reorganization of its company and a separation from its partner, the Isetan Company, a large Japanese retailer. Chapter 11 refers to the provisions in the Federal Bankruptcy Act for court-supervised reorganization of debtor companies.

COMPANY FILES FOR CHAPTER 11 PROTECTION

Usually when it can no longer pay its creditors; sometimes when it expects future liabilities it cannot hope to pay; or when it wants to break a burdensome contract.

THE CHAPTER 11 PROCESS

1. Judge issues automatic stay
- Creditors cannot press suits for repayment.
- Debts are frozen.
- Company's day-to-day operations continue.
- Secured creditors can ask the court for a hardship exemption from the debt freeze.

2. Unsecured creditors form a committee
- Representatives are chosen to deal with the company.
- Creditors can ask the court to appoint an examiner to investigate possible fraud or mismanagement.
- Creditors, with the court's permission, can name a trustee to run the company .

3. The committee and company negotiate a reorganization plan.
- Parties work out a repayment plan for frozen debts. This step can take months or years.

4. Creditors approve the plan
- Must have assent of majority of creditors as well as creditors who are owed two-thirds of the debt.

5. Judge approves the plan

REORGANIZED COMPANY EMERGES

- It must meet the terms of the agreed repayment plan, which can require major changes in operation.
- It performs as a normal company.

THE NEW YORK TIMES, TUESDAY, MARCH 18, 2003

Big Credit Default Rate Forces Spiegel Bankruptcy Filing

By TRACIE ROZHON

In 1871, the Great Chicago Fire destroyed the first Spiegel furniture warehouse, but by 1885, business was racing along again, and the founder, Joseph Spiegel, started offering credit to his customers under the slogan: "We Trust the People."

Yesterday, the **Spiegel Group** — which owns the famous Spiegel catalog, Eddie Bauer and Newport News, another direct-mail clothing business — filed for bankruptcy. The reason given was that the company had trusted too many people, and some did not pay their credit card bills.

Analysts estimated the default rate at 17 percent to 20 percent of all Spiegel credit card receivables. Forty-one percent of purchases companywide, — and 73 percent at the Spiegel catalog, were made with Spiegel's private-label charge cards, which were issued through a Spiegel-owned bank.

"The straw that broke the camel's back at Spiegel was the credit card business, not the retail and the catalog," said Robert M. Miller, president of the Financo Restructuring Group, based in New York. "They had a very high default rate."

In its Chapter 11 filing yesterday, the company listed $1.74 billion in assets and $1.71 billion in debts. All stores and the catalog operations will remain open while the restructuring proceeds, said Debbie Koopman, a spokeswoman.

According to David Robertson, publisher of The Nilson Report, a trade journal that reports on the credit card industry, Spiegel had become, in effect, a subprime lender, offering credit to lower-income consumers who, in many cases, would not qualify for the more mainstream Visa or MasterCard.

For decades, the credit business fueled Spiegel. But then, several years ago, the furnace stopped blasting. Spiegel's fortunes tipped, along with those of Sears, who, Mr. Robertson said, "makes virtually all its money from credit card financing, not from selling products."

When the economy started worsening, Visa and MasterCard started loosening their previously extremely tight standards across the country, Mr. Robertson said, "casting a wider and wider net for customers." The retail companies, trying to compete for a share of the lucrative plastic business, had to lower their own standards even further.

Not that the credit card issue was the retailer's only problem. Spiegel's catalog, once reaching more than $1 billion a year in sales, dropped to $522 million in 2002, and while Spiegel had hurried to sell its products online, the company is also still pro-

Shoppers entered a Spiegel outlet store in Naperville, Ill., yesterday. The Spiegel Group also owns the Newport News and Eddie Bauer clothing businesses.

Bloomberg News

ducing a catalog of more than 500 pages several times a year. Newport News, the less-well-known catalog merchant, took in $337 million, and Eddie Bauer sold $1.4 billion. Although the combined sales at the division totaled a hefty $2.3 billion, that was 18 percent less than the $2.8 billion the Spiegel Group brought in the year before.

Yesterday, analysts zeroed in on the lucrative Eddie Bauer casual clothing chain as a prime candidate to be sold by Spiegel in its efforts to improve its balance sheet.

Although Eddie Bauer is still regarded as a strong brand name, the store has stumbled badly over the last five years, failing to differentiate itself from competitors like the Gap, Banana Republic, American Eagle Outfitters and others. Now, Eddie Bauer is trying to go to its outdoorsy roots, the spokeswoman said. Same-store sales, which compare recent performance to those of the same stores a year ago, were down 12 percent for 2002.

Yesterday, several analysts, including Walter Loeb, of the company that bears his name, speculated that the company's new interim chief executive, William C. Kosturos, a restructuring expert who came from the New York firm of Alvarez & Marsal on March 1, will try to find a buyer for Eddie Bauer — and possibly, for the Newport News division as well. Ms. Koopman said no decision

had been made on Eddie Bauer's future, and she refused to speculate on what she called "what ifs."

According to a statement released by Mr. Kosturos, the Chapter 11 petition, which was filed yesterday in United States Bankruptcy Court of the Southern District of New York, "will allow the Spiegel Group to address its immediate liquidity needs, restructure its debt and improve its

---

Analysts say 17 to 20 percent of credit card receivables went unpaid.

---

prospects for future growth and profitability."

Earlier this month, Spiegel entered into an agreement with the Securities and Exchange Commission, which had charged the company had not fully disclosed to investors how precarious the company's financial position really was. An independent court-appointed examiner will study the company's financial records since January 2000 and report to the court.

In 1982, Spiegel was acquired by

Otto Versand, the world's largest catalog company, and according to a company history issued by Spiegel, later transferred its shares "to a group of individual investors."

Yesterday, an investment banker said that Dr. Michael Otto, a German billionaire who controls the voting shares of Spiegel, had been assuring German lenders that there was no chance that the company's well-reported problems would ever result in a bankruptcy filing. The investment banker said that the German banks said they had been caught by surprise by the filing and that it had been the American banks who had "pulled the trigger."

Actually, the company had little choice. Because of an existing agreement, investors had to be paid immediately if the expected credit card receivables fell below certain amounts. Recently, the company was forced to discontinue its private-label credit cards.

Despite the gloom, Spiegel announced yesterday that it had found $40⁰ million of new financing. The Bank of America, which has already lent Spiegel $85 million (the fourth-biggest creditor, behind Commerzbank, Dresdner Kleinwort Wasserstein and DZ Bank), had agreed, with several other institutions, to extend another $400 million in "debtor in possession" financing; the spending of that money will be closely supervised by the bankruptcy judge.

CHAPTER ONE

SOME PRELIMINARY BACKGROUND INFORMATION

A. What Is Chapter 11 Bankruptcy?

A Chapter 11 bankruptcy (also known as reorganization bankruptcy) could, in a word, be defined as follows: a judicial procedure undertaken under Chapter 11 of the 1978 Federal Bankruptcy Code, by which a *business debtor* (as opposed to a personal debtor) is allowed, by virtue of the protection provided by the court, to continue operations free of interference by his creditors while he devises a plan of reorganization to rehabilitate the company and repay his debts—usually under terms that are somewhat more favorable and more manageable for the debtor. The bankruptcy laws are a federal law, hence bankruptcy matters are federal (not state) matters, handled by federal courts.

To secure bankruptcy, however, you (or your representative) would have to prepare and file a "petition" for bankruptcy in the bankruptcy court of the federal district in your area, detailing your financial affairs, condition and prospects. Once the petition is filed in court, you are legally protected and your creditors may not, under the law, start or continue any collection actions in respect to your indebtedness; they must now work through the bankruptcy court and abide by whatever the court eventually decides on the matter. You'll then negotiate terms with your creditors and shareholders and present a feasible "plan" of settlement that is acceptable to most of your creditors, shareholders, and other interested parties. If the court should view the proposed plan of reorganization favorably, it will then approve ("confirm") it, thereby directing the execution of its provisions. Your only obligation thereafter, will be to carry out the repayment and other provisions in the confirmed plan—just to the extent provided therein—and your total indebtedness shall have been discharged.

B. What Is The Nature Of The Reliefs Obtainable From Filing Chapter 11 Bankruptcy?

The first and probably the foremost relief of filing for bankruptcy would be that your mere filing of the petition papers in court immediately stops your creditors from either commencing or continuing any collection actions against you—from the very day you take your petition forms to the bankruptcy court and file them with the court clerk and pay the necessary filing fee ($839 or a part of it)! Just about all of your business creditors are, in effect, "frozen cold"—they can't collect or even try to collect your indebtedness to them, they can't ask for, harrass, or threaten you about it; they can't sue or threaten to sue you in any other court about it, and any suit they might have brought or judgment they might have gotten against you before you filed for bankruptcy, may not be enforced or pressed forward, and they can't seize or threaten to seize your property or assets. (It's tantamount to "contempt of court"—violation of a court order, if they do any of these!) In short, just about the only thing your creditor could do thereafter is to file his claims with the bankruptcy court and wait, along with everybody else, to have his day in court (in the bankruptcy court) about how and when you can pay him, if at all.

But what is most important and advantageous from the standpoint of any debtor is this: while you enjoy this rare freedom from harrassment by your creditors, you (or, more appropriately, your company's management) would have had a freer atmosphere—and a clearer head—to work on formulating a more convenient arrangement ("plan of reorganization") that would better enable you to rehabilitate your company and straighten out its financial affairs, and to repay your debts over time, at least in part. (For the kinds of actual reliefs enjoyed by a company in a real case, see the Itel Corporation Case, Chapter Two, pp. 19-24 .)

As one long-term expert and legal practitioner of bankruptcy law sums it up, "A Chapter 11 reorganization allows the management [of the debtor company] to concentrate on the crucial decisions that must be made without the diversion of time and effort to meet creditors' demands."

A Summary:

The various important ways by which filing for Chapter 11 could offer helpful reliefs of sorts to a troubled company, may be summarized as follows:
- — You do not pay interest on your debts during the time that the bankruptcy proceedings are going on.
- — Your debt payments to both secured and unsecured creditors can be modified in any number of ways—scaled down, rescheduled, some cancelled totally or in part, etc.
- — You may reorganize or streamline management.

— You are protected from lawsuits and collection actions; and all pending lawsuits are automatically "stayed" (frozen).

— All claims against you are consolidated and dealt with in one shot, through the single bankruptcy case.

— You are allowed to continue operation of the business (free of the interference of creditors and other interested parties).

— You may close unprofitable portions or subsidiaries of your business, or dispose assets no longer needed to gain some needed cash flow.

— You get rehabilitated and given a "new lease on life" so that you can repay your debts in some form or another.

C. What Could Lead A Company To File For Chapter 11?

In attempting to account for America's current record high rates of business failures and bankruptcy filings (see pp. i-ii, 2), experts point, at one time or another, to different factors as the potential or actual precipitators:

i) financial strains (in the nature of stifled sales and dampened consumer spending) resulting from a steep or prolonged recession in the American economy;

ii) record-high rates of interest (of up to a prime rate of 20½% at one point in Sept. 1981) which make business loans—the essential fuel for business growth and expansion—too costly for most businesses, and devastating to an industry like construction;

iii) escalating wages and social costs of doing business in recent American history, all of which add to the overall cost of doing business;

iv) excessive dependence of American businesses on short-term debt for financing business operations and expansion;

v) the impact of foreign competition in recent years which has forced American industries (e.g., the automotive and textile industries) into prolonged structural shifts as many markets they formerly served either disappear or are saturated with an influx of lower priced, often better made or more functional products from overseas competitors;

vi) record level rates of unemployment (up to a 50-year record at 10.1% as of this writing in October 1982) which saps the consumer's ability to make purchases and effectively squelches business sales and growth. And so on and so forth.

One thing about this question is certain: on one point is everyone unanimously agreed—namely, that national economic conditions (factors such as recession, high interest rates or unemployment) are almost always a major causative factor which underlies business failures and business bankruptcies.

George Washington University's **Professor Eric Fredland**, who conducted a study of business failures for the Congressionally-commissioned Commission on the Bankruptcy Laws of the United States, did an empirical comparison of the key characteristics of 2,080 firms which failed in 1971 as against another group of 1978 businesses of the same characteristics which didn't fail. The central question to which Fredland sought some answers was: Why did one business fail while its counterpart did not? On this, he drew the following conclusions:

i) that business failures, though not necessarily likely among smaller businesses as compared to larger ones, is much more likely among relatively young and inexperienced firms;

ii) that the predominance of business failures are among retail establishments; and

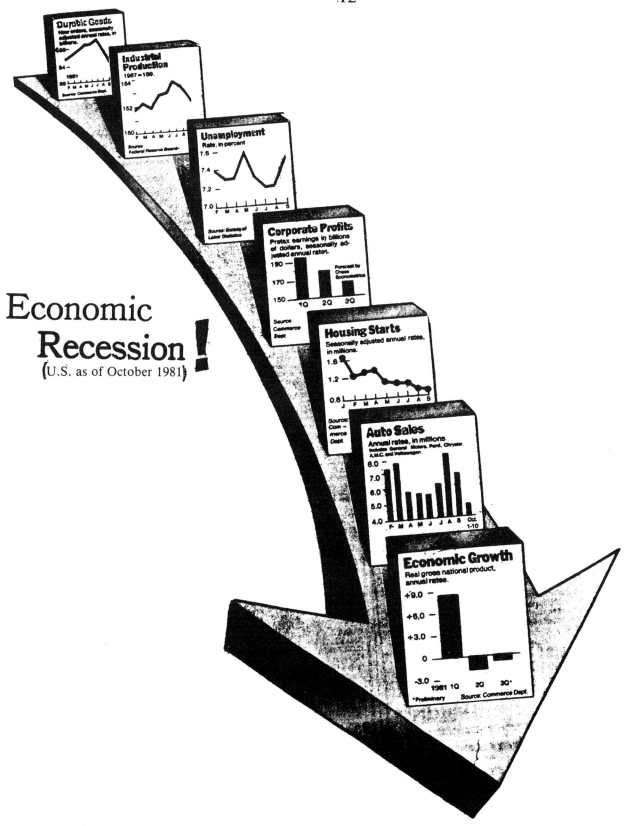

Economic
Recession !
(U.S. as of October 1981)

iii) that both a sluggish, declining economic situation and a rapidly expanding, progressively changing one produce greater numbers of failures than more stable conditions do induce.*

To **Dr. Francis A. Lees**, a professor of finance at St. Johns University who did a study of corporate debt published by the Conference Board, the nation's elite business research group, the rise in the business failures of the early 1980s, was at least partly a reflection of the overall deterioration of the "debt quality" in American business. (According to figures cited by Lees, of the 50 large and medium-sized companies he studied, almost all had increased the ratio of their debts to assets from 1979 to 1981, accompanied by profitability ratios that were generally down and internal costs that stayed up.)

Other theorists see rapid overexpansion of business over too short a period of time, or even extension of business into many directions as the chief culprits for business failures.

And, finally, there is a body of theory which attributes financial failures (for businesses and non-businesses alike) principally to so-called "internal causes"—meaning causes which originate with the debtor and over which he does have control: incompetence, mismanagement, irresponsibility, dishonesty, and inadequate size and vulnerable stage of growth of a business, and the like.**

D. Should You File For Chapter 11?

Make no mistake about it, while bankruptcy is just about the most powerful and promising remedy that an overburdened debtor (whether in business or outside of it) may seek under the law, it is, by the same token, just about the most serious and drastic financial measure that a business debtor could undertake. It would be the gravest error for you—for any individual or company with money problems—to think of bankruptcy as either the easy, pain-free panacea, or the automatic solution or answer in every instance. The truth is that, like most other things of some value in life which might on the surface seem overly easy and attractive to obtain, business bankruptcy is not without some serious risks or costs.

*While it should be rather obvious why a declining economic situation is likely to produce business failures, not so obvious might be the reason why the same result would be true from a rapidly expanding economic situation. The reason would be that a rapidly expanding economic situation attracts new ventures, some of which are risky and some of which do not survive the changing conditions associated with rapid expansions.

**In a report by Dun & Bradstreet titled "The Failure Record Through 1970", for example, the following were offered as the "underlying causes" of business failure: "lack of experience in the line," "lack of managerial experience," "unbalanced [not too well rounded] experience," and, for nearly 50 percent of the cases, "incompetence." And the proof that these were the causes was said to be "evidenced by inability to avoid conditions which resulted in...inadequate sales, heavy operating expenses, receivable difficulties, inventory difficulties, excessive fixed assets, poor location, competitive weakness, and other [factors]."

For one thing, a Chapter 11 filing would almost invariably mean a huge (sometimes over 50 percent) cutback in the size and activities of your company and personnel. And for another thing, the observation of Tony Haboian, a vicepresident of the Chicago-based Sim's Motor Transport Lines, which filed for Chapter 11 in early 1982, still remains relatively and generally accurate even in this day and age of growing bankruptcy "respectability": "There's [still] a certain negative attitude when you file Chapter 11. Other companies don't want to do business with you. They're afraid of you." Thirdly, the prospect of having to turn over control of your company to an outsider (e.g., a court-appointed trustee), and of having to go through the process of long, complicated, searching creditors' meetings or the scrutiny of the court, may not exactly be the most pleasant thing for a debtor. A Chapter 11 filing invariably has an adverse and disruptive effect on the company's credit rating and stock prices—at least, in the initial stages of the process. Your company must, in effect, operate under close supervision by outsiders, and you must be able to come up, within a limited period, with a reorganization plan that meets with the satisfaction of your creditors (or at least the court), or you may be forced to accept the creditors' own plan (which may not be too palatable for you) or have the company dissolved and liquidated.

The point of all these, simply, is that bankruptcy is not—and should not be—something one jumps into casually, lightly or at the drop of a hat. It is a drastic, "last resort" type remedy—one intended and meant for use only when it is genuinely and absolutely necessary, as when all other viable alternative avenues for solution are closed and not readily available to the debtor. *By the same token, however, delay or hesitation in vigorously initiating and proceeding with Chapter 11 are just as greatly ill advised and costly for a business debtor who genuinely qualifies because he really lacks other viable alternative!*

Fortunately, though, the evidence is almost universal that the overwhelming majority of debtors who go into bankruptcy do so on nothing other than the absolute "last resort" basis! As the Congressionally-commissioned 1973 Report of the Commission on the Bankruptcy Laws of the United States put it:

"Notwithstanding the notoriety of "scam" bankruptcies, absconding and concealing debtors, and other instances of egregious conduct in, and in anticipation of (bankruptcy) cases. . . . the Commission has found little empirical substantiation that dishonest conduct is a cause of bankruptcy in a significant number of cases."

Indeed, some insightful financial analysts have noted that it is, after all, in the best and inherent self-interest of a business operator that he should avoid, not undertake, bankruptcy—if at all he could remotely help it. "Generally," says Winston Williams, a *New York Times* financial analyst, "businesses turn to bankruptcy as a last resort when there is no other way to meet their debts. Corporations strive above all else for continuous growth in profits, revenues and corporate influence. Consequently, even gravely ill companies usually try to avoid bankruptcy (since this would) mean the end of their growth"*—e.g., amputation of important parts of the company, or even complete liquidation.

E. Some Alternatives To Chapter 11

But let's say that you've studied the facts of your financial situation. You've given it a most careful analysis and in the end, you've somehow decided, for whatever your reasons (moral, legal, philosophical, whatever), that bankruptcy is not quite for you and that you'd rather find an alternative.

---

*Quoted from "Debt Burden Takes Big Toll on Businesses," *The New York Times*, Oct. 4, 1982, p. D10.

Now, you might ask, are there any real, viable alternatives? There are some alternatives, for sure, somewhat less extreme remedies you might want to consider. Whether in fact you'll find these alternatives to be a **viable** one in terms of effectively addressing your financial problems relative to your creditors is quite another matter altogether, however!

Alternatives? For one thing, you may negotiate directly with your creditors without having to go through the formal process of filing for or going through bankruptcy. You simply make a solemn plea with your creditors, probably by forwarding a formal letter to them, asking that they exercise a little more patience with you while, say, a better business climate you anticipate comes around, and the like. If you could then work out with your creditors a more stretched out, less burdensome debt repayment arrangement, where you might, for example, make repayments over a longer time schedule at a lower rate per repayment period, or have the past or future interest on the indebtedness reduced or completely forgiven, then you are in real luck!

Another "alternative" of some kind would be to decide that the financial state of your business—and the future prospects for its rehabilitation—is simply too hopeless to merit the further time, expense and hassle of undergoing the Chapter 11 proceedings to keep the business alive. You might then elect to file for total liquidation of the business—under the so-called Chapter 7 of the bankruptcy code.*

They, Among Many, Survived Chapter 11

	Date of filing under Chapter 11	Liabilities at filing (in millions)	Date of Emergence from Chapter 11	1981 Revenues (in millions)	1981 Earnings (in millions)
Penn Central	June '70	$2,900	Oct. '78	$3,300	$169
Toys 'R' Us*	May '74	173	April '78	783	49
Miller-Wohl	Sept. '72	44	Nov. '73	221	18
Continental Steel**	April '80	118	Mar. '82	158	(14)
Dynamics Corp. of America	Aug. '72	52	Nov. '74	153	6

(Loss)   * Formerly Interstate Stores Inc.   ** Formerly Penn-Dixie Steel Corp.

David G. Klein

The liquidation alternative may be accomplished under Chapter 7 or 13* of the Bankruptcy Code, or even under the liquidation provisions of the State corporation, partnership, or limited liability company laws under the Assignment for the Benefit of Creditors, or, informally, with or without an agreement with creditors.

---

*Chapter 7 bankruptcy (also known as total liquidation or straight bankruptcy), is the subject matter of the sister volume to the present one, titled **How To File Your Own Personal Bankruptcy Without A Lawyer,** authored by the same author and published by the Do-It-Yourself Legal Publishers.

F. How Does Chapter 11 Bankruptcy Basically Work in a Summary Nutshell?

Basically, to commence a "Voluntary" Chapter 11 case, you'll prepare a **"petition"** (and other documents) for Chapter 11 bankruptcy, detailing your (i.e., the debtor company's) financial condition and prospects, and listing all of its creditors and interest holders, and all of its property and other assets, and other relevant financial information about the debtor. The debtor then files this petition with its area bankruptcy court.

Upon filing the petition with the bankruptcy court, the debtor immediately, gets the critical **"automatic stay"** relief by the mere act of filing the Chapter 11 petition. Immediately upon filing the petition, all foreclosures, collection actions, civil litigations and creditor actions of any kind against the debtor are automatically "stayed" — i.e., automatically prohibited from being undertaken by the creditors against the debtor or its property — in court or out of court. The automatic stay which comes with the filing of the Chapter 11 case, in effect gives the debtor an immediate moratorium (i.e., suspension) on payments for most of its bills and debts for at least the period between the filing of the case and the confirmation of the plan, an average of some 6 to 8 months.

Upon filing for Chapter 11 bankruptcy, the court will usually allow the debtor to remain as **"debtor in possession"**, meaning that the debtor continues to manage and operate its business during the course of the bankruptcy case, subject, of course, to its compliance with certain rules and standards prescribed under the law and to the orders of the court.

Next, the debtor prepares a **Chapter 11 Plan** (see samples on pp. 151-169) and files it with the court, usually within 120 days from the date the case was filed. The debtor must also prepare and file with the court for the court's consideration and approval, a **"Disclosure Statement"** — basically, a detailed financial statement that should adequately inform the debtor's creditors and interest holders about the financial condition of the debtor and its future plans. (Samples of this Statement are reproduced on pp. 132-142)

Upon the debtor obtaining the court's approval of the disclosure statement — but NOT <u>before</u> then — copies of the Disclosure Statement, as well as of the proposed Chapter 11 Plan, are distributed to the creditors and interest holders who may then vote on whether to **"accept"** or to **"reject"** the debtor's plan. If the voting shows acceptance of the plan by at least one class of creditors whose claims are "impaired"[*] under the plan, the plan may be "confirmed" (i.e., approved) by the court. Following the completion of the voting process, the court holds a **"confirmation hearing"** on the proposed Chapter 11 plan for the purpose of determining whether the plan should be confirmed (approved). At the confirmation hearing, the debtor must present evidence showing that the Plan complies with the Chapter 11 confirmation requirements under the law (see pp. 85-88 for such requirements). *Basically, a plan may be confirmed by the court in one of two ways:*
EITHER through the **regular confirmation method** (see pp. 144-153 of the manual), OR through a **"cramdown"** method (p. 165 of the manual). Briefly stated, the regular method applies in situations when the plan has been accepted by <u>every</u> class of creditors with impaired claims and the interest holders, while the cramdown method is applicable in situations when the plan has been rejected by one or more classes of creditors with impaired claims or interest holders, but has been accepted by at least one class of creditors with impaired claims.

Upon confirmation of the plan by the court, the debtor becomes obligated to implement and carry out the provisions of the plan; at the same time, the debtor promptly receives a Chapter

---

[*]See pp. 195-6 for full definition.

11 discharge promptly upon such confirmation. The confirmed plan may, for example, call for the debtor to be reorganized, or for a new corporation to be formed; it may call for property to be transferred or for liens to be created or modified, and for specific claims of creditors to be paid in a manner specified in the plan, and so on and so forth.

Finally, when months or years later all the provisions and requirements of the Chapter 11 plan have been carried out by the debtor, the plan is said to be **"consummated"** — that is, fulfilled. At that point, the debtor files a final report and accounting with the court and the case is closed by the court.

What if the debtor is unable to fulfill the provisions of the Chapter 11 plan, though? To put it briefly, a debtor who fails to carry out its obligations under the plan can simply expect to be sued anew by its creditors or for its property and assets to be seized or foreclosed on, either in the bankruptcy court or in other courts. However, as a practical matter, a debtor confronted with the prospect of not being able to carry out its Chapter 11 plan obligations would usually seek to file an "amended" plan with the court which it may be more able to fulfill, assuming sufficient grounds exist for winning the court's approval of such amendment. However, if all fails in the end, the Chapter 11 case will be dismissed or be converted to a Chapter 7 liquidation case.

G. HOW DOES CHAPTER 11 BANKRUPTCY COMPARE AGAINST CHAPTER 13 BANKRUPTCY?

A comparison between filing for bankruptcy under Chapter 11 and Chapter 13 of the Bankruptcy Code would seem to be a natural one to make for the simple reason that both types of bankruptcy primarily embody the principle of **"reorganization"** of the debtor's debt obligations and rehabilitation of the debtor — as differentiated, for example, from filing under Chapter 7 of the Code, which primarily involves liquidation of the debtor's affairs, on the other hand.

Firstly, there are differences between Chapter 11 and 13 in terms of the size and type of debts that are permissible under the respective types of bankruptcy. With respect to Chapter 13 cases, the debtor must have unsecured debts which total <u>no more than</u> $250,000, and secured debts which total <u>no more than</u> $750,000. With regard to the Chapter 11 debtor, on the other hand, there is no restriction as to the type and size of debt obligation it may have; it may have as much or as little in debt as it can.

The second major area of difference is this. Under Chapter 13, only an individual (i.e., a natural human person) is eligible, and corporations, partnerships and other non-individual entities are not eligible to file under Chapter 13. The Chapter 11 bankruptcy case, on the other hand, permits any entity whatsoever, whether it be a person or a business (sole proprietorship, partnership, or a corporation), and whether it is big or small, to file under it.

Thirdly, in a Chapter 13 case, the debtor is required to have a regular income — defined as income sufficiently stable and regular as to enable the debtor to make the payments called for under a Chapter 13 payment plan. To be eligible to file a Chapter 11 case, on the other hand, no financial or insolvency requirements apply; such a debtor may be solvent or insolvent, its assets may exceed its liabilities by any amounts, or vice versa, and its income may be substantial, meager or even none.

From the facts set forth above, certain relevant conclusions can be immediately drawn. First, the use of Chapter 13 is obviously precluded as far as most small businesses are concerned,

18

as only sole proprietorships (and marital partnerships), but no corporations, partnerships or other non-individual debtors are permitted to file under chapter 13. Secondly, whereas individual debtors may file under chapter 11 as well as under chapter 13, debtors who may file under chapter 13 are limited to only those having only relatively small debts and relatively small income with which to finance a repayment plan — those having less than $250,000 in unsecured debts and $750,000 in secured debts. Middle and upper income debtors having relatively large debts and large incomes or assets (e.g., substantial personal investments in real estate, stocks, or what have you) are, as a practical matter, left with no other choice but to file for reorganization or rehabilitation of their affairs under chapter 11 only. As one experienced bankruptcy legal practitioner recently put it, "The limits of $250,000 in unsecured debts and $750,000 in secured debts for a chapter 13 debtor, used to be reasonable limits But nowadays (in the 1990s and early 2000's), a professional with some real estate can easily go over those limits."*

In any event, it must be stated however, that all of the above facts aside, *for those who qualify, chapter 13 still has several advantages over chapter 11.* First of all, a chapter 13 proceeding is much simpler and less protracted or time consuming than a chapter 11 case. Such elaborate and often expensive and time-consuming formalities as the filing of "disclosure statements", appointment of "creditors' committees" and "solicitations" and "acceptance" of votes for the payment plan, for example, are not required in chapter 13 cases. In chapter 13 cases, it is not necessary that the approval of any class of unsecured creditors be obtained for the plan to be approvable, as is the case in a chapter 11 case. Also, the requirements needed for securing the court's confirmation for a payment plan under chapter 13 are mush simpler and easier to meet than those under chapter 11. Finally, the discharge offered in chapter 13 is considered to be the broadest discharge in all of bankruptcy; it is considerably broader than the chapter 11 discharge, discharging virtually all debts except for alimony, maintenance or support, student loans, and debts arising from criminal restitution or personal injuries or death that are caused by drunk driving.

Finally, with respect to a qualified small business debtor whose objective is to reorganize and rehabilitate his business and remain in business, in general chapter 13 is almost always preferable to chapter 11. In a chapter 13 case, the debtor pays much of his "disposable income" (income left over after allowing for the support of the debtor and his dependents or the operation of his business) to the court-appointed chapter 13 trustee who then makes the required payments to the creditors as stipulated under the debtor's plan. By law, such payments to the trustee by the debtor lasts for a maximum period of 3 years (5 years for debtors having real property) in chapter 13 cases. Such a period is shorter than for most Chapter 11 Plans. And, given the more protracted time schedule involved in the processing of the Chapter 11 cases, the legal expenses of handling Chapter 13 cases are generally a mere fraction of the expenses of doing Chapter 11 cases.

---

*"More Assets Shielded by Bankruptcy Ruling," *New York Times*, June 14, 1991, P.D. 5, quoting a statement attributed to Weldon Ponder, an Austin, Texas bankruptcy lawyer.

CHAPTER TWO

LET'S LEARN A FEW THINGS FROM THE CASE HISTORY OF A MAJOR AMERICAN COMPANY THAT WENT THROUGH CHAP. 11: THE ITEL CORPORATION

In this chapter, we attempt, for the illustrative purposes of exposing the processes and procedures involved in a typical Chapter 11 case, the case history of a major American corporation which had to seek the legal shelter of bankruptcy—the case of the Itel Corporation. This case would seem particularly suited for our needs: it is recent, it is one of the biggest business bankruptcies ever, and by many accounts, it is one of the most complex bankruptcies on record. And, above all, it fits into the category of companies which, as *Barron's* Magazine writer Stan Kulp fittingly put it, "like corporate Lazaruses, have put on new garb, reorganized their fiscal affairs, and risen from the dead."

Business bankruptcies, says *Barron's** writer Stan Kulp, a specialist in bankruptcy issues, are often "a great cleansing process." Kulp adds that, "Sometimes all the company needs is pruning in the reorganization process to blossom again."

Why would this be so? One expert, Eugene Lerner, a professor of finance at Northwestern University's Kellogg Graduate School of Management, explains it this way: "There's an awful lot of nonsense that goes on when the economy is good. Companies start making money and egos take over. You could say that bankruptcies are purifying [in that sense]."**

One thing could be said about the Itel bankruptcy experience: the facts of its case would tend to support that school of bankruptcy theorists who hold that, as painful and unpleasant as bankruptcies may often be for debtors, creditors, or stockholders, they nevertheless do have some positive "purifying" or "cleansing" import for the economy in general, and the company in particular—in terms, for example, of ridding the economy of dead wood in troubled industries, and of forcing companies to act more rationally.

---

*Cited from "Life After Bankruptcy," *Barron's*, Feb. 8, 1982, p. 8.

**Cited from *The New York Times*. Oct. 4. 1982. p. D-10.

In January, 1981, the Itel Corporation, a San Francisco-based company which leased everything from computers and aircraft to containers and rail cars, filed a petition in San Francisco for protection under Chapter 11. From Aug. 1980 to then it had tried several other means to refloat the company, all to no avail.

Factors That Led To Itel's Financial Woes

Through most of the 1970's, Itel expanded rapidly in its capital-intensive, but highly profitable equipment leasing business. To bankroll the growth, it relied on income from the sale and leasing of computer equipment to government agencies, manufacturers and other businesses. Itel failed when it overstretched its computer business. In 1977, Itel had begun marketing computers in head-on competition with the International Business Machines Corporation (I.B.M.) in the so-called plug-compatible market. Sales of its computers increased from 40 in 1977 to 240 a year in 1978, and the company predicted that sales would continue to grow rapidly. But early in 1979, I.B.M. shocked the computer industry with the announcement of a new line of computers, the E Series, before it was actually available. Customers stopped taking rival equipment until they could see just what the new I.B.M. machines offered. (What I.B.M. offered turned out to be a line of faster, more efficient computers.)

A major contributing negative factor for Itel was that its old clients had all along been given **the option of returning Itel's equipment** before the leases expired. And, since the Itel equipment was a combination of earlier I.B.M. systems and equipment designed to be "plug-compatible"—meaning it worked like and could be used with I.B.M. systems—nearly all of Itel's clients wasted no time in taking advantage of the option, rapidly returning the now outmoded Itel equipment as soon as I.B.M. introduced its new equipment.

Then there was **the problem with Lloyd's of London**, the international insurance underwriter. Itel had bought some $300 million in insurance coverage from Lloyd's against losses on the computer it leased, to protect Itel should a customer cancel a lease agreement. However, after the London underwriters had reimbursed the company for about $7 million in losses that year for the stampede of Itel clients who turned in their leased computer equipment, it balked, contesting its liability to Itel on several grounds, among which was that Itel had failed to exercise "due diligence" in avoiding losses.

Itel Reshuffles Its Personnel

Suddenly, Itel was in deep financial trouble. For, virtually overnight, the new I.B.M. computers made Itel's equipment obsolete, and the demand for it disappeared. One initial response of Itel was swift: it swept out its old management. And, in April 1980, **James H. Maloon**, a 54-year-old specialist in managing troubled companies who had been executive vicepresident for finance at Pan American World Airways where he was deeply involved in Pan Am's financial woes of the 1970's, was appointed chairman of the board and chief executive officer by Itel.

Rapid Fall In Itel's Earnings

The company's earnings came tumbling down nevertheless. By August of that year (1980), Itel was warning that its operating losses for 1979 would be more than $430 million. The actual figure turned out to be a loss of $443 million (compared to a net income of $21.5 million the year before)!

The company's total debt was $1.3 billion, plus another $300 million of contingencies. Some $500 million of that debt paid a floating interest rate of around 25 percent. With its debt exceeding its net worth by around $260 million, the company was technically bankrupt.

Itel's Lawsuit Problem

On top of the myriad of Itel's other problems (overnight and heavy loss of business and earnings, the dispute with Lloyd's, rapid turnover within the management ranks, lowered personnel morale, etc.), the company also had to contend with a torrent of lawsuits filed on behalf of its more than 6,000 individual shareholders. The suits, which eventually sought damages of more than $200 million, charged that the company, in the year before its collapse, had issued financial reports with false information on its profits, financial condition and prospects.

In a word, then, when Itel filed its petition for protection under the federal bankruptcy code, the company's chances of successful reorganization were dim at best!

Nevertheless, the company confidently went about doing whatever it could still do to keep alive in one form or another. "I'm afraid it's about one of the biggest bankruptcies ever," declared the cool-headed, widely respected, hard-working, new Itel Chairman Maloon, the man whose direct involvement in the detailed negotiations with the Itel creditors is widely credited with the company's ability to eventually survive bankruptcy when bankruptcy eventually became inevitable. "It is a complex situation, but we have to move fairly promptly to get it resolved so that we can get back to running a business. That is in everybody's general interest."

Itel Filed For Chapter 11 After Its Efforts To Refloat The Company Without Bankruptcy Failed

Mr. Maloon had first tried several other means to refloat the company. Efforts were made to persuade the company's 6,000 creditors, led by 100 major banks and institutions, to refinance the enormous debt. That failed. Then Itel tried to offer some of the debt at a substantial discount. That too failed because the holders of public debt would have received much more than holders of similar classes of private debt. Those last round of talks ended on January 5, 1981, and four days later—on January 9th—the company filed the petition in San Francisco's bankruptcy court for protection under Chapter 11, with Mr. Maloon declaring: "I would have preferred not to have gone to [bankruptcy] court. But in the end, I was not willing to pay the kind of premium necessary to make this approach [of having to pay holders of public debt much more than holders of similar classes of private debt] work."

Itel Gets Some Immediate Relief Just For Filing

What happened thereafter? The court ordered Itel to produce a plan of reorganization by the end of March 1981. Itel's first important "break" as a direct result of filing for Chapter 11, was swift and most helpful. Immediately after the filing, the company's creditors, in accordance with the rules of procedure prescribed under the bankruptcy law, agreed to set up a **Creditors' Committee**, a committee of only three members, to negotiate for and act on behalf of Itel's creditors—an obviously much more flexible and manageable arrangement for Itel than the pre-petition situation when it would have had to deal one-by-one with its 6,000 or so individual creditors! And it was with this Committee (backed, of course, by their lawyers, accountants, and other professional aides) that the Itel management had to sit down, negotiate and work out acceptable terms of settlement—a so-called "plan" of reorganization.

There was another immediate "break" which accrued to Itel upon filing its bankruptcy petition in court: the torrent of lawsuits against the company was brought to an immediate halt, giving the Itel management the respite it badly needed to address the tough decisions that needed its undivided attention about the continued life of the company, or its death; Itel now had an atmosphere that was free of creditor and stockholder pressures!

Itel Adopts Some "Purification" And Cost-Cutting Measures

Along the way, Itel, which in its heydays was reputed to be one of the most extravagant of companies ("And don't forget, Itel wasn't known for being tight with a nickel," said Itel's Chairman Maloon), adopted extensive cost-cutting and austerity measures. The payroll was slimmed down to 1,400 from more than 7,000. The old company Mercedes cars were jettisoned, and Perrier mineral water on tap in the water coolers was gone. The new chairman, Mr. Maloon, took a pay cut to $250,000 a year—about a third of the $734,000 his ousted predecessor, Peter S. Redfield, was getting.

'We're in a very, very deep hole.'

James H. Maloon, the Itel President who expertly guided the company through the early Chapter 11 bankruptcy years, as he appeared in a July 1982 article in *The New York Times*.

Itel Works Out Separate Deals With
Different Classes Of Creditors & Shareholders

Itel's bankruptcy proved to be one of the largest, and perhaps the most complicated of American bankruptcies on record. The most difficult parts of its reorganization plan concerned negotiations with its creditors (both of secured and unsecured types) holding $1.2 billion in debt.

The agreements—each negotiated separately with the Creditors' Committee representing the given class of creditors—were negotiated in separate parts.

On The Secured Debts: In May 1982, the company announced that it had reached an agreement "in principle" with its secured lenders' committees (representing investors and creditors who provided loans secured by liens on the company's rail cars) on the terms by which most of its $330 million in secured debt was to be treated under the plan of reorganization Itel planned to propose. Primarily, the announced agreement—worked out with the Creditors' Committees representing Itel's secured and unsecured creditors—provided for changes in the terms of Itel's equipment trust certificates, secured by railroad cars, while leaving payment terms of the certificates unchanged. (The certificates accounted for more than 80% of Itel's secured debt.) A new and separate subsidiary was created in rail freight cars and railroad equipment that would eventually pay off the debt. This new unit (which principally consisted of Itel's rail-related assets valued at $483 million; $6 million in unrestricted cash; and $8 million in rail-related restricted cash) was to assume obligations associated with Itel's rail-related secured debts, and could defer up to $40 million of certain scheduled payments from 1982 through 1988 without incurring additional interest, but only to the extent that Itel's cash flow would otherwise be negative—i.e., only to the extent that the company does not achieve a specified level of profitability.

On Itel's Unsecured Debts: A satisfactory arrangement with Itel's $900 million in unsecured debt holders (lenders or suppliers who were owed monies for loans or supplies that were not secured by liens on Itel's assets) was the biggest element in the company's reorganization. There were 100 banks, suppliers and others who fell into this category. For this group of creditors, Itel struck a preliminary agreement with the unsecured creditors' committee representing them, for them to receive payment of $654 million in cash, preferred stock and bonds. In addition, this group was to receive 79 percent of the common stock in the reorganized company—tying this group's fate and the size of their fortunes, to the fate of the company after reorganization, since, given the large holdings of this group in the new Itel, the better the new company does in terms of future profitability, the better would the group's return in terms of dividends and share of profits.

On The Matter With Lloyd's of London: Itel struck an agreement with the London-based insurance company (announced in December 1981) by which Lloyd's was to pay Itel $4 million and settle other claims for payments with the banks that financed Itel's computer leasing business.

The above enumerated agreements represented an understanding with parties representing the three main constituencies in Itel's reorganization bid. They reflect the extent of the agreements Itel's management had worked out as of this writing in July of 1982, after the first 18 months of negotiations. Negotiations leading to these agreements were, for sure, protracted and often difficult, invariably described by lawyers and other participants in such terms as "extremely complicated" and "agonizing." (The price tag of this initial 18 months of negotiations—in fees to lawyers, investment bankers, consultants and accountants, etc.—was put at $5 million!) Still to be negotiated as of then, were the terms of settlement with shareholders on the more than a dozen lawsuits they still had pending against the company—a matter in which a team of 13 lawyers were engaged on behalf of the shareholders alone.

Eventually, after having attained agreements with all the principal creditors, shareholders and other interested parties, Itel shall have been finally ready to submit to the court *a plan of reorganization* incorporating the various agreements and understandings for the court's "confirmation" or approval. (See requirements and procedures for confirmation on pp. 93-98 of the manual.)

The "New" Itel Already Showing Greater Financial Health

As of this account, Itel had not yet concluded its bankruptcy proceedings—it was yet to present a "plan of reorganization" to the court for confirmation. Yet, even at that stage, Itel had already begun to show many significant positive effects to a point where, by July 1982, some Itel executives were, by one account, beginning to say that "the company could well emerge from court protection by the end of this [1982] year." For one thing, the new slimmed-down Itel, which had been heavily stripped as part of the process of its Chapter 11 reorganization, suddenly found itself $300 million in cash richer*—thanks to the disposal of the less profitable segments of its businesses in computer sales and leasing, ships and aircraft and other equipment leasing ventures. Operating under the basic belief that Itel's problems "were largely isolated in computers," as one of the experts representing a major Itel lender put it, the central strategy the Itel executives had adopted in fashioning out a plan of reorganization had been to "tailor a company with two businesses"—with one part of the Itel operations, the computer-oriented part, cut away from the company and sold, and the remaining part of the operations (in railroad freight cars and cargo shipping container leasing) continued. For another thing, the new slimmed-down version of Itel had begun to show signs of revival and profitability before long: in the first quarter of 1982, the most recent for which figures were available as of this writing, Itel showed a net income of $6 million—compared with a loss of $600,000 in the first quarter of a year earlier for the comparative segment of the old Itel's companies. The new Itel has, as one newspaper headline aptly put it, "returned, slim and profitable"! [See below for a graphic depiction of the "new", slimmed down Itel relative to the old "bloated" (pre-bankruptcy) Itel!]

---

*Although the bulk of this $300 million would have to be claimed by Itel's creditors under the terms of its reorganization plan, Itel still stood to get needed operating cash flow, for the plan still called for Itel to keep about $25 million to finance its remaining businesses.

Itel Returns, Slim and Profitable.

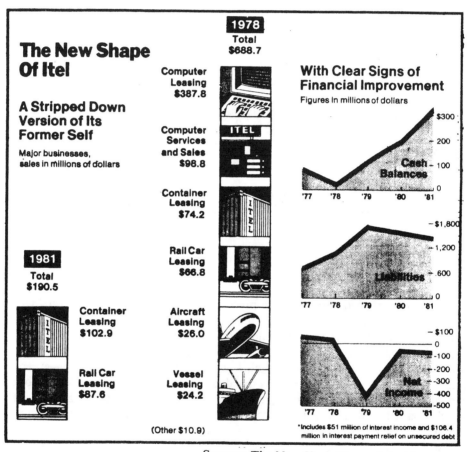

Source: *The New York Times*, July 18, 1982.

25

CHAPTER THREE

THE STEP-BY-STEP PROCEDURES FOR FILING FOR & PROCESSING A CHAPTER 11 CASE FROM START TO FINISH

As briefly explained elsewhere in a preceding section of this manual (pp. vii-viii , esp. the footnote therein), and much for the same reasons given therein, by and large it would probably not be practicable, and perhaps it would be even ill-advised, as a business debtor, to undertake the complete filing and processing of your Chapter 11 case from start to finish solely by yourself, without employing outside expert legal, financial, and other expert help—except, perhaps, for companies of very small size with a simple debt structure. Nevertheless, it cannot be emphasized enough that your informed knowledge of what is involved in such undertakings—of what the "experts" you'll hire to help you out do and how they'll probably go about it—still remains invaluable to you as a debtor or intending Chapter 11 filer.

Listed below, in this chapter, are a series of 16 simple "steps" which, taken together, take the reader through the complete procedures involved in filing and processing a Chapter 11 case through the bankruptcy court system, from start to finish. **But be cautioned:** To get and make the most out of the information provided in this chapter (or, for that matter, in any part of this manual), it is necessary that you take the "steps" one (and only *one*) at a time, following them *exactly* in the same numerical order in which they are listed in this chapter. Do not skip around from step to step, or from page to page (unless so instructed in the manual).

HERE ARE THE 16 SIMPLE SYSTEMATIC STEPS INVOLVED IN PROCESSING A CHAPTER 11 CASE:

step 1: DETERMINE THAT YOU MEET THE ELIGIBILITY REQUIREMENTS TO FILE UNDER CHAPTER 11.

Who is eligible? Basically, you would be eligible to file under Chapter 11 (business reorganization) provisions of the bankruptcy code if you meet the following three simple conditions:

   1. If you are either an individual (or a married couple) engaged in business, or you are business partnership, a limited liability company, or a corporation; and

   2. If you are NOT any of these: a governmental unit or agency, an estate or nonbusiness trust, a stockbroker, a commodity broker, a domestic or foreign insurance company, a bank, savings and loan association, a credit union, a small business investment company licensed by the S.B.A., or, in some states, a defunct corporation whose charter has been revoked by the state for nonpayment of fees or failure to file reports. (Such a defunct corporation which is not eligible for Chapter 11 reorganization relief, depending on the specific corporation's local state law, may **simply reinstate the debtor's charter with the state prior to filing under Chapter 11); and**

   3. If the Chapter 11 case is filed by the debtor "in good faith" -- that is, not as a means of obtaining relief that the Bankruptcy Code was not intended to provide, such as any other purposes other than an effective reorganization.

What does the "bad faith" requirement mean? Under a judicially-imposed standard, the courts have held that a Chapter 11 case that is found to have been filed in bad faith is subject to dismissal for cause under the Section 1112 (b) of the U.S. Bankruptcy Code. As articulated by the courts*, the concept of bad faith implies strong evidence of intent on the part of the debtor to abuse or misuse the judicial process and the primary reorganization purposes of Chapter 11. factors which indicate such an intent include the following

   (1) The lack of a realistic possibility of an effective reorganization of the debtor's business;

   (2) Evidence that the debtor seeks merely to delay or frustrate creditors or prevent foreclosure, or the legitimate efforts of secured creditors to enforce their rights;

   (3) Evidence that the debtor is seeking to use chapter 11 to create and organize a new business and not to reorganize or rehabilitate an existing business;

   (4) The timing of the debtor's relevant actions;

   (5) Evidence that the debtor is merely a shell corporation; and

   (6) Evidence that the debtor was created, or that important property was transferred to the debtor, for the sole purpose of obtaining protection under the automatic stay provided by a chapter 11 filing.

To determine whether a Chapter 11 case was filed in bad faith, however, a judicial inquiry must first have been conducted by the court which must take into account the totality of the circumstances.

   Does an individual have to be engaged in business to qualify to file under chapter 11? The answer is, No! A person need not be "engaged in an ongoing business" (or in any business of any kind) in the traditional sense in order to be eligible to file under Chapter 11. Quite to the contrary, any individual, whether in business or otherwise, is eligible to file under chapter 11.**

---

*See, for example, Trident Assocs. Ltd Partnership v. Metropolitan Life Insurance Co., 52 F.3d 127 (CA 6, 1995); National Land Corp, 825 F. 2d 296 (CA 11, 1987); and In re Kerr, 9089 F.2d 400 (CA 8, 1990)

**On June 13, 1991, in an opinion by Justice Blackman, the U.S. Supreme Court, by an 8 to 1 decision, ruled in favor of one Sheldon B. Teibb, by overturning a decision of the Federal Appeals Court in St. Louis, Mo., which had held that chapter 11 of the Bankruptcy Code could not be used by an individual not "engaged in an ongoing business". Thus, the Supreme Court established one uniform national standard that Chapter 11 is available to individuals who are not engaged in an established and continuing business.

However, in practical terms it just works out that in real life those who use Chapter 11 the most are persons with relatively larger debts and relatively large incomes and more complex financial structures than ordinarily possessed by the average individuals. As one bankruptcy expert put it, "as a practical matter, however, the person filing under chapter 11 must have something to reorganize, rehabilitate, or liquidate before chapter 11 (will make economic sense or be practicable).*" Non-business debtors with substantial personal investments or assets in real estate or stocks, for example, or middle or upper-income individuals who have enough assets to negotiate a repayment plan with the creditors, will be perfect candidates qualified to file under Chapter 11.

To sum is up in one word, just about anyone – whether in or out of business – is eligible, except a governmental unit or agency, a stockbroker or commodity broker, an insurance company, a banking institution, or an S.B.A. licensed small business company.

step 2 : GATHER NECESSARY INFORMATION AND IDENTIFY THE CAUSES OF THE DEBTOR'S FINANCIAL PROBLEMS

In order to be able to make a sound, informed decision on whether to reorganize under Chapter 11, or alternatively to undertake other remedies (e.g., selling the business or liquidating it, abandoning it, etc), it is most essential that you gain a reasonable knowledge and determination of the real, underlying causes of the business's financial difficulties and shortcomings. To begin the process of ascertaining the true causes of the business's financial difficulties, one central tool you will need it this: You must obtain and gather accurate financial and organizational data relating to the business. It does not matter if the business owner(s) think or claim they already know the answer to the basic question of the cause of their financial problem. It will still be useful and necessary that you go ahead and gather the data, in any case. For one thing, such data will still serve to confirm and verify (or refute) the owner(s) prejudgment And, even more importantly, such a data will serve to justify any plan of reorganization that may latter the proposed by and on behalf of the business owner(s).

What kinds of data will be required? The following are the kinds of data you should have .assembled on the business:

(1) A complete list of all debts owed by the business, including the name and address of each creditor, the exact amount and current status of each debt, a description of any actual or threatened action taken by each creditor, a description of the collateral, if any, securing each debt, and the names and addresses of any other persons or entities liable with the business on each debt.

(2) Copies of all notes, mortgages, security agreements, finance statements, and other financial agreements of the business currently in effect.

(3) Copies of all leases and executory contracts under which the business is currently obligated.

(4) A detailed statement of the current status of the business's trade credit, relationships with commercial lenders, and general credit rating.

(5) A list of all court actions, executions, attachments, foreclosures, and other creditor action presently pending against the business in any court or forum, and a statement of the current status of each proceeding.

(6) A list of all bank accounts, deposits with financial institutions, negotiable instruments, documents of title, securities, or other sources of cash or cash equivalent currently owned or possessed by the business, together with a statement as to the amount or value and the secured status of each item listed.

(7) An accurate and up-to-date balance sheet and profit and loss statement for the business, and copies of all such documents issued by or on behalf of the business during the previous two years.

---

* John H. Williamson, *The Attorney's Handbook on Bankruptcy*, p. 2

(8) Copies of the business's federal income tax returns for each of the last three years, and copies of any other documents available that show the income or expenses of the business during the last three years.

(9) Copies of the following: all documents under which the business was organized (e.g., articles of incorporation, bylaws, operating agreements, partnership agreements, etc.), minutes of all official meetings held by the business owners, and any agreements or other documents in any way dealing with the organizational or capital structure of the business.

(10) A list of all officers, directors, shareholders, partners, members, or other owners or persons in control of the business, and a description of the share of the business entity, if any, held by each person listed.

(11) A list of all significant management personnel of the business, a brief job description for each person listed, the compensation (current and deferred) paid to each, and copies of all employment contracts.

(12) A list of all other employees by class and a description of the compensation (current and deferred) paid to each class, together with a copy or complete description of the terms of any collective bargaining or similar agreements currently in effect.

(13) The names, addresses, and telephone numbers of all accountants, attorneys, and independent financial advisors employed or used by the business during the past two years.

How do you gather such data? A good practice will be for you to simply consult with your accountant or independent financial advisors presently (or previously) employed by the business, and have them do this for you. Such professionals are ideal for this in that they are generally likely to have a more objective evaluation and a better understanding of the business, and of its financial or management, ills, than the average business owner. Furthermore, an important part of such data, must include separate personal interviews by the evaluating professional (and by the business owners, as well) with key employees or managers of the business on the day-to-day business practices of the debtor and the business. And lastly, it may be necessary, especially in cases where conflicts exists as to the cause of the debtor's financial difficulties, to consult with industry experts, important creditors, financial or tax consultants, former employees, and assorted other persons, before a full picture of the actual causes of the debtor's financial problems may finally be determined. The causes of the business financial problems which may be indicated, may range widely: poor or dishonest management, lack of managerial experience, disagreement among the business owners, a general slump in the field of the company's business, chronic undercapitalization, a general rise in the cost of labor or supplies, or plain incompetence or other causes such as those listed under Section C of Chapter 1 of the manual above. Nevertheless, what is important here, is that once the above-listed documents and information are assembled, they should be carefully but objectively and truthfully analyzed, and such information should enable (the debtor) or anyone else to make an informed determination of the underlying causes of the business financial difficulties, and hence to formulate a workable plan of reorganization for the business, assuming a reorganization is the best available remedy indicated by such facts, or other causes such as those listed under Section C, chapter 1 of this manual.

step 3: MAKE PRELIMINARY ASSESSMENT OF THE CASE

After you shall have gathered the necessary information and made some fair determination of the underlying causes of your (the debtor's) financial difficulties – Step 2 above – you are now in the position to take the next step: namely, to make an assessment of your proposed Chapter 11 case. That is, there are a fair preliminary matters and functions you should address in advance of the actual filing of your chapter 11 case in order to ensure a proper and effective filing when you actually do so. These preliminary matters and functions include the following.

A. Collect the Information Needed to Prepare the Chapter 11 Forms and Documents for Filing.
    You will need to gather all the information that will be needed to prepare the chapter 11 forms (see p. 32 for the list of forms) for filing. To do this, simply use some worksheets or questionnaires that ask for all

the required information without repetition or omission. For this, you may · simply make an extra copy of the Chapter 11 forms and use them for that.

As for the source of such information, by and large the debtor's bookkeeper or accountant will be able to provide most of the necessary information at least for the average small or medium size business.

B. Determine If Preferential or Fraudulent Transfers Have Been Made.

It is important to discover early in the Chapter 11 case, all of the debtor's significant preferential or fraudulent transfers made to principal owners or key employees of the business, if any, and to appropriately address them. Under Section 547(b) of the Bankruptcy Code, a "preferential" transfer is defined as a transfer by the debtor, of an interest in property to or for the benefit of a creditor for payment of debt owed by the debtor prior to the transfer that was made while the debtor was insolvent and within 90 days before the date of filing of the Chapter 11 petition, and that enables such creditor to received more than it would have received in a Chapter 7 liquidation of the debtor's estate. The 90-day preferential look back period is increased to one year for transfers to "insiders" of the debtors (e.g., the debtor's relative, a general partner, a director in the business, if a corporation, or their relatives thereof, a person in control of the debtor, managing agent or affiliate of the debtor.)* And a "fraudulent" transfer is defined (see Section 548(a) of the Bankruptcy Code) as a transfer of an interest of the debtor in property or an obligation incurred by the debtor, which was made or incurred within one year prior to the date of the Chapter 11 filing, wherein the debtor made the transfer or incurred the obligation: **1)** With actual intent to hinder, delay, or defraud its present or future creditors; or **2)** the debtor received less than a reasonably equivalent value in exchange for the transfer or obligation; or **3)** the debtor was insolvent at the time of the transaction or became insolvent, undercapitalized, or unable to pay its debts as a result of that transaction..

The reasons why it's very important that you make a thorough review of all significant transfers and select out any preferential or fraudulent transfers, if any, even in advance of your filing the Chapter 11 petition, are basically two old. First, in order to determine early on what might be the personal liability of the persons to whom the transfers were made for the return of the funds or property transferred; and, secondly in order to prevent such transfers from later becoming grounds for having a trustee appointed in your bankruptcy case thereby taking away many of the management functions of the business from the debtor in bankruptcy. (see Step 9 on p. 79 for the negative effects of having a trustee appointed in a Chapter 11 case). Typically, in situations involving discovery of substantial preferential or fraudulent transfers, the filing of a chapter 11 case may result in the setting aside of such transfers by the courts and an order for its repayment by the transferees. Consequently, here's what you must do in advance of the filing of the Chapter 11 petition.

❖ All significant transfers of funds or property to insiders of the debtor made within the 12 month period prior to the proposed date of chapter 11 filing, should be closely scrutinized. And if it appears that a significant part of such transfer to an insider may have been preferentially or fraudulently made, then both you (the debtor) and the transferee had at least better be advised and forewarned of the potential consequences of that for your planned Chapter 11 case. In deed, in addition to some of the negative consequences already mentioned above, such matters often have an important bearing on determining when a chapter 11 case should be filed, or even whether at all it should be filed. This is true especially in situations involving small business debtors. For example, you could have a situation where it is in the best interest of the debtor to file the chapter 11 case immediately, while the interest of the insider-transferee who is the recipient of the transferred funds or property is best served by postponing the filing for a few months in order to protect the transfer from being "avoidable" (cancellable) by the court in bankruptcy. What do you do in such situation? The best practice would be for you (the debtor) and the insider-transferees to fully examine the possible ramifications, and then to decide on how and when best to proceed.

❖ All transfers of funds or property by the debtor to anyone within 90 days prior to proposed filing of the chapter 11, should be carefully examined for any preferential or fraudulent content, especially if the transfer was substantial and was not made in the ordinary course of the debtor's business. With small business debtors, particularly, it is common to find that often one or more of the principal owners is personally liable for an obligation paid off by a transfer that is probably preferential and thereby "avoidable" in bankruptcy. In such a situation, see whether it may be necessary to delay the filing of the chapter 11 case to protect such a transfer.

---

*See Section 101 (3) of the Bankruptcy Code for the definition of the "insider"

❖ Examine all significant transfers or obligations incurred by the debtor within one year of the bankruptcy filing, more particularly those that might have been made or incurred outside the ordinary course of the debtor's business. Realistically evaluate the consideration received by the debtor for any such transfer or obligation, especially if the transferee or oblige is an insider. Any transfers made to insiders or to companies owned or controlled by insiders, or important creditors of the debtor for insufficient consideration, would probably be deemed a fraudulent transfer or obligation by the courts.

C. Determine If You Should Elect To Be Treated As A "Small Business"

Under the Bankruptcy code [see Section 101 (51c) thereof] there are several advantages which apply for a debtor who qualifies to be treated as a "small business debtor." And in order to be able to take advantage of such provisions, a debtor who qualifies as a small business is required to affirmatively "elect" to be treated as a SMALL BUSINESS in the Chapter 11 case. In light of that, one important determination you will need to make prior to your filing your chapter 11 petition, is to determine whether or not you can qualify to file as a small business debtor.

You qualify as a small business for the purposes of chapter 11 filing, if you meet the following two requirements: 1) You are a person or entity engaged in a commercial or business activity, other than owning or operating a real estate business; and 2) your aggregate non-contingent liquidated and unsecured debts as of the date of the chapter 11 filing, do not exceed $2,000,000

Generally speaking, for a debtor filing as a small business, the handling of the case will be speedier, and therefore less expensive for the debtor. An electing small business debtor is permitted, for example, not to have a Creditor's Committee, such debtor is allowed a 100 day exclusive period in which to file a Chapter 11 Plan, and is subject to less restrictive provisions with respect to the Disclosure Statements and the solicitation of acceptances of a proposed Plan.

Under the bankruptcy rules, however, for you to be treated as a qualifying "small business" in a Chapter 11 case, assuming you are so qualified, you would have to actual "elect" to do so by filing a notice of the election with the bankruptcy court **within** 60 days from the date of the filing of the bankruptcy petition. In practice, such election is normally made when the petition is filed, as a provision for making the election is contained on the petition itself. **Hence, you should simply be sure to analyze your situation in advance and to determine, prior to the filing, whether you are qualified as a small business, and if you will elect to be treated as one in the case.**

D. Determine Whether And When To Employ An Attorney And Other Professionals In the Case.

It is worth noting that nothing in the Bankruptcy Code or Rules necessarily requires (or restricts) employment of an attorney or other professionals in a Chapter 11 bankruptcy case, and a debtor does not necessarily have to have legal representation in a Chapter 11 case, at least at the pre-filing stages of the case. [See, for example, Section 327 of the Code, Rule 9010 and 9011 of the Rules of Bankruptcy Procedures, and Kressel V. Kotts, 34 BR 388, 392 (MN, 1983)]. Nevertheless, whether out of custom or otherwise, it is common for debtors to engage the services of an attorney even in the pre-filing stages of the Chapter 11 case.

In any event, one of the important matters for you (the debtor) to determine even before the actual Filing of the chapter 11 petition, is whether you need immediate employment of an attorney (or some other professional) particularly in the pre-filing stages of your case, if at all. Assuming that you will be employing an attorney in your case, you should know that for most small business debtors, the principal expense of a Chapter 11 proceeding are usually attorney and other professional fees. In deed, in many small business chapter 11 cases the only professional that is employed is the debtor's attorney. Much of which other professionals, if any, get employed, will depend on the size and financial structure of the debtor's business and the extend of the reorganization contemplated. The services of other professionals such as an accountant, financial consultant, stockbroker, tax specialist, appraiser, or others, may be needed in particular senses. There are three basic options for you may explore on the issue of attorney employment. (1) You may hire an attorney to do the pre-filing bankruptcy paperwork for you; or (2) you may hire one to represent your bankruptcy interests AFTER the filing of the case (the post-filing era representation); or, (3)

---

*Indeed, the Federal Rules of Bankruptcy Procedures explicitly allows for explicit personal representation by the debtors, creditors or others themselves, in a bankruptcy case, if and when preferred. Rule 9010 provides as follows: "(a) AUTHORITY TO ACT PERSONALLY OR BY ATTORNEY. A debtor, creditor, equity security holder... may (1) appear in a case under the Code and act either in the entity's own behalf or by an attorney authorized to practiced in the court, and perform any act not constituting the practice of law, by an authorized agent, attorney in fact, or proxy."

you may, if you prefer, personally represent yourself in bankruptcy proceedings. In any case, given the fact that the principal expense of Chapter 11 proceedings, are usually attorney (and other professional) fees, it will be important for you to have your accountant determine the anticipated amount of these fees, especially those that will have to be paid during the 6 month period after the filing of the case. Both the filing fees and the Chapter 11 quarterly fee payable to the U.S. Bankruptcy Trustee during the pendency of the Chapter 11 case, should be taken into account (see p. 69 for the amount of the fees) in making the necessary calculation and budgeting for the debtor's post filing supply of cash. In answering the question of when to employ an attorney or other professionals, or even whether at all to hire one, much will largely depend therefore on to what extent it can be ascertained that the debtor will have sufficient funds especially during the several months after the commencement of the case to both maintain its business activities and pay the expenses of a chapter 11 proceeding.

(See pp 185, 187 for a sample copy of the form., titled, *"Application For Order Approving Employment of Attorney."*

step 4: ORDER THE INITIAL FORMS YOU'LL NEED TO FILE THE BANKRUPTCY PETITION.

OK., let's say you've now come to the decision to file for bankruptcy and that the type you choose to go for is "straight" Chapter11. Your next order of business is, of course, to get started: GET THE NECESSARY FILING FORMS.

You may order from the Publisher a complete package of the appropriate forms that are usable in every state. The package of petition forms – the initial forms you'll need to commence the case and thereby bring your company under the legal protection of the Code – are enumerated in "STEP FIVE" below, and are sampled on p. 32 of the manual. Our posture in this manuals is, of course, that the average Chapter 11 debtor should not be expected to undertake the complete procedures involved in declaring Chapter 11 bankruptcy (meaning all 18 "steps" of this chapter) all by himself. Nevertheless, the extent of such limitations that we suggest should not be mistaken. For one thing, a debtor in an average case can all alone on his own, competently initiate the Chapter 11 action – and automatically begin to enjoy all the legal protections for a company in bankruptcy – simply by preparing the initial petition papers (Step 5 below), and filing them in court (Step 6 below).

For the added convenience of the readers, The **Do-It-Yourself legal Publishers** makes available to its readership the standard, fully pre-sorted, all-in-one package of forms – containing a complete set with 2 true copies plus one "practice" copy of each of the necessary forms. The Publisher supplied forms are pre-carbonized for easy handling and are identical to the forms used for illustration on pp.53-67 of this manual. They are suitable for use in every state of the nation.

To order the publisher's standard "all-in-one" bankruptcy kit of forms, just complete the **Order Form** on p. 228 and send it away to the Publisher's legal forms Division therein.

NOTE: Clearly specify that you want the "Bankruptcy Petition forms for Chapter 11 business re-organization".

step 5: FILL OUT THE INITIAL PETITION FORMS

The initial forms which need to be completed to initiate a Chapter 11 case, are listed below. You'll find blank copies of each of these forms in the kit you ordered in "STEP FOUR" above. (Disregard, for now, any other forms you may find in the kit, unless they are specifically required of you by your local district's court clerk.)

Generally, the forms obtained from this Publisher ("Step above) would include one extra copy beyond the minimum number of copies required to be filed – look for the yellow or canary color sheet. Use these for practice work sheet purposes

To complete the forms, fill out the forms contained in the kit in the exact order in which they are listed below in this chapter. For each form, tear out the singly 'practice sheets" (the yellow or canary color copies), and use a pencil to complete them first, closely following the illustrations or instructions on the sample forms in this manual. Then, check them through to make sure that you have everything pretty much in order. Thereafter, using a typewriter, you may then transfer the information to the final, actual forms (the write sheets) that will get filed with the court. You will notice that in most instances, instructions on what information to fill in are already printed in, right on the blank pre-printed forms. And the sample forms that are used for illustrations in this manual only add to those instructions, as and when necessary.

The forms you are to complete (from the bankruptcy kit of forms you ordered), are now listed below.

IMPORTANT: COMPLETE THESE FORMS IN THE **EXACT** SEQUENTIAL ORDER IN WHICH THEY ARE LISTED BELOW.
1. VOLUNTARY PETITION:
(See p.63-4 for a sample illustrating the preparation of this form).

Schedule A—Real Property..35
Schedule B---Personal Property...35
Schedule C---Property Claimed As Exempt...37
Schedule D---Creditors Holding Secured Claims....................................39
Schedule E---Creditors Holding Unsecured Priority Claims...................41
Schedule F---Creditors Holding Unsecured NonPriority Claims............43
Schedule G--- Executory Contracts & Unexpired Leases.......................45
Schedule H---Co-debtors...47
Schedule I---Current Income of Business Debtors..................................48
Schedule J---Current Expenditures of Business Debtors........................49
Summary of Schedules..50
Declaration Concerning Debtor's Schedules...51
Statement of Financial Affairs..52
List of Creditors Holding 20 Largest Unsecured Claims......................57-8
List of Equity Security Holders..59
Exhibit "A" To Voluntary Petition..60
Notice to Individual Consumers...61
Address Matrix...62
Form 1 –Voluntary Petition...63-4
Debtor's Resolution Authorizing Commencement of Case....................65
Request For Order That Creditors' Committee Not Be Appointed.........66
The Blue Backer/Cover..67

AN IMPORTANT NOTE ABOUT THE FORMS:

Although, broadly speaking, the bankruptcy courts are operated under the same basic laws and rules all across the country, nevertheless, each court in each Federal district has it's own "local court rules" which govern minor issues of details and specifics -- matters such as the format of the forms, the number of copies required, the specific sequence of procedures, etc. Occasionally, a bankruptcy filer, especially one filing pro se without an attorney, may encounter a court clerk in a given bankruptcy court district who would insist that the debtor must use certain specific 'local forms' exclusively, and nothing else.

It is important, under the circumstance, that our readers know that the illustrative sample forms used by this publisher in this manual, and those sold by the Publisher to its readership for use for their bankruptcy filings, have been painstakingly designed by bankruptcy experts and professional legal forms drafters so as to meet the "substantial compliance" standard as prescribed under the bankruptcy rules.

Essentially, every bankruptcy court is required to use certain "Official Forms" designed and designated for use nationally by the U.S Supreme Court, basically establishing the contents and numbering of the forms. Under the controlling bankruptcy rule in this matter (Rule 9009 of the Rules of Bankruptcy Procedure), the user of the Official Forms (or any private publishers of bankruptcy forms) are permitted to modify the format of the official forms as they may deem appropriate, so long as any such modified forms still basically ask the same questions and provide the same information in the same order. This is the so-called "substantial compliance" rule.

Furthermore, Rule 9029 of the Rules of Bankruptcy Procedure, further state that courts may NOT reject documents or forms presented to them for filing, if indeed (i.e., so long as) those documents or forms contain the essential substance prescribed by the "Official Forms" and meet the requirements for one-sided printing, pre-punched holes, and adequate top margins. Nor do the courts have the legal authority to impose local rules which vary in substance from the official forms on the claim by them that the proffered papers or documents differ from the locally preferred version. Furthermore, under Rule 5005(a), the *"clerk (or Court) shall not refuse to accept for filing any paper presented for the purpose solely because it is not presented in proper form as required by these rules or any local rules or practices"*; only the Bankruptcy Judge may do so.

INSTRUCTIONS: ON COMPLETING THE VOLUNTARY PETITION (Sampled on p. 63 & 64)

This 2-page form is used to commence a voluntary case under Chapter 7, 11, 12 or 13 of the Bankruptcy Code. This form is largely self-explanatory. You merely have to check off the rectangular boxes which apply to you, and enter "NONE" where they do not apply to you. Simply use Exhibit 3-G on pp.   as a guide in preparing this petition form.

Exhibit A To The Petition (p.60 of the form) is to be completed and attached but ONLY IF the debtor has issued publicly traded securities or bonds. And Exhibit B (p.2 of the form) is to be completed ONLY IF the debtor is an individual whose debts are primarily **consumer debts.** By and large, if you are a SMALL BUSINESS debtor, you probably would not need to file Exhibit A.

NOTE THE FOLLOWING POINTERS IN PREPARING THIS FORM

- Be sure to check the appropriate boxes for "election" for you to be treated as a SMALL BUSINESS debtor (p.1 of the Voluntary Petition form), assuming that you qualify as a small business and wish to file as one. (See Section C of Step 3 above, for information of the advantages of filing as a "small business" debtor.)

- If you do not wish to have a Creditor Committee appointed in the case (it's bad for a creditor to have a Creditors' Committee present in virtually every case, as fully explained in Step 3, Section C of this chapter), then this may be the time to request for an order by the Court for a Creditors Committee NOT to be appointed. Local rules of some jurisdictions make such a specific request unnecessary, however.

- In the very first item on the form, be sure to enter the proper "venue" – that is, the proper Bankruptcy Court and location in which you are to file (Appendix E).

- The Petition is to be signed by you, the Debtor; or by a principal or chief executive officer of the debtor company and by the debtor's attorney, if any is employed in the case, or has been employed as of that point. If the debtor is a partnership, it is to be signed by ALL the general partners.

INSTRUCTIONS: ON COMPLETING SCHEDULE A
(Sampled on p.35))

Except as otherwise directed below, you are required to list in this schedule all **REAL PROPERTY** in which you (or a co-debtor) have any legal, equitable, or future interests, including all real property you own as co-tenant or community property, or in which you have "life estate" rights. *Include any of the following, if applicable to you:*

- A house or dwelling structure
- Duplex Boat or marina dock space
- Residence Airplane hangar
- Mobile home
- Vacation cabin
- Unimproved land
- Mobile home park space
- Rental property
- Agricultural land or farm land
- Crops in the ground
- Condominium or coop unit

TO COMPLETE SCHEDULE A

In completing this Schedule, see the Worksheet (p.35) for the required Schedule A information. In the column marked **(1)**, you should enter the type of property (e.g., "a 2-family house," or "an unimproved lot measuring 100 ft. by 95 ft." or a "condominium unit"), as well as the address. If you own NO real property, simply enter "NONE." In the column marked **(2)**, enter the kind of ownership interest you have in the property (e.g., you may own title to the property under "joint tenancy" or "tenancy by the entirety" or in "fee simple" or "life estate"). If you are married, indicate in the column marked **(3)**, whether ONLY the husband owns the property by entering "H", or ONLY the wife "W", or both spouses JOINTLY own it "J". If you live in a "COMMUNITY PROPERTY state, enter "C". In column **(4)**, simply enter the current fair MARKET VALUE your interest in the property will fetch today — that is, without figuring in the mortgage still outstanding on the property, if any, or the applicable homestead exemption to which you're entitled. [Get the current price estimates from a local real estate broker in the property's neighborhood.] In column **(5)**, enter the amount for any lien or secured interest (i.e., mortgage) held by any entities in the property, or enter "NONE" if the property is fully paid for.

NOTE: Real estate interests resulting from Executory Contracts or Unexpired Leases should be listed in Schedule G, and not here in Schedule A. And if the debtor is an individual, or if a joint petition is being filed, state the amount of the EXEMPTION claimed in the property ONLY in Schedule C.

INSTRUCTIONS: ON COMPLETING SCHEDULE B (Sampled on p. 35-6)

This Schedule is for the listing of all PERSONAL PROPERTY, of whatever kind, owned by you – EXCEPT Executory Contracts and Unexpired leases (which are to be listed, by the way, in Schedule G). In the column marked **(2)**, place an 'X' against any property category for which you have no property. [If additional space is needed for any property category, attach a separate continuation sheet properly identified with the case name, case #, and the number for the category]. In the column marked **(3)**, list the items of the property involved, to the extent possessed by you, and give a brief description and location thereof. Property being held for you by someone else, if any, also goes here (enter that person's name and address). In column **(4)**, enter the letter "H", if the designated property category is owned ONLY by the husband, or the letter "W", if it's owned ONLY by the wife, or the letter "J", if it's owned jointly by BOTH spouses, or if you are filing in a COMMUNITY PROPERTY state, enter the letter "C". In column **(5)**, simply enter the current fair MARKET VALUE of each property – that is, what you calculate the property would fetch today in a fair, open 'garage sale' market; NOT what you paid for it, or even what you may still be owing on it, or the applicable property exemption, if any, [For example, let's say you own a boat which you list on the Schedule, and that it's worth (i.e. it is reasonably saleable for) $5,000 in today's market, and that you still owe $2,000 on it, and are entitled to an exemption of $1,000 for boats under the state or federal exemption law in which you file. You will disregard every other detail and only put down the figure $5,000 in column **(5)**, representing just the boat's present market value.]

In completing schedule B, property such as accounts receivable, licenses, office equipment, and inventory, should be itemized with reasonable particularity.

NOTE: **If you own interest in EXECUTORY CONTRACTS or UNEXPIRED LEASES, do not list them in this (or other); rather, list them in Schedule G ONLY.**

[Debtor's Name]

In re: <u>New Hope, Inc.</u>

35

(Get this from Court clerk at the time of filing)

Debtor(s)   Case No. 92-B11146 ____ (if known)

SCHEDULE A - REAL PROPERTY

DESCRIPTION AND LOCATION OF PROPERTY (1)	NATURE OF DEBTOR'S INTEREST IN PROPERTY (2)	H W J C (3)	CURRENT MARKET VALUE OF DEBTOR'S INTEREST IN PROPERTY WITHOUT DEDUCTING ANY SECURED CLAIM OR EXEMPTION (4)	AMOUNT OF SECURED CLAIM (5)
A commercial building at 2 Park Place, New York, N.Y. 10002	Owned by debtor in fee simple		$197,000	Ist Mortgage $140,000 2nd Mortgage - $25,000

Total -> $ 197,000

(Report also on Summary of Schedules.)

SCHEDULE B - PERSONAL PROPERTY

TYPE OF PROPERTY (1)	N O N E (2)	DESCRIPTION AND LOCATION OF PROPERTY (3)	H W J C (4)	CURRENT MARKET VALUE OF DEBTOR'S INTEREST IN PROPERTY WITHOUT DEDUCTING ANY SECURED CLAIM OR EXEMPTION (5)
1. Cash on hand		Petty cash fund	N/A	$210
2. Checking, savings or other financial accounts, certificates of deposit, or shares in banks, savings and loan, thrift, building and loan, and homestead associations, or credit unions, brokerage houses, or cooperatives.		company checking account, Friendly Bank, 2 Mall St., N.Y. N.Y. 10016		$900
3. Security deposits with public utilities, telephone companies, landlords, and others.		Deposit, Manhattan Electric Co., 10 Manhattan St. N.Y. N.Y. 10005 ($200); Security deposit with landlord for store,Landlord Corp. of N.Y. Inc,100 5th Ave., N.Y. N.Y. 10012 ($2800)		$3,000
4. Household goods and furnishings including audio, video and computer equipment.	X			
5. Books; pictures and other art objects; antiques; stamp, coin, record, tape, compact disc, and other collections or collectibles.	X			
6. Wearing apparel.	X			
7. Furs and jewelry.	X			
8. Firearms and sports, photographic, and other hobby equipment.	X			
9. Interests in insurance policies. Name insurance company of each policy and itemize surrender or refund value of each.		Life insurance, Equity Insurance Co., 12 Orchard Rd. Boston MA 02118. Policy #19-1888 (Current surrender value on life of the President)*		$1,900

[Name of Debtor]

In re: New Hope,Inc., DEBTORS.   36

SCHEDULE B
PERSONAL PROPERTY

Case No. _92-B11146_ (if known)

TYPE OF PROPERTY (1)	NONE (2)	DESCRIPTION AND LOCATION OF PROPERTY (3)	HWJC (4)	CURRENT MARKET VALUE OF DEBTOR'S INTEREST IN PROPERTY WITHOUT DEDUCTING ANY SECURED CLAIM OR EXEMPTION (5)
10. Annuities. Itemize and name each issuer.	X		N/A	-0-
11. Interests in IRA, ERISA, Keogh, or other pension or profit sharing plans. Itemize	X			_0_
12. Stock and interests in incorporated and unincorporated businesses. Itemize.		100 shares of Texco Corporation stock, assigned to & kept by Amico Factoring Co(1 Wall St., N.Y. N.Y.) as loan security.		$3,000*
13. Interest in partnerships or joint ventures. Itemize.	X			-0-
14. Government and corporate bonds and other negotiable and nonegotiable instruments.		U.S. Savings Bonds,Series "E", in Safe deposit box, National Bank,190 E. 40th St. N.Y. 10016.		$4,000
15. Accounts receivable.		See attached List, "ACCOUNTS RECEIVABLE"		$10,000
16. Alimony, maintenance, support, and property settlements to which the debtor is or may be entitled. Give particulars.	X			-0-
17. Other liquidated debts owing debtor including tax refunds. Give particulars.	X	*[Will include: wages or fees due the debtor, tax refunds due you from returns already filed, vacation or sick pay earned, judgments won but not yet collected, commission already earned but not collected, disability benefits or life insurance proceeds due you for which the insured had already died].*		-0-
18. Equitable or future interests, life estates, and rights or powers exercisable for the benefit of the debtor other than those listed in Schedule of Real Property.	X	*[Refers to money/property not in debtor's possession at this time but due the debtor in the future].*		-0-
19. Contingent and noncontingent interests in estate of a decedent, death benefit plan, life insurance policy, or trust.	X	*[Inheritance from an estate of a person who has died but for which you are just awaiting distribution, workers compensation due you, earned but unpaid wages].*		-0-
20. Other contingent and unliquidated claims of every nature, including tax refunds, counterclaims of the debtor, and rights to setoff claims. Give estimated value of each.	X	*[Refers to claims or debts owed to you by government, corporation, businesses, or individuals, but which are still in dispute, e.g. expected tax refunds. In general, any claims you think you may have against any entity for which you haven't yet obtained a court judgment on].*		-0
21. Patents, copyrights, and other intellectual property. Give particulars.	X	*[Will include: trade secrets, trademarks, tradenames].*		-0-
22. Licenses, franchises, and other general intangibles. Give particulars.	X	*[Will include: liquor licenses, exclusive or non-exclusive licenses].*		-0-
23. Automobiles, trucks, trailers, and other vehicles and accessories.		1988 Dodge delivery truck,ID #AP 42778 (Repossessed) 1990 Ford pick-up van,ID#2889147 1989 Chevy Camero ID #122568		$5,000 $8,000 $2,500
24. Boats, motors, and accessories.	X			
25. Aircraft and accessories.	X			
26. Office equipment, furnishings, and supplies.		Office furnitures(desks,chairs,file cabinets),copy machine,2 typewriters, 2 computers,with printers,miscallaneous variety store supplies& warehouse equipmts.		$6000
27. Machinery, fixtures, equipment, and supplies used in business.				
28. Inventory.				
29. Animals.	X	Store supplies & variety store goods for sale[Attach listing if necessary]		$20,000
30. Crops - growing or harvested. Give particulars.	X			
31. Farming equipment and implements.	X			
32. Farm supplies, chemicals, and feed.	X			
33. Other personal property of any kind not already listed. Itemize.	X			

(Include amounts from any continuation sheets attached. Report total also on Summary of Schedules)   Total -> $ 64,510

_____ continuation sheets attached

*Get current price quote from stock broker or today's newspaper.

[Name of Debtors]

In re: New Hope, Inc., DEBTOR

37

Case No. _____ (if known)

[Enter this]

SCHEDULE C - PROPERTY CLAIMED AS EXEMPT

Debtor elects the exemptions to which debtor is entitled under (Check one box)

☐ 11 U.S.C. § 522(b)(1): Exemptions provided in 11 U.S.C. § 522(d). Note: These exemptions are available only in certain states.

☐ 11 U.S.C. § 522(b)(2): Exemptions available under applicable nonbankruptcy federal laws, state or local law.

DESCRIPTION OF PROPERTY (1)	SPECIFY LAW PROVIDING EACH EXEMPTION (2)	VALUE OF CLAIMED EXEMPTION (3)	CURRENT MARKET VALUE OF PROPERTY WITHOUT DEDUCTING EXEMPTION (4)
NOT APPLICABLE – DEBTOR IS A CORPORATION.	NOTE: [Only persons conducting business as sole individual proprietorships may claim exemption in such business property -- and only if the property is solely owned by such debtor. Debtors conducting business as partnerships or corporations may not, therefore, claim exemptions for partnership assets or corporate property. The general rule is simple: if you are an individual debtor, you may not keep any "exempt" property, unless you list and claim it as exempt -- on this page. If the debtor is filing as an individual, then see Anosike, "How To Declare Your Personal Bankruptcy," especially Chapter B thereof, for details on the claiming of exemptions.]		

INSTRUCTIONS: ON COMPLETING SCHEDULE D (Sampled on p. 39)

Simply defined, SECURED debts (or claims) are those kinds of debts or financial obligations for which you might have put up or pledged certain property (a "collateral") as a guarantee ("security") that if you fail to pay, the creditor can take, repossess or sell that pledged property to recoup its claim. The three Schedules that are known as the *Schedules of Liabilities* – namely, Schedules D, E, and F -- are largely self-explanatory, only that they may take some time to complete if the debtor has a large number of creditors. The names and addresses of ALL creditors with secured claims (claims secured, in whole or in part, by property of the debtor's estate or by a right of set-off) should be listed in Schedule D; those for ALL creditors holding claims which are unsecured but are entitled to PRIORITY under the Bankruptcy Code, should be listed in Schedule E; and those of ALL creditors holding claims which are UNSECURED and also NOT entitled to PRIORITY under the bankruptcy Code (i.e., creditors holding general unsecured claims), should be listed in Schedule F. Each particular claim must be listed only once, in just one among the three Schedules of Liabilities.

To complete the Schedule D (sample on p.39), list the creditors alphabetically by surname or company name. Enter in appropriate spaces provided in the column marked **(1)**, the name, mailing address (include zip code), and account number, if any, of each of your creditors whose claims are of SECURED type. Include secured creditors having secured interests of any kind -- judgment liens, garnishments, statutory liens, mortgages, deeds of trust, etc. (If all will not contain on the page, use a continuation sheet properly labeled). In the column marked **(2)**, labeled "CODT," place an 'X' therein if the claim listed has any other co-debtors (other than a spouse in a joint case) who may be jointly liable with you for the claim ---guarantors, co-signers, and the like. *You're required simply to indicate in this scheduled that such a co-debtor exists, but details about the co-debtor are reserved for and provided in scheduled H ONLY.*

If your petition is a joint petition, indicate in the column marked **(3)**, whether the husband ONLY ("H"), or wife ONLY ("W") or BOTH spouses ("J"), is liable on each claim by placing the appropriate letter in the column marked **(3)**; or if your state is a Community Property state, enter "C" therein. In column **(4)**, enter date when debt was incurred or the judgment lien was recorded; the nature of the debt (including the secured property or collateral pledged or the property subject to lien); the secured property's present fair MARKET VALUE,* given its age and present condition – that is, the price the property would fetch in the market today in a forced or garage sale.

In the column marked **(5)**, place a "C" therein, if the claim is contingent,* or a "U", if the claim is unliquidated*, or a "D", if it is disputed.* (You may need to place more than one letter for a claim, if applicable). In column **(6)**, simply enter here what the creditor says you owe him – that is, in full, what the creditor is asking for to pay off the debt. In column **(7)**, enter that part of the secured claim which is NOT secured, if there is any – simply, the amount by which the claim is greater than the market value of the property.**

NOTE: The 'market value' of the secured property (Column **(4)** of the Schedule], is listed somewhat differently when and where the secured item has MORE THAN ONE claim on it – e.g., say a house has a mortgage, plus a second deed of trust, and a judicial lien. To calculate a 'market value' in such situation, what you'll do will be to apportion that market value of the item in such a way that, when you add all the various claims together, the combined total will be equal to the market value of the item. Such apportionment is made in one of two different ways, depending on one factor: if the combined totals of all the claims is LESS than the market value of the item, it is made in one way, and if the combined totals is MORE than the market value of the item, it is made another way.

Procedure when the combined totals of all claims against the property is LESS than the property's market value.

You list as the market value of that claim, as well, the full value of each additional claim other than the first claim. Then total up these additional claims and deduct this total from the market value of the secured property and list the leftover thereof as the market value for the first claim.

Example: Let's say your house has a market value of $100.000 and an $80.000 mortgage. But also has a $13,000 secured deed of trust and a $3,000 judgment lien against the property. First, you'll list under column **(4)** of Schedule D each of the additional claims: $13,000 as the market value of the second deed of trust, then $3,000 as the market value of the judgment lien. And, upon your subtracting these additional claims ($13,000 and $3,000 or $16,000) from the $100,000 market value of the property, what you get is the market value of the main claim (the mortgage), that is, $84,000. [Countercheck: if you add all the claims on the property (i.e., $13,000 and $3,000 and $84,000), this amount should equal the full market value of the property, which is $100,000.]

Procedure when the combined totals of all claims against the property is MORE than the market value of the property. You list as the market value of the first claim the full value of that claim. Then, deduct this amount from the

---

*See Appendix F, the Glossary of Termss, for definition. Note that if you (a debtor) wish to dispute a claim, it is only necessary for you to place an "X" in the appropriate column in the Schedule; it is not necessary that you file a detailed statement of your contention.

** A claim (debt) may not be fully secured, but may be only partially secured, leaving the balance of the debt to be treated as unsecured portion. A partially secured debt is one secured by a lien (collateral) whose value is LESS than the amount of the claim — that is, where the value (amount) of the claim exceeds the value of the collateral securing the claim. To put it another way, if the value of a creditor's interest in the collateral securing the claim is less than the amount of its claim, then only the value of the creditor's interest in the collateral is regarded as a secured claim; the balance of it's claim is treated as unsecured claim. Example: Say a creditor's claim against a debtor is for the amount of $10,000, and the market value of the collateral securing it is worth only $7,000. Then, only the $7,000 portion (i.e., to the extent of the present fair market value of the creditor's interest in the collateral) is treated as secured claim, and the remainder of the claim, the $3,000, is treated as an "unsecured" claim.

[The Debtor's Name]

39

[Enter this]

In re: New Hope, Inc., DEBTOR

Case No._____ (if known)

SCHEDULE D - CREDITORS HOLDING SECURED CLAIMS

CREDITOR'S NAME AND MAILING ADDRESS INCLUDING ZIP CODE (1)	CO DEB T (2)	H W J C (3)	DATE CLAIM WAS INCURRED, NATURE OF LIEN, AND DESCRIPTION AND MARKET VALUE OF PROPERTY SUBJECT TO LIEN (4)	C U D (5)	AMOUNT OF CLAIM WITHOUT DEDUCTING VALUE OF COLLATERAL (6)	UNSECURED PORTION IF ANY (7)
ACCOUNT NO AL-29756-90 Americar Loan Corp. 114 20th St., Bronx N.Y. 10456			Loan for purchase of used 1990 Ford pick-up van, 5/90 VALUE $ 6000	U	$8,000	$2000
ACCOUNT NO 86705 Amico Factoring Corp. 1 Wall St., N.Y. N.Y. 10007			Secured interest in Accounts Receivable obtained, incurred 6/20/91 VALUE $ 4000	U	$5,800	$1,800
ACCOUNT NO. W-68345-88 Americar Loan Corp. 114 20th St., Bronx N.Y.10456			Loan obtained 5/88, for purchase of del'vry truck,1988 Dodge(Rep-ossessed)* VALUE $5,000	U	$6000	$1000
ACCOUNT NO A-45321 Alton Zinger Realty, 250 Plaza Place, Bronx N.Y. 10456			2nd mortgage on bldg. at 2 Park Pl. N.Y. NY 10002, per loan cont-ract 4/1/90 VALUE $25,000**	U	$25,000	–
ACCOUNT NO. BF-292776 Business Finance, Inc 290 Lexington Ave. N.Y. N.Y. 10036			Secured interest in furnitures & computers; loan obtained 2/2/89 VALUE $ 10,000	U	$16,000	$6000
ACCOUNT NO ML107410 Maple Leasing,Ltd 410 Maple St., Yonkers N.Y. 10710			Fixtures at busines offices obtained 3/90 VALUE $ 3000	U	$5000	$2000
ACCOUNT NO. WV-4278-91 Walden Variety Wholesalers 10 Jerico St., Jersey City, NJ 07122			Claim in merchandise inventory obtained, incurred 2/1/91 VALUE $7,000	U	$10,000	$3,000
ACCOUNT NO. RE-12354 Wellington Bank, 119 Mab-Ave., N.Y. N.Y. 10012			Ist Mortgage on Bldg. at 2 Park Pl.N.Y. N.Y. 10002,per loan contr-act 4/1/88 VALUE $ 172,000**	U	$140,000	–
ACCOUNT NO. VALUE $						

____ no continuation sheets attached

Subtotal -> (Total of this page) $ 215,800

Total -> (use only on last page) $ 215,800

Report this (the final total) on Summary of Schedules

(Report total also on Summary of Schedules)

*

market value of the property. Repeat this procedure for each succeeding claim until the item's value has been used up, simply listing the leftover amount in each round (if any) as the market value of each such succeeding claim.

Example: Let's say your home has a market value of $100,000, and an $80,000 mortgage, but also has an $18,000 second deed of trust and a $10,000 judgment lien against the property. In this case, first, you'll list as the market value of the first claim (the mortgage) in column (4) of Schedule D, the full amount of $80,000. Then, upon subtracting the $80,000 from $100,000 (the full market value of the property), this leaves you with a leftover of $20,000. Now, you deduct the $18,000 (representing the market value of the second deed of trust) from the $20,000 leftover, giving you a final left over of $2,000. This time, you'll simply list this final leftover amount ($2,000) as the market value of the next succeeding claim, the judgment lien. [Countercheck: if you add all the claims on the property (i.e., $80,000 and $18,000 and $2,000), this amount should equal the full market value of the property, or $100,000.]

IMPORTANT: Be sure not to omit any creditors, and that the correct address of each creditor be listed, on the particular appropriate liability Schedule (schedule D, E, or F). Under a very important rule of the Bankruptcy procedure, if a creditor is not listed in the bankruptcy schedules, and winds up not receiving notice of the bankruptcy procedures in time for him to be able to file a proof of claim, then such creditor's claim will generally remain undischarged in the case, meaning that the debtor will still remain liable for it.

INSTRUCTIONS: ON COMPLETING SCHEDULE
E (Sampled on p. 41)

What is a "**PRIORITY**" debt or claim? In a word, priority debts are simply some designated categories and types of debts which, by definition of the bankruptcy law, are given the privilege of being the <u>FIRST</u> in line to be paid off – if (just if) the bankruptcy filer were to still have some non exempt property left over to be distributed to creditors. You are simply to list here, alphabetically by surname or company name, ALL <u>unsecured</u> claims that are or may be entitled to <u>priority</u> of payment.

Note, however, that as a rule, most priority-type debts are usually business-oriented debts, as a glance at the different categories of debts or claims listed on 'Schedule E (See sample on p.41) will immediately indicate.

To complete Schedule E, first put a check mark ☑ next to each of the boxes which designates the types of priority debts owed by you, if any. [Or, if you have NONE of the kinds of debts or claims listed therein, simply check off the very first box and proceed next to Schedule F.] Next, enter within the spaces in the column marked (**I**), the name, mailing address (include zip code), and account or case number, if any, of each party. In column (**2**) labeled "CO DEBT", place an "X" therein if the claim listed has any other co-debtors (other than the spouse in a joint case) who may be jointly liable with you for the claim — guarantors, co-signers, and the like. You're required simply to indicate here that such a co-debtor exists, but the details about the co-debtor are reserved for and provided in Schedule H ONLY. If your petition is a **joint** petition, indicate in the column marked (**3**), whether the husband ONLY ("H"), or wife ONLY ("W"), or BOTH spouses ("J"), or the COMMUNITY PROPERTY, if your state is a so-called community property state ("C"), is liable on each claim by placing the appropriate letter in column (**3**). In the column marked (**4**), enter the date when the claim against you was incurred or officially recorded, and the nature of the claim (what the claim is for). You could be general in your description. In Column (**5**), place a "C" therein, if the claim is contingent,** or a "U", if the claim is unliquidated,** or a "D", if the claim is disputed.** (You may need to place more than one letter for a claim, if applicable). In column (**6**), simply enter here what the creditor claims you owe him — the full amount the creditor is asking for to pay off the debt. Column (**7**) is the amount of the creditor's claim, up to the maximum limit allowable for such claim under the applicable law — e.g. $2,000 for wages, or $900 for deposit by individuals. It will generally be the same amount as in column (**6**), but is <u>not always</u> the same..

**See the Glossary of Terms appendix   for definitions.

[Enter this]
↓

In re: New Hope, Inc., DEBTOR.   .41   Case No._____ (if known)

SCHEDULE E - CREDITORS HOLDING UNSECURED PRIORITY CLAIMS

☐ Check this box if debtor has no creditors holding unsecured priority claims to report on this Schedule E.

TYPE OF PRIORITY CLAIMS (Check the appropriate box(es) below if claims in that category are listed on the attached sheets)

☐ Extensions of credit in an involuntary case
Claims arising in the ordinary course of the debtor's business or financial affairs after the commencement of the case but before the earlier of the appointment of a trustee or the order for relief. 11 U.S.C § 507(a)(2).

☑ Wages, salaries, and commissions
Wages, salaries, and commissions, including vacation, severance, and sick leave pay owing to employees, up to a maximum of $2000 per employee, earned within 90 days immediately preceding the filing of the original petition, or the cessation of business, whichever occured first, to the extent provided in 11 U.S.C. § 507(a)(3)

☐ Contributions to employee benefit plans
Money owed to employee benefit plans for services rendered within 180 days immediately preceding the filing of the original petition, or the cessation of business, whichever occured first, to the extent provided in 11 U.S.C. § 507(a)(4).

☐ Certain farmers and fishermen
Claims of certain farmers and fishermen, up to a maximum of $2000 per farmer or fisherman, against the debtor, as provided in 11 U.S.C. § 507(a)(5).

☐ Deposits by individuals
Claims of individuals up to a maximum of $900 for deposits for the purchase, lease, or rental of property or services for personal, family, or household use, that were not delivered or provided. 11 U.S.C. § 507(a)(6)

☑ Taxes and Certain Other Debts Owed to Governmental Units
Taxes, customs duties, and penalties owing to federal, state, and local governmental units as set forth in 11 U.S.C. § 507(a)(7).

CREDITOR'S NAME AND MAILING ADDRESS INCLUDING ZIP CODE (1)	CO DEBT (2)	H W J C (3)	DATE CLAIM WAS INCURRED AND CONSIDERATION FOR CLAIM (4)	C U D (5)	TOTAL AMOUNT OF CLAIM (6)	AMOUNT ENTITLED TO PRIORITY (7)
ACCOUNT NO. Martin Rusk, 10 Beverly Place, N.Y. N.Y. 10015		N/A	Wages due employee 1/1 to 1/30/92	U	$900	$900
ACCOUNT NO. Julian Mans, 15 Lords St., Brooklyn N.Y. 11216		N/A	Wages due Jan. 15 to 31st 1992	U	$3,200	$1,200*
ACCOUNT NO. 022971/91 IRS, 120 Church St., New York, N.Y. 10010		N/A	Income tax on corporate income for 1991	U D	$1000	$1000
ACCOUNT NO. S-257981 N.Y. State Dept. of Taxation, 2 World Trade Center, N.Y. N.Y. 10047		N/A	Sales taxes for 6/1 to 12/31/91	U D	$300	$300
ACCOUNT NO.						

Subtotal -> $5,400
(Total of this page)

Total -> $ 5,400 ← Report this (the final total) on the Summary of Schedules Form

NO Continuation sheets attached.
(use only on last page of the completed Schedule E.) (Report total also on Summary of Schedules)

INSTRUCTIONS: ON COMPLETING SCHEDULE
F (Sampled on pp. 43-4)

In this schedule, the type of debts you are to list are those that are NON-SECURED but **NON-PRIORITY** in nature. To put it very simply, except perhaps for obligations that may qualify as executory contracts and unexpired leases (Schedule G below), virtually any and all other debts, personal as well as business debts, that you haven't already listed (and can't be listed) in the two preceding "liability" schedules of Schedules D and E, should go on this schedule.

To complete Schedule F, list the creditors (all general unsecured claims) alphabetically by surname or company name .Include here any unsecured non priority claims resulting solely from breaches of executory contracts or expired leases (which should also be listed on schedule G); and unsecured claims of co-debtors and persons who have guaranteed or became liable for debts of the debtor. Simply enter the same details in Column **(1) through (6)** of schedule F, in the proceeding schedule. Additionally, you are to "affirmatively" state if the claim is subject to a "set off," if applicable to a given debt, by so indicating in Schedule F's column **(4)**. DO NOT include in this schedule any claims you might have listed in schedules D or E. And if all applicable creditors will not contain on this page, attach continuation sheet properly labeled and identified.]

INSTRUCTIONS: ON COMPLETING SCHEDULE
G (Sampled on p. 45)

In a word, basically a contract is "EXECUTORY" (or "UNEXPIRED") when there is still a portion of the contract that is yet unperformed by one party or the other or both, and the creditor is, in effect, still to provide you something sometime in the future in return for some payment on your part. Some common examples of executory contracts are things like: health club memberships; book, magazine and record club contracts; service contracts, business contracts or leases or obligations, time share contracts or leases, contracts for real estate sale, copyright leases, car leases, and residence leases.

The basic purpose behind this Schedule, is to enable the trustee to determine whether such a contract, if any exists, ought to be continued in force, or should be "rejected" (terminated), so that, in effect, you'd be freed from further liability for such obligations. Cancellation will simply mean that you won't get the future goods or services in question, but you won't have to pay for them either!

Schedule G is essentially self-explanatory. *To complete this Schedule,* simply list all executory contracts of any kind, and all unexpired leases of either real or personal property to which you are a party, if any; give the names and mailing addresses of the other parties to each lease or contract, the nature of your interest in the contract (i.e., "purchaser", "agent", "sub-contractor", etc.), and whether you are the lessor or lessee of a lease.

NOTE: Creditors listed on the Schedule G may not generally be listed on other schedules also. However, as a rule, a party listed only on this schedule will not receive notice of the filing of this case UNLESS such party is also listed on the appropriate schedules of creditors.

SCHEDULE F - CREDITORS HOLDING UNSECURED NONPRIORITY CLAIMS

NOTE: List the <u>actual</u> original creditor, not the attorney or collection agent.

☐ Check this box if debtor has no creditors holding unsecured nonpriority claims to report on this Schedule F

CREDITOR'S NAME AND MAILING ADDRESS INCLUDING ZIP CODE (1)	CODEBTOR (2)	HWJC (3)	DATE CLAIM WAS INCURRED AND CONSIDERATION FOR CLAIM. IF CLAIM IS SUBJECT TO SETOFF, SO STATE. (4)	CUD (5)	AMOUNT OF CLAIM (6)
ACCOUNT NO. A11290 ABC Cleaning Services, Inc., 200 Broadway, Brooklyn N.Y. 11234		N/A	Cleaning services incurred 2/90	U	$750
ACCOUNT NO. 88874 Bank of America,10 Madison Ave., N.Y. N.Y. 10001		N/A	Revolving signature loan taken 8/8/89 for operating expenses	U	$12,000
ACCOUNT NO. APC-2929/91 Apple Computer Co. 75 Grant St., N.Y. N.Y. 10030		N/A	Installation & repair work on office computer system, incurred 1/92	U	$2,500
ACCOUNT NO. 2145-569-789 Chase National Bank,195 E. 42nd St., N.Y. N.Y. 10016		N/A	Overdrawn account, incurred 10/91	U	$2,400
ACCOUNT NO. Michael Chin, 4 Park Lane Jersey City, N.J. 08891		N/A	Claims resulting from automobile accident with company vehicle.lawsuit commenced 4/90 & still pending	C D	$60,000
ACCOUNT NO.10047-5591/88 Citibank, P.O. Box 800. Melville, N.Y. 11801		N/A	Unsecured operating loan incurred, per contract dated 1/1/88; account assigned to Anything Goes Collection Co..22 Main St., NY NY 10021	D	$2000
ACCOUNT NO. Landlord Corporation of New York. Inc.. 100 5th Ave., N.Y. N.Y.10012		N/A	4-months rents for debtor's store at 100 5th Ave.,N.Y. N.Y, from 1/1/92 to date of bankruptcy filing	U	$5600
ACCOUNT NO. 77980-2 Elgin N. Michaelson,Esq. 4 Park Ave., N.Y. N.Y. 10015		N/A	Legal services rendered to debtor in 1990 & 1991	U	$5000
ACCOUNT NO.44117-ADV New York Daily Express, 1 Madison Ave., N.Y. N.Y. 10021		N/A	Advertising services done 6/90	U	$800

_1_ Continuation Sheets attached.

Subtotal -> $ 91,050
(Total of this page)

Total -> $ — —
(use only on last page of completed Schedule F.)
(Report total also on Summary of Schedules) Carry over to the next (continuation)sheet.

In re: New Hope, Inc., DEBTOR   44   Case No._____ (if known)

SCHEDULE F - CREDITORS HOLDING UNSECURED NONPRIORITY CLAIMS
(Continuation Sheet)

CREDITOR'S NAME AND MAILING ADDRESS INCLUDING ZIP CODE (1)	CODEBTOR (2)	HWJC (3)	DATE CLAIM WAS INCURRED AND CONSIDERATION FOR CLAIM. IF CLAIM IS SUBJECT TO SETOFF, SO STATE. (4)	CUD (5)	AMOUNT OF CLAIM (6)
ACCOUNT NO. 69578-568 Opera Radio Station, 2 Combus St., N.Y. N.Y. 10017		N/A	Business advertising incurred 12/90	U	$1,300
ACCOUNT NO. PA-25051 Paramount Suppliers.Inc. 88 Aple BLVD., Queens N.Y. 11431		N/A	Miscallaneous office supplies & merchandise purchased from 6/90 to date	U	$750
ACCOUNT NO. IDL-44059-2 Patranage Gas & Electric Co., 10 Montaque St.. Brooklyn, N.Y. 11201		N/A	Electricity supply from 9/91 to	D	$2,200
ACCOUNT NO. J995897-24 Paycity Bureau of Motor Vehicles,Div. of Parking Violation,c51 Chambers St N.Y. N.Y. 10007		N/A	Tickets outstanding on company de-livery truck, Plate #XYZ-1448NY	D	$600
ACCOUNT NO. DSA-92-115798 ✓ Sachs New York, Inc. 2480 Grand Concourse.. Bronx, N.Y. 10469		N/A	Purchases of office furnitures & store supplies incurred 1/92. Co-signed for by President in his personal capacity	U	$1,500
ACCOUNT NO.					
ACCOUNT NO.					
ACCOUNT NO.					
ACCOUNT NO.					

Sheet no. 2 of 2 sheets attached to Schedule of Creditors Holding Nonpriority Claims.

Subtotal -> $ 6,350
(Total of this page)

Total -> $97,400
(use only on last page of completed Schedule F.)
(Report total also on Summary of Schedules)

Report this on the Summary of Schedules Form

[Debtor's Name]

In re: New Hope, Inc., DEBTOR

45

Case No._____ (if known)

SCHEDULE G - EXECUTORY CONTRACTS AND UNEXPIRED LEASES

☐ Check this box if debtor has no executory contracts or unexpired leases.

NAME AND MAILING ADDRESS, INCLUDING ZIP CODE, OF OTHER PARTIES TO LEASE OR CONTRACT.	DESCRIPTION OF CONTRACT OR LEASE AND NATURE OF DEBTOR'S INTEREST. STATE WHETHER LEASE IS FOR NONRESIDENTIAL REAL PROPERTY. STATE CONTRACT NUMBER OF ANY GOVERNMENT CONTRACT.
Landlord Corporation of New York,Inc 100 5th Ave. Suite 400 New York, N.Y. 10012	Lease dated 5/1/84 with the Landlord Corporation 9of New York, Inc., for lease of store space used by debtor for its business at 100 5th Ave.,N.Y. N.Y. (Ground floor). Terms of lease: lease expires 4/30/96; debtor pays $1400 per month and pays all utilities & other charges and cleaning costs; debtor is currently 4 months in arrears on rents.

NOTE: All interests of the debtor in personal property should be listed in Schedule B, except interests resulting solely from executory contracts or leases. Interests resulting solely from executory contracts or leases are to be listed here on Schedule G.

INSTRUCTIONS: COMPLETING SCHEDULE H (Sampled on p. 47)

This Schedule is designed to provide the bankruptcy trustee and creditors information about **co-debtors** of any types in the case, other than the spouse in joint cases.

To complete Schedule H, simply provide the information asked for in Schedule H concerning anybody else (other than a spouse in a joint case) that is also liable on any debts listed in Schedules D, E and F — i.e., on persons who are either co-applicants, guarantors or co-signers for the debts. In **community property states,** a married debtor not filing a joint petition should still list in this schedule the name and address of the non-debtor spouse, regardless.

INSTRUCTIONS: COMPLETING SCHEDULES I & J (Sampled on pp. 48 & 49)

As can be seen from the sample Schedules I & J on pp. 48 & 49 , respectively, in most Chapter 11 cases, especially where the debtor is a corporation or partnership (as opposed to an individual) and is actively engaged in business with probably many sources of current income and expenditures, the information provided in these two forms is usually scanty and of little use. Consult your district court clerk as to whether you are required to file these schedules under your local rules. And, if they happen to be required, then simply use the samples on pp. 48 & 49 below as your general guide in preparing one.

See Glossary of Terms appendix for definition. Community property states are the following states: Arizona, California, Indiana, Louisiana, Nevada, New Mexico, Texas, Washington and Wisconsin.

re: New Hope, Inc., DEBTOR.   47   Case No. _____?_____ (if known)

SCHEDULE H - CODEBTORS

☐ Check this box if debtor has no codebtors.

NAME AND ADDRESS OF CODEBTOR	NAME AND ADDRESS OF CREDITOR
John Lee Doe, 1 President St., Staten Island, N.Y. 10314	Sachs New York, Inc. 2480 Grand Concourse, Bronx N.Y. 10469

In re: NEW HOPE, INC., DEBTOR.   .48   Case No. _____:_____ (if known)

SCHEDULE I - CURRENT INCOME OF ~~INDIVIDUAL~~ BUSINESS DEBTOR(S)

The column labeled "Spouse" must be completed in all cases filed by joint debtors and by a married debtor in a chapter 12 or 13 case whether or not a joint petition is filed, unless the spouses are separated and a joint petition is not filed.

Debtor's Marital Status:	DEPENDENTS OF DEBTOR AND SPOUSE		
	NAMES	AGE	RELATIONSHIP
N/A (Corporation/ Business)	NOT APPLICABLE (N/A)	–	–

Employment: N/A	DEBTOR	SPOUSE
Occupation		
Name of Employer		
How long employed		
Address of Employer		

Income: (Estimate of average monthly income)   DEBTOR   SPOUSE

	DEBTOR	SPOUSE
Current monthly gross wages, salary, and commissions (pro rate if not paid monthly.)	$	$
Estimate monthly overtime		
SUBTOTAL	$ _____	$ _____
LESS PAYROLL DEDUCTIONS		
a. Payroll taxes and social security		
b. Insurance		
c. Union dues		
d. Other (Specify)		
SUBTOTAL OF PAYROLL DEDUCTIONS	$ _____	$ _____
TOTAL NET MONTHLY TAKE HOME PAY	$ _____	$ _____

Regular income from operation of business or profession or farm
(attach detailed statement) $9000
Income from real property (from office bldg. at 2 Park Pl. NY, NY) $1200*
Interest and dividends
Alimony, maintenance or support payments payable to the debtor for the debtor's
    use or that of dependents listed above.
Social security or other government assistance (Specify)

Pension or retirement income
Other monthly income (Specify) ....

	DEBTOR	SPOUSE
TOTAL MONTHLY INCOME	$ _____	$ _____

TOTAL COMBINED MONTHLY INCOME $ 10,200* _____   (Report also on Summary of Schedules)

Describe any increase or decrease of more than 10% in any of the above categories anticipated to occur within the year following the filing of this document:

*NOTE that this rental income has been assigned to a creditor as of 9/91.(see Statement of Financial Affairs, Questions 2 & 6), precluding it from being counted as debtor's income as of time of bankruptcy filing.

In re: NEW HOPE, INC., DEBTOR.

J 49   Case No. _____?_____ (if known)

SCHEDULE J - CURRENT EXPENDITURES OF ~~INDIVIDUAL~~ *BUSINESS* DEBTOR(S)

Complete this schedule by estimating the average monthly expenses of the debtor and the debtor's family. Pro rate any payments made bi-weekly, quarterly, semi-annually, or annually to show monthly rate.

☐ Check this box if a joint petition is filed and debtor's spouse maintains a separate household. Complete a separate schedule of expenditures labeled "Spouse".

Rent or home mortgage payment (include lot rented for mobile home) .... $

Are real estate taxes included? ☐ Yes ☐ No   Is property insurance included? ☐ Yes ☐ No

Utilities Electricity and heating fuel ....

     Water and sewer ....

     Telephone ....

     Other

Home maintenance (repairs and upkeep) ....

Food ....

Clothing ....

Laundry and dry cleaning ....

Medical and dental expenses ....

Transportation (not including car payments) ....

Recreation, clubs and entertainment, newspapers, magazines, etc. ....

Charitable contributions ....

Insurance (not deducted from wages or included in home mortgage payments)

     Homeowner's or renter's ....

     Life ....

     Health ....

     Auto ....

     Other

Taxes (not deducted from wages or included in home mortgage payments)

(Specify)

Installment payments: (In chapter 12 and 13 cases, do not list payments to be included in the plan)

     Auto ....

     Other ....

Alimony, maintenance, and support paid to others ....

Payments for support of additional dependents not living at your home ....

Regular expenses from operation of business, profession, or farm (attach detailed statement) ....

Other   Normal business expenses $11,000

TOTAL MONTHLY EXPENSES (Report also on Summary of Schedules) $11,000

(FOR CHAPTER 12 AND 13 DEBTORS ONLY)
Provide the information requested below, including whether plan payments are to be made bi-weekly, monthly, annually, or at some other regular interval.

A. Total projected monthly income .... $

B. Total projected monthly expenses .... $ _____

C. Excess income (A minus B) .... $ _____

D. Total amount to be paid into plan each .... $ _____
                        (interval)

Form B6 (6-90)

UNITED STATES BANKRUPTCY COURT   Southern   **50**   DISTRICT OF   New York

In re: New Hope, Inc., DEBTOR.   Case No. 92-B11146   (If Known)

NOTE See summary below for the list of schedules. Include Unsworn Declaration under Penalty of Perjury at the end.

GENERAL INSTRUCTIONS: Schedules D, E and F have been designed for the listing of each claim only once. Even when a claim is secured only in part, or entitled to priority only in part, it still should be listed only once. A claim which is secured in whole or in part should be listed on Schedule D only, and a claim which is entitled to priority in whole or in part should be listed in Schedule E only. Do not list the same claim twice. If a creditor has more than one claim, such as claims arising from separate transactions, each claim should be scheduled separately.

Review the specific instructions for each schedule before completing the schedule.

SUMMARY OF SCHEDULES

Indicate as to each schedule whether that schedule is attached and state the number of pages in each. Report the totals from Schedules A, B, D, E, F, I and J in the boxes provided. Add the amounts from Schedules A and B to determine the total amount of the debtor's assets. Add the amounts from Schedules D, E, and F to determine the total amount of the debtor's liabilities.

Name of Schedule	Attached (Yes\No)	Number of sheets	Assets	Liabilities	Other
A - Real Property	No	1	$197,000		
B - Personal Property	No	2	$64,510		
C - Property Claimed as Exempt	No	1			
D - Creditors Holding Secured Claims	No	1		$215,800	
E - Creditors Holding Unsecured Priority Claims	No	1		$5,400	
F - Creditors Holding Unsecured Nonpriority Claims	Yes	2		$97,400	
G - Executory Contracts and Unexpired Leases	No	1			
H - Codebtors	No	1			
I - Current Income of Individual Debtor(s)	No	1			$10,000
J - Current Expenditures of Individual Debtor(s)	No	1			$11,000
Total Number of Sheets of All Schedules →		12			
Total Assets (Add up Schedules A & B) →			$261,510		
Total Liabilities (Add up Schedules D, E & F) →				$ $318,600	

NOTE: For completing of this SUMMARY OF SCHEDULES form (when you shall have, of course, completed the preceding forms, namely, The Voluntary Petition and Schedules A to J), simply transpose the applicable TOTALS of each Schedule to this Summary of Schedules form. Note, however, that this Summary of Schedules form (which must, of necessity, be prepared last), should be placed as the FIRST page among all the Schedules before you file the papers. And, finally, to complete the preparation of the SCHEDULES, you, the Debtor (or the appropriate representative of the debtor) are now to sign the Declaration Concerning the Debtor's Schedules form.

In re: New Hope, Inc., DEBTOR.

51

Case No._____ _[Enter it]_↓

(if known)

DECLARATION CONCERNING DEBTOR'S SCHEDULES

DECLARATION UNDER PENALTY OF PERJURY BY INDIVIDUAL DEBTOR

I declare under penalty of perjury that I have read the foregoing summary and schedules, consisting of _____ sheets, and that they are true and correct to the best of my knowledge, information, and belief.

(Total shown on summary page plus 1.)

Date

Signature:_____
Debtor

Date

Signature:_____
(Joint Debtor, if any)
(If joint case, both spouses must sign.)

[Count the number of pages for your schedules, including any continuation sheets attached.]

DECLARATION UNDER PENALTY OF PERJURY ON BEHALF OF CORPORATION OR PARTNERSHIP

Use this in corporate or partnership filings.

I, the _____ (the president or other officer or an authorized agent of the corporation or a member or an authorized agent of the partnership) of the _____ New Hope, Inc _____ (corporation or partnership) named as debtor in this case, declare under penalty of perjury that I have read the foregoing summary and schedules, consisting of _____ 12 _____ sheets, and that they are true and correct to the best of my knowledge, information, and belief.

(Total shown on summary page plus 1.)

[Date when signed] ↓

Date _____ 19__

Signature: X_____

SAME PARTY'S NAME(PRINTED): _____
(Pint or type name of individual signing on behalf of debtor.)

(An individual signing on behalf of a partnership or corporation must indicate position or relationship to debtor.)

Penalty for making a false statement or concealing property: Fine of up to $500,000 or imprisonment for up to 5 years or both. 18 U.S.C. §§ 152 and 3571.

Affairs (8-91)

[Debtor or Debtors enter
full name/names & your]

UNITED STATES BANKRUPTCY COURT,

[District of filing,
as in Appendix E]
Southern

52

DISTRICT OF

[Your state]

New York

[Basically, to complete this whole form ("Statement of Financial Affairs..."), all you need to do is to answer the question asked, item by item, per the instruction.]

In re: New Hope, Inc., DEBTOR.

Case No. _____ *[Enter it]*

STATEMENT OF FINANCIAL AFFFAIRS

Please Read and Note this

This statement is to be completed by every debtor. Spouses filing a joint petition may file a single statement on which the information for both spouses is combined. If the case is filed under chapter 12 or chapter 13, a married debtor must furnish information for both spouses whether or not a joint petition is filed, unless the spouses are separated and a joint petition is not filed. An individual debtor engaged in business as a sole proprietor, partner, family farmer, or self-employed professional, should provide the information requested on this statement concerning all such activities as well as the inviddual's personal affairs.

Questions 1-15 are to be completed by all debtors. Debtors that are or have been in business, as defined below, also must complete Questions 16-21. Each question must be answered. If the answer to any question is "None," or the question is not applicable, mark the box labeled "None." If additional space is needed for the answer to any question, use and attach a separate sheet properly identified with the case name, case number (if known), and the number of the question.

DEFINITIONS:

"In business." A debtor is "in business" for the purpose of this form if the debtor is a corporation or partnership. An individual debtor is "in business" for the purpose of this form if the debtor is or has been, within the two years immediately preceding the filing of this bankruptcy case, any of the following: an officer, director, managing executive, or person in control of a corporation; a partner, other than a limited partner, of a partnership; a sole proprietor or self-employed.

"Insider." The term "insider" includes but is not limited to: relatives of the debtor; general partners of the debtor and their relatives; corporations of which the debtor is an officer, director, or person in control; officers, directors, and any person in control of a corporate debtor and their relatives; affiliates of the debtor and insiders of such affiliates; any managing agent of the debtor. 11 U.S.C. §101(30).

☐ None **1. Income from Employment or Operation of Business**

State the gross amount of income the debtor has received from employment, trade, or profession, or from operation of the debtor's business from the beginning of this calendar year to the date this case was commenced. State also the gross amounts received during the **two years** immediately preceding this calendar year. (A debtor that maintains, or has maintained, financial records on the basis of a fiscal rather than a calendar year may report fiscal year income. Identify the beginning and ending dates of the debtor's fiscal year.) If a joint petition is filed, state income for each spouse separately. (Married debtors filing under chapter 12 or chapter 13 must state income of both spouses whether or not a joint petition is filed, unless the spouses are separated and a joint petition is not filed.) Give AMOUNT and SOURCE (If more than one).

Debtor's (Corporation's) gross income from Jan.1 to date of filing on 4/1/92 - $30,000. Gross income for the 2 yrs before this calendar yr. - 1990 & 1991, $250,000

☐ None **2. Income Other than from Employment or Operation of Business**

State the amount of income received by the debtor other than from employment, trade, profession, or operation of the debtor's business during the **two years** immediately preceding the commencement of this case. Give particulars. If a joint petition is filed, state income for each spouse separately. (Married debtors filing under chapter 12 or chapter 13 must state income for each spouse whether or not a joint petition is filed, unless the spouses are separated and a joint petition is not filed.) Give AMOUNT and SOURCE.

Rental income from office bldg. at 2 Park Pl., N.Y N.Y., $12,000 in 1990 & $600 in 1991 (see Question #6 below)

3. Payments to Creditors

☐ None a. List all payments on loans, installment purchases of goods or services, and other debts, aggregating more than $600 to any creditor, made within **90 days** immediately preceding the commencement of this case. (Married debtors filing under chapter 12 or chapter 13 must include payments by either or both spouses whether or not a joint petition is filed, unless the spouses are separated and a joint petition is not filed.) Give NAME AND ADDRESS OF CREDITOR, DATES OF PAYMENTS, AMOUNT PAID, and AMOUNT STILL OWING.

America Loan Corp., 114 20th St. Bronx NY, was paid $300 in each of Jan.,Feb., & Mar., 1992,still owing $8000; Amico Factoring Corp. 1 Wall St. NY NY paid $400 2/1/92, $300 3/15/92, for continued supply of merchandise,still owed $5800; Wellington Ban 119 Mable Ave. NY NY - $900in each of Jan.,Feb., Mar., 1992, still owing $140,000.

☑ None b. List all payments made within **one year** immediately preceding the commencement of this case to or for the benefit of creditors who are or were insiders. (Married debtors filing under chapter 12 or chapter 13 must include payments by either or both spouses whether or not a joint petition is filed, unless the spouses are separated and a joint petition is not filed.) Give NAME AND ADDRESS OF CREDITOR AND RELATIONSHIP TO DEBTOR, DATE OF PAYMENT, AMOUNT PAID and AMOUNT STILL OWING.

4. Suits, Executions, Garnishments and Attachments

☐ None a. List all suits to which the debtor is or was a party within **one year** immediately preceding the filing of this bankruptcy case. (Married debtors filing under chapter 12 or chapter 13 must include information concerning either or both spouses whether or not a joint petition is filed, unless the spouses are separated and a joint petition is not filed.) Give CAPTION OF SUIT AND CASE NUMBER, NATURE OF PROCEEDING, COURT AND LOCATION and STATUS OR DISPOSTION.

(See attached sheet captioned, "CONTINUATION, STATEMENT OF AFFAIRS, PARAGRAPH # 4")

☐ None b. Describe all property that has been attached, garnished, or seized under any legal or equitable process within **one year**

$900 seized 11/91 by Chase Nat. Bank, 195 E. 42nd st NY NY 10016 for debt - levy against checking acct. held at Amico Bank, 1 Wall St NY NY 1007

immediately preceding the commencement of this case. (Married debtors filing under chapter 12 or chapter 13 must include information concerning property of either or both spouses whether or not a joint petition is filed, unless the spouses are separated and a joint petition is not filed.)

Give NAME AND ADDRESS OF PERSON FOR WHOSE BENEFIT PROPERTY WAS SEIZED, DATE OF SEIZURE and DESCRIPTION AND VALUE OF PROPERTY.

☐ None   **5. Repossessions, Foreclosures, and Returns**

List all property that has been repossessed by a creditor, sold at a foreclosure sale, transferred through a deed in lieu of foreclosure or returned to the seller, within **one year** immediately preceding the commencement of this case. (Married debtors filing under chapter 12 or chapter 13 must include information concerning property of either or both spouses whether or not a joint petition is filed, unless the spouses are separated and a joint petition is not filed.)

Give NAME AND ADDRESS OF CREDITOR OR SELLER, DATE OF REPOSSESSION, FORECLOSURE SALE, TRANSFER OR RETURN and DESCRIPTION AND VALUE OF PROPERTY.

```
Company delivery truck, 1988 Dodge, repossessed by
Americar Loan Corp., 114 20th St., Bronx NY 10456
on 2/9/92. Estimated Mkt. value of truck $5000
```

6. Assignments and Receiverships

☐ None   a. Describe any assignment of property for the benefit of creditors made within **120 days** immediately preceding the commencement of this case. (Married debtors filing under chapter 12 or chapter 13 must include any assignment by either or both spouses whether or not a joint petition is filed, unless the spouses are separated and a joint petition is not filed.)

Give NAME AND ADDRESS OF ASSIGNEE, DATE OF ASSIGNMENT and TERMS OF ASSIGNMENT OR SETTLEMENT.

```
Rental income from company's real estate (2 Park
Pl., NY NY), assigned to Amico Factoring Co., 1
Wall St., NY NY 10007., in amount of $1200 monthly
to secure continued extension of credit line as of
9/91
```

☐ None   b. List all property which has been in the hands of a custodian, receiver, or court-appointed official within **one year** immediately preceding the commencement of this case. (Married debtors filing under chapter 12 or chapter 13 must include information concerning property of either or both spouses whether or not a joint petition is filed, unless the spouses are separated and a joint petition is not filed.)

Give NAME AND ADDRESS OF CUSTODIAN, NAME AND LOCATION OF COURT, CASE TITLE & NUMBER, DATE OF ORDER and DESCRIPTION AND VALUE OF PROPERTY.

```
Security deposit with landlord, Landlord Corporat-
ion of N.Y. Inc,100 5th Ave. NY NY 10012 - $2800;
100 shares of Texco corporate stock pledged to
Amico Factoring Co., 1 Wall St. NY NY as  loan
security.
```

☑ None   **7. Gifts**

List all gifts or charitable contributions made within **one year** immediately preceding the commencement of this case except ordinary and usual gifts to family members aggregating less than $200 in value per individual family member and charitable contributions aggregating less than $100 per recipient. (Married debtors filing under chapter 12 or chapter 13 must include gifts or contributions by either or both spouses whether or not a joint petition is filed, unless the spouses are separated and a joint petition is not filed.)

Give NAME AND ADDRESS OF PERSON OR ORGANIZATION, RELATIONSHIP TO DEBTOR, IF ANY, DATE OF GIFT, and DESCRIPTION AND VALUE OF GIFT.

[Intended to aid the court (the trustee) in determining that you didn't improperly give out or waste away any property before filing for bankruptcy, or that you didn't recently receive insurance proceeds that your creditors might have been entitled to.]

☑ None   **8. Losses**

List all losses from fire, theft, other casualty or gambling within **one year** immediately preceding the commencement of this case **or since the commencement of this case.** (Married debtors filing under chapter 12 or chapter 13 must include losses by either or both spouses whether or not a joint petition is filed, unless the spouses are separated and a joint petition is not filed.)

Give DESCRIPTION AND VALUE OF PROPERTY, DESCRIPTION OF CIRCUMSTANCES AND, IF LOSS WAS COVERED IN WHOLE OR IN PART BY INSURANCE, GIVE PARTICULARS and DATE OF LOSS.

☐ None   **9. Payments Related to Debt Counseling or Bankruptcy**

List all payments made or property transferred by or on behalf of the debtor to any persons, including attorneys, for consultation concerning debt consolidation, relief under the bankruptcy law or preparation of a petition in bankruptcy within **one year** immediately preceding the commencement of this case.

Give NAME AND ADDRESS OF PAYEE, DATE OF PAYMENT, NAME OF PAYOR IF OTHER THAN DEBTOR and AMOUNT OF MONEY OR DESCRIPTION AND VALUE OF PROPERTY.

```
Paid to John Benson, attorney, 96 Broadway, N.Y. NY
in 6/91 for consultation regarding bankruptcy fil-
ing.  Paid $60 to Budget & Credit Counseling Servi-
ce.,Inc., 100 Park Ave. South, NY NY in 7/91 for
credit, debt and financial counseling.
```

☑ None   **10. Other Transfers**

List all other property, other than property transferred in the ordinary course of the business or financial affairs of the debtor, transferred either absolutely or as security within **one year** immediately preceding the commencement of this case. (Married debtors filing under chapter 12 or chapter 13 must include transfers by either or both spouses whether or not a joint petition is filed, unless the spouses are separated and a joint petition is not filed.)

Give NAME AND ADDRESS OF TRANSFEREE, RELATIONSHIP TO DEBTOR, DATE, and DESCRIBE PROPERTY TRANSFERRED AND VALUE RECEIVED.

[Refers to all real or personal property you've disposed of WITHIN the past 12 months that haven't already been listed anywhere in the bankruptcy petition, if any. E.g., say you sold or junked a car, or put up your house as security for a loan or traded property.]

☐ None   **11. Closed Financial Accounts**

List all financial accounts and instruments held in the name of the debtor or for the benefit of the debtor which were closed, sold, or otherwise transferred within **one year** immediately preceding the commencement of this case. Include checking, savings, or other financial accounts, certificates of deposit, or other instruments; shares and share accounts held in banks, credit unions, pension funds, cooperatives, associations, brokerage houses and other financial institutions. (Married debtors filing under chapter 12 or chapter 13 must include information concerning accounts or instruments held by or for either or both spouses whether or not a joint petition is filed, unless the spouses are separated and a joint petition is not filed.)

Give NAME AND ADDRESS OF INSTITUTION, TYPE AND NUMBER OF ACCOUNT AND AMOUNT OF FINAL BALANCE and AMOUNT AND DATE OF SALE OR CLOSING.

Checking account held with Chase National Bank, 195 E. 42nd. St., N.Y. N.Y. Acct. No. 885740 closed 2/9/92, balance at closing, zero. Checking account with Amico Bank, 1 Wall St., N.Y. N.Y. closed 11/91, balance at time of closing $900 was seized by Chase National Bank.

☐ None   **12. Safe Deposit Boxes**

List each safe deposit or other box or depository in which the debtor has or had securities, cash, or other valuables within **one year** immediately preceding the commencement of this case. (Married debtors filing under chapter 12 or chapter 13 must include boxes or depositories of either or both spouses whether or not a joint petition is filed, unless the spouses are separated and a joint petition is not filed.)

Give NAME AND ADDRESS OF BANK OR OTHER DEPOSITORY, NAMES AND ADDRESSES OF THOSE WITH ACCESS TO BOX OR DEPOSITORY, DESCRIPTION OF CONTENTS and DATE OF TRANSFER OR SURRENDER, IF ANY.

Safe deposit box at National Bank, 190 E. 40th St., N.Y. N.Y. 10016. Contents: U.S. Bond & Corp. documents. Acess to box by John Lee Doe, President.

☐ None   **13. Setoffs**

List all setoffs made by any creditor, including a bank, against a debt or deposit of the debtor within **90 days** preceding the commencement of this case. (Married debtors filing under chapter 12 or chapter 13 must include information concerning either or both spouses whether or not a joint petition is filed, unless the spouses are separated and a joint petition is not filed.)

Give NAME AND ADDRESS OR CREDITOR, DATE OF SETOFF and AMOUNT OF SETOFF.

Citibank, PO Box 800 Melville, N.Y. 11801, made setoff in amount of $1200 in 2/92 against funds in debtor's acct. at Citibank for indebtedness to bank, as listed in Schedule F.

☑ None   **14. Property Held for Another Person**

List all property owned by another person that the debtor holds or controls.

Give NAME AND ADDRESS OF OWNER, DESCRIPTION AND VALUE OF PROPERTY and LOCATION OF PROPERTY.

[Refers to all property, if any, that you've borrowed from or are holding in trust for someone else, e.g. fund in irrevocable trusts which you hold in trust for another person as a trustee, or property you are holding as an estate administrator, or a property (say a house or a car) owned by someone else but which is in your name].

☑ None   **15. Prior Address of Debtor**

If the debtor has moved within the two years immediately preceding the commencement of this case, list all premises which the debtor occupied during that period and vacated prior to the commencement of this case. If a joint petition is filed, report also any separate address of either spouse.

Give ADDRESS, NAME USED and DATES OF OCCUPANCY.

The following questions are to be completed as shown below.*

16. Nature, Location and Name of Business*

☑ None   a. If the debtor is an individual, list the names and addresses of all businesses in which the debtor was an officer, director, partner, or managing executive of a corporation, partnership, sole proprietorship or was a self-employed professional within the **two years** immediately preceding the commencement of this case, or in which the debtor owned 5 percent or more of the voting or equity securities within the two years immediately preceding the commencement of this case.

b. If the debtor is a partnership, list the names and addresses of all businesses in which the debtor was a partner or owned 5 percent or more of the voting securities, within the **two years** immediately preceding the commencement of this case.

c. If the debtor is a corporation, list the names and addresses of all businesses in which the debtor was a partner or owned 5 percent or more of the voting securities within the **two years** immediately preceding the commencement of this case.

Give NAME, ADDRESS, NATURE OF BUSINESS and BEGINNING AND ENDING DATES OF OPERATION.

None other except debtor's current business operations as retail variety store, commenced Feb. 1980.

17. Books, Records, and Financial Statements

☐ None   a. List all bookkeepers and accountants who within the **six years** immediately preceding the filing of this bankruptcy case kept or supervised the keeping of books of account and records of the debtor.

Give NAME AND ADDRESS and DATES SERVICES RENDERED.

Anne Maxwell, bookkeeper 2/1/86 to present, 100 Hollis St., QUEENS N.Y. David N. Anderson, CPA., 20 Business St., N.Y. N.Y. 10014, accountant for past 6 years.

*These questions are to be completed by every debtor that is a corporation or partnership and by any individual debtor who is or has been, within the two years immediately preceding the commencement of this case, any of the following: an officer, director, managing executive, or owner of more than 5 percent of the voting securities of a corporation; a partner, other than a limited partner, of a partnership; a sole proprietor or otherwise self-employed. (An individual or joint debtor should complete this portion of the statement only if the debtor is or has been in business, as defined above, within the two years immediately preceding the commencement of this case.)

☐ None b. List all firms or individuals who within u.. .wo years immediately preceding the filing of this bankruptcy case have audited the books of account and records, or prepared a financial statement of the debtor.
Give NAME, ADDRESS and DATES SERVICES RENDERED.

Davidson & Benson, Auditors, 70 Corporate St., New York, N.Y. 10002. Served for the last 3 years.

☐ None c. List all firms or individuals who at the time of the commencement of this case were in possession of the books of account and records of the debtor. If any of the books of account and records are not available, explain.
Give NAME and ADDRESS.

New Hope, Inc., the debtor, at its business address, 100 5th Ave., N.Y. N.Y. 10001.

☐ None d. List all financial institutions, creditors and other parties, including mercantile and trade agencies, to whom a financial statement was issued within the **two years** immediately preceding the commencement of this case by the debtor.
Give NAME AND ADDRESS and DATE ISSUED.

Maple Leasing Ltd., 410 Maple St., Yonkers, N.Y. 10710, in 4/90; and Amico Factoring Corp., 1 Wall St N.Y. N.Y. 10007, 6/20/91.

18. Inventories

☐ None a. List the dates of the last two inventories taken of your property, the name of the person who supervised the taking of each inventory, and the dollar amount and basis of each inventory.
Give DATE OF INVENTORY, INVENTORY, SUPERVISOR and DOLLAR AMOUNT OF INVENTORY (specify cost, market or other basis).

Last taken Dec. 31, 1990 & 1991; under supervision of John Davis,a company employee; valuation $25,000 at cost.

☐ None b. List the name and address of the person having possession of the records of each of the two inventories reported in a., above.
Give DATE OF INVENTORY and NAME AND ADDRESSES OF CUSTODIAN OF INVENTORY RECORDS.

New Hope,Inc., the debtor, at its business address. By John Lee Doe, President, & Anne Maxwell, bkkeeper

19. Current Partners, Officers, Directors and Shareholders

☐ None a. If the debtor is a partnership, list the nature and percentage of partnership interest of each member of the partnership.
Give NAME AND ADDRESS, NATURE OF INTEREST and PERCENTAGE OF INTEREST.

☐ None b. If the debtor is a corporation, list all officers and directors of the corporation, and each stockholder who directly or indirectly owns, controls, or holds 5 percent or more of the voting securities of the corporation.
Give NAME AND ADDRESS, TITLE and NATURE AND PERCENTAGE OF STOCK OWNERSHIP.

John Lee Doe,President, 1 President St., Staten Island, N.Y.(55% stock ownership); David Mills,vice-pres. 20 Fulton St., Brooklyn, N.Y. 11201(35%); and Edward Miller, 10 Victory Blvd., Queens, N.Y. 11436, (10%), Secretary-Treasurer. All constitute the board of directors.

20. Former Partners, Officers, Directors and Shareholders

☐ None a. If the debtor is a partnership, list each member who withdrew from the partnership within **one year** immediately preceding the commencement of this case.
Give NAME, ADDRESS and DATE OF WITHDRAWAL.

☑ None b. If the debtor is a corporation, list all officers or directors whose relationship with the corporation terminated within **one year** immediately preceding the commencement of this case.
Give NAME AND ADDRESS, TITLE and DATE OF TERMINATION.

☐ None **21. Withdrawals from a Partnership or Distributions by a Corporation**

If the debtor is a partnership or corporation, list all withdrawals or distributions credited or given to an insider, including compensation in any form, bonuses, loans, stock redemptions, options exercised and any other perquisite during **one year** immediately preceding the commencement of this case.
Give NAME & ADDRESS OF RECIPIENT, RELATIONSHIP TO DEBTOR, DATE AND PURPOSE OF WITHDRAWAL, and AMOUNT OF MONEY OR DESCRIPTION AND VALUE OF PROPERTY.

John L. Doe,President, has withdrawn the sum of $45-000 during the last year as compensation, & David Mills, $30,000, as follows:

	DOE	MILLS		DOE	MILLS
4/4/91 -	$4000	$3000	10/5/91 -	$7000	$3000
5/5/	5000	3000	11/7/	$7000	5000
6/2/	7000	5000	1/3/92	4000	3000
7/5/	8000	5000	3/2/92	3000	3000

Unsworn Declaration under Penalty of Perjury.

(If completed by an individual or individual and spouse) I declare under penalty of perjury that I have read the answers contained in the foregoing statement of financial affairs and any attachments thereto and that they are true and correct.

_____ _____ _____ _____
Date Signature of Debtor Date Signature of Joint Debtor (if any)

(If completed on behalf of a partnership or corporation) I declare under penalty of perjury that I have read the answers contained in the foregoing statement of financial affairs and any attachments thereto and that they are true and correct to the best of my knowledge, information and belief.

[Date of signing this] [Principal Officer signs here] [Same officer prints name & title here]

_____ X _____
Date Signature John Lee Doe, President, New Hope, Inc
Print Name and Title

(An individual signing on behalf of a partnership or corporation must indicate position or relationship to debtor.)

_____ *I* _____ continuation sheets attached

Penalty for making a false statement: Fine of up to $500,000 or imprisonment for up to 5 years, or both. 18 U.S.C. §§152 and 3571.

DEBTOR(S): New Hope, Inc.   Docket No. _____

CONTINUATION, STATEMENT OF FINANCIAL AFFAIRS, Question #4

1. Business Finance, Inc. vs. New Hope, Inc., N.Y. City Civil Court, New York County, Case No. 41441/91. Suit for payment of loan. Judgment against debtor 11/91

2. Landlord Corporation of New York, Inc. vs. New Hope, Inc., N.Y. City Housing Court, New York County. Case #92-1005, for rents; case pending.

3. Michael Chin vs. New Hope, Inc. New York State Supreme Court, Bronx County. Case #17998/91. Suit for personal injury from automobile accident. Judgment against debtor 1/92.

4. Opera Radio Station vs. New Hope, Inc. New York City Civil Court,, New York County, Case #51229/91. Suit 10/91 for business advertising. Still pending.

Form B4 (6-90)

57

UNITED STATES BANKRUPTCY COURT, Southern   DISTRICT OF New York

In re: New Hope., Inc.,DEBTOR.   Debtor(s)   Case No. ___?___   (If Known)

LIST OF CREDITORS HOLDING 20 LARGEST UNSECURED CLAIMS

Following is the list of the debtor's creditors holding the 20 largest unsecured claims. The list is prepared in accordance with Fed. R. Bankr. P. 1007(d) for filing in this chapter 11 [or chapter 9] case. The list does not include (1) persons who come within the definition of "insider" set forth in 11 U.S.C. § 101(30), or (2) secured creditors unless the value of the collateral is such that the unsecured deficiency places the creditor among the holders of the 20 largest unsecured claims

(1) NAME OF CREDITOR AND COMPLETE MAILING ADDRESS INCLUDING ZIP CODE	(2) NAME, TELEPHONE NUMBER AND COMPLETE MAILING ADDRESS, INCLUDING ZIP CODE OF EMPLOYEE, AGENT, OR DEPARTMENT OF CREDITOR FAMILIAR WITH CLAIM.	(3) NATURE OF CLAIM (trade debt, bank loan, government contract, etc)	(4) C U D S	(5) AMOUNT OF CLAIM (If secured also state value of security)
NOTE: *[To complete this form, simply transfer onto this sheet, preferably in alphabetical order, the names, addresses and claims of the 20 LARGEST CREDITORS listed in your Schedule F [one name/address to each box and column]. (Exclude any "insiders" therein, if any, from this listing.) List ALL unsecured claim holders, if you have fewer than 20 unsecured claims.]*				
ABC CLEANING SERVICE, INC 200 Broadway, Brooklyn, N.Y. 11234	Michael Johnston,Credit Manager, same address. 1-718-229 4545	service supply	U	$750
Bank of America,10 Madison Ave., N.Y. N.Y. 10001	Monica Jones,ACCOUNTS PAYABLE DEPT. Same address. 212-2689919	loan	U	$12000

"(4) C U D S" If contingent, enter C; if unliquidated, enter U; if disputed, enter D; if subject to setoff, enter S.

OVER →

58

LIST OF CREDITORS HOLDING 20 LARGEST UNSECURED CLAIMS (continuation)

(1)	(2)	(3)	(4)	(5)
[Continue the listing of unsecured debts on this page, if necessary.]				

Unsworn Declaration under Penalty of Perjury (partnership or corporation) I declare under penalty of perjury that I have read the answers contained in the foregoing list of creditors and that they are true and corrrect to the best of my knowledge, information and belief.

_____ X_____ _____
Date   Signature   Print Name and Title

(An individual signing on behalf of a partnership or corporation must indicate position or relationship to debtor.)

Penalty for making a false statement: Fine of up to $500.00 or imprisonment for up to 5 years, or both. 18 U.S.C. § § 152 and 3571

UNITED STATES BANKRUPTCY COURT   Southern   59   **DISTRICT OF**   New York

In re New Hope, Inc., DEBTOR   Debtor(s)   Case No. _____?_____ (If Known)

LIST OF EQUITY SECURITY HOLDERS

Registered name of holder of security Last know address or place business	Class of security	Number registered	Kind of interest registered
John Lee Doe, 1 President St., Staten Island, N.Y. 10314	Class A Common Stock	550 shares	Common stock
David Mills 20 Fulton St., Brooklyn N.Y. 11201	Class A	350 shares	Common Stock
Edward Miller. 10 Victory Blvd.,Queens N.Y.11436	Class A	100 shares	Common Stock
NOTE: *[Complete this form, LARGELY IF debtor is a corporation. Simply show the name/address of EACH holder of an "equity security" in the debtor, the number of shares of stock held by each stockholder, the percentage of the total issued and outstanding stock held by each, and the type or class of stock ("common stock", "1st preferred stock", "2nd preferred stock", etc.) held by each stockholder. Equity security are such things as the stock of a corporation, limited partnership interests, and the right to purchase, sell or subscribe to either. If the debtor company has more than one class (i.e., type) of equity security holder, then list the holders by class or type. NOTE: if debtor is an individual or a general partnership or other entity with no equity holders, attach, instead, a statement stating that you do not have any equity security holders.]*			

EXHIBIT 'A'

UNITED STATES BANKRUPTCY COURT   Southern   DISTRICT OF New York

In re: New Hope, Inc., DEBTOR.   Case No. _____?____

                                                                   Chapter 11

(If debtor is a corporation filing under chapter 11 of the Code, this Exhibit 'A' shall be completed and attached to the petition)

EXHIBIT "A" to Voluntary Petition

1. Debtor's employer identification number is   13-98476
2. If any of debtor's securities are registered under § 12 of the Securities and Exchange Act of 1934, the SEC file number is   N/A
3. The following financial data is the latest available information and refers to debtor's condition on . . . . . . .19 . . . ?

Get these from Summary of Schedules

		Approximate number of holders
a. Total assets $261,510		
b. Total liabilities 318,600		

Make these out from Schedule D.

Fixed, liquidated secured debt	–	
Contingent secured debt	–	
Disputed secured claims	–	
Unliquidated secured debt $215,800		8

Make these out from Schedule F.

Fixed, liquidated unsecured debt	–	
Contingent unsecured debt $60,000		1
Disputed unsecured claims $64,800		4
Unliquidated unsecured debt $32,000		10

Number of shares of preferred stock........ none
Number of shares of common stock 1,000

Comments, if any:

4. Brief description of debtor's business: retail sales of variety store, personal, household goods and items.

5. List the name of any person who directly or indirectly owns, controls or holds, with power to vote, 20% or more of the voting securities of debtor:

JOHN LEE DOE
DAVID MILLS

6. List the names of all corporations 20% or more of the outstanding voting securities of which are directly or indirectly owned, controlled, or held, with power to vote, by debtor: none other

61

United States Bankruptcy Court

NOTICE TO INDIVIDUAL CONSUMER DEBTOR(S)

If you intend to file a petition for relief under the bankruptcy laws of the United States, and your debts are primarily consumer debts, the Clerk of Court is required to notify you of each chapter of the Bankruptcy Code under which you may seek relief. You may proceed under:

Chapter 7—Liquidation, or
Chapter 11—Reorganization, or
Chapter 13—Adjustment of Debts of an Individual
with Regular Income

If you have any questions regarding the information contained in this notice, you should consult with your attorney.

Clerk of Court

ACKNOWLEDGMENT

I hereby certify that I have read this notice.

(Date of Signing)

DATED: _____

X (Sign this, only if your debts are
primarily "consumer debts")

Debtor

_____,
Joint Debtor, if any

INSTRUCTIONS: *If the debtor is an individual, a copy of this notice personally signed by the debtor must accompany any bankruptcy petition filed with the Clerk. If filed by joint debtors, the notice must be personally signed by each. Failure to comply may result in the petition not being accepted for filing.*

New Hope, Inc (DEBTOR
100 Fifth Ave.,
N.Y. N.Y. 10001

62
ADDRESS MATRIX

BANKRUPT/DEBTOR NO.

DISTRICT DIRECTOR
INTERNAL REVENUE SERVICE
225 Cadman Plaza
Brooklyn N.Y. 11201

START A-Z LIST OF
CREDITORS

NOTE: *[This information is for use by the court in sending notices to creditors and others. To complete this form, simply transfer onto this sheet, preferably in alphabetical order, the names and addresses of EACH and EVERY creditor listed in your Schedules D, E, F, G & H. You must include, also, YOUR OWN (the debtor's) name and address. In many local court districts, the following parties are also required to be included in this sheet for a Chapter 11 case: name and address of the debtor's attorney (if debtor is using any), of the U.S. trustee, the U.S. Attorney for the local district, the District Director of the IRS and of applicable federal, state and local taxing authorities. (If necessary, check with the clerk of your local bankruptcy court for the exact local requirements.)]*

DO NOT TYPE IN THIS AREA

If a debt is disclosed to the United States other than one for taxes, type an address for the United States Attorney for the district in which the case is pending and to the department, agent or instrumentality of the United States through which the bankrupt became indebted.

Check with your local district for addresses of state or local government agencies to which addressed label must be prepared.

FORM 1 VOLUNTARY PETITION

[Full names (NO initials) of the Debtor or Debtors]

[Enter name of your District of filing, from Appendix E]

[Name of your state]

United States Bankruptcy Court	VOLUNTARY PETITION
Southern **District of** NEW YORK	

IN RE (Name of debtor-If individual, enter Last, First, Middle)	NAME OF JOINT DEBTOR (Spouse) (Last, First, Middle)
New Hope, Inc.	
ALL OTHER NAMES used by debtor in the last 6 years (Include married, maiden and trade names) none	ALL OTHER NAMES used by the joint debtor in the last 6 years (Include married, maiden and trade names.)
SOC. SEC./TAX I.D. NO. (If more than one, state all) 13-98476	SOC. SEC./TAX I.D. NO.(If more than one, state all)
STREET ADDRESS OF DEBTOR (No. and street, city, state, zip) 100 5th Ave., New York, N.Y. 10001	STREET ADDRESS OF JOINT DEBTOR (No. and street, city, state, zip)
COUNTY OF RESIDENCE OR PRINCIPAL PLACE OF BUSINESS New York	COUNTY OF RESIDENCE OR PRINCIPAL PLACE OF BUSINESS
MAILING ADDRESS OF DEBTOR (If different from street address) Same as above	MAILING ADDRESS OF JOINT DEBTOR (If different from street address)

LOCATION OF PRINCIPAL ASSETS OF BUSINESS DEBTOR (If different from addresses listed above) Same as above	☑ Debtor has been domiciled or has had a residence, principal place of business or principal assets in this District for 180 days immediately preceding the date of this petition or for a longer part of such 180 days than in any other District. ☐ There is a bankruptcy case concerning debtor's affiliate, general partner or partnership pending in this District.

INFORMATION REGARDING DEBTOR (Check applicable boxes)

TYPE OF DEBTOR		CHAPTER OR SECTION OF BANKRUPTCY CODE UNDER WHICH THE PETITION IS FILED (Check one box)
☐ Individual	☐ Corporation Publicly Held	☐ Chapter 7 ☑ Chapter 11 ☐ Chapter 13
☐ Joint (H&W)	☑ Corporation Not Publicly Held	☐ Chapter 9 ☐ Chapter 12 ☐ § 304-Case Ancillary to Foreign Proceeding
☐ Partnership	☐ Municipality	FILING FEE (Check one box)
☐ Other _____		☑ Filing fee attached.

NATURE OF DEBT
☐ Non-Business Consumer ☑ Business - Complete A&B below

☐ Filing fee to be paid in installments. (Applicable to individuals only) Must attach signed application for the court's consideration certifying that the debtor is unable to pay fee except in installments. Rule 1006(b). see Offical Form No..3

A. TYPE OF BUSINESS (check one box)

☐ Farming	☐ Transportation	☐ Commodity Broker
☐ Professional	☐ Manufacturing/ Mining	☐ Construction
☑ Retail/Wholesale		☐ Real Estate
☐ Railroad	☐ Stockbroker	☐ Other Business

NAME AND ADDRESS OF LAW FIRM OR ATTORNEY

B. BRIEFLY DESCRIBE NATURE OF BUSINESS

Retail sales of variety store items & personal. and household goods

Telephone No.

NAME(S) OF ATTORNEY(S) DESIGNATED TO REPRESENT THE DEBTOR

☑ Debtor is not represented by an attorney

STATISTICAL ADMINISTRATIVE INFORMATION (28 U.S.C. § 604) (Estimates only) (Check applicable boxes)	THIS SPACE FOR COURT USE ONLY

☑ Debtor estimates that funds will be available for distribution to unsecured creditors.

☐ Debtor estimates that after any exempt property is excluded and administrative expenses paid, there will be no funds available for distribution to unsecured creditors.

ESTIMATED NUMBER OF CREDITORS
☐ 1-15 ☑ 16-49 ☐ 50-99 ☐ 100-199 ☐ 200-999 ☐ 1000-over

{ Get this count from your Schedules D, E, F.

ESTIMATED ASSETS (in thousands of dollars)
☐ Under 50 ☐ 50-99 ☑ 100-499 ☐ 500-999 ☐ 1000-9999 ☐ 10,000-99,000 ☐ over 100,000

{ Figure this from the bottom of the Summary of Schedules.

ESTIMATED LIABILITIES (in thousands of dollars)
☐ Under 50 ☐ 50-99 ☑ 100-499 ☐ 500-999 ☐ 1000-9999 ☐ 10,000-99,000 ☐ over 100,000

{ Figure this from the bottom of the Summary of Schedules.

ESTIMATED NUMBER OF EMPLOYEES -CH 11 & 12 ONLY
☐ 0 ☑ 1-19 ☐ 20-99 ☐ 100-999 ☐ 1000-over

ESTIMATED NO . OF EQUITY SECURITY HOLDERS - CH 11 & 12 ONLY
☐ 0 ☑ 1-19 ☐ 20-99 ☐ 100-499 ☐ 500-over

Chapter 11 Small Business (Check all boxes that apply)
☑ Debtor is a small business as defined in 11 U.S.C. § 101
☑ Debtor is and elects to be considered a small business under 11 U.S.C. § 1121(e) (Optional)

Page 1 of 2 pages

[Debtor's Names]

64 [Get this from the Court clerk at time of Filing]

Name of Debtor __New Hope, Inc., DEBTOR.__ Case No 92-B11174

(Court use only)

FILING OF PLAN

For Chapter 9, 11, 12 and 13 cases only. Check appropriate box.

☐ A copy of debtor's proposed plan dated _____ is attached.

☑ Debtor intends to file a plan within the time allowed by statute, rule, or order of the court.

PRIOR BANKRUPTCY CASE FILED WITHIN LAST 6 YEARS (If more than one, attach additional sheet)

Location Where Filed	Case Number	Date Filed
NOT APPLICABLE (N/A)		

PENDING BANKRUPTCY CASE FILED BY ANY SPOUSE, PARTNER, OR AFFILIATE OF THIS DEBTOR (if more than one, attach additional sheet.)

Name of Debtor	Case Number	Date
(N/A)		

Relationship	District	Judge

REQUEST FOR RELIEF

Debtor requests relief in accordance with the chapter of title II, United States Code, specified in this petition.

SIGNATURES

ATTORNEY

X _____   Date _____

Signature

INDIVIDUAL /JOINT DEBTOR(S)	CORPORATE OR PARTNERSHIP DEBTOR
I declare under penalty of perjury that the information provided in this petition is true and correct.	I declare under penalty of perjury that the information provided in this petition is true and correct, and that the filing of this petition on behalf of the debtor has been authorized.
X _____ Signature of Debtor Date	X _John Lee Doe_____ Signature of Authorized Individual John Lee Doe Print or Type Name of Authorized Individual President
X _____ Signature of Joint Debtor Date	Title of Individual Authorized by Debtor to File this Petition Date (Date when signed)

EXHIBIT "A" (To be completed if debtor is a corporation requesting relief under chapter 11.)

☑ Exhibit "A" is attached and made a part of this petition.

TO BE COMPLETED BY INDIVIDUAL CHAPTER 7 DEBTOR WITH PRIMARILY CONSUMER DEBTS (See P.L. 98-353 § 322)

I am aware that I may proceed under chapter 7,11,12 or 13 of title 11, United States Code, understand the relief available under each such chapter, and choose to proceed under chapter 7 of such title.

If I am represented by an attorney, exhibit "B" has been completed.

X _____   Date _____

Signature of Debtor

X _____   Date _____

Signature of Joint Debtor

EXHIBIT "B" (To be completed by attorney for individual chapter 7 debtor(s) with primarily consumer debts.)

I, the attorney for the debtor(s) named in the foregoing petition, declare that I have informed the debtor(s) that (he, she, or they) may proceed under chapter 7, 11, 12, or 13 of title 11, United States Code, and have explained the relief availabe under each such chapter.

X _____   Date _____

Signature of Attorney

Debtor's Resolution Authorizing Commencement of Case [Use, If Required by Your Area's Local Court Rules]

CERTIFICATE OF CORPORATE RESOLUTION
AUTHORIZING COMMENCEMENT OF CHAPTER 11 CASE

I, Mary M. Jones, the Secretary of HARDTIMES SUPPLY CO, INC., an Illinois corporation, hereby certify and declare under penalty of perjury that the following is a true and correct excerpt from the official records and minutes of the said corporation, truly and correctly reflecting the matters transacted by the board of directors of the said corporation at a special meeting duly called and held on January 3, 1998:

"WHEREAS, from the information presented to the board of directors it appears that the corporation is no longer able to pay or meet its debts and obligations as they become due, that the corporation qualifies as a debtor under Chapter 11 of the United States Bankruptcy Code, and that it is in the best interest of the corporation to file a petition under Chapter 11; therefore,

IT WAS UNANIMOUSLY RESOLVED and voted by the board of directors of HARDTIMES SUPPLY CO., INC., an Illinois corporation, that the corporation should file a petition under Chapter 11 of the United States Bankruptcy Code and thereafter file a plan to reorganize its business under Chapter 11.

IT WAS FURTHER RESOLVED and voted by the board of directors of the corporation that Leo E. Lawnoer, Attorney at Law, and the law firm of Reddy, Willing & Able be retained to represent the corporation on all matters related to the Chapter 11 case, including the filing of the petition and initial pleadings.

IT WAS FURTHER RESOLVED and voted that Joseph P. Jones, the President of the corporation, be authorized and directed to execute any and all petitions, statements, schedules, plans, and other necessary documents in the Chapter 11 case on behalf of the corporation.

The foregoing matters were transacted and approved on behalf of the corporation by the entire board of directors at a special meeting duly called and held on the 3rd day of January, 1998."

Certified under penalty of perjury this 5th day of January 1998 by

_____
Mary M. Jones, Secretary

PARTNERSHIP RESOLUTION AUTHORIZING COMMENCEMENT OF CHAPTER 11 CASE

WHEREAS, at a special meeting of the general partners duly called and held, it appeared to the general partners of the SMITH BROTHERS SUPPLY COMPANY, a general partnership engaged in the oil field supply business, that the partnership is no longer able to meet its debts and obligations as they become due, that the partnership qualifies as a debtor under Chapter 11 of the United States Bankruptcy Code, and that the best interest of the partnership would be served by filing a petition under Chapter 11 and reorganizing its business thereunder; therefore,

IT IS UNANIMOUSLY RESOLVED by the general partners of the SMITH BROTHERS SUPPLY COMPANY that the partnership file a petition under Chapter 11 of the United States Bankruptcy Code and thereafter file a plan of reorganization for the partnership business.

IT WAS FURTHER RESOLVED by the general partners that John H. Jones, Attorney at Law, be retained to represent the partnership on all matters related to the Chapter 11 case and that Sidney S. Smith be authorized and appointed to execute any and all petitions, schedules, statements, plans, and other necessary documents in the Chapter 11 case on behalf of the partnership.

The foregoing matters were transacted and unanimously approved by all of the general partners on behalf of the partnership at a special meeting duly called and held on this 10th day of January, 1998.

_____ _____ _____
Joseph P. Smith   Sidney S. Smith   Henry H. Smith
General Partner   General Partner   General Partner

CERTIFICATION

I, Joseph P. Smith, a general partner of the SMITH BROTHERS SUPPLY COMPANY, a general partnership, certify and declare under penalty of perjury that the above is a true and correct account of a resolution duly passed and adopted by the partnership on the date therein reflected.

Certified under penalty of perjury on this 12th day of January, 1998 by

_____
Joseph P. Smith, General Partner,
Smith Brothers Supply Company

Request For Order That Creditors' Committee NOT Be Appointed [Necessary, Unless Your Area's Local Court Rules Do Not Require this in a Case]

DEBT FORM

Instructions: Complete one of these forms for each debt of any kind. If possible, attach a copy of the creditor's most recent statement or bill to the completed form. Respond to every question on this form. Write "N/A" in the blank after each question that does not apply to a particular debt. If more space is needed to answer a question, use the back of the form.

1. List the complete name and address of the party to whom this debt is owed. _____
    _____ name

    _____
    address

    _____
    city   state   zipcode

2. What is the creditor's account number for this debt? _____

3. Is this debt covered or secured by a mortgage, lien, pledge, or other security interest on any property? _____
    If so, is this property listed elsewhere in these Work Sheets? _____ In what question? _____
    If it is not listed in these Work Sheets, describe the property and list its owner, value and location. _____

    _____

4. Is this debt entitled to priority of payment under the Bankruptcy Code? _____ If so, describe the type of
    priority (wage claim, tax claim, etc.; see questions 69-73). _____

5. Is anyone beside the debtor liable for this debt? _____ If so, list that person's name and address.

    _____

6. Has this debt been turned over to anyone for collection? _____ If so, to whom? _____
    name

    _____
    address   city   state   zipcode

7. When was this debt incurred? Month _____ Year _____

8. What did the debtor receive in consideration for this debt? _____

    _____

9. Does this creditor owe the debtor a debt? _____ If so, can the creditor's debt be setoff against this debt? _____

10. Is this debt contingent upon anything? _____ If so, explain _____

    _____

11. Has the final amount of this debt been determined? _____

12. Does the debtor admit liability for the full amount of this debt? _____ If not, explain. _____

    _____

13. Do the debtor and the creditor agree on the amount of this debt? _____ If not, explain. _____

    _____

14. Has the debtor given a written financial statement in connection with this debt? _____ If so, attach a copy of
    the statement to this form and state to whom and when the statement was given. _____

    _____

15. If this debt is a continuing obligation, are the payments on this debt current or delinquent? _____
    If delinquent, what is the total amount of the arrearage? $_____

16. Is this a debt of someone else that the debtor has guaranteed, secured, or otherwise became liable for? _____
    If so, list the other person's name, address and relationship to the debtor. _____

    _____

17. What is the total amount of this debt? $_____

67

Case No. _____ [Enter it] ↓ _____

United States Bankruptcy Court

Name of your filing District,
from Appendix E. →

Southern _____ **DISTRICT OF** New York _____

[Enter the name of your state.] ↙

In re _____ NEW HOPE., INC _____ Debtor ←

[Give the business name, the Tax I.D. # of business.] ←

[Enter here the figure "11"] → Chapter 11

Soc. Sec. No(s) _____ _____ ...and all ↙

Employer's Tax Identification Nos. (if any) _____ 13 – 98476 _____

Petition, Schedules and Statement of Financial Affairs

[Name of the principal officer & the address of business.] →

~~Attorney(s)~~ for Petitioner(s) PRO SE
Office & Post Office Address & Telephone Number

JOHN LEE DOE, President,
New Hope, INc.
100 5th Ave., Ground Floor
New York, N.Y. 10001
PHONE:(212) 967-1212

REFERRED TO

_____

_____
Clerk

_____
Date

3010, 3020, 3021 & 3050

step 6: PROPERLY SIGN THE FORMS & FILE THEM WITH THE COURT

Signing of the Papers

After having prepared the Voluntary Petition papers as instructed in "Step Five" above, one or more persons with official authority to act for the business (i.e., one or more authorized officers or partners) should simply sign them in the five (or four) places – at the equivalent spots marked "X" of pp. 51, 55, 58, 61, 64 of the manual. Sign the forms directly on the papers themselves – not through a carbon sheet.

The next order of business would be for you to submit them to ("file" them with) the court. But wait a minute! First, make a photocopy of all the completed forms and put those away for your own records and future reference. Next, before you take the papers to court, you've got to arrange them in a proper manner. Here's how you do it: First put the "Address Matrix" form aside to be submitted singly to the court clerk along with the rest of the papers; then sort out all the forms into five or six* different sets, arranged in the same EXACT order in which they are listed in STEP THREE above., except that the 2-page "Form 1 Voluntary Petition" cover sheet forms should come first (i.e., should be on top of each set and be the first to be read), followed by the "Summary of Schedules" form. (All the other forms should simply remain in the same sequential order as they are listed in STEP THREE above)*

Next, take each set of forms and place the set on top of the Blue (or Green) Backer/Cover, with the forms facing up so that the backer gets read last in each set. Now, staple each set of forms together at the top right hand and left hand corners. (All the originals should be in one set.)

Venue, The proper Place/Court District Where To File

The papers are finally in shape for submission. Where do you submit the papers? You submit them to the Clerk of the Bankruptcy Court which handles cases for the area in which your domicile, residence, principal place of business or assets are located for the last 180-day period immediately prior to the filing of the petition papers. Or, if the principal place of business or principal assets of the debtor have been located in more than one district during that 180-day period, then the proper venue on which to file is in the Federal Court District in which the debtor's domicile, residence, principal place of business, or principal assets, have been located for the longest portion of that 180-day period.* (See Appendix E for a listing of the court locations in each State.) You merely submit the papers to the Court Clerk, and you do not have to see or to go before any judge then.

What happens then? The bankruptcy clerk will check over your papers to make sure they are complete and properly filled out and signed. The clerks in this court have a well-earned reputation for being very knowledgeable and helpful, and many bankruptcy courts will often have a "pro se" clerk, meaning one that is especially set aside to attend to the filing needs of petitioners who file without a lawyer. So, if you should have any questions, don't ever hesitate to ask the clerk whether then or at any time later.

More often than not, the papers you submit to the clerk will check out. However, don't always count on it. If the clerk should tell you there is some necessary information or additional paper that's missing or improperly filled out, don't even worry about it. (The same clerk will also tell you—if you corner him or her in private, of course!—that even the lawyers themselves, who are supposed to be the know-it-alls in such matters, have a record of making more errors than lay petitioners like you!!) Simply ask the clerk to tell you *specifically* what needs to be corrected or supplied, and make a note of what he says. Then make the corrections or obtain the missing documents and resubmit the papers. (Always try to resubmit to the same clerk, if possible.)

After the clerk gives his o.k. to your petition papers, you pay him $839 for the filing fee. [Or, if you're unable to make the full payment at once, you can make a partial payment; you simply submit an application to the court, through the bankruptcy clerk, and request to pay up the balance by periodic installments.] The clerk will stamp an assigned **"Docket Number"** for your case on your papers, meaning the number by which your case is to be officially identified at all times thereafter.

---

*Different localities require different numbers of copies. New York's is 6 sets of copies. You can always make additional xerox copies to meet your local requirements, however.

Chapter 11 Fees

The filing fee for any Chapter 11 case except a railroad case, is $839 (as of this writing in early 2004). This fee will almost always be paid by the debtor when the petition is filed in that, while it is legally permissible for the debtor to make an application to be allowed to pay the filing fee in installments, it is seldom practicable to do so: if the debtor can't even afford to pay the filing fee, it makes it difficult to convince the creditors and the court that he/she will be able to successfully reorganize under Chapter 11.

Then, in addition to the regular filing fee ($839) payable to the Court Clerk, as a Chapter 11 debtor you also must pay a Quarterly fee to the U.S. Trustee for each quarter, or a fraction thereof, that the case is pending until a Chapter 11 Plan is "confirmed" by the Court, or the case is dismissed or converted to a case under another chapter. This fee, which is payable NOT to the court clerk but to the U.S. Bankruptcy Trustee, is required to be paid on the last day of the calendar month following the calendar quarter for which the fee is owed.

The Chapter 11 quarterly fees are set forth in the following Chart:

Total Amount of Disbursements in Quarter	Quarterly Fee
Less than $15,000	$250
$15,000 to $75,000	$500
$75,000 to $150,000	$750
$150,000 to $225,000	$1,250
$225,000 to $300,000	$1,500
$300,000 to $1,000,000	$3,750
$1,000,000 to $2,000,000	$5,000
$2,000,000 to $3,000,000	$7,500
$3,000,000 to $5,000,000	$8,000
$5,000,000 or more	$10,000

Documents To File

In a Chapter 11 case not filed on an emergency basis, the forms and documents you file in order to commence the Chapter 11 case, are the following:

- The Voluntary Petition form (sample on pp. 63, 64)
- Schedules A through J, and other forms listed under "Step 5" above. (Samples on pp.35-67)
- Debtor's Resolution Authorizing Commencement of Case (include this, if required by your local bankruptcy court). See sample of this form on p.65)
- Request For Order That Creditors' Committee Not Be Appointed. (Include this if debtor elected to be treated as a "Small Business" and hence wishes not to have a Creditors' Committee appointed in the case.) (See "Step 7", and sample of the form on p. 66). Note that this application is filed either when the case is filed or shortly thereafter.
- Application For Order Approving Employment of Attorney. Include this if debtor elects to employ an attorney to represent the debtor as a debtor-in-possession during the actual bankruptcy proceedings. The application should be filed either with the petition when the case is filed, or shortly thereafter. See Step 3, Section (d) thereof, for background information on employment of an attorney, and pp. 185, 187 for sample of this form.

NOTE: You should recognize that if you are filing the Chapter 11 case in an "emergency" situation rather than in a normal situation, you will not need initially to file most of the forms and documents enumerated above. Rather, in such a situation you will only need to file just the 2-page Voluntary Petition form, and one or two other lists in order to commence the case. By "emergency situation," we mean a situation where the debtor faces an immediate threat posed by by hostile creditors to the income or I portent assets of the business.

Filing an "Emergency"Case Situation

A situation, for example, where creditor actions that may curtail the debtor's income or deprive it of important business assets, such as a foreclosure, an attachment, impoundment of funds, or repossession are pending or likely to be carried out in the immediate future, would qualify as an "emergency" bankruptcy filing situation. And, in such a situation, the debtor's immediate concern would usually be to secure an emergency bankruptcy relief – that is, to stop any potential creditor action in the meantime from occurring which may curtail a major portion of the debtor's business assets even before it would be able to gather all the necessary facts and information upon which to file the Chapter 11 petition.

In an emergency filing situation, here's what is usually done. You simply hurry and prepare and file the 2-page Voluntary Petition form only, accompanied by the following: a List of all the debtor's creditors, a list of the Creditors Holding 20 largest unsecured claims, excluding insiders; a resolution authorizing the filing of the petition (if the debtor is a corporation or partnership and the local rules require this), and any other documents as the local rules may require. Such limited petition papers, once filed by the debtor, promptly commences the bankruptcy case, whereupon the debtor immediately receives the legal protection ("relief:") accorded by the "automatic stay" provision of the bankruptcy law.

Time and Notice Requirements

In the event that you had filed on an emergency basis, then here's what you must further do: you must be sure to file all the Schedules and the other remaining papers (the rest of the papers listed in Step 5 above) within 15 days thereafter. [See Bankruptcy Rules 1007(a)(4) and 1007(c) for circumstances and procures under which can get further time extension for filing this]

NOTE: Under Section 1112(e) of the Bankruptcy Code and Bankruptcy Rule 1017(d), if you fail to file within 15 days of filing the petition or within such additional time as the court has allowed the required schedules and lists, the court may, on the request of the U.S. Trustee, and after notice and hearing, dismiss the case or convert it to a Chapter 7 case.

Court Notifies Creditors of the Bankruptcy Filing & Of Its Order of Relief

Under Section 301 and 302 of the Bankruptcy Code, the sole act of your filing the Voluntary Chapter 11 petition, as outlined above in this Section, constitutes an "**Order of Relief**" for the Debtor – that is, it immediately accords the debtor the "Automatic stay" protection of the court against any creditors by prohibiting such creditors from making collection efforts against the debtor with immediate effect. Consequently, upon your filing the Chapter 11 petition with the court, the next move is for the court (the bankruptcy court clerk or some other person the court may direct), to immediately give a notice of that, in writing, to the various parties interest to formally inform them, accompanied by the Court's Order of Relief. The court sends the written notice, by mail, to parties such as the following: the Debtor, the creditors and equity security holders, and any indenture trustees.

NOW THAT YOU'VE FILED YOUR BANKRUPTCY PETITION, YOU MAY NOW GO HOME AND GET YOURSELF READY FOR THE OTHER SUCCEEDING PROCEDURES.

NOTE: After the commencement of your Chapter 11 case—i.e., upon the filing of the petition papers—and while the processing of your case drags on and on through the court channels in the days and months thereafter, you, the debtor, will ordinarily remain "in possession"—that is, in control and management—of the business or its property, unless, of course, the court orders that a trustee be appointed to serve that function. In other words, in general (unless the court orders otherwise), the debtor retains all the rights and powers in a reorganization that a trustee would usually have, including the power to operate his business, except perhaps the right to a compensation or to conduct an investigation of his own business. (See pp. 82-83 for a fuller treatment of this.)

step 7: UNLESS YOU ARE A "SMALL BUSINESS" DEBTOR, THE U.S. TRUSTEE WILL PROBABLY APPOINT THE COMMITTEE OF CREDITORS.

Now that you (the debtor) have filed the initial petition papers to commence your Chapter 11 case (Step 6 above), the next move is the Court's. Under the provisions of the Bode, the United States Trustee,* unless the Court orders otherwise, is required to automatically appoint a body called **Committee of Creditors Holding Unsecured Claims** "as soon as practicable" – usually within a few days of the filing of the case. In other words, the debtor, on his own, need not affirmatively do anything in order to bring this (i.e., the appointment) about. It's the U.S. Trustee's and the Court's responsibility. The U.S. Trustee is a Court official independently appointed by the Justice Department and acting totally independently from the court, who is charged with handling the administration of the bankruptcy cases. Upon the making of the appointment, the debtor will get from the court a written notification of such appointment, giving the name, identity and affiliation of the parties appointed.

The Committee of Creditors Holding Unsecured Claims will NOT need to be appointed, however, if and when certain circumstances exist. If the debtor is a debtor who is electing to be treated as a "Small Business" for the purposes of Chapter 11 petition (see Subsection C of Step 3 of the Chapter), upon the request of any party in interest in the case (e.g., a debtor, creditor, etc.) for that, and for cause shown, the court may order that a Committee of Creditors not be appointed in the case. Therefore, assuming that you qualify for and have elected to be treated as a small business so as to take advantage of the many important advantages attached to filing as a Small Business debtor, then you should request the court for an order not to appoint a Creditors' Committee in your case. To do this, simply complete and file with the court a form such as the sample Form on p. 66 , stating a good, reasonable cause or reason why the court should not make such appointment of a Creditors' Committee in your case – e.g., for the reason that it will save the debtor's bankruptcy estate funds, that it will be more speedy, and therefore less expensive for the debtor, and the like.

In any case, unless the court orders otherwise, the U.S. Trustee will appoint an Unsecured Creditors' Committee as a matter of course.

Who makes up such a committee? It will ordinarily consist of the persons willing to serve, that hold the seven largest unsecured claims against the debtor. "Persons" are broadly defined here to include individuals, partnerships, or corporations. It should be pointed out, however, that persons may at times be appointed who are not necessarily holders of the seven largest unsecured nonpriority claims against the debtor. The court (i.e., the U.S. Trustee) may, when it prefers, choose to appoint as members of the committee certain creditors – particular creditors it feels will best represent the holders of unsecured claims – even if such persons are not among the seven largest creditors.** In most cases, the Unsecured Creditors' Committee is appointed from the list of the Creditors Holding the 20 Largest Unsecured Claims which you shall have filed with the court.

---

*In certain few districts, no U.S. Trustee is yet serving. However, in all such districts where no U.S. trustee is serving, all committees are appointed by the court.

* *Note that nothing in the law prohibits the appointment to this committee of persons who hold both unsecured claims and secured claims or ownership interests. If the holders of the seven largest unsecured claims also happen to be holders of the seven largest secured claims (or of ownership interests) in a case, the court would just as well be within its rights if it were to appoint such creditors to the committee. And should a party in interest object to the committee being dominated by holders of secured claims (or if, for that matter, he has any objection about anything whatsoever), such objector may file a complaint with the court and request that the size or composition of the committee be changed. The court would then give notice of this complaint to the various interested parties and hold a hearing on the complaint; it may then leave the committee unchanged, or modify it as to the size and composition, if it determines at that point that the committee is not representative of unsecured claimants.

True, in so far as the matter of appointing creditors committees in Chapter 11 cases is concerned, it is only ONE committee that the Bankruptcy Code expressly requires being appointed in a case – the Committee of Unsecured Creditors. (Apparently, this seeming bias in favor of unsecured creditors is borne out of the belief by the Congress that the interest of the "little guy," the creditor with the least security or safeguard within the whole creditor group's pecking order, as represented by the unsecured creditors, is more needy of protection, and more representative and reflective of the creditor classes as a whole.)

It should be noted, though, that a case may not necessarily have just the Committee of Unsecured Creditors, the one committee of creditors that is specifically authorized in the Code. Quite to the contrary, some other additional committees may be appointed in a case – though such additional committees are seldom appointed in small business Chapter 11 cases, and such appointment may not, any way, be done except on an order of the Court, which must in turn be made upon the request of a party in interest. If, for example, the court should determine from the facts of a particular case, that separate representation of particular classes of creditors or equity security holders is necessary to assure adequate representation of the special interest of such groups, that would be one circumstance where the court may find it compelling to order the appointment of additional or multiple committees.

There are various forms the *additional* committees could take. The additional committees that U.S. Trustee, the appoints, may, for instance, be additional committees of unsecured creditors, or it may be some **Committees of Equity Security Holders** (holders of securities in the debtor's business, such as stocks or warrants) depending on what parties the trustee and for the court deems legitimately needy of separate representation.

Why Would Additional Committees Be Warranted?

What kind of situation would warrant the appointment of additional committees? In an average Chapter 11 case involving a relatively small business or medium-sized corporate debtor, which has no public security holders and no substantial number of secured creditors, there would ordinarily be no need to appoint additional committees and only one committee of unsecured creditors should be sufficient. On the other hand, in a large case involving a publicly owned corporate debtor with a variety of issues of publicly held senior and subordinated debts, or involving significant groups of creditors or equity holders with a variety of conflicting claims whose fate would most likely be affected by the Chapter 11 plan of reorganization, the appointment of additional committees may become necessary to the court. Such would be the case in a situation, for example, where there are numerous consumer creditors holding claims that are entitled to "priority" under Section 507(a)(5) of the bankruptcy code.

Take note of the fact, however, that the court (or the U.S. trustee) may make such appointment of additional committees, or make changes in the membership or size of any committee, only if certain conditions are present: first, only if the court (or the U.S. trustee) initiated the action upon the request of "a party in interest," and secondly, only after the bankruptcy court (i.e., the judge) shall have had the routine "notice and hearing" on that request.

As in the case of the Committee of Unsecured Creditors, a Committee of Equity Security Holders, if and when one is appointed in a case, would ordinarily consist of persons holding the seven largest amounts of equity securities of the debtor for each given class, who are also willing to serve on the committee. And should an issue of potential conflict of interest arise among such 7 creditors (e.g., say one or more of the seven shareholders are also creditors of the debtor or past or present officers or directors of the debtor), that issue may, again, be raised with the court by "a party in interest" and may be resolved by the court through the routine procedure of giving a notice and holding a hearing on the issues raised.

The Powers & Duties of the Creditors' Committees

The role and scope of committees in Chapter 11 cases will vary from case to case depending on such factors as these: i) the size of the case; ii) the complexity of the debtor's financial affairs; iii) the class or classes of creditors represented; iv) whether the debtor remains "in possession" of his property and business; v) whether an examiner is appointed to investigate the affairs of the debtor; and vi) whether the court orders the appointment of a trustee in a case.

If we were to sum it up in one sentence, the central purpose for which the bankruptcy code created the committee system in Chapter 11 cases could be defined as follows: to provide the debtor with a representative body of his creditors with whom to put heads together and evaluate the financial condition of the business as a basis for negotiating a plan of reorganization with each other—a body which has the power, legitimacy and representativeness to represent and speak for the major economic interests in the case. The theory behind the use of a committee method is that a limited group of persons (a "committee") composed of and representing the dominant creditor interests would be much more easy and flexible for a debtor to work and negotiate with than a system which requires the debtor to negotiate individually with every creditor (or security holder) in the case.

Of paramount importance and permeating everything the committee does, however, in the eyes of the law, is the principle that committee members owe what is known as a **"fiduciary obligation"** (i.e., a position of extreme trust) to the class of creditors represented by the committee. And, to serve in a committee, a creditor should not have an interest which is in conflict with the interest of the debtor and its attempt to reorganize. Hence, for example, based on this ground, a creditor with a priority claim should not normally serve on a committee of unsecured, nonpriority creditors, nor should a creditor whose claim is only partially secured serve on a committee of unsecured creditors.* Similarly, competitors of a debtor may not usually serve on committees, and unions may sometimes be excluded from serving on committee since such connection, it is held, could provide the union operatives access to confidential financial information about the debtor bearing on a pending or future labor negotiation.

The following are the basic procedures and main powers and duties of the committee under the Bankruptcy Code:

1. As required under section 1103(d) of the Bankruptcy Code, as a Debtor-in-Possession you are to meet with the Creditors' Committee "as soon as practicable" after such a committee is appointed, to transact such business as may be necessary and proper. And thereafter, the committee is to maintain communications with the debtor-in-possession and its attorney, if any, and other agents.

2. A committee may, if it determines that such employment is necessary, select and authorize the employment of one (or more attornies, accountants, appraisers, and any other types of agents it may consider necessary, to represent or assist it in performing its duties. A decision to make any such employment of professionals must, however, be taken at a scheduled meeting of the committee at which a majority of the committee members are present, and finally, the decision must have the court's approval.

   must have the court's approval.

   NOTE: Though not mandated by "the letter" of the Code, "the spirit" of the law requires that a Committee may not employ more than one attorney or law firm to serve as the "committee attorney" (as differentiated from a lawyer or lawyers the individual creditors may want to engage to represent their individual interests). Exceptions to the general rule would be made and employment of more than one attorney permissible, only in situations where, for "good cause" shown to the court, the court authorizes employment of more than one. Anyone employed to represent a Chapter 11 case committee may not represent any other entity in the case, and must be a "disinterested person"—i.e., one who is not a creditor or stockholder of the debtor, a previous or present underwriter of any outstanding securities of the debtor within the past five years, or a present or previous officer, director or employee of the debtor within the past 2 years.

3. The Committee may consult with the trustee or with a debtor-in-in-possession concerning the administration of the Chapter 11 case. It is customary in many court districts for the debtor-in-possession and/or its attorney (if he is using any) to send proposed orders and other bankruptcy papers to the Committee (or its attorney) for approval before submitting them to the Court.

4. The committee has the legal responsibility to do the following: i) determine the desirability of the continuance of the debtor company's business; ii) negotiate terms of a plan of reorganiza-

---

*See <u>Bohack Corp. v. Gulf & Western Industries, Inc.</u>, 607 F.2d 258 (CA 2, 1979), In re <u>Glendale Woods Apts. Ltd.</u>, 25 B.R. 414 (MD, 1982), In re <u>Wilson Foods Corp.</u>, 31 B.R. 272 (WD OK, 1983), In re <u>National Equipment & Mold Corp.</u>, 33 B.R. 574 (ND OH, 1983).

tion with the debtor; iii) make recommendations with respect to the plan or plans that are filed in the case; and iv) determine whether the committee should request the court to order the appointment of a trustee or examiner.

5. In a Chapter 11 case where neither a trustee nor an examiner is appointed, it becomes essential for the committee involved to examine the debtor's financial condition if a committee is to intelligently represent the interests of creditors in the reorganization case. In such instances, the committee has the right and power to investigate the nature of the debtor's assets and liabilities, the debtor's financial condition, and the strengths and weaknesses of the debtor's business inasmuch as it is only with such information and knowledge that the committee can possibly make an intelligent determination regarding the viability of the debtor's business or the plan of reorganization submitted, and whether the business merits being continued or rehabilitated, or deserves to be completely liquidated.

Where, however, there is a trustee appointed in the case, the responsibility to investigate the acts, conduct, assets, liabilities, and financial condition of the debtor's business—any matter whatsoever that might bear on the case and on the formulation of a viable reorganization plan—would primarily be the responsibility of the trustee. Hence, in such a situation, the investigative role which a committee would ordinarily have had, would be limited, if not totally eliminated, and the committee would merely limit itself to closely consulting with the trustee (or examiner) and debtor concerning the affairs of the case or any investigations being undertaken, but it may not actually carry out such investigations. That is to say that, in general, only if and when it should happen that the trustee or debtor in possession unjustifiably fails to take a necessary action on behalf of the estate, may the committee usually bring an independent action.*

Likewise, the committee's scope of responsibilities with respect to financial (or other) investigations would be limited in a case in which an **"examiner"** (pp. 81-82   ) is appointed, since the primary responsibility of an examiner is usually investigative—to investigate and evaluate the assets, affairs and prospects of the debtor and render a report of same to the court.

6. The committee is required to collect and file with the court acceptances or rejections of plans of reorganization submitted to creditors for consideration, and, when and where circumstances warrant, it may investigate the circumstances surrounding the debtor's solicitation of those acceptances so as to ensure that such consents were properly solicited and that the requisite majorities of each class of creditors and equity security holders did properly consent to the plan.

7. The committee may, if it determines it to be necessary, request the court to order the appointment of a trustee, or that of an examiner, in a case.

8. Pursuant to Section 1121(c) of the Bankruptcy Code, the committee is empowered to file with the court a chapter 11 plan of its own, if a trustee is appointed in the case; or, it may do so if the debtor fails to file a plan within 120 days after the initial filing of the bankruptcy petition, or if a filed plan has not been accepted within 180 days after the filing of a plan. However, in this connection, it should further be noted that when a committee files a plan, it must also file the disclosure statement and carry out the requirements necessary to solicit the votes and to obtain the acceptance and confirmation of the plan.

All said and done, however, as a practical matter, probably the most common and vital task of all often undertaken by the creditors' committee in many cases, is to participate in the formulation of a chapter 11 plan. This derives from the responsibilities assigned to the creditors' committee under Section 1103(c)(3) of the Bankruptcy Code (basically, item #4 on p. 73), whereby the said committee is charged with the duties of advising the creditors it

---

*See, for example, *In re Toledo Equipment Co.*, 35 B.R. 315 (ND OH, 1983), and *In Re Wesco Products Co.*, 22 B.R. 107 (ND IL, 1982).

represents of its (the committee's) findings and making informed assessments as to the desirability of any plan proposed by the debtor. Indeed, in this connection, some bankruptcy experts vastly knowledgeable in the inner workings of successful chapter 11 plan formulation, contend that advisory and fact-finding functions are the one principal area of responsibility to which the creditors' committee should devote much of its attention and energies relative to the debtor, arguing that the committee system is uniquely suited to and most effective in such task, to the overall benefit of the creditors and the debtors alike. As one such expert put it, "if a (creditors') committee is permitted to actively participate in the formulation of a plan, it is more likely to recommend acceptance of the plan (to the creditors). The best practice, therefore, is to permit the unsecured creditors' committee to participate actively in the formulation of a plan, either directly, through an attorney, or through a negotiating subcommittee appointed by the committee to deal with the debtor in possession."[*]

To sum it all up, the primary role of a creditors' committee is to assess the company's situation and the plan for reorganization proposed by the company or a trustee, and to identify what creditors would realistically settle for in light of the committee's assessment of the financial condition and prospects of the debtor company. It may — and usually does — engage in direct negotiations with the debtor on the reorganization or settlement terms. It may raise, and may appear on and/or be heard on any issues in the Chapter 11 case, such as action to set aside an avoidable transfer, or to intervene in an adversary proceeding brought by a third party, or to request the court to convert a Chapter 11 case to Chapter 7 for liquidation.[**] However, its main role, as statutorily granted under the code, is essentially advisory; it may not operate the debtor's business or attempt to assume its management, and where it feels that the officers and directors of a debtor corporation are either unwilling or incapable of properly managing the debtor company's business, all the committee may do is to make application to the court for a trustee to be appointed.[***]

As soon as practicable after the appointment of a committee under this Chapter, the trustee or debtor shall meet with such committee to transact such business as may be necessary and proper [as in "Step 8" below) , regarding the Meeting(s) of Creditors and Stockholders].

NOTE: It would appear, though, that while a Committee may not actually or directly operate or take over the management of the debtor company, it may select a person (or persons) to act on its behalf as its so-called "custodian" in instances where the debtor is in possession, and that upon approval by the court, such a person could perform various duties and exercise rights and obligations that are, nevertheless, sweeping in nature and scope.

As could be seen from the duties and responsibilities delegated to one such Creditors' Committee-appointed "custodian" in a Chapter 11 case, set forth in Article IV of the Plan of Reorganization on pp. 163-5 of this manual, a custodian's powers—of supervision, if not of direct control of the debtor's business affairs—could nevertheless be far-reaching and drastic. Under the provisions of the said Article IV of the Plan (pp. 163-5), the custodian's power ranges from the power to keep custody of duly executed documents vital to the sale or transfer of title of major debtor property, to the power to act as the major depository of business receipts or proceeds as well as disbursement agent to creditors, the power to require, at his sole discretion, the sale by the debtor of any or all of the debtor's property, and, to approve all major dispositions of property by the debtor or applications for loans and other financing measures on behalf of the debtor company.

---

[*]Williamson, *The Attorney's Handbook on Chapter 11 Bankruptcy*, p. 136.

[**]See, for example, *In re Joyanna Holitogs, Inc.*, 21 B.R. 323 (SD NY, 1982); *In re Graf Brothers, Inc.*, 19 B.R. 269 (ME, 1982).

[***]On the power of the Committee to obtain financial information from the debtor or the parties employed by it, see, for example, *Matter of International Horizons, Inc.*, 689 F.2d 996 (CA 11, 1982). And on the committee's lack of power to intervene in the day-to-day affairs of the debtor's business, see, for example, *In re UNR Industries, Inc.*, 30 B.R. 609 (ND IL, 1983).

step 8: ATTEND THE MEETING OR MEET-INGS OF CREDITORS

Under the Bankruptcy Rule X-1006 and Section 341(a) of the Code, following the filing of the chapter 11 bankruptcy petition by the debtor which commences the case, the United States trustee is required to call a meeting of creditors (and, of equity security holders as well, if necessary or so ordered by the court)* , to be held not less than 20 days nor more than 40 days from the date of the filing of the bankruptcy petition. [If there is an appeal from or a Motion to Vacate the order of relief, or if a motion to dismiss the case is filed, a later time may be set for the meeting]. This meeting is also called **Section 341(a) Meeting,** referring to Section 341(a) of the Bankruptcy Code which authorizes it.

In practice, shortly after the bankruptcy petition has been filed, the clerk of court or the United States trustee sends a written notice of this meeting by mail to the debtors, all the creditors, the equity security holders,* if applicable, and other parties in interest in the case.** [When deemed desirable or necessary, (such as when notice by mail is either impracticable or is necessary only as a supplement), the court may order that notice of this meeting be given by publication].

The written notices go by different names in different local districts, such as *"Order for the Meeting of Creditors, Fixing Time for Filing Objections to Discharge, Filing Complaints to Determine Dischargeability of Certain Debts, Combined with Notice Thereof and of Automatic Stay",* or, more simply, *"Notice of First Meeting of Creditors and Stockholders, of Automatic Stay, and Related Matters".* But, basically, it specifies the date, time and place designated for the meeting, and the general agenda thereof. (See a sample copy of this notice on p. 123).

---

* As a rule, Meetings of Equity Security Holders are seldom called in small business cases. However, if and when such a meeting is desired, the procedure is simply to request the U.S. trustee to call a meeting of the debtor's equity security holders. Basically, the same rules applicable to the Meeting of Creditor also apply to the Meeting of Equity Security Holders. (See Section 341(b) of the Code, and Bankruptcy Rule X-1006).

** In any and all instances in which a notice is required to be given to parties in the case, copies of such notice should always be mailed to each of the following entities also: to the Securities and Exchange Commission, Washington D.C., if the debtor is a corporation (or, preferably, at such other address it may designate in any notice of appearance or in writing filed with the court); to the District Director of the IRS covering the district in which the case is pending; to the U.S. Attorney for the district in which the case is pending whenever the debtor owes an outstanding debt to the United States other than taxes, or to a department, agency or instrument of the United States; and to the Secretary of the Treasury, Washington D.C., if the papers filed with the court indicate a stock interest of the United States.

What Are the Purposes of this Meeting?

As stated, this U.S. Trustee, or a designee thereof, is the one who must convene this meeting and preside therein. When and where appropriate, a trustee for the Chapter 11 case may be elected at such meetings. However, the essential purpose and business of the meeting is to conduct an **examination** of the debtor. The Code (Section 343) and the Bankruptcy Rule [X-1006(b)(1)], provide that the debtor (and/or responsible and knowledgeable representatives of the debtor acting in his behalf) must appear at this meeting and submit to an "examination" under Oath. Creditors, any indenture trustee, the U.S. trustee, or the trustee or examiner (if one is serving in the case), may appear at the meeting and may ask any questions of the debtor, or request certain proofs, clarifications or documentations. If the debtor is a corporation, the president and other responsible executive officers, for example, will be appropriate representatives to attend the meeting. For a partnership, one or more of the general partners must be in attendance. The United States trustee (or the Clerk of the Bankruptcy Court in certain districts or instances), is designated to preside at such meetings, and by provision of the law the bankruptcy judge may neither preside at nor even attend any such meetings. A meeting of creditors may be adjourned from time to time by announcement at the meeting and without further written notice.

The scope of examination of the debtor and the debtor's affairs in reorganization cases covers a broad area of investigation. As summarized by a relevant Senate Report, it would include "inquiry into the liabilities and financial condition of the debtor, the operation of his business, and the desirability of the continuance thereof, and other matters relevant to the case and to the formulation of the plan [of reorganization]."* The examination cannot be used to delve into the private affairs of a debtor or witness, however, as such affairs have no connection with the acts, conduct or property of the debtor. Hence, the court ultimately reserves the discretion to make a determination as to what questions, or line of inquiry is relevant or what facts are deserving of disclosure.

Have your books, papers and documents ready and organized, therefore, for you may at any time be asked to produce them for examination by an inquirer. A witness other than the debtor may be asked to testify at the hearing, or to produce books, papers and documents which relate to the debtor's business, unless such papers are not in his possession. The officers of a debtor corporation (or of another corporation), members of the board of directors or trustees, or a controlling stockholder may be called upon by the court to undergo an examination as a representative of the debtor as to the dealings of the corporation.

From the standpoint of the debtor in possession (or simply the debtor), perhaps the most important questions of relevance are these: What is the primary significance of this meeting to the debtor? To what use should the debtor put the meeting of creditors (or of equity security holders), and how should the debtor conduct itself with respect to the meeting?

Experts experienced in Chapter 11 bankruptcy procedures see the major significance of the meeting of creditors to the debtor as being primarily public relations-oriented, as being a tool or forum to be seized upon by the intelligent debtor and effectively used to reassure the creditors and to create a favorable disposition in the creditors minds towards the debtor and its reorganization goals.

---

*Senate Report No. 989, 95th Congress 2nd Session 43(1978).

John H. Williamson, a Lakewood Colorado bankruptcy law practitioner and author with a vast practical experience with chapter 11 bankruptcy procedures, sums up how a debtor should best conduct itself at such meetings and the most fruitful uses and purposes to which the debtor should put such meetings this way:*

> "For the debtor, the meeting of creditors is an excellent, and often the first, opportunity to clarify and personally explain the debtor's situation to its creditors. A clear and realistic explanation of the debtor's financial condition, prospects, and plans may answer many of the creditors' potential questions and help to shorten the debtor's examination. If permitted by the presiding officer, it is a good practice for the debtor or its attorney to begin the meeting of creditors with an opening statement touching on the following matters:
>
> (1) the debtor's present financial condition and the underlying reasons therefore;
> (2) the prospects for the debtor's business in the foreseeable future and a description of the obstacles that must be overcome if the business is to succeed;
> (3) the debtor's reasons for seeking reorganizational relief under chapter 11; and
> (4) the reorganizational alternatives being considered by the debtor.
>
> It is important for the debtor to create a favorable reaction among its creditors to its reorganizational effort. By so doing the debtor may insure continuing business relationships with important creditors, diminish the potential for contested matters during the course of the case, and increase the chances for creditor acceptance of its reorganizational plan. With careful preparation and a property attitude, a knowledgeable debtor can make great strides toward accomplishing these objectives at the meeting of creditors...
>
> The meeting of creditors serves the practical function of bringing the debtor and its creditors together in the same room on a face-to-face basis. As such, it presents an opportunity for the parties to begin negotiating on the practical issues that are likely to arise during the course of the case. Such matters as adequate protection for secured creditors, the use of cash collateral by the debtor in possession, and the formulation of a mutually-acceptable plan of reorganization can be discussed in a professional atmosphere. *In many cases the negotiations that later produce a workable reorganizational plan begin at the meeting of creditors.*"

Williamson gives an idea of what you'd expect from the creditors at such a meeting in terms of their attitude and their examination of the debtor's affairs:**

> "[First, with respect to the unsecured creditors of the debtor], as a class, unsecured creditors, who usually receive little or nothing in liquidation proceedings, tend to favor reorganization as opposed to liquidation.*** For these creditors, the meeting of creditors is an opportunity to determine the reorganizational alternatives that will result in the most favorable treatment of their claims. *When examining the debtor, unsecured creditors are generally most concerned with matters pertaining to the condition of the debtor's business, its prospects for the future, and the reorganizational alternatives being considered by the debtor.* In most cases the unsecured creditors' committee will have been appointed prior to the meeting of creditors, and the presiding officer will often permit the committee or its attorney to examine the debtor on behalf of its constituency...
>
> [Next, with respect to the secured class of creditors], secured creditors, on the other hand, are often hostile to a debtor's reorganizational efforts because liquidation of the debtor's assets will usually satisfy their claims. At the meeting of creditors, *a secured creditor is likely to examine the debtor on matters pertaining to the condition of the creditor's collateral, whether the collateral is deteriorating, whether it is covered by insurance, whether taxes against it have been paid, and what steps are being taken to protect and preserve the property.* Secured creditors are also likely to question the debtor as to the role their collateral will play in any reorganizational plans being considered by the debtor."

---

*Williamson, *The Attorney's Handbook on Chapter 11 Bankruptcy*, pp. 138 & 139.

**Williamson, *The Attorney's Handbook on Chapter 11 Bankruptcy*, pp. 138 & 139.

***The reasons why the unsecured creditor — the holder of the allowed claim that is not secured by alien on property of the estate and which is not subject to a setoff — should generally, even naturally, favor the Chapter 11 reorganization, is simple. Primarily, most unsecured creditors realize that if the debtor company were to file instead for chapter 7 bankruptcy (i.e., for liquidation), or to simply close down its business, they (the unsecured creditors) would likely receive little, perhaps even nothing, on their claims. But that, with chapter 11, on the other hand, not only would the unsecured creditor usually receive payment of at least a part of its claim, but the possibility would still remain open for the unsecured creditor to recoup its claims in full at a future date since the debtor remains in business with a reorganization.

step 9: IF THE COURT SHOULD APPOINT A TRUSTEE IN THE CASE, HERE'S WHAT TO DO

A. What's the Significance to you of a Trustee Being Appointed?

This point can safely be made outright: *No other decision in a Chapter 11 case is more critical, certainly from the standpoint of the debtor company, than the decision as to whether or not a trustee is appointed in a case.* The reason this decision is of such great importance is this: If a trustee is appointed in any Chapter 11 case, it would be the trustee, rather than the debtor company, that takes control of the debtor's assets and operates the debtor's business, among other things, unless the court orders otherwise.

In other words, the decision to appoint a trustee would automatically mean, in effect, that the debtor would *not* be "in possession" of his assets and business during the bankruptcy proceedings, and must have the trustee handle those matters. Furthermore, if a trustee is appointed in a case, that automatically terminates the debtor's exclusive right to file a Reorganization Plan. And, thirdly, the trustee, immediately upon being appointed, has the exclusive right to control all litigation by and against the debtor, including the right to bring actions against the debtor's owners and management.

Ordinarily, unless the court does specifically order otherwise, it would be the debtor corporation and its board of directors that would continue to operate the debtor's business while the company is undergoing Chapter 11 bankruptcy proceedings. The court has the authority to order the appointment of a trustee (or, if not that, an "examiner") at any time from the start of the case up to the time before the plan is confirmed. *The court may make such appointment of a trustee in a case, however, only under certain strict conditions.*

B. Typically, A Trustee Would Probably Not Be Appointed in Your Case

But what are the chances, though, that a trustee would likely be appointed in your case, in the first place? Not much of a chance, particularly if you are a small business debtor! Simply summed up, in the vast majority of small business Chapter 11 cases, neither a trustee nor an "examiner" (Step 10 below) is appointed. This is so because the general rule in Chapter 11 cases, is that the debtor is to remain "in possession" (i.e., in control and management) of its assets and business during the course of the case.

Under the provisions of the Code, the court's decision on whether to appoint a trustee in a Chapter 11 case is intended to be flexible, to be undertaken purely on a case-by-case basis according to the facts of each case. There's more than ample evidence, however, that a primary Congressional intent in the 1978 Bankruptcy Code was to make it as easy and frequent as possible for the Chapter 11 debtor to remain **"in possession"**—i.e., for the debtor himself to continue to manage and control the company's business or assets during the period of the Chapter 11 reorganization rather than to have the debtor turn over such control to his creditors or a court official. The need to generally leave the debtor company "in possession" was born out of the need to achieve what has been described as "the chief purpose"* of the business bankruptcy laws—which is, in a word, to attempt to keep and rehabilitate, rather than to in any way hamper the recovery of, or to liquidate an otherwise salvageable company. The law aims, therefore, at preserving and strengthening the hands

---

*"The chief purpose of corporate reorganization is to preserve, if possible, the going-concern value of the debtor in contrast to forced sales and depressed values of liquidation. To accomplish this purpose, the debtor's business must be maintained in operation."—13A *Collier on Bankruptcy*, #10-207.03 (14th ed. 1977).

of an otherwise honest but already existing management, the rationale being that continuity of a management team is often an important ingredient in making possible a successful operation and reorganization of a business.

Out of this basic belief, therefore, the draftsmen of the Code sought to see to it that the appointment of a trustee in a Chapter 11 case—which would, in effect, mean that the debtor would be displaced from remaining in possession—would be done only as a last resort, only in a limited and exceptional number of cases. They reasoned as follows, that: "Very often, the creditor will be benefitted [by maintaining the debtor in possession] both because the expense of a trustee will not be required, and [also because] the debtor, who is familiar with his business, will be better able to operate it during the reorganization case."*

Hence, the Code stipulates that before the court may order the appointment of a trustee in a Chapter 11 case, one of two stringent conditions must be met: i) it has to be either *"for cause"* shown—that is, on the basis of convincing evidence of fraud, dishonesty, incompetence, or gross mismanagement of the debtor's affairs on the part of the *current* (as opposed to past) management, presented to the judge by "a party in interest" in a formal hearing; or ii) such appointment has to be made based on a determination by the court (on a request of a party in interest to appoint a trustee, and made after "notice and hearing" by the court) that appointing a trustee would be "in the best interest" of each of the following groups: creditors, equity security holders, and ownership interests. Thus, for example, in deciding whether to appoint a trustee on the "best interest" grounds, the court may balance the added expense of having a trustee against any possible savings to the estate and creditors that may result from the appointment of a trustee, and if such appointment would impose a substantial financial hardship, a trustee will not be appointed.

A mere showing that the *current* management of the debtor company had mismanaged the debtor's affairs *prior* to the time of the filing for Chapter 11, if based solely on that ground, would be insufficient to warrant the court to appoint a trustee "for cause", whatever the strength of the evidence presented. The law seemingly admits to a tacit recognition that some degree of mismanagement exists in almost every insolvency case, and secondly, given the fact that a central philosophy of the Chapter 11 code is to give the debtor company a "second chance," a trustee would not necessarily be appointed solely because of the current management's mismanagement of the company previously, rather, the current management would be permitted a continued opportunity to identify and correct its past mistakes. Continued mismanagement of the company's affairs by the *current* management after Chapter 11 petition has been filed, would, however, constitute a good ground for appointment of a trustee and displacing the existing management-for incompetence.** In deed, in practice in most proceedings for the appointment of a trustee in Chapter 11 cases, the courts have almost always had a strong presumption in favor of retaining the debtor in possession.***

For details on the powers and responsibilities granted the trustee under the code, see Appendix B on pp. 197-8 , "The Legal Powers and Responsibility of a Trustee." The model samples of the trustee's Report of Investigation, a key product of a trustee in any Chapter 11 case, are reproduced on pp. 139-143 (for corporate debtor).

Other grounds which the courts have found for appointing a trustee, beside fraud, dishonesty, incompetence or gross mismanagement, include the following: the death of an individual Chapter 11 debtor; debtor's failure to disclose post-petition income and liabilities; debtor's failure for a prolonged period to file tax returns and pay taxes; failure by debtor to bring an action against its president to recover a large preferential transfer; and failure by the debtor during the Chapter 11 case to keep adequate books and records and to maintain its property.

---

*House Committee Report No. 595, 95th Congress 1st Session, 232-33 (1977). The report further went on: ". . .a trustee frequently has to take time to familiarize himself with the business before the reorganization can get under way. Thus, a debtor continued in possession may lead to a greater likelihood of success in the reorganization. Moreover, the need for reorganization of a public company today often results from simple business reverses, not from any fraud, dishonesty, or gross mismanagement on the part of the debtor's management. . . ."

**To put it another way, the Code essentially views both the misdeeds of the past management and the past misdeeds of the present management as irrelevant. Congress indicated its reasoning for the need to differentiate between the pre- and post-reorganization conditions this way: "Even if the cause (for reorganization) is fraud or dishonesty, very frequently the fraudulent management will have been ousted shortly before the filing of the reorganization case, and the new management, very capable of running the business, should not be ousted by a trustee because of the sins of former management."—The House Report, Report No. 595, 95th Congress 1st Session 232-33 (1977).

***See, for example, In re: Colorado-Ute Electric Assn., 120 B.R. 164 (Co, 1990).

C. How the Trustee's Appointment Could be Terminated

Can a debtor regain control and management of his business from a trustee once a trustee has been appointed? Yes he can. Under the Code (Section 1105) the court may, at any time before the Chapter 11 plan of reorganization is confirmed, and on request of "a party in interest" (the debtor himself, the trustee, a creditors' committee, a creditor, an equity security holder, etc.), order the termination of a trustee's appointment, and restore the debtor to possession and management of the property and operations of his business. The court would do this if it could determine that, based upon any new facts or evidence that are subsequently brought to his attention after the trustee had originally been appointed, or based on changed conditions subsequent to the time of the trustee's appointment, the continued use of a trustee is either no more warranted, or not in the best interests of creditors, equity security holders and others concerned.

step10: IF THE COURT SHOULD APPOINT AN EXAMINER IN THE CASE, HERE'S WHAT TO DO

A. The Conditions Under Which an Examiner may be Appointed

If no trustee is appointed in a Chapter 11 case (say, because, in the court's judgment, the displacement of management by appointing a trustee would be unwarranted), the law requires that the court should go ahead and order the appointment of an "examiner"—if one of these two conditions obtain: i) if a request for such an appointment is made to the court by the U.S. Trustee or a party in interest at any time before the confirmation pf a reorganization Plan, and the court finds that such an appointment would be in the interest of creditors, any equity security holders, and other interests in the estate; or ii) if a request for such an appointment is made to the court and the party in interest making that request can present evidence showing the court that the debtor's fixed, liquidated, unsecured debts (exclusive of debts for goods, services, or taxes, or debts owing to an "insider") exceed $5,000,000. In practice, the Court has considerable discretion in such determinations.

Thus, an examiner may be appointed only if a trustee is not serving in a case, and in the event of the appointment of a Trustee, the appointment of an Examiner in a Chapter 111 case is an extraordinary matter and is done only if there are grounds clearly justifying such an appointment. The standards for the appointment of an examiner are identical to those for the appointment of a trustee under the "best interest" grounds, namely: protection of the interests of creditors and the estate must be needed; and the benefits to the estate and creditors to be provided by an examiner, must outweigh the expenses of such an appointment. As in the case of the appointment of a trustee, a proceeding to appoint an examiner is a contested matter and is initiated by the filing of a motion for the appointment of an examiner.

B. What a Chapter 11 Examiner Does

The Chapter 11 examiner's role in a case is a far more specific and limited one than that of the trustee. Unlike the trustee, an examiner does not displace the existing management of the debtor company, nor does he take control of the debtor's assets or the operation of the business. The primary responsibilities of the examiner (who could be an individual, a partnership, a corporation, a law or accounting firm, or what have you), are, in a word, investigatory: He (or she) is to conduct an investigation of any allegations or suspicions of fraud, gross mismanagement, incompetence, or other misconduct made against the debtor or the current or former management; or, as is more usually the case, he may merely conduct an investigation of the debtor's actions, financial affairs, and condition. And thereafter he submits a report of the results of such investigations to the court as an aid to enable the court to make an informed decision regarding a proposed reorganization plan.

In other words, the Code's provision for use of an examiner in the Chapter 11 case is intended to provide an alternative to having to use a trustee frequently—a more limited, less expensive, and less drastic but equally effective alternative. And, in view of the fact that the Code favors permitting the debtor to remain in charge of his business except under the most extreme of circumstances, generally the court would decide in favor of appointing an examiner rather than a trustee whenever it seems even remotely likely that the displacement of management (by appointing a trustee) would not be in the best interest of the creditors and the ownership interests, or that such would entail unnecessarily greater costs of administration than the appointment of an examiner. Even then, where the court determines that not even the costs of employing an examiner would be justified in the circumstances of a particular case, or that such an appointment would not be in the interest of creditors and other ownership interests, not even that appointment would be authorized and the court could deny such a request to appoint an examiner and a trustee alike.

If the court were to order the appointment of an Examiner in a case, the court would direct the U.S. Trustee to make the appointment. The U.S. Trustee, after consultation with the parties in interest, must then appoint one disinterested person, other than the US Trustee, to serve as an examiner in the case, subject to the approval of the court.

The model sample copies of the Trustee's Report of Investigation, reproduced on pp. 139-143 *(for corporate debtor), are adaptable (with a little modification) as an Examiner's Report of Investigation, a key product of an examiner, when one is appointed in a Chapter 11 case.*

step11: YOU'LL PROBABLY REMAIN AS "DEBTOR IN POSSESSION": HERE ARE YOUR LEGAL RIGHTS, POWERS & DUTIES

First, what is a **"debtor in possession"** status? This is, in a word, the term used to describe the status of a debtor when the debtor and his company's management are allowed to remain in control ("in possession") of the debtor's own business and affairs, and to continue to operate and manage the affairs of such business even as the bankruptcy proceedings run their normal course. Put in a more technical term, in a Chapter 11 case, the debtor-in-possession, except when a trustee is serving in the case. However, even though the Debtor and the Debtor-in-Possession are one and the same entity in both physical and practical terms, for purposes of the Bankruptcy Code, the Debtor-in-Possession is regarded as a legal entity that is separate and apart from the Debtor.

As more fully pointed out earlier in this manual in relation to appointment of a trustee in a case, the debtor-in-possession arrangement is, for reasons basically related to the Congressional intent of the Code's drafters, the arrangement most commonly used and encouraged in Chapter 11 cases, and it is only occasionally that a court-appointed trustee is used and made to displace the debtor from remaining in possession.

When left to function in a debtor-in-possession capacity, your powers and duties in this status would be just as sweeping, varied and vitally determinative of the success or failure of the company's reorganization as those of the trustee. *To sum it all up, you have as a debtor-in-possession exactly the same powers, duties and responsibilities designated for Chapter 11 trustees (pp. 197-8 of this manual), except i) the trustee's right to compensation; and ii) those powers pursuant to which the trustee is required to file the list, schedule and statement required under the code when the debtor has not previously filed such, or, those powers pursuant to which he is required to investigate the affairs of the debtor and file a statement of the result of such investigation (since one cannot investigate and report on oneself).*

result of such investigation with the court (since one cannot investigate one self!). Thus, a Debtor-in-possession must set aside its own fraudulent or preferential transfers (if there are any) and may reject its own executory contracts. In short, for all practical purposes, a debtor-in-possession in a Chapter 11 case has the same rights, powers and duties, as a trustee in the operation of the debtor's business and the handling of the debtor's property during the course of the Chapter 11 case.

Thus, like the trustee, the debtor in possession is empowered to, among other things, perform the following duties:

i) he may employ, with the court's approval, one or more attorneys, accountants, appraisers, auctioneers, or other professional persons to assist him in undertaking the Chapter 11 case, so long as such persons are "disinterested persons" and do not hold or represent interests adverse to the estate. [See Chapter 6, at pp. 116-132 for the basic procedures in doing this]

ii) he may, after notice and a hearing, use, sell or lease property of the estate, other than in the ordinary course of business. [See Chapter 6, at pp. 123-6 for the basic procedures involved]

iii) he has the power to sell property of the estate free and clear of any interest and lien in such property, providing that the debtor complies with those requirements under the Code (Sec. 363) that would ensure that "adequate protection" is accorded to entities with an interest in such property. [However, where the property concerned is "cash collateral" (e.g., cash, negotiable instruments, documents of title, securities, deposit accounts, and such similar cash equivalents), the debtor in possession, like the Chapter 11 trustee, may not use, sell or lease them unless each entity with an interest in the cash collateral consents or the court, after notice and a hearing, authorizes such use, sale or lease. The aim of this restriction is to provide protections against the possible dissipation of such property of unique nature.] [See Chapter 6, at p. 123-6 for the basic procedures in doing this]

iv) unless the court orders otherwise, the debtor in possession has the power to obtain credit on behalf of the business, as well as the power to reject, affirm, and assign executory contracts and unexpired leases in accordance with the conditions set forth in the Code (Section 365). [See Chapter 6, at p. 120-3 for the basic procedures involved]

v) the debtor in possession has the rights of a trustee under Section 544(a) of the Code. By this, not only is he allowed those powers granted him under other sections of the Code to set aside preferential or fraudulent transfer or transfers otherwise voidable under applicable or federal law, but he also gets the additional "strong-arm" powers to set aside or "avoid" (i.e., invalidate) transfers of, or encumbrances on, the debtor's property, even where such transfers or encumbrances are invulnerable to assault on the usual grounds of illegal or fraudulent transfers.* And under Section 544(b) of the Code, the debtor in possession (as with the trustee) has the powers to exercise whatever rights of avoidance any creditor holding an unsecured allowable claim could have exercised on his own behalf under applicable state or federal law regarding any transfer of an interest of the debtor in property or any obligation incurred by the debtor.

vi) like the trustee, the debtor has the same rights, under Section 544 of the Code, to abandon property that is burdensome to the estate or that is of inconsequential value to the estate.

NOTE: For an elaborate discussion of the rights, duties, and functions of a debtor-in-possession in a Chapter 11 case, and the various procedures involved in operating the debtor's business by the debtor-in-possession during the course of the Chapter 11 case, turn to Chapter 5.

---

*The primary purpose of all the Section 544 provisions is to give the trustee (or the debtor in possession) the capacity to secure, marshall, or increase the potential assets of the estate for an equal distribution according to the terms of the Code.
IMPORTANT: See the paragraph captioned "NOTE" at the end of Step 7 above, p. 75 for some indications that, in practice, the debtor-in-possession may, under certain circumstances, not quite be able to exercise all the powers theoretically assigned to him under the Code.

step 12: WORK ON PUTTING TOGETHER A PLAN OF REORGANIZATION WITHIN THE TIME REQUIRED

Under the stipulations set forth by the Code, the debtor in a Chapter 11 case may file his own plan of reorganization either with the petition at the commencement of the case, or at any time thereafter. In theory, the Chapter 11 debtor may file a plan of reorganization with, and at the same time as, the filing of the petition commencing the case—providing the debtor has complied with applicable non-bankruptcy law concerning adequacy of disclosure in soliciting acceptance of such plan. In practice, however, a Chapter 11 case where a plan of reorganization is filed along with the petition will be the rare exception. This is because negotiations with respect to proposed plans will have to be conducted through creditors' committees, and the consents (acceptances) of various parties obtained to the plan, before a reorganization plan could be formulated and ready for filing with the court.

Similarly, Under the Code, a debtor-in-possession is a limited time during which he would have the sole and *exclusive* right to propose a Plan – within the first 120 days from the date of the filing of the petition.* If the Debtor is a qualifying small business who has elected to be treated as a Small Business (see Step 11 above), only the debtor may file a plan during the first 100 days from the date of the filing of the petition, and all plans must be filed within 180 days of the date of the filing of the petition. Upon the request of a party in interest made within the respective periods, and after notice and a hearing, the court may, for cause, reduce or increase the 120-day or 180-day exclusive period for filing the plan if the need for the increase is caused by circumstances for which the debtor should not be held accountable but which impeded the debtor's ability to formulate a plan.

The primary objective in making this provision is said to be to put the debtor involved in a case under pressure, and to put him on notice to engage in serious, meaningful negotiations with his creditors at once—in the early stages of the case. A debtor in this situation shall have been aware, the reasoning goes, that failure or continued delay on his part to come up with an acceptable plan within the initial period, may well bring forth an application by a party in interest for the appointment of a trustee, thereby ending the debtor's exclusivity with respect to filing a plan and warranting the creditors and other parties in interest to file plans of reorganization of their own.

The law provides that if at the end of the 120 day period of debtor exclusivity (or at the end of any other time limit the court may set), the debtor has not filed a plan, or if the debtor had filed a plan on time but the plan fails to win an adequate number of acceptances** before the end of 180 days from the date of the filing of the petition (or within any other expanded length of time the court may fix), then any party in interest may formulate and file a plan of reorganization of his own.

---

*Depending on the circumstances, the court may, for cause (e.g., an unusually large or unusually small case, justifiable delay of the debtor, the showing of some probable success with allowance of additional time, or recalcitrance among creditors), increase the 120 day period in which the debtor has the exclusive right to file a plan; or, on the other hand, the court may, on the request of a party in interest and after notice and a hearing, reduce the 120 day period of the debtor exclusivity. The nature of the court's action would depend, in each instance, on the facts of each situation—i.e., whether or not the court finds, on the basis of the facts presented, that the delay with respect to either obtaining acceptances to a plan or filing a plan is attributable to inaction on the part of the debtor. *In any and all cases, however, at any time whatsoever when a trustee gets appointed in a Chapter 11 case, the debtor's right to exclusively file a plan terminates.*

**A plan is "accepted" if it has received the approval of: i) two-thirds in amount and more than one-half in number of allowed claims of each class of creditors whose claims are "impaired" under the terms of the plan; and ii) at least two-thirds in amount of the allowed interests of each class of equity security holders, if it is a corporation, or two-thirds in amount of the partnership interests, if it is a partnership.

Stan Kulp, a Barron's magazine financial writer, summed the plan formulation principle up rather well but simply: "There aren't that many hard and fast rules. It's whatever kind of package (the mix of cash, new debt and new stock) the company can work out for the different classes of creditors."

step 13 : KNOW THE BASIC REQUIRE- MENTS FOR AN ACCEPTABLE RE- ORGANIZATION PLAN

To begin with, it is relevant to remind oneself, once again, of the fundamental objective of a Chapter 11 proceeding: What it's all about is, in a word, to "buy" you, the debtor, some extra time and opportunity, under the protection and supervision of the court, to enter into good faith negotiations with your creditors and equity security holders, hopefully culminating in a reasonable arrangement ("a plan") of reorganizing and rehabilitating the debtor's business that would win, or at least merit, the consent of a requisite number of the creditors and shareholders, and/or the court's approval.

Before a proposed plan of reorganization could win the approval of the creditors or ownership interests, however, or the signature of the judge, the plan must first meet certain conditions of fairness and feasibility and must contain certain elements as set forth under the bankruptcy code. *That's why it's so important that before you even start formulating, negotiating and actually drawing up your proposed plan of reorganization, you should first set forth and be fairly clear in your own mind (as well as on paper) what the contents of that plan would look like.*

Outlined below are the main elements of a proper Chapter 11 reorganization plan under the Code:

1. Any proposed plan you put forth should **classify** the *"claims"* and *"interests"* separately. That is, it should designate the "interest" items within it *separately*, by classes, and the "claim" items within it *separately*, by classes, *except* for the claims of the kinds specified in Section 507(a)(1), 507(a)(2), or 507(a)(6) of the Code —which have to do with allowed "priority" claims items for administrative expenses and allowed unsecured claims for governmental

*See 11 U.S.C. 1123(a)(b).

units for income or gross receipts taxes, property taxes, collected taxes (for wages, sales, etc.) withheld by the debtor, and the like. Such "priority" items are the exempt "claims" items which are not required to be classified, the reason being that under the Code, the holders of such priority claims are not entitled to vote as a class with respect to the plan since the plan cannot "impair" (i.e., adversely affect) the right of such parties to receive full payment of their claims. A claim is a right to payment or a right to equitable remedy in lieu of payment. An the term "interest" as used in the context of a Chapter 11 Plan, refers to the equity security rights of shareholders and limited partners. In a word, in Chapter 11 cases creditors have "claims," and security holders have "interests." [See "Classification of Claims or Interests," pp. 199-204 for details of the manner in which a plan is to classify such claims and interests; see also Articles I of the Sample Model plans,   pp. 158, 162 & 167   of the manual.]

2. Having assigned every interest and every claim to a particular class [except, of course, for Section 507(a)(1), (a)(2), and (a)(6) claims], the proposed plan must then specify every class in terms of whether it is either *"impaired"* or *"unimpaired"* under the plan. [See Appendix D on pp.   205-6 , "Impairment of Claims or Interests," for details about the concept of impairment; see also Articles II of the Sample Model plans, on pp. 158, 162 & 167 of the manual.]

3. With respect to any and every class that is designated as "impaired" under the plan—i.e., for any class of claims or interests whose legal, equitable or contractual rights are altered in one direction or the other, e.g., where the claims of a class are not to be paid in full under the plan—the plan must specifically state why and how such class is impaired, and specify the treatment to be accorded that class under the Plan. It may, for example, provide for any one of the following modes of treatment, among others: for payment of claims in full over time to creditors of the class (what payments in amounts and on what specific dates); for a partial payment in satisfaction of a claim; for conversion of all or part of claims to equity; transfer of claims to a new entity; exchange of one kind of security of the debtor for another kind of security; exchange of securities of a new entity for securities of the debtor; outright cancellation of unsecured claims; cancellation of claims in kind (e.g., two pounds of chocolate for each one dollar of claims), and so forth and so on. [See Articles III of the Sample Model plans, pp.158, 162 & 168 of the manual for an illustrative treatment.]

The central point here is that you must spell out in the plan the terms, reasons and details of whatever treatment you propose for each given class of claims and interests that is to be impaired under the plan—whatever class of claims or interests, if any, whose legal, equitable, and contractual rights would in any way be altered by the plan after the effective date of the plan.

4. The proposed plan must provide the same and **equal** treatment (a non-discriminatory treatment) for all claims or interests within the same class. Except, however, that a differential treatment would be proper if the holder of a particular claim or interest voluntarily agrees to a less favorable treatment than is accorded the other members of its class under the plan, or if the claim is part of a separate class of unsecured claims of less than a specified dollar amount established for the purpose of making a classification under the "administrative convenience" provision of the Code.

5. The proposed plan shall provide **"adequate means for its execution"**—i.e., means for carrying out the provisions of the plan. For example, it could provide for one or more of the following:
   i) retention by the debtor of all or any part of its property.
   ii) transfer of all or any part of the debtor's property to one or more entities, whether they existed before or were formed after the confirmation of the plan.
   iii) merger or consolidation of the debtor with one or more other individuals, partnerships or corporations—the debtor corporation may be terminated or liquidated and securities issued to creditors and stockholders by a newly formed corporation, for example.
   iv) sale of all or any part of the debtor's estate, either subject to or free of any lien, or the distribution of all or any part of the property among those who have an interest in the

property, or among holders of claims and interests generally. (Note that a plan may provide for sale of all or part of the property of the estate while not providing that the proceeds be distributed.)

v) satisfaction or modification of any lien.

vi) cancellation or modification of any indenture or similar instrument.

vii) curing or waiving any default.

viii) extension of a maturity date or a change in an interest rate and other terms of outstanding securities.

ix) amendment of the debtor's charter.

x) issuance of securities of the debtor or such other corporations for cash, for property, for existing securities, or in exchange for claims or interests, or for any other appropriate purpose.

[See Articles IV of the Sample Model plans pp. 158, 163 & 168 for some typical "plan execution" provisions usable in a plan.]

6. If the debtor is a corporation, the proposed Plan must *equitably* allocate the voting power of old and new securities – the control of the company—among the several classes of equity securities so as to properly recognize the respective positions of the claimants and stockholders according to the rank and rights they surrender. No non-voting equity securities may be issued. [See Articles V of the Sample Model plans, pp. 159, 165 & 168 of the manual, for an example.]

7. The reorganization plan must contain only provisions that are equitable to the parties, and consistent with the interests of creditors and equity security holders and with public policy—e.g., the manner of the selection of any officer, director, or trustee under the plan must be fairly representative, and discredited management may not be selected. [See Articles V of the Sample Model plans, pp. 159, 165, & 168 of the manual, for an example.]

8. The plan *may* impair (i.e., adversely modify or affect the entitlement of) any class of interests or claims (secured or unsecured), or leave any such class unimpaired—depending, basically, on the needs of the given debtor. For example, if all you propose is simply an extension agreement with your trade creditors, you would be "impairing" just one class—that class of creditors in the plan whose claims would be extended—but not the other classes. The claims of such other classes would therefore remain "unimpaired." [See Articles III of the Sample Model plan on pp. 158, 162 & 168, for example.]

9. You *may* (this is strictly discretionary) propose to assume any **executory contract(s)** or unexpired lease(s) of the debtor (which has not already been rejected by the trustee), or, alternatively, you may propose to reject such yourself. Whatever your plan proposes to do with these contracts or leases would be alright so long as it meets with the court's approval. [See Article VII of the Sample Model plans on p. 160 Art. V. on p. 165 & on p. 168, for an example.]

10. Your plan may propose terms of settlement or compromise either on the debtor's personal claim or interest ("property of the debtor"), or on those of the estate ("property of the estate" which is defined to include all property or ownership interests of the debtor in property as of the time of the commencement of the bankruptcy case). The maker of a plan may, at his option, choose not to settle a claim or interest. When such is the case, however, the plan would have to provide for the retention and enforcement of any such claim or interest. [See Article VIII of the Sample Model plan on p. 160 of the manual, for an example.]

NOTE: In most small business Chapter 11 cases, the equity security holders are the individual business owners and their equity security interests are not ordinarily dealt with in the Plan. Thus, in most small business cases the plan deals, rather, exclusively with creditors and does not affect the interests of equity security holders. However, if the debtor's business is to be transferred to a new entity under the plan, if additional equity stock is to be issued under the plan, or if the plan proposes the buyout or termination of the equity interests of certain owners, then the interests of the security holders may have to be dealt with in the plan. And, in any event, if the plan is to be confirmed under the "cramdown" provisions of the Code (see pp. 105), which may mean that the claims of a nonaccepting class of creditors are not paid in full under the plan,, the rule of absolute priority may render it necessary for the plan to eliminate the interests of equity security holders, any way, in such situations.

In a case concerning an individual, a plan proposed by an entity other than the debtor may not provide for the use, sale, or lease of property exempted to the debtor (property which the debtor is allowed to keep and which, by state or federal law, is "exempt" from being seized from him by a creditor), unless the debtor consents to such use, sale or lease.

The Practical Aspects of a Chapter 11 Plan Preparation

How do you practically put together a decent Chapter 11 plan? John H. Williamson, a nationally respected legal practitioner with a long bankruptcy experience who has successfully put together hundreds of Chapter 11 plans, sums up the core fundamentals necessary for putting together a good plan this way: *

> *"[Discussions about the preparation of the Chapter 11 plan often concentrate] primarily on the legal aspects of Chapter 11 plans. In many cases, however, the most difficult aspect of preparing a Chapter 11 plan is the practical or business aspect.* Such basic matters as how the debtor should restructure its business, how much money the debtor will be able to put into a plan, when funds will be available for use under a plan, and the amounts and terms that creditors will accept in satisfaction of their claims, must be resolved before a realistic plan can be devised. In resolving these matters, input should come from three sources: the debtor's owners and management, the attorney for the debtor or other plan proponent, and the debtor's creditors, either individually or through committees.
>
> The debtor's owners and management should start by disclosing to creditors a realistic account of the debtor's financial situation, the extent of the debtor's resources, and the debtor's plans or intentions for reorganizing. The principal function of the debtor's attorney [or, if none is retained, the debtor in possession] at this stage is to advise the parties as to the legal requirements of Chapter 11. The main function of creditors in the formulation of a plan is to satisfy themselves as to the ability of the debtor to reorganize and pay claims and to agree to some extent among themselves on how the debtor's resources should be allocated.
>
> It is important to involve creditors in the plan preparation process for two reasons: (1) at least one class of impaired claims must accept the plan if it is to be confirmed, and (2) discontented creditors can make a Chapter 11 case both difficult and expensive for a debtor by opposing the debtor at every opportunity, including such matters as the use of cash collateral, the use or sale of secured property, and the obtaining of credit. If creditors, either individually or through committees, are realistically involved in the preparation of the debtor's plan, they are more likely to be cooperative in all aspects of the case.
>
> Especially if they have not previously done so, the best practice is for the three interests to meet, preferably after the debtor has had a few weeks of uninterrupted operational experience under Chapter 11. The purpose of such a meeting is to commence working on a compromise that, hopefully, will ultimately result in a mutually acceptable plan. In approaching such a meeting, it is important for the debtor and its attorney [if any is retained in the case] to have conferred extensively and to be thoroughly prepared. The primary objectives of the debtor and its attorney at such a meeting should be to convince creditors of the soundness of the decision to file under Chapter 11 and to create a favorable impression among the creditors as to the debtor's reorganizational effort. These tasks are best accomplished if those in attendance on behalf of the debtor have a thorough understanding of both the present condition of the debtor and what the debtor intends to accomplish under Chapter 11."*

IMPORTANT: REPRODUCED IN APPENDIX A OF THE MANUAL, FOR THE ILLUS-TRATIVE PURPOSES OF SHOWING WHAT A GOOD PLAN OF REORGANIZATION SHOULD TYPICALLY CONTAIN AND GENERALLY LOOK LIKE, ARE THREE MODEL SAMPLE PLANS OF REORGANIZATION—TWO, FOR A CORPORATE DEBTOR, ON PP. 157 & 167, AND THE OTHER, FOR AN INDIVIDUAL DEBTOR, ON PP. 161-6 .

Readers should carefully examine and analyze the contents, structure and format of these model samples, but be equally careful to use them merely as a guide in the understanding and formulation of an acceptable plan particular to their own unique conditions.

Note that the Plan for the corporate debtor (pp. 157-160) involves a case in which a trustee is appointed and exercises complete control, while the Plan for the individual debtor (pp. 101-106) involves a case in which the debtor remains "in possession."

---

* Williamson, <u>The Attorney's Handbook on Chapter 11 Bankruptcy</u>, pp. 158 & 159

step 14: FULFILL THE DISCLOSURE REQUIREMENTS FIRST, BEFORE YOU MAY BEGIN SOLICITATIONS FOR PLAN ACCEPTANCES FROM CREDITORS & OTHERS

Ordinarily, for a plan of reorganization to be confirmed by the court, the plan must first have or enjoy the acceptances of the requisite majority* of the classes of claims and interests (see the Confirmation Conditions outlined on pp. 101-106). The Code stipulates, however, that the proponent of a proposed plan may not even *begin* to solicit any acceptances or rejections to a plan from any party *unless*, at the time of or before making such solicitation, the plan's proponent had first furnished each and every such party (every holder of claim or interest of a particular class being solicited) with a written **disclosure statement** which shall have been approved by the court as containing **adequate information**, along with a copy of the proposed plan or a summary of it.

This is one of the most fundamental precepts of Chapter 11, namely, that the creditors and equity security holders may not be required to accept or reject a proposed plan until they have been provided with information sufficient to enable them to make an informed decision on the matter – the "DISCLOSURE STATEMENT." And before this disclosure statement may be distributed to the creditors and equity security holders by the party proposing the Chapter 11 Plan, this Statement must FIRST have been examined and approved by the Court as containing accurate and sufficient information.

A. The Disclosure Statement & Hearing

Briefly, the procedure is for whoever is the party proposing the Chapter 11 Plan to put together a sufficiently informative "***Disclosure Statement***." [See a model sample of such a Statement reproduced on pp. 144 & 153 of this manual]. The plan's proponent then files the Statement with the Court for its review. The Disclosure Statement is required to be filed with the Court either together with the proposed Chapter 11 Plan or within a time fixed by the court for the filing of the disclosure statement. Where the Debtor is filing as a "Small Business" in the case, the debtor must file the Disclosure Statement with the Plan or within a time fixed by the court, and must file an application with the court for "conditional" approval of the disclosure statement asking the Statement be "conditionally" approved subject to its final approval later after notice and a hearing.

Briefly, the procedure is for whoever is the proponent of the plan to put together a sufficiently informative *"Disclosure Statement."* [See a model sample of such a statement reproduced on pp. 144 & 153 of this manual.] The plan's proponent then files the Statement with the court for its review.

The court will then set a date for a hearing to be held on examining the "adequacy" of the Statement, on at least 25 days notice to the debtor, creditors, equity security holders and other parties in interest. Depending on who is ordered to do it by a particular court, the transmission of the notices of this hearing (plus the accompanying plan or its summary) to the parties in interest may have to be done by the clerk of the bankruptcy court, the trustee, debtor in possession, or the proponent of the plan. [See a sample copy of *"Notice of Hearing On Disclosure Statement"* on p. 156 of the manual.]

At this hearing, the court will consider the Statement and any objections filed with the court against the Statement or any modifications requested or deemed desirable thereto.

---

*Under Sec. 1126(c) of the Code, the requisite majority of a class of claims is two-thirds in amount and more than one-half in number of allowed claims of the class who are entitled to vote and that accept or reject the plan. And with respect to a class of interests, the Code (Sec. 1126(d)) gives the requisite majority as two-thirds in amount of the allowed interests that are entitled to vote and that accept or reject the plan.

Following this hearing*—which, it should be noted, is one of the few major procedural hearings in any reorganization case—the court will approve the Statement, assuming, of course, that the court finds it acceptable overall. That is, if the court is satisfied that the Statement contains "adequate information"   —information of a kind, and in sufficient detail, that would, in the court's opinion, enable a typical holder of claims or interests to make an informed judgment about the plan, given the nature and history of the particular debtor company and the condition of its books and records.

Only thereafter (i.e., if the court has approved the disclosure statement as adequately informative following its hearing on it) would the proponent of the proposed plan have attained the legally right time frame to submit the court-approved Disclosure Statement (with a copy of the plan or a summary thereof attached) to the creditors and other interests for their own consideration—clearing the way for solicitation of acceptances for the plan to commence.

Objections & Hearing Requirements

Any party in interest raising an objection to matters contained in or omitted from the Disclosure Statement, must file such objections with the Court and serve same upon the debtor, the Trustee (if one is serving in the case), any committee appointed in the case, the U.S. Trustee, and any other entities designated by the Court. Such objections may be filed and served at any time prior to the approval (or final approval, in the case of an electing Small Business debtor) of the disclosure statement by the court. Most objections relate to the adequacy of the information contained in the Statement or to the sufficiency or validity of the opinions or conclusions set forth in the Statement. Such matters may often be resolved by amending the disputed opinions or inserting a counter opinion of the objecting party in the disclosure statement.

Under the bankruptcy Rule 3017(a), in cases where the debtor has not filed as a Small Business, the court must hold a hearing on the Disclosure Statement. However, where the debtor has filed as a Small business, the court must hold a disclosure hearing in such a case ONLY IF a timely objection to the conditionally approved disclosure statement is filed, and may combine the disclosure hearing with the CONFIRMATION hearing.

The same disclosure statement may be given to each member of the same class of claims or interests. However, in recognition of the fact that the information needed for an informed judgment about a plan may differ for different classes, the law allows that different statements (differing as to amounts, details, or kinds of information) may be used for different classes—if that would be the cheaper, more convenient or more effective method in the debtor's or the trustee's judgment. (A class whose rights under the plan center on a particular fund or asset, for example, would have no use for an extensive description of other matters that could not affect them, while another different class may require a more extensive disclosure.)

To reach the acceptable standard of adequacy, a disclosure statement does not have to contain a "going concern" valuation of the business. In general, it is sufficient if the statement merely goes as far as disclosing what creditors will receive in a straight liquidation situation if confirmation for a Chapter 11 plan were to be denied. Furthermore, though the Code does not prohibit a valuation of the debtor, the court may (and does generally) approve a disclosure statement without a valuation of the debtor or an appraisal of the debtor's assets.

---

*Ordinarily, the disclosure hearing will not—at least should not—be necessary in every instance, and a hearing need not necessarily be automatic each time a disclosure statement is submitted to the court. Indeed, as stipulated by Section 102(1) of the Code, only if there has been an objection raised by a legitimate party in the case against the Disclosure Statement would a formal hearing on it be absolutely necessary. Strictly speaking, therefore, in instances where no objection is raised by anyone against the debtor's application for approval of his disclosure statement, the court really ought not hold an independent review ("notice and a hearing") on the statement, as it is the central intent of the bankruptcy code that the bankruptcy judge should "stay removed from the administration of the bankruptcy or reorganization case, and to become involved only when there is a dispute about a proposed action, that is, only when there is an objection." (House of Representatives Report No. 595, 95th Congress 1st Session (1977) on p. 315).

In any and all events, however, a public agency or official (such as the Securities and Exchange Commission) has the right under the Code to "be heard on the issue of whether a disclosure statement contains adequate information." In a case involving a corporation with outstanding public creditors or stockholders, for example, the SEC may, if it desires, advise the court on the adequacy of the proposed disclosure statement. It may also participate in a disclosure hearing, if there is one, and may present evidence therein. However, the SEC (or any like public agency or official that does not qualify as "a party in interest" in the case) may not *initiate* an appeal of any approval order that arises from such a disclosure hearing, as this would be going against the Code's general purpose of avoiding protracted hearings which might unduly prolong a reorganization case.

B. The Great Importance of Disclosure Statements in Chapter 11 Cases

The importance attached to the presentation of a disclosure statement containing "adequate information" in Chapter 11 proceedings cannot be overemphasized. The importance with which this matter is viewed derives directly from the fact that the concept of disclosure goes to the very heart of the primary purposes and goals embodied in the Chapter 11 reorganization practice: to, among other things, i) remove, or at least restrict, the courts and administrative or governmental agencies (such as the SEC, for example) from excessive involvement in the negotiation and formulation of reorganization plans; ii) correspondingly, to give to creditors and stockholders themselves a greater role in making decisions on the plan of reorganization of the debtor company; and, iii) to enhance the survivability of the debtor company by curtailing unnecessary delays and rigid or costly formalities in reorganization proceedings.

In recognizing that under the previous bankruptcy procedures,* certain problems often came about simply from the fact of long delays, the Congressional drafters of the present (1978) Code apparently concluded that rigid formalities which unnecessarily delay confirmation of plans of reorganization are detrimental to the interest of creditors and shareholders alike—detrimental in ways such as reduction in the value of distributions received by creditors under such a plan and, often, the making of the debtor's continued existence as a competitive force in the marketplace additionally difficult, if not impossible. Hence the present Code seeks to avoid such problems and to encourage negotiated, speedy settlements in reorganization cases by allowing for a reorganization plan, once having been duly negotiated by the holders of claims and interest in the plan, to be confirmable by the court, subject only to a minimum of restrictions.

A look at a few statements of policy by the Congressional drafters of the Code would show how strongly Congress views the disclosure requirement as the pivotal concept in achieving the primary purposes desired in reorganization cases. One part of the House Report put it thus:

> The premise underlying the consolidated Chapter 11 of this bill is [that]...if adequate disclosure is provided to all creditors and stockholders whose rights are affected, then they shall be able to make an informed judgment of their own, rather than having the court or the Securities and Exchange Commission inform them in advance of whether the proposed plan is a good plan. *Therefore, the key to the consolidated Chapter is the disclosure section.* **

Another part of the House Report notes:

> The premise of the bill's financial standard for confirmation is the same as the premise of the securities law: *parties should be given adequate disclosure of relevant information and they should make their own decision on the acceptability of the proposed plan of reorganization.* The bill does not impose a rigid financial rule for the plan. The parties are left to their own to negotiate a fair settlement.... negotiation among the parties after full disclosure will govern how the value of the reorganizing company will be distributed among creditors and stockholders.***

Coming Up With An Acceptable Disclosure Statement – Providing "Adequate Information"

The primary requirement stipulated under the Bankruptcy Code for a Disclosure Statement [See Section 1125(a)(1) thereof], is that the said statement must contain **"adequate**

---

*The sponsors of the Bankruptcy Code declared thus: "The primary problem posed by Chapter 10 (the Chap. 11 equivalent under the previous bankruptcy law) is delay. The modern corporation is a complex and multifaceted entity.... The success, and even the survival, of a corporation in contemporary markets depends on three elements: First, the ability to attract and hold skilled management; second, the ability to obtain credit; and third, the corporation's ability to project to the public an image of vitality. Over and over again, **it is demonstrated that corporations which must avail themselves of the provisions of the Bankruptcy Act suffer appreciable deterioration if they are caught in a Chapter 10 proceeding for any substantial period of time."** 124 Congressional Record H11,101; 124 Congressional Record S17,418.

**H.R. Report No. 595, 95th Congress, 1st Session, p. 226 (1977)

*** H.R. Report No. 595, p. 224

information" — basically, information of the kind and in sufficient detail, that would enable the typical holder of claims or interests to make an informed judgment about the proposed plan, given the nature and history of the particular debtor-company and the conditio of its books and records. Consequently, *a most important question for a debtor or debtor in possession faced with the task of having to put together a disclosure statement is: how do you determine what constitutes "adequate information" for your disclosure statement?*

As a practical matter, from the standpoint of the way the courts have approached the issue, the standard for what constitutes adequate information is a variable and flexible one applied on a case-by-case basis and generally based on the SUBJECTIVE views of the court involved, rather than on any objective criteria as to the degree of information required.* In practice, there are no concrete standards as to what constitutes adequate information in a particular case, nor are there specific requirements as to the degree of disclosure required or exactly what information must be included in a particular disclosure statement. This reality aside, however, it is a fact that the courts in deciding on the adequacy of a disclosure statement, have often looked for certain fundamental information that need to be included in the statement.**

What A Good Disclosure Statement With "Adequate Information" Should Contain

John H. Williamson, a Lakewood, Colorado Chapter 11 bankruptcy legal practitioner and author, sums up the vital information generally contained in what the courts have considered to be well written disclosure statements as the following:***

> "(1)   A history and *general description of the debtor's business.* Included here should be such matters as how and when the business was organized, who the founders were, who ultimately evolved as the principal owners, how each branch of the business evolved or developed, how and when the debtor's present financial difficulties arose, and any other historical information that might give creditors and other parties insight on the background of the debtor's business activities and financial difficulties. The type of business or industry in which the debtor competes should also be described, and the debtor's competitive position in the business or industry explained.

> (2)   A general description of the *debtor's assets, liabilities, and capital structure.* Major assets should be described and realistically evaluated, and any encumbrances against them should be listed. Third party guarantors on debts or liabilities of the debtor should be identified.

> (3)   A description of *all pending litigation by and against the debtor.* The importance of each case to the debtor's reorganizational attempt should be explained. If the debtor possesses important claims or causes of action upon which litigation has not been commenced, they should also be identified and described.

> (4)   *A projection of the debtor's future earnings, income, and expenses.* This is especially important if the debtor proposes to pay creditors from future earnings. Both current and projected balance sheets should be prepared and included. Income statements and cash flow statements should also be included, if feasible. Estimates of such items as administrative expenses (including legal fees), court costs, and other expenses of the Chapter 11 case should be given. The source of all information used in the projects should be identified.

> (5)   *A liquidation analysis of the debtor* should the debtor file under chapter 7 of the Bankruptcy Code. This is needed because the holder of each impaired claim or interest must either accept the plan or receive a value under the plan that is not less than what the creditor or interest holder would receive in a chapter 7 liquidation of

---

*See 11 U.S.C. 1125(a); In re <u>A. C. Williams Co.</u>, 25 B.R. 173 (ND OH, 1982); <u>Matter of Northwest Recreational Activities, Inc.</u>, 8 B.R. 10 (ND GA, 1980); and In re <u>The Stanley Hotel, Inc.</u>, 13 B.R. 926 (CO, 1981).

**See, for example, <u>A.C. Williams Co.</u>, 25 B.R. 173 (ND OH, 1982).

*** Williamson, <u>The Attorney's Handbook on Chapter 11 Bankruptcy</u>, pp. 173-4.

the debtor. Realistically, creditors must be shown that they will receive more under the plan than in a chapter 7 liquidation if they are to accept the plan.

(6) A list of all parent companies and subsidiaries of the debtor.

(7) *A list of all officers, directors, major shareholders, general partners,* or other persons in control of the debtor, both at present and in the proposed reorganization. The role of each significant person in the operation or management of the debtor's business should be explained and his or her compensation disclosed. The disclosure requirements of 11 U.S.C. 1129(a)(5) should be complied with.

(8) *A general description of the debtor's chapter 11 case.* Included here should be the reasons for filling the case, how the debtor is faring under chapter 11, the debtor's ultimate goals in the case, and how the debtor intends to accomplish; its goals.

(9) *A summary of the debtor's plan or reorganization* and an explanation of the plan. An explanation of how the various classes of claims and interests are dealt with under the plan, how the debtor's business will be reorganized under the plan, the sources of funds for making payments under the plan, and the estimated length of the plan should be given." (Emphasis added by the author).

Williamson added: "A well-written disclosure statement (which, ideally, should be a coordinated task jointly put together by the debtor's management, its accountant or other financial record keeper, and its attorney, if any is employed, or other plan proponent) should be divided into three general segments. The first segment should consist of a history of the debtor's business and a description of its present business operation. The second segment should consist of factual and financial information about the debtor and its business operations. The third segment should consist of an explanation and summary of the debtor's proposed plan...*it is important to remember that the statement should contain as many facts and as few opinions as possible. A disclosure statement containing too much opinion and too little fact will not be approved by the court.* While opinions must, of necessity, be rendered on such matters as the value of property and anticipated future income, such opinions should be supported by fact and rendered by persons competent to do so."

NOTE: In drafting a disclosure statement, it is very, very important to remember this: the statement should contain as many FACTS and as few OPINIONS as possible. A disclosure statement containing too much opinion and too little facts, is not likely to be approved by the Court. When opinions are unavoidable with respect to certain matters (as in the value of a property and anticipated future income, for example), such may be supported by facts rendered by experts or persons competent to do so.

IMPORTANT: REPRODUCED IN APPENDIX A (PP.144 & 153) OF THE MANUAL, FOR THE ILLUSTRATIVE PURPOSES OF SHOWING WHAT A GOOD DISCLOSURE STATEMENT SHOULD TYPICALLY CONTAIN AND GENERALLY LOOK LIKE, IS A MODEL SAMPLE DISCLOSURE STATEMENT.

Readers should carefully examine and analyze this model sample statement; but be equally careful to use it merely as a guide in the understanding and formulation of an acceptable statement of disclosure particular to their own special conditions.

Williamson, *The Attorney's Handbook on Chapter 11 Bankruptcy*, pp. 172 & 174.

step 15: YOU MAY NOW COMMENCE SOLICITATIONS OF ACCEPTANCE VOTES FOR YOUR PROPOSED PLAN FROM CREDITORS & OTHERS

The next step in the Chapter 11 Plan confirmation process, after the court approval of the Disclosure Statement, is ACCEPTANCES of the Plan by creditors, and, if they are dealt with in the plan, by interest holders. Thus, assuming that you've secured the court's approval of the written Disclosure Statement ("Step 14 above), you are now in an eligible position to take the next step—begin to solicit acceptances (or rejections) of the plan from holders of claims or interests. The reason why solicitations could not have been commenced earlier than now, is because, under the procedures of **Chapter 11** cases, vote solicitations for a plan may only be commenced if the following are transmitted to the party being solicited at the time or before such solicitation is made: i) the Chapter 11 Plan or a summary of it; and ii) a court-approved Disclosure Statement. In other words, creditors and interest holders may vote on the acceptance or rejection of a plan only after they shall have been provided with a court-approved disclosure statement and related documents.

A. Procedures for Formal Solicitation of Votes on the Plan

At the time of the approval of the disclosure statement, the court shall have fixed a time (contained in its *Order Approving Disclosure Statement*) within which creditors and holders of interests have to accept or reject the plan. And to commence solicitation of acceptances (or rejections), therefore, all that you—i.e., the proponent of the plan—have to do, is mail, within the time fixed and by the method prescribed by the court, the following materials to all creditors and interest holders:

i) a Notice of Time for Filing Acceptances or Rejections of Plan, and of the date and time fixed for the Confirmation Hearing. (See illustrative sample of this form reproduced on p. 170.)

ii) Ballot for Accepting or Rejection of Plan. (See illustrative sample on p. 171)

   NOTE: This document need be mailed ONLY to those creditors and interest holders who are entitled to vote on the Plan – i.e., it need not be mailed to creditors or interest holders in unimpaired classes of claims or interests, or to creditors or interest holders in classes receiving nothing under the plan, because the former are deemed to have accepted the plan, and the latter are deemed to have rejected it. (See Advisory Committee's Notes to Bankruptcy Rule 3017(d).

iii) copy of the Plan, or a court-approved summary of that.

iv) copy of the Disclosure Statement as approved by the Court, or as conditionally approved by the court, where applicable

v) such other information as the court may direct, which may include any opinion of the court approving the disclosure statement or a court-approved summary of such opinion. (For example, where the disclosure statement is too lengthy or technical to be readily understood by a typical creditor, it is common for the court to approve a summary of the statement to be mailed with the Disclosure Statement.

vi) a cover letter accompanying transmission of the materials for Plan Solicitation (see Exhibit on p. 135

vii) a letter from the Creditors' Committee soliciting the acceptance of the plan, where such a committee has been appointed in the case and the committee does approve of the plan.

You are to transmit (usually but by no means always by mailing) such material to each and every holder of a claim or interest "allowed" under the proposed plan, as well as to the U.S. Trustee. As a debtor, or other plan proponent, if you are directed by the court to mail the above materials, the best practice would be fore you to write up a cover letter and send the materials with such letter, clearly explaining the purpose of each of the document enclosed and soliciting acceptance of the Plan. (See item vi above for a sample of such letter).

B. Who Are Eligible to Cast Ballots of Acceptance (or Rejection) on the Plan?

As required by the Bankruptcy Code (see Section 1125(b) thereof), only AFTER the items described in A above shall have been transmitted to the creditors and equity holders and the U.S. Trustee, may solicitations for acceptances or rejections be made. Hence, now that you have transmitted the above materials to the parties, you should commence active solicitation for the acceptance of the Plan. Commence this IMMEDIATELY: the date of the confirmation hearing and voting deadline is likely to be only about a month after the date of the bankruptcy judge's order approving the disclosure statement.

To begin with, what constitutes an "acceptance" of a proposed plan by a creditor, stockholder, or any other party? An acceptance is more easily understood if it is simply viewed in terms of an eligible voter (i.e., stockholder, creditor, and the like) casting an affirmative or "yes" vote on a proposed plan. (By the same token, a "rejection" is a negative or "no" vote on a plan, cast by an eligible holder of a claim or interest.) Formal indication (vote casting) of the acceptance—or rejection—of a proposed plan will usually be made in writing, entered on the ballot form (such as the "Ballot for Accepting or Rejecting Plan" form on p. 171), and signed by the creditor or stockholder concerned or his authorized agent, and, where applicable, further signed by representatives of the interests of the debtor and partners of the debtor partnership. The ballot form will then be returned, within the time stipulated for filing ballots, to the party designated therein as the party to whom the ballot should be returned.

But who is eligible to cast such a vote (of acceptance or rejection) on the proposed plan of reorganization?

The general rule is that the holder of a claim or interest may vote such claim or interest to either accept or reject a plan of reorganization—if, and only if, the given claim or interest is "allowed" as defined under the Code. To put it another way, the holder of any impaired claim or interest that has been allowed (or deemed allowed) under the Code (and who are of record as of the date of the entry of the court's order approving the Disclosure Statement), may vote to accept or reject a plan within the time fixed by the court. In order words, **whether a claim or interest is eligible to vote on a proposed plan depends upon the claim or interest being "allowed" or deemed "allowed" under the Code.**

And what is an *"allowed"* claim or interest? Here's the simple criterion as set forth under the relevant section of the Code (Sec. 502): *generally speaking, a claim or interest is deemed to qualify as an "allowed" claim or interest if it is filed and no objection has been filed or raised against it by a party in interest.* To put it another way, if a claim or interest has been properly filed in a Chapter 11 bankruptcy case and no party in interest (i.e., the debtor, a creditor, trustee, shareholder, the Secretary of the Treasury on the government's behalf, when applicable, and the like) raises an objection* to its allowance, that claim or interest is "deemed" allowed – as to its validity as well as the amount of the claim or interest. And, in any event, however, only creditors and interest holders of record as of the date of the entry of the court's order approving the disclosure statement, are entitled to case votes.

C. How a Ballot is Counted as an Acceptance or a Rejection

How are the number of acceptances and rejections determined and tabulated? First, if there are any class or classes of claims or ownership interests which are *not* "impaired" under the plan (pp. 2?5-6 of the manual), those classes would be considered and counted as acceptances in support of the proposed plan,** and no formal vote or solicitation thereof would be required with respect to such classes. Secondly, if, on the other hand, there are any class or classes which receive no payment or compensation under the plan for their claims or interests, those classes are deemed to have rejected—and would be counted as rejections against—the proposed plan. (As one Senate report*** put it, "There is obviously no need to submit a plan for a vote by a class that is to receive nothing.")

In sum, if any holder of a claim or interest is *either unimpaired or uncompensated* under a proposed plan, such holder or class would not have to formally vote on the plan (nor would solicitation of votes from such holders or classes be necessary), since their "votes" are already predetermined as a matter of law—one (the unimpaired's) as an acceptance vote, and the other (the uncompensated's), as a rejection of the plan.****

D. What Constitutes a Binding Acceptance of a Plan?

To be a decisive vote, one which legally binds a particular *class of claims* to a proposed plan, that plan is required to get a specified number and amount of acceptances ("yes" votes) from among those voting in the class; and with respect to interests, every *class of interests* in a plan must also muster a specified amount of acceptances from amongst those voting in the class in order to make that vote binding on that particular class.

With respect to a class of claims (for creditors), the vote on a proposed plan is binding—i.e., the class is considered to have accepted it—if at least two-thirds in amount, and a majority (more than one-half) in number of the allowed claims of the particular class that are voted are cast in favor of the plan, with any claims disqualified by the court, if any, fully excluded from all these calculations in making this computation. It should be noted that

---

*Only a valid "objection" would, of course, count. To be a properly raised objection which qualifies as valid, the objecting party would have to make it in writing detailing the bases and supporting grounds and evidence for it. A copy of the objection document together with a written notice of the time and place for a hearing to be held on the objection would be served on the claimant. The court would then hold such a hearing on the object of the objection and render a ruling one way or the other as to whether the claim or interest is to be accepted as "allowed"—or not.

**As more fully explained on p. 206 of the manual, under Section 1126(f) of the Code, a class which is *not* "impaired" under the Code is automatically "deemed" to have accepted the plan. Hence, even if a class that is not impaired votes to reject a plan, the effect of Sec. 1126(f) is to make such a "no" vote inconsequential anyway, since acceptance by the class is conclusively presumed as a matter of law.

***Senate Report, No. 95-989, 95th Congress, 2nd Session (1978), p. 123.

****Take note of the fact that, under Sec. 1126(b) of the Code, an acceptance or rejection solicited **prior** to the commencement of the Chapter 11 case (i.e., through a so-called *"pre-petition" solicitation*) may be legitimately taken account of in computing whether a class of claims or interests has accepted a given plan—*providing* that the pre-petition solicitation was: i) in compliance with the applicable non-bankruptcy law, rules or regulations (i.e., the proxy rules of the Securities and Exchange Act of 1934), or, otherwise, that it is in compliance with the requirements governing adequacy of disclosure rule under the bankruptcy code; and ii) that the solicitation meets the "good faith" requirements of the Code and was conducted after disclosure of "adequate information" as discussed on pp. 89-93 of the manual.

the number and amount here are computed on the basis of *claims* (or, where appropriate, interests) *actually voted for or against the plan*—not on the basis of the allowed claims (or interests) in the class.

And with respect to any class of equity securities (for ownership interests), the vote on a proposed plan is binding—i.e., the class is considered to have accepted it—if at least two-thirds* in the amount of the outstanding securities actually voted are voted for the plan (with the same exclusions also made in making this computation, for any interests the court may have disqualified).

E. How Does the Court Compute Whether the Requisite Majorities have been Achieved?

In determining whether the requisite number and amount of claims or interests required to bind a particular class of claims or interests to a proposed plan has been attained, the court may, in its discretion, disqualify certain claims or interests, thereby disallowing any acceptance or rejection votes that holders of such claims or interests may have cast or been entitled to, and excluding them in the computation to determine whether the requisite majorities for binding acceptance of the plan is obtained. For the court to so disqualify an entity, however, two basic conditions set forth under the Code must be present: i) the court may act to disqualify the person only "on the request of a party in interest," and only after a notice has been given and a hearing held on the substance of such a request; and ii) only in the event that the court shall have found (from the hearing held) that the person or entity's acceptance or rejection of the plan had not been done *"in good faith,"** or was not solicited or procured in good faith or in accordance with the provisions of the bankruptcy code.

step 15: DO YOU WANT TO MODIFY THE PLAN? HERE'S HOW.

If, for some reason, you wish to modify your original plan, you are permitted to do so (but only a plan's proponents are qualified to undertake it) at any time before the plan is ever confirmed. This is called a *pre-confirmation modification*. Such a new plan, as modified, would, upon its being filed with the court, be viewed and treated as though it were an original plan, providing it satisfies the requirements of the Code (Sec. 1122 & 1123) concerning the proper classification and contents of reorganization plans (pp. 85-8 & 199-204 of this manual). And should additional acceptances and solicitations be found to be necessary to secure an approval of the new modified

---

*If a corporate debtor, this would mean ⅔ in number of shares of common and preferred stock of the particular class, and if a partnership, it would mean ⅔ in amount of partnership interests of a particular class.

**The term "good faith" in this context is meant to be construed by the courts in the broadest possible light, taking into consideration the given facts and circumstances of each case. However, the general test seems to be whether it can be shown that there's reason to believe that a party had an "ulterior," less-than-honest motive for his action, with an eye to gaining some special advantage thereby—as in where a stockholder who rejects a plan purposely obstructs confirmation of a plan with the intent to buy time until such a point when he could sell his interest at a profit, for example, or as in where there's a strong reason to believe that creditors in a reorganization situation have not been afforded a fair opportunity to vote regarding the plan, etc. As was noted by the court in a case which dealt with the issue, one should be extremely careful not to confuse mere "selfishness" (self-interest) as being a case of bad faith, but "pure malice, 'strikes' and blackmail, and the purpose to destroy an enterprise in order to advance the interest of a competing business, all plainly constituting bad faith, are motives which may be accurately described as ulterior." [In re Pine Hill Collieries Co., 46 F. Supp. 669 (E.D. Pa. 1942) as cited in Collier on Bankruptcy (15th ed.), #1129-15].

plan, the proponents of the modified plan must comply with the disclosure requirements (pp. 89-93 of this manual) in making such additional solicitations for such new acceptances. (The court may determine, however, that additional disclosure is not required under certain circumstances—e.g., where the proposed modification is substantially minor, or where information previously furnished to members of the class to be solicited is deemed adequate.)

Aside from modification *before* the confirmation (known as pre-confirmation modification), a proposed plan may be modified *after* it has been confirmed (*post-confirmation modification*). A post-confirmation modification is permitted to be made either by the plan's proponents or by the reorganized debtor. A post-confirmation modification must, however, be done before there's a "substantial consummation"* of the plan, and, furthermore, such new plan, as modified, must satisfy the same requirements of the Code concerning proper classification and the contents of a plan (pp. 199-204 of this manual).

Whether in a pre-confirmation or a post-confirmation situation, any creditor or equity security holder that has already accepted or rejected a given plan is deemed to have also accepted or rejected the modification, *unless* such person changes his previous acceptance or rejection within the time fixed by the court. Unlike the situation in a pre-confirmation modification, in a post-confirmation modification the modified plan is treated as though it is a "new" plan that is filed, and the court is therefore required to give formal notice of, and to hold a hearing on such proposed post-confirmation modifications before it may confirm such modified plans, assuming the court finds that circumstances warrant a modification in the first place. The proponents of a post-confirmation modification are not necessarily required to re-solicit the consent of each class in all cases. Such determinations would depend on the nature of the modifications proposed and the adequacy of information previously furnished members of the class who the proponents intend to solicit. When and where it should become necessary for proponents of a modification to solicit new acceptances from a given class, however, the proponents should have to comply with the provisions of Section 1125 of the Code: Members of the class will have to be supplied with a disclosure statement containing "adequate information" (irrespective of whether the proposed modification will substantially affect the position of any class under the plan), and be further supplied with a copy of the proposed modified plan (or its summary) before or concurrently with the new solicitation.

step 17 : ATTEND THE COURT CONFIRMATION HEARINGS ON THE PROPOSED PLAN

At the time of the court's approval of the Disclosure Statement (pp. 81-5 of the manual), the court, by written order whose substance shall have also been noticed to the creditors and holders of interest in the case (pp. 94-97 of the manual on solicitation procedures), shall have usually fixed a time within which creditors and holders of interests may accept or reject such

---

*Defined in Sec. 1101(2) of the Code as follows: "A) transfer of all or substantially all of the property proposed by the plan to be transferred; B) assumption by the debtor or by the successor to the debtor under the plan of the business or of the management of all or substantially all of the property dealt with by the plan; and C) commencement of distribution under the plan."

plans. The court shall have also fixed the time at which a hearing on confirmation (approval) of the plan is to be held—the so-called Confirmation Hearing.* A sample copy of such notice titled *Notice of Time for Filing Acceptances or Rejections of Plan, of Time of Hearing on Confirmation, and of Time for Filing Objections to Confirmation*, is reproduced on p. 170 of this manual to give the reader an idea.

And now comes the time for the court to hold the hearing on confirmation of one out of any number of reorganization plans that may possibly have been filed with the court. (Although the court may consider a number of plans filed by parties in interest in a case, only one plan may be confirmed in the end.**)

What happens at this confirmation hearing? Basically, the judge will examine the acceptances and rejections of any claims (or interests) that may have been filed, and the provisions of the plan, in terms of its fairness, feasibility, and general suitability for confirmation. The rules permit any party in interest in a case (e.g., the debtor, trustee, creditors' committee, equity security holders' committee) or any indentured trustee or the Securities and Exchange Commission who wishes to, to raise an objection to the confirmation of a proposed plan at the confirmation hearings and such objections, if raised by any such entities, would be given full consideration by the court. In the end, however, if the court decides that a proposed plan meets the legal requirements for confirming a plan (pp. 101-106 below), the court would, by a written order, "confirm" (i.e., approve) such plan and order its implementation.

Sample copies of *"Order Confirming Plan of Reorganization of Corporate Debtor"* is reproduced on pp.174 & 176, for illustrative purposes and guidance. *Notice of Entry* of this Order is usually required to be mailed promptly to all parties in interest in the case, and atimes to persons

---

*Under the Bankruptcy Rule, 2002(b) and (d)(6), however, such notice is not always separately given but is often given in the combined order and notice issued following the court's approval of the disclosure statement. Under the rules, the clerk (or some other person as the court may direct), must give at least 25 days notice of the confirmation hearing to the debtor, the trustee (if one is serving in the case), all creditors and indenture trustees, all committees, the U.S. Trustee, and all equity security holders.

**As discussed on p. 84 of the manual, in any Chapter 11 case where a trustee happens to be appointed or where the debtor fails to file or to obtain acceptances for its plan of reorganization within the time required by the court, the court would be at liberty to consider any number of plans filed by the parties in interest in the case.

who opposed its making, if stipulated by the order of the court. Practices of certain localities may also require that this order should be noticed to the parties in interest for settlement.

What are the procedures in such confirmation hearings? In the first place, it is important that you take careful note of the fact that *confirmation hearings usually come in TWO categories:* in the first category, there is a hearing held on the plans that have been **accepted** by all impaired classes of claims and interests; and in the second category, is a hearing held on plans that have been **rejected** by one or more impaired classes of claims or interests. In cases of the first category, the plan advocate is required to meet the 13 requirements of Section 1129(a) plan confirmation standards (see pp. 101-4 below) in order to obtain the court's confirmation approval of that segment of the plan; and since in this instance all impaired classes of claims and interests shall have accepted the proposed plan, the only opposition to the plan is normally from minority creditors in the classes of claims that have accepted the plan. In the cases of the second category, on the other hand, the plan proponent is required to meet all but one [paragraph 8 thereof] of the 13 requirements set forth for confirmation under Section 1129(a) of the Code, as well as comply with the "cramdown" confirmation requirements set forth under Section 1129(b) of the Code (pp.105-6 below); and, since in this instance some impaired classes of claims or interests shall have rejected the proposed plan, the plan proponent would have to get the plan confirmed over the opposition of one or more classes of creditors or equity security holders.

In either category of cases, the court must hold a hearing and the plan's proponents must present evidence that the plain is confirmable. What specifically happens at a hearing, it's course, duration and contents, will by and large depend on whether or not there's opposition to the plan, and if so to what extent, the nature of any objections to the confirmation which have not been ruled upon by the court, and on the scope and provisions of the proposed plan. *Nevertheless, in general, in a confirmation hearing in either of the above mentioned two categories, the plan proponent (or the debtor's attorney or accountant or other professional representing it) must be present at the hearing and should be fully prepared to present evidence and factual information showing that the plan is confirmable.*

The said plan proponent would generally be expected to present evidence, facts, figures and documentations (or even expert testimony) to show the following:[*]

(1) That all the relevant parties in interest required to be given notice of the confirmation hearing under the rules have been given such notice (e.g., by furnishing sworn affidavits of service or mailings).

(2) That the plan complies, one-by-one, with each and every one of the 13 specific requirements for winning confirmation approval set forth under Section 1129(a) of the Bankruptcy Code (pp.101-4 of the manual). Or, if on the other hand the debtor is rather seeking confirmation under the "cramdown" confirmation standards of Section 1129(b) of the Code (pp.105-6 below), then the plan proponent would not only have to present evidence showing that the plan meets all the 13 confirmation requirements of Section 1129(a) of the Code, except for the provision of paragraph 8 thereof, but would also present sufficient evidence and arguments showing that the plan also meets the so-called "cramdown" requirements of Section 1129(b) of the Code — which has to do, in a word, with showing that the plan does not discriminate unfairly, and is fair and equitable with respect to each impaired class of claims or interests that has not accepted the plan.

(3) That the issues of fact or law raised in any objections to confirmation which have not previously been ruled upon by the court, and any impairment disputes that have·not been resolved, should legitimately be resolved in the plan proponent's favor.

---

[*]Account as summarized from Williamson, The Attorney's Handbook on Chapter 11 Bankruptcy, pp. 183-84.

(4) If the court has ordered the deposit of any funds or other considerations in the case, that such required deposits have been made, or at least evidence showing the ability of the debtor to make any payments required to be made in the case upon confirmation of the plan.

THE TWO SEPARATE CATEGORIES UNDER WHICH A REORGANIZATION PLAN MAY BE CONFIRMED:

The hallmark of Chapter 11 of the 1978 bankruptcy code is said to be flexibility. Under its procedures, creditors and equity security holders who are affected by the plan of reorganization are expected to engage in negotiations with the debtor and among themselves concerning the terms of the proposed plan of reorganization. The parties are expected to compromise their positions in order to preserve the "going concern" value of the debtor's assets and maximize the present value of their recoveries. But what if the parties are unable to reach a compromise? Then, in such event, the Code provides a mechanism, through the so-called "cram down" clause of the Code (pp. 105-6 of the manual), for the court itself to make the determination of the rights of the parties in an adversary context, allowing the court therefrom to confirm a plan even over the opposition of one or more classes of creditors or equity security holders.

In short, there are, then, *two basic* standards by which a plan could be confirmed by the court: a) confirmation when each class of claims and interest affected by a plan has either accepted the plan or is unimpaired under it. This method we shall call *Section 1129(a) Confirmation Standards*—pp. 101-104 of the manual; or b) confirmation of a plan by the court over the opposition of one or more classes of claims or interests. This is the so-called *"cram down" (or Section 1129(b))* alternative Confirmation Standard—pp. 105-6 of this manual.

A. Section 1129(a) Confirmation Standards

Under this standard, fully set out in Section 1129(a) of the Code, the court shall confirm a plan if – and only if – **ALL** of the following 13 confirmation requirements are met:

1. The Plan must comply with the applicable provisions of the Bankruptcy Code – matters such as whether the plan includes all the mandatory provisions required under Section 1123(a) of the Code, whether the plan classifies claims and interests as required by Section 1122 of the Code, whether any modifications of the plan were carried out in compliance with Section 1127 of the Code, whether the plan proponent has complied with the disclosure and solicitation requirements of Sections 1125 and 1126(b) of the Code, and similar matters.

The plan shall have properly *classified* the claims and interests therein as they are required to be classified by Section 1122 of the Code [See pp. 199-204 of manual on classification procedures; and Article I of the model sample plan (p.158 & 162)];

2. The plan shall have included all the major *"plan execution"* means and other provisions required to be included in a plan of reorganization under Section 1123 of the Code [See pp. 85-88 of the manual on the basic contents required of a reorganization plan];

3. The plan's proponents shall have *properly solicited* its acceptances or the rejections of competing plans, if any, and shall have disclosed *"adequate information"* to all the parties concerned as required under Section 1125 of the Code [See pp. 94-97 of this manual on proper solicitation procedures];

4. The plan shall have been proposed "**in good faith**" and not by any means forbidden by law [See footnote on pp.97 for an idea of what constitutes "good faith"]. In general, this is deemed to mean that the court is empowered to deny confirmation if it finds that any illegal activity or bad faith exists in connection with the case. Matters such as a finding by the court, for example, that the primary purpose of a plan is to avoid taxes, to settle a contract dispute, or to achieve an objective other than reorganization or liquidation, would qualify as items of **bad faith**. As a rule, a plan it deemed to be proposed in good faith when there is a reasonable likelihood that the plan will achieve a result consistent with the objectives and purposes of the Bankruptcy Code, such as reorganization or liquidation of a company.

5. The plan shall have disclosed, in full, all payments or promises of payments, made to anyone (including any "insider"* of the debtor company) for services, costs, expenses and other dealings in connection with the Chapter 11 case, and all such payments or promises of payments, if any, shall have been "reasonable."
(The court is, among other things, charged with the obligation of policing the awarding of fees in a bankruptcy case, and must ensure that the debtor company's estate will not be unreasonably siphoned off to various persons or firms in fees for "professional services" thereby leaving the creditors and equity securities holders with diminished resources to share in. This provision is apparently meant to serve this protective purpose.)

6. The plan shall have fully disclosed the identity and affiliations of the persons who are proposed therein to serve as director, officers, or voting trustees of the debtor, or of any "insider" of the debtor who will be employed or retained by the reorganized debtor (as in Article V of the Model Sample Plan, p. 159 of the manual); and the court shall have been satisfied that the use or appointment of the persons or firms named is "consistent with the interests of creditors and equity security holders, and with public policy"—that is, that the appointment of the given functionaries is not likely to constitute or bring about a pattern of incompetence or lack of discretion, active misconduct, inexperience, connections or affiliations with repudiated personnel or groups that would be harmful either to the best interests of the debtor or to those of the reorganized company or the public at large.

7. Where the debtor is a regulated company, and where the plan for such a company proposes to alter rates normally regulated by the regulatory commission, then the proposed rate change shall have received the approval of the regulatory commission, or, alternatively, the proposed rate change may be conditioned upon the regulatory agency's approval being obtained. (This provision is meant to discourage the use of Chapter 11 as a device for circumventing the regulatory powers of duly established regulatory authorities under state or other federal law.)

8. *Each* holder of a claim or interest of *every* class (as classified along the principles outlined on pp. 199-204 of this manual), has to have accepted the proposed plan. Or if, alternatively, there happens to be a class (or more than one class) which has not granted its unanimous consent, then, for the plan to be acceptable, the proponents of the plan shall have outlined within the plan a comparison between what each member of that class will receive under the proposed Chapter 11 plan, on the one hand, and what such member would receive if the debtor company were totally liquidated under Chapter 7 of the Code, on the other hand.* [To put it another way,

---

*Full technical definition of the term "insider" is to be found in Section 101(25) of the Code. As defined here, however, the term is extremely broad and inclusive, and includes affiliates and insiders of affiliates.

*NOTE: Somewhat special situations arise where the claims of certain creditors are *"subordinated"* in favor of the claims of other creditors. In such situations, some special problems may just as equally be presented. Take, for example, a situation where all the secured creditors are part of a single class and the claims of certain unsecured creditors are subordinated in favor of other unsecured creditors. In such a situation the court would have to consider the effect of Section 510(a) of the Code (which requires that the court enforce subordination agreements) in determining whether the plan satisfies "the best interest of creditors" principle of the Code, the central objective test of this provision. The court must also compare the amount which will ultimately be received (or receivable) by senior creditors under the plan to the amount which such creditors would receive in a total liquidation situation after complying with the subordination agreement.

A problem does not generally arise when a plan does not affect the rights of senior creditors to claim distributions that are allocable to junior creditors—senior creditors may, as a matter of right, ask the court to exercise the power granted it under Section 501(a) of the Code and enforce the subordination. It is where the plan attempts to "settle" the relative rights of senior creditors as against the rights of subordinated creditors that a problem often arises. *In all situations, however, the key question is almost always this: does the plan meet the "best interest of creditors" test*—i.e., would the senior creditors be receiving in reorganization (Chap. 11) more than they would receive in liquidation (Chap. 7)? In other words, a plan may, in the eyes of the court, still comply with the "best interests of creditors" requirement even though it does not enforce a subordination agreement, and even though the majority of the class does not grant its consent to the failure to enforce the subordination. It all depends on the facts of each particular case. **In any given case, so long as each member of a particular class will receive more (or, to put it another way, as long as he would not receive less) under the Chapter 11 reorganization plan than he would receive in a Chapter 7 liquidation, the best interests of that class of creditors is deemed to have been served.**

in the absence of a unanimous consent of a class, the class must receive under the plan at least what such class would receive in a liquidation under Chapter 7 of the Code. If, however, the class exercises the Section 1111(b)(2) election, the class must receive property with the present value of the class' secured claims.]

9. The above-outlined general rule barring confirmation of a plan if a class within it will receive less than it would receive in a Chapter 7 liquidation, may not apply under the following two *exceptions*, however:
   a) where each holder of a claim or interest of a particular class accepts the plan in spite of the fact that it makes such a provision; and
   b) where the class (for which the plan provides that it is to receive or retain less than it would receive in a Chapter 7 case) exercises its Section 1111(b)(2) election— which, except for a few exempt situations,* generally permits a class to "elect" to have its entire allowed amount of claim to be treated as a secured claim irrespective of the court's valuation of the collateral securing those claims.**

In situations where the above two conditions apply, the general rule barring confirmation of a plan if a class will receive or retain less than that class would receive in a Chapter 7 liquidation, may not apply, and such a plan may nevertheless be granted confirmation therefore even if it makes such a provision.

10. Each class of claims or interests in the plan shall either have accepted the plan (in the sense of a binding consent as outlined on pp. 96-97 of this manual), or be "unimpaired" under the plan. [See pp. 205-206 of the manual on the concept of impairment in Chapter 11 cases.]

11. The plan shall have provided for payment of claims as follows (except to the extent the holder of a particular claim has agreed to a different treatment):
   i) With respect to those *allowed unsecured claims entitled to "priority"*, those of the type specified in Sections 507(a)(1), (2), or (6) of the Code,*** the plan must provide for such claims, to the extent that they are allowed, to be paid in full in cash on the effective date of the plan (as in Article VI of the Sample Model Plan on pp. 160 & 165 of the manual, for example).

---

*There are certain exceptions when Section 1111(b)(2) elections may not be taken: if the property securing the claims of the particular class is either of inconsequential value, or is sold under the plan or otherwise.

**The provision of this paragraph is made in recognition by the Code that a Chapter 11 creditor whose collateral is worth less than the creditor's allowed claim which is secured by such collateral will have an allowed secured claim in an amount equal to the value of the collateral, and, an unsecured claim for the deficiency. And by providing for the exercise of the Section 111(b)(2) election option—enabling the whole allowed amount of the class to be treated as secured claims—the effect for the class is to waive the right which the class would otherwise have to a deficiency claim and to distributions in compensation for such deficiency claims. (The class of creditors waive their unsecured deficiency claims and are not holders of unsecured claims.)

***These would include debts or claims such as the following: allowed expenses for the administration of the case or in preserving the debtor company's estate (wages, salaries, or commissions for administrative services received), fees and charges, assessed against the estate or awarded as compensation or reimbursement for professional services received after the commencement of the case; taxes included as administrative expenses of the estate and any fines or penalties related thereto; and in a situation where the Chapter 11 petition was filed "involuntarily" (i.e., where the debtor was "thrown into bankruptcy" filing because his creditors took the initiative in filng for one), claims which arise in the ordinary course of the debtor's business or financial affairs at any time between the filing of such petition and the date of the granting of the Order of Relief by the court, would all be includable within this category of debts and claims.

ii) With regard to so-called *"sixth priority tax claim"* items* [items covered by Section 507(a)(6) of the Code], the plan is permitted to provide for payment on such items over a period not to exceed 6 years from the date when such claims had been assessed (as in Article VI of the Sample Model Plan on pp.160 & 165 of manual, for example).

iii) With regard to such claims as outstanding employee compensations (wages, salaries, commissions, vacation, severance and sick leave pay, pension benefit claims, and the like), and with respect to certain consumer claims entitled to priority under the Code (i.e., up to $900 in claims of individuals arising from the pre-petition deposit of money in connection to the purchase or rental of property or the purchase of services which were never delivered or rendered), the plan must either provide that such claims be paid on the effective date of the plan, or that they be paid in full over a period of time based on whatever negotiated terms were acceptable to the requisite majority of the particular class of claim holders. [This sub-paragraph refers to claims of the kind specified in Section 507(a)(3) of the Code.]

12.   A further condition of confirmation of a plan is that *at least one class of claims* shall have accepted the plan, determined without including any acceptance of the plan by any insider.**

13.   Finally, the proposed plan must be *feasible* and must have a reasonable prospect of attaining financial stability and success. It must, in a word, seem likely to the court that the proposed plan offers the debtor, when reorganized, a reasonable prospect of operating at a financial profit and keeping his business in a solvent condition with sufficient projected cash flow reasonably capable of sustaining the debtor's business while permitting him to meet the payments and other obligations required under the plan.***

---

*This is so called because it covers items designated in Section 507(a)(6) of the Code. The items covered by this category include the following, all of which are pre-petition unsecured tax claims of governmental units: allowed taxes for claims for a tax upon or measured by income or gross receipts, for property tax assessed before the commencement of the case, for tax required to be collected or withheld and for which the debtor is liable, employment taxes on wages and other compensation earned by or due to others from the debtor before the date of the filing of the petition; and excise taxes of varying types due or payable.

Take careful note of the fact that this paragraph apparently seeks to reconcile, on the one hand, the needs of the confirmation precondition outlined in Item 10 above (i.e., the requirement that a plan must either be accepted by each class or be unimpaired under the plan), with another relevant requirement (Section 1126(f) of the Code) which states that a class which is unimpaired under a plan is deemed to have accepted the plan. The issues presented are whether, on the one hand, this paragraph requires an active *affirmative* act of acceptance and that leaving a class unimpaired is different from obtaining its affirmative acceptance; or, whether, on the other hand, this paragraph implies consent and does not therefore require an affirmative vote since, presumably, an unimpaired class would surely vote to accept the plan if given an opportunity to express its position. Ultimately, this issue will have to be resolved by the courts. However, it might be helpful to remember the fact that the entire purpose of Section 1126(f) of the Code was to avoid situations wherein proponents of a plan would be compelled to engage in unwarranted delaying tactics of slightly impairing a class by extension or composition and obtaining the almost certain acceptance of that class, after a costly solicitation. **And given this reality, only an interpretation of this paragraph which accepts that Section 1126(f) means implied consent will seem to be consistent with the central purpose of avoiding delaying or wasteful exercises in solicitation of acceptances.

***It is vitally important to understand the primary purpose of the "feasibility" provision of this paragraph: it is, in a word, to try to avoid confirmation of visionary but impracticable plans of reorganization which have little or no realistic prospect of attaining what the plan promises its creditors and shareholders. **A plan of reorganization which the court believes would merely continue in business a company hopelessly insolvent and unable to prosecute its business with any reasonable prospect of success, would not get the court's confirmation.** Among the tests of "feasibility" which various courts have considered in various decisions involving such questions, are the following: the post-confirmation soundness and adequacy of the capital structure of the business reasonably to be anticipated; the earning power and general financial prospects of the business; the future economic conditions, the ability of management, the probability of a continuation of the same management, and any other related matters bearing on the prospects of a sufficiently successful operation to enable performance of the provisions of the plan.

B. Section 1129(b) or "Cram Down" Alternative Confirmation Standards

The so-called *"cram down"* provisions of the Code [Sec. 1129(b)] give an alternative standard for winning a plan's confirmation—alternative to the standards just outlined in the preceding passage above. Essentially, the "cram down" rule provides as follows: that the court may still confirm a plan if the plan were to meet all the confirmation requirements of Section 1129(a) above, except the provision of Item 10 above requiring acceptance of the plan by all impaired classes of claims and interests. To put it differently, the "cram down" alternative confirmation standard is one that permits confirmation of a proposed plan even when a class (or classes) that is impaired under the plan objects to the plan and does not grant its acceptance thereto. Thus, the proponent of a plan which fails to win the requisite number of acceptances to the plan may still find a way, nevertheless, to get his plan confirmed—by invoking the "cram down" provisions of the Code!

Conditions for a 'Cram Down' Confirmation

To qualify for this "cram down" alternative confirmation path, however, the plan must meet certain standards. Briefly, these standards, which are essentially standards of fairness to dissenting creditors or equity security holder, may be summarized as follows:

First, the proposed plan must meet all the other conditions of subsection 1129(a)—i.e., pp. 101-4 of this manual—*except* for one: the provision represented by Item 10 on p. 95 above-- which has to do with the requirement that the plan must be accepted by all impaired classes of claims and interests.

Second, the court may consider confirmation of a proposed plan under the "cram down" alternative standard only "on request of the proponent of the plan"—and not at the instance of either the court or any other entity.

Third, in a broad sense of the term, the proposed plan must meet certain standards of fairness to those classes of claims or interests which are **both** impaired and non-accepting under the plan: more specifically, the plan shall not have *"discriminated unfairly"* against any such classes, and it must be *"fair and equitable"* to each such impaired and non-accepting class thereof.

NOTE: The legal requirements here that a plan not "discriminate" and that the plan be "fair and equitable" apply *only* to the dissenting class or classes—not to any accepting classes. That is, if senior classes which are accepting choose to do so, they may give up value to junior classes so long as no dissenting intervening classes receive less than the amount of its claims in full. However, though senior accepting classes may so give up value to junior classes, to remain "fair and equitable," no such senior class may have received more than 100% of the amount of its claims.

The important question is this: by what criteria does the court determine that a plan satisfied the "non-discrimination" and "fairness-equitability" tests regarding impaired and dissenting classes? The Code provides certain guidelines by which a court may attempt to make this determination. In general, the underlying principle of the so-called cram down confirmation standard is that an impaired, non-accepting class is considered to have been treated "fairly and equitably" if that class and all below it in priority (pp. 199-204) are treated according to the so-called *absolute priority rule.*" Briefly described, this rule warrants that the impaired dissenting class must first have been paid in full before any class junior to it may share under the plan; and that if that class is paid in full, then junior classes may share.

Unsecured Claims: Where the dissenting class involved is an unsecured class (which do not, as a rule, fall in the priority ladder), the proposed plan would have met the fairness and equitability test to that class if the members of such unsecured class are not impaired, or if they are to receive payment of a value equal to the allowed amount of their secured claims as of the effective date of the plan.*

Secured Claims: Where the dissenting class involved is a secured class (which, as a rule, do fall in the priority ladder), the proposed plan would have met the fairness and equitability test to that class if the members of such secured class, including priority claims, are unimpaired (i.e., if they will receive payment of a value equal to the allowed amount of their claims), or if, alternatively, no class junior to the given secured class will share under the plan. In other words, if the class is impaired, then they must be paid in full or, if paid less than in full, then no class junior to it may have received anything under the plan.

Equity Holders*: Where the dissenting class involved is a class of equity holders, the proposed plan would have met the fairness and equitability test to that class if the members of such class are unimpaired, or if they receive their fixed liquidation preference or fixed redemption rights in respect to their interests, if any, or, in the event that the class has none of these rights (i.e., if the class holds no preferred stock or stocks entitled to fixed payment), then no class junior to the dissenting equity class shall have received anything under the plan.***

FOR THE LEGAL EFFECTS AND IMPLICATIONS OF COURT CONFIRMATION OF A REORGANIZATION PLAN, SEE CHAPTER 4, ON PP. 109-110

IMPORTANT: Reproduced on pp. 157, 161 & 167 of the manual are three model sample Chapter 11 plans for illustrative purposes.

---

*If, on the other hand, a class of *secured* claims were to be *impaired* and has not accepted the plan, the plan may be "crammed down" and confirmed over the dissent of that class only if the plan complies with the following:

  i) if it provides for that dissenting class of secured claims to retain its lien (which secures the allowed secured claims) on the property, whether the property is retained by the debtor or transferred. In addition, the plan must provide for the "allowed secured claim" holder to receive payments, either present or deferred, of a principal face value equal to the amount of the debt and of a present value equal to the value of the collateral;

  ii) if it provides for the sale of any property that is subject to the lien securing such claims, free and clear of such lien, with such lien to attach to the proceeds of the sale; or

  iii) if it provides for the realization, by the secured class, of the "indubitable equivalence" of the secured claims—e.g., an abandonment of the collateral to the creditor, or a lien on similar collateral.

**Equity holders would include the following: interests of general or limited partners in a partnership, sole proprietor in a proprietorship, or common or preferred stock shareholders in a corporation.

***For example, a plan which provides for distributions to holders of preferred stock and grants nothing to holders of common stock would be considered "fair and equitable" if the corporation's reorganization value is less than the aggregate of the allowed claims or is less than the allowed claims and the value of the preferred stock interests. However, the plan is not fair and equitable with respect to a dissenting class of stock holders if the senior classes as a group receive more than 100% of their allowed claims and interests.

step 18 : CARRY OUT THE PROVISIONS OF THE COURT-CONFIRMED REORGANIZATION PLAN

As more elaborately explained in Chapter 4, "The Effects of Confirmation...," pp. 109-110, , an order confirming a plan is somewhat like a judicial judgment—a binding determination as to the rights and liabilities created by, and arising out of the plan of reorganization. *Once having been approved ("confirmed"), however, the provisions of the plan of reorganization—and of the order of the court confirming the plan—would still need to be fully carried out if the whole exercise is to be of any value.* The next major order of business following the plan's confirmation, therefore, is its "execution"—the carrying out or implementation of the plan.

As provided by the bankruptcy code, confirmation of a plan of reorganization by the bankruptcy court does not close the case, but the case still remains "open" after such confirmation. Whenever the case eventually runs its course and deserves to be closed—which, by the Code's stipulation, would be only "after an estate is fully administered and the court has discharged the trustee"*—the court would enter a formal order closing the case.

For the debtor, the trustee, creditors, shareholders and all others concerned, however, **what is most relevant to recognize in the context of this chapter is that until such a time that the case is formally closed, which may take months or years, at all times prior to such closing by the bankruptcy court, the court retains continued, and virtually sweeping and unlimited jurisdiction over any and all civil matters arising in or related to the case.**

Suffice it to say, for the sake of brevity, that in attempting to carry out the provisions of the plan, it is routinely customary for the debtor or any entity responsible for carrying out the plan, to seek and obtain specific authorizations (court orders) from the court from time to time on virtually every issue deemed necessary and useful for carrying out the provisions of the plan: matters such as fixing the time and manner for the deposit and distribution of the cash or other consideration under the plan; or directing the debtor, trustee, mortgagees and the like, to execute and deliver documents which might become necessary to effect a retention or transfer of property covered in the plan; directing the satisfaction of liens; issuing of such orders as may be necessary to enjoin any act inconsistent with or interfering with the reorganization plan; ordering an accounting of funds not properly distributed, and so on and on. And, armed with such court orders,

---

*Language of Section 350(a). As this section requires a case to be closed only after two elements are present [i) after the estate is fully administered, and ii) after the trustee is discharged], a key related question is how does one (or the court) determine that these conditions have been met? Of these two conditions, only the first one is more fundamental since, as a rule, the full administration of the estate by the trustee is a condition precedent to the discharge of the trustee anyway. Rule 514 of the 1973 Rules of Bankruptcy Procedure, which continues to be effective under the current 1978 code, seems to intimate that much of what could be interpreted as constituting "full administration" of an estate or case is left largely to the individual judge's discretion: an estate is fully administered "whenever it appears (to the court) that an estate has been administered and the court has passed upon the final account...." And Bankruptcy Rule 3022 under the current rules (i.e., under the rules which superseded the 1973 Rules), sheds more light on the matter as follows: "Final Decree — after an estate is fully administered, including distribution of any deposit required by the plan, the court shall enter a decree (1) discharging any trustee...and (3) closing the case."

the debtor-in-possession (or the trustee, as the case may be), would be able to carry out the tasks of reorganization for as long as it might take—whether in a matter of months, or possibly years.*

See Chapter 5, **Handling Some of the Practical Problems Involved In Implementing The Chapter 11 Plan,** for the primary issues involved in implementing the Plan. Also, see Appendix A for sample forms of some of the more routine kinds of court orders frequently applicable in plan execution and post-confirmation Chapter 11 proceedings.

An Order of Confirmation of a plan, once granted, may be revoked by the court solely on one ground: if evidence is turned up that the order was fraudulently obtained. The move to so revoke an order of confirmation may be undertaken by the court, however, only if certain conditions are present: i) if it is prompted by a request by a party in interest; ii) if this request is made within 180 days from the date of the entry of the confirmation order; and iii) if a notice and a hearing are had by the court on the substance of the request to revoke confirmation.

---

*Note that under the Code (Section 1143 thereof), any entity required by the plan to present or surrender a security, or to perform any other act as a condition to share in distribution under the plan, must undertake such action *not later than 5 years* from the date of the entry of the order confirming the plan. Otherwise, such entity may not participate in distribution under the plan. The term 'security' is broadly defined in this context to include, as in Section 101(35) of the Code, the following: notes, stocks, treasury stock, bonds, debenture, trust certificates, voting-trust certificates, certificates of deposit, investment contracts or certificates of interest or participation in a profit-sharing agreement or in an oil, gas, or mineral royalty or lease registered with the SEC, interests of a limited partner in a limited partnership, certificates of interest or participation in temporary or interim certificate for, receipt for, or warrant or right to subscribe to or purchase or sell a security.

CHAPTER FOUR

THE LEGAL EFFECT OF COURT CONFIRMATION OF A REORGANIZATION PLAN FOR THE DEBTOR, CREDITORS, SHAREHOLDERS AND OTHERS

The Confirmation by a bankruptcy court of a plan of reorganization has many automatic, far-reaching legal implications—for the debtor company, the creditors, and the shareholder or ownership interests in the debtor company. We outline below the general rules governing the effects of such a confirmation in a Chapter 11 bankruptcy case.

1. Except for a few exceptions*, the provisions of a plan are, once confirmed, legally binding upon all parties—on the debtor, any entity issuing securities or acquiring property under the plan, and every creditor or equity security holder of the debtor or general partner thereof, etc.

---

*Chapter 11 confirmation does not discharge an individual debtor (as opposed to a business debtor) from debts designated as "non-dischargeable" under the Code—e.g., certain personal taxes, alimony or child support arrears, certain government-guaranteed student loans,and the like. And, if a plan of liquidation (as opposed to a plan of reorganization) is confirmed under the Chapter 11 filing, then an individual debtor, or a debtor partnership or corporation which, after consummation of the plan, does not engage in business will not be discharged in such a circumstance.

And, with specific respect to any entity that holds a claim or interest of whatever kind against the debtor, the plan, once confirmed, would be just as equally binding upon that holder even if he is not scheduled, or has not filed a claim, does not have notice of, or never appeared in the case*, does not receive a distribution under the plan, or is not entitled to retain an interest under the plan. To sum it all up, any and all questions which could have been raised with respect to a plan are, after the plan's confirmation, said to be "res judicate"—i.e., considered to be, in the eyes of the law, a matter that has been judicially decided upon and settled as final, and about which the parties are forbidden from instituting a new suit or court action to fight over again.

2. After confirmation, if property covered in the confirmed plan gets transferred by the trustee or debtor in possession, or is retained under the plan by the debtor, that property is transferred or retained (as the case may be) "free and clear" of all claims and interests (e.g., liens or encumbrances) of the debtor, creditors and shareholders, except as otherwise specifically provided in the plan or in the court order approving it , if any.

3. In general, confirmation of a plan vests all of the property of the estate—i.e., in any cause of action whatsoever that the debtor could assert as of the commencement of the case—in the debtor (unless, of course, otherwise provided in the plan or the court order approving it).

4. Another major binding effect of confirmation is this: except as might otherwise be provided by the plan or the court order approving the plan, confirmation of a Chapter 11 plan of reorganization discharges you, the debtor (or debtor company), from any debt or claim that arose before the date of such confirmation, and also terminates all rights and interests of equity security holders and general partners covered in the plan. It also terminates the debtor's debts and thereby discharges him from any debt which arose by reason of rejection of executory contract or unexpired lease, recovery of property under Sections 522(i), 550, or 553 of the Code (having to do with the debtor's avoidance power in respect to property, preferences, fraudulent transfers, statutory liens, pre-petition set-off recovery, and the like), or by reason of any tax claims arising after commencement of the case even if the debt technically arises after confirmation. The one main exception when this rule does not apply (i.e., when confirmation would not entitle a corporate, partnership or individual debtor to a discharge) would be under the following circumstances: where the confirmed Chapter 11 plan provides, not for reorganization, but for liquidation (whether of all or substantially all of the property of the estate), and the debtor does not continue in business thereafter.

---

*Note, however, that when the creditors involved are a secured creditor, often the proponents of the plan would either have to leave such claims unimpaired or would have to establish that they (the proponents) attempted to give such creditors adequate notice. In other words, proponents of a plan may, in any event, find it unavoidable to make a good faith effort to give notice to the necessary claimants and interests. For one thing, the Code requires actual notice of the confirmation hearing to parties in interest in advance of a confirmation hearing.

EXAMPLES: Take, for instance, a situation involving a secured creditor not scheduled under the plan and thus never participating in the case. The collateral will, in such case, vest in the reorganized debtor free and clear of the creditor's lien; and should the property be retained by the debtor, the property would be free and clear of all claims, encumbrances, and interests not specifically provided for in the plan or the court order approving it. In a case involving a corporate debtor, for another example, in which the plan provides, say, for no distribution to holders of equity securities and provides for distribution of new common stock to creditors, confirmation of the plan would mean automatic termination of the rights and interests of equity security holders as well as termination of the interests of former shareholders in the debtor's property.

CHAPTER 5

HANDLING SOME OF THE PRACTICAL PROBLEMS INVOLVED IN IMPLEMENTING THE CHAPTER 11 PLAN

With the confirmation of the Plan, the principal objective of most Chapter 11 cases is attained. That does not, by any means, mean the end of the case, however. To the contrary, in many small business cases, for example, there are nearly as many functions to be performed after confirmation (**post-confirmation**), as before confirmation (**pre-confirmation**). Fundamentally, the plan would now have to be implemented by the reorganized debtor or the debtor's successor under the plan, and its provisions carried out: the claims of creditors would have to be reviewed, objected to, and allowed; the distributions would have to be made on the allowed claims as provided under the plan; and the plan would have to be consummated, a final decree entered, and the case closed.

The Effects Of the Order of Confirmation

The court's Order of Confirmation has the following significant effects in a Chapter 111 case:

1. It terminates the debtor's estate and reverts the estate property to the reorganized debtor. Except as otherwise provided in the plan or in the order confirming the plan, the confirmation of a plan rests all property of the estate in the debtor. Thus, if there is an estate property that is not dealt with in the Plan or in the Order Confirming the Plan, ownership of the property is vested in the debtor after confirmation. The confirmation of a plan binds the debtor and all parties to the terms of the Plan regardless of whether the claim or interest of a party is impaired under the plan and regardless of whether party has accepted the Plan.

2. It terminates the "debtor in possession" status of the debtor

3. It serves as a discharge of the debtor. A Chapter 11 discharge, it should be noted, is not contingent upon the success of the Plan. As long as the Order of Confirmation is not revoked, a Chapter 11 discharge is not affected by the subsequent failure of the debtor to consummate its plan. (see below)

4. Because Chapter 11 Order of Confirmation serves to discharge the debtor, it has the effect of terminating the "automatic stay," except as it applies to acts against property of the estate.

Nature of Chapter 11 Discharge

Basically, the extent of a Chapter 11 discharge depends on two factors: whether the debtor is an individual, and whether the Plan confirmed is a plan of reorganization (Chapter 11) or a plan of liquidation (Chapter 7).

If the debtor is an individual (i.e., a natural person), and if the plan confirmed is a plan of reorganization, a Chapter 11 Confirmation Order discharges the debtor from all pre-confirmation debts, except those set forth in Section 523(a) of the Bankruptcy Code (which basically has to do with debts that are not dischargeable in a Chapter 7 case). In order words, the Chapter 11 discharge received by a reorganizing individual debtor, discharges only such debts as are dischargeable in a Chapter 7 case; however, a reorganizing individual debtor receives a Chapter 11 discharge whether or not the debtor is eligible for a Chapter 7 discharge.

If the plan provides for the liquidation of all or substantially all of the debtor's property, and if the debtor does not engage in business after consummation of the plan, a Chapter 11 order of confirmation does not discharge the debtor. Therefore, an individual debtor who obtains confirmation of a Chapter 11 of plan of liquidation, receives a Chapter 11 discharge if the individual either remains in business after consummation of the plan or is eligible for a Chapter 11 discharge. An individual Chapter 11 debtor with a confirmed plan of liquidation who engages in business after consummation of the plan, receives the same discharge as an individual Chapter 11 debtor with a confirmed plan of reorganization. An individual debtor having a confirmed Chapter 11 plan of liquidation who does not engage in business after consummation of the plan, is discharged to the same extent and under the same circumstances as an individual debtor in a Chapter 7 case.

On the other hand, if a debtor is a non-individual (i.e., a corporation, etc), and if the plan confirmed is a plan of reorganization, a Chapter 11 Order of Confirmation discharges the debtor from all scheduled pre-confirmation debts without exception, whether or not a proof of claim is filed, or the claim is allowed, or the holder of the claim has accepted the plan. Thus, a reorganizing corporate or other non-individual debtor is discharged from all scheduled debts regardless of the nature of the debts. However, if the debtor is a non-individual and does not engage in business after consummation of the plan, and if the plan confirmed is a plan of liquidation, a Chapter 11 order of confirmation does not discharge the debtor from any debts whatsoever.

Implementation, Distribution and Consummation of the Plan

As a general proposition, the supervisory powers of the bankruptcy courts over the property and business operations of the reorganized debtor, are substantially reduced after confirmation. Unless the Plan or the Order of Confirmation provides otherwise, the reorganized debtor which emerges after confirmation may enter into contracts, obtain secured or unsecured credit, open business bank accounts in its own names without reference to Chapter 11 case, or buy and sell property, and pay professional fees, all without the approval of the bankruptcy court. Except, however, that atimes the plan or order of confirmation may, if desired, provide for the continued supervision of the bankruptcy court over one or two more post-confirmation activities of the reorganized debtor.

In general, regarding the issue of the post-confirmation justification of the bankruptcy court, a bankruptcy court retains sufficient post-confirmation jurisdiction to interpret and administer a confirmed plan. Thus, aside from matters involving the post-confirmation supervisory powers of the court over the property and business operations of the reorganized debtor, the second most questionable area of post-confirmation bankruptcy court jurisdiction, are those involving liquidation related solely to post-confirmation defaults by the reorganized debtor.

Typical post-confirmation litigation involving the reorganized debtor or the debtor's successor under the plan, are issues such as breach of contract actions, eviction actions, and lien foreclosure actions resulting from the failure of the debtor or its successor to comply with the requirements of the plan.

Post-Confirmation Functions To Be Performed Under the Plan

It is convenient to break post-confirmation matters down into categories such as implementation, distribution, and consummation. In practice, however, such clear-cut categories of activities seldom exist. In reality, post confirmation activities take the form of functions that must be performed if the plan is become effective and its provisions carried out. The post-confirmation functions to be performed by the reorganized debtor or the debtor's successor under the plan in a typical small business Chapter 11 case, include the following:

(1) Prepare and file any postconfirmation reports required by the court or the U.S. Trustee.

(2) Perform the acts or functions, if any, upon which the implementation of the plan is expressly conditioned or contingent.

(3) Distribute the deposit or other funds or property required under the plan to be distributed upon confirmation.

(4) If necessary, prepare the corporate and other documents needed to revise or restructure the reorganized debtor, incorporate or otherwise organize the successor to the debtor under the plan, or complete any merger, consolidation, or other reorganization required under the plan.

(5) Prepare any documents needed to transfer assets or property of the debtor as provided in the plan, and, if necessary, prepare the documents needed to transfer the assets or liabilities of the debtor to the successor to the debtor under the plan.

(6) If necessary, prepare the pleadings and other documents needed to extinguish, modify, or create liens or other security interests in accordance with the provisions of the plan.

(7) Examine all claims and interests that have been filed or deemed filed, file objections to the allowance of claims or interests where necessary, resolve each objection either by negotiation or court ruling, and prepare a final list of claims and interests for each class of claims and interests provided for in the plan.

(8) Prepare, file, and obtain court approval of any necessary modifications to the confirmed plan. See infra, this section, for further reading on postconfirmation plan modifications.

(9) Substantially consummate the plan and, if desired, obtain an order of substantial consummation.

(10) Prepare and file a final report and a final account of the administration of the debtor's estate with the court and U.S. Trustee.

(11) After the completion of all matters provided for in the plan and the confirmation order, obtain from the court a final decree and an order closing the case.

Conditions Precedent To Plan Implementation

If, under the plan, there are conditions or contingencies to the implementation of the plan, the first matter of business after confirmation should be to fulfill the required conditions or contingencies. For example, if implementation of the plan is contingent upon the approval of a specified rate change for the debtor by a governmental regulatory commission, the initiation of a proceeding to obtain approval of the rate change should be the first order of business after confirmation. Other contingencies to the implementation of a plan, might be matters such as the resolution of certain pending litigation or the obtaining of a particular patent, copyright, or contract.

As soon as any contingencies or conditions precedent to implementation of the plan have been satisfied, any funds or property distributable upon confirmation of the plan should be distributed in accordance with the plan. If the debtor was required, under Bankruptcy Rule 3020(a), to deposit funds or property prior to confirmation, distributions should be made from the deposit. Otherwise, the debtor must provide the funds or property to be distributed.

Actual Implementation of the Plan

After complying with any contingencies or conditions precedent to implementation, the actual implementation of the Plan may commence. Implementation will typically include the following:
- Formation of the reorganized entity that is to be the successor to the debtor under the plan, or the restructuring of the debtor as required under the Plan. (These are usually the first matters to be performed in implementing a plan).
- Transfers of assets and property, either to the reorganized debtor or its successor under the plan, or to its creditors; the extinguishment or modification of liens, and the creation of new liens.
- The preparation of the final list of creditors. Preparation, as well, of a final list of interest holders, if they are dealt with in the plan. (Note that it is not necessary for a creditor to file a Proof of Claim in a Chapter 11 case unless the creditor's claim is either not scheduled or listed in the debtor's schedule of liabilities.)
- Payment of claims, and liquidation under the plan.

In regard to matters such as conveyances of assets or property, extinguishment or modification of liens, and the like, it should be noted that an important element would probably be that you (the debtor) or any other necessary party, may have to execute or deliver, or to join in the execution or delivery of, any instrument required to effect the transfer of property dealt with by the plan, and to perform any act, such as satisfaction of any lien, that is necessary for the consummation of the plan. And in regard to matters relating to payment of claims, it should be noted that the claims dealt with at this post-confirmation stage of the case, are usually nonpriority unsecured type of claims, since the allowance of secured and priority claims shall normally have been determined prior to the confirmation. (See Step 15, and Appendix C, for more on the handling of claims and the filing of objections to the allowance of claims).

In general, the procedure is that it is not necessary for a creditor to file a Proof of Claim in a Chapter 11 case unless the creditor's claim is either not scheduled or listed in the debtor's Schedule of Liabilities. [Section 1111(a) of the Bankruptcy Code and Bankruptcy Rule 3003(c)(2)]. However, if a Proof of Claim has been filed for any claim listed on the debtor's schedules, an appropriate objection should be filed unless an agreement can be reached with the creditor as to the amount and status of the claim.

A usual practice, after all objections to the allowance of claims have been prepared, is to file and serve notice of the objections as a group, and, if possible, obtain a common hearing date for all of the objections. Then, when all such objections have been ruled upon by the court, a final list of claims may be prepared for each class of claims provided for in the plan. If the rights interest holders are dealt with in the plan, a final list of them must likewise be prepared.

Thereupon, after that distributions must be made to creditors whose claims have been allowed (see Bankruptcy Rule 3021). Especially if there are a large number of claims to be paid, the best practice is to obtain a court order in aid of consummation authorizing distribution in accordance with the plan to creditors as set forth in the final list of creditors. Disbursement checks should contain a notice stating that the check is void if not presented for payment within a specified period, such as 60 days from the date of the check. After all distributions have been made, the debtor or its attorney should file an affidavit with the court confirming that distributions have been made in accordance with the plan and orders of the court.

Normally distributions should not be made to creditors until all objections to the allowance of claims have been ruled upon and the final list of creditors has been approved by the court. However, if appeals or other delays prevent the finalization of the final list of creditors for a prolonged period, the court may grant permission to make an earlier distribution to the holders of allowed claims, provided that sufficient funds or other property is reserved for the later payment of contested claims.

Modifying plan after confirmation. The proponent of a plan or the reorganized debtor may, for cause shown, modify a confirmed plan at any time prior to substantial consummation✱of the plan. See 11 U.S.C. 1127(b). The modification of a confirmed plan is usually attempted when the reorganized debtor is unable to perform its obligations under the existing plan, but could perform under a modified plan. A postconfirmation modification may also be warranted in situations where certain provisions or matters were inadvertently omitted from a confirmed plan.

In any event, modification of a confirmed Plan may occur, however, only if circumstances warrant such modification, and the court, after notice and a hearing, confirms the plan as modified. Thus, the proponent of a post-confirmation Plan modification, especially if extensive or substantive, must show good cause in order to warrant the modification of a confirmed plan over the objection of adversely affected creditors, such as significant and uncontrollable intervening circumstances. Only the debtor and the plan proponent have a standing to seek modification of a confirmed plan.

Assuming that the conditions for modification of a confirmed plan are present (i.e., that substantial consummation has not occurred and that sufficient cause is shown to warrant modification), then the following requirements must further be met: the modified plan must comply with the classification requirements of Section 1122 of the Code and the plan provision requirements of Section 1123 of the Code; proponents of the modification must comply with the disclosure and solicitation in requirements of the Code (see Section 1125 thereof) with respect to the modified plan; all creditors and other parties in interest must be given at least 20 days notice by mail of the time fixed by the court for accepting or rejecting the proposed modification; and the plan, as modified, must be reconfirmed by the court, after notice and a hearing.

Closing the Chapter 11 Case

When a plan has been substantially consummated, a good and advisable practice is for the debtor or other plan proponent to file a motion with the court for an Order of substantial consummation, although the fil-

---

✱A plan is deemed to be "substantially consummated" when: (1) substantially all of the property proposed to be transferred under the plan has been transferred, (2) the reorganized debtor or the successor to the debtor under the plan has assumed the business or the management of all or substantially all of the property dealt with by the plan, and (3) distribution under the plan has commenced. See 11 U.S.C. 1101(2). Once substantial consummation of a plan has occurred, the plan may not be modified. See In re Northampton Corp., 37 B.R. 110 (ED PA, 1984). Whether substantial confirmation has occurred is a question of fact to be determined on a case-by-case basis. See In re Jorgenson, 66 B.R. 104 (BAP 9, 1986), In re Modern Steel Treating Co., 130 BR 60 (ND IL, 1991), and In re Fansal Shoe Corp., 119 BR 28 (SD NY, 1990). Under plans that provide for transfers of property or money upon confirmation or shortly thereafter and for distributions to creditors from earnings over an extended period, substantial confirmation is generally held to require completion or near completion of the former but only commencement of the latter. See In re Hayball Trucking, Inc., 67 B.R. 681 (ED MI, 1986), and In re Bedford Springs Hotel, Inc., 99 B.R. 302 (WD PA, 1989).

ing of such a motion is not required by either the Bankruptcy Code or the Rules of Bankruptcy Procedure. Substantial consummation is a significant event in a Chapter 11 case in that it denotes that substantially all of the provisions of the plan have been complied with and that only minor or ministerial matters are yet to be performed.

When all the statutory requirements for "substantial consummation" (as listed above in the footnote on p. 114), have been satisfied, a "motion" (written application) for an order of substantial consummation may be filed with the court. The motion should comply with the notice and other requirements of Bankruptcy Rule 9014 (and any applicable local rules and practices) relating to the filing of such a motion.

The debtor is required to make a final report and file a final account of the administration of the estate with the court and with the U.S. Trustee. See 11 U.S.C. 1106(a)(1), 704(9), which are made applicable to a debtor in possession by 11 U.S.C. 1107(a). The final account may normally be filed after substantial consummation of the plan. The local rules should be checked for requirements and forms relating to the filing of the final report and final account.

After an estate has been fully administered, the court, on its own motion or on the motion of a party in interest, must enter a final decree closing the case. See Bankruptcy Rule 3022 and 11 U.S.C. 350(a). A case may be reopened in the court in which the case was closed to administer assets, to accord relief to the debtor, or for other cause. See 11 U.S.C. 350(b). In many districts the final decree in a Chapter 11 case customarily contains a broad injunction prohibiting parties from asserting preconfirmation claims or interests against the reorganized debtor or against the property or assets of the reorganized debtor.

An application for a final decree may be filed, if desired, when all matters requiring court approval or court action have been resolved, and when the jurisdiction of the bankruptcy court is no longer needed in the rehabilitation of the debtor or the consummation of the plan. If certain minor provisions of the plan have yet to be completed, the application should set forth such matters and request the court to retain jurisdiction with respect to such matters. In small business cases the application for a final decree is often filed with the final account of the debtor.

CHAPTER 6

HANDLING SOME COMMON PRACTICAL PROBLEMS YOU MAY ENCOUNTER AS A DEBTOR-IN-POSSESSION·

In "STEP‖" of Chapter 3 (pp.82-3 of the manual), we sketched in essentially brief terms the basic rights, powers and duties legally exercisable under the bankruptcy code by the debtor who functions as a **"debtor in possession"** in a Chapter 11 bankruptcy case. As was explained in that section, *the act of serving as a "debtor in possession" describes a situation where and when the debtor itself and the company's management are allowed to remain in control ("in possession") of the debtor's business and affairs, and to continue to operate and manage the business during the course of the bankruptcy proceedings.* In the overwhelming number of Chapter 11 cases, the debtor is left to remain in possession of the debtor's business. Hence, it is deemed necessary and useful, especially to the do-it-yourself debtor, that a more detailed discussion of the more common practical, procedural and legal issues often confronted by the debtor in possession (or the trustee) in the course of administering the Chapter 11 case be provided, including the precise procedures and mechanics practically involved in tackling such situations.

This Chapter deals, therefore, with issues relating to the mechanics and procedures involved in handling some of the more common practical problems often arising in Chapter 11 cases following the initial filing of the bankruptcy petition.

For our purpose here, the topics to be addressed in this chapter are the following:

A) Handling of Automatic Stay (pp. 117-120)
B) Operation of the business by the debtor following the filing of the petition (pp. 117-123)
C) Use, sale or lease of cash collaterals by the debtor in possession (pp.123-125)
D) Use, sale or lease of other estate property other than cash collateral by debtor in possession (pp.125-6)
E) Handling of claims and security interests of creditors (pp. 126-9)
F) Handling of executory contracts and unexpired leases held by the debtor (pp. 130-2)

A. Handling of Automatic Stay Matters

As has been explained elsewhere in this manual (see pp. 8-10 & 15, for example), as a matter of law, the filing of the Chapter 11 bankruptcy petition by the debtor immediately operates as an **"automatic stay"** prohibiting any initiation or continuation of all foreclosures, collection actions, setoff of debts, civil litigation, and credit for actions of any kind (lawsuits, seizures, repossessions, even a mere phone call or letters, etc) against the debtor or the debtor's property.** *Suffice it to say, simply, that the automatic stay accompanying the filing of Chapter 11 bankruptcy is probably the single most important and fundamental protection provided the debtor by the act of filing for bankruptcy, and without which protection the entire system would not possibly work.* Fundamentally, by stopping harassment of the debtor and halting virtually all collection efforts and creditor actions against the debtor, the automatic stay mechanism provides the debtor a breathing space from its creditors. In deed, the underlying purposes of the automatic stay mechanism are said to be to shield the debtor from a multitude of lawsuits and legal actions in numerous forums, to prevent piecemeal liquidation or dismemberment of debtor's property by creditors, and to freeze the respective claims of creditors so that, and until, the bankruptcy court can examine and determine the issues.

For our limited purposes in this chapter, the most common form of problem that a debtor typically confronts relative to the issue of automatic stay relief would typically have to do with fighting off creditors' demands and efforts for them (the creditors) to be relieved from the automatic stay. That is, as it often happens in many bankruptcy cases, a creditor or a number of creditors, may file a motion with the court asking that the creditor be relieved (excused) from the automatic stay imposed upon it by the debtor's filing of bankruptcy, which would thereby allow the creditor to undertake certain debt collection actions against the debtor.

Under the Bankruptcy Code (see Section 362 thereof), **there are two grounds under which the court may grant a creditor relief from the automatic stay: 1) "for cause"**, which typically means proof of lack of adequate protection of an interest in the property of the creditor seeking the relief; and **2)** a showing, in situations when the relief being sought is against the stay of acts against property, that the debtor has no equity in the property and that the property is not necessary for an effective reorganization.

1. Relief From Automatic Stay Based on Debtor's Lack of Equity in Property

We shall address this ground for relief first, as this ground is somewhat easier and more straightforward to dispose of: namely, *a showing that the debtor has no equity in the property constituting the collateral and that the property is not necessary for an effective*

---

*11 U.S. Code 362.

It is important for the reader to note, however, that with respect to Chapter 11 cases, the **automatic stay applies only to acts directly against the debtor and does not apply against third parties. Thus, for example, the automatic stay has been held not to prevent an issuing bank from honoring a prepetition letter of credit in favor of a creditor (In re M. J. Sales & Distributing Co., 25 B.R. 608 (SD NY, 1982); that a creditor is not prohibited by the automatic stay from collecting a prepetition claim from a third party guarantor (Otoe County Nat'l Bank v. W & P Trucking, Inc., 754 F.2d 881 (CA 10, 1985); and that the automatic stay does not protect the general partners of a partnership debtor from actions to collect partnership debts (see in re Cloud Nine, Ltd., 3 B.R. 202 (NM, 1980). All those notwithstanding, it is commonly customary, however, for the bankruptcy court to issue injunctions under Section 105(a) of the Code effectively barring a creditor from engaging in certain acts or proceeding in another court against third parties, if it should seem that such a relief is necessary to prevent an irreparable harm to the debtor estate or protect an otherwise effective reorganization. [See, for example, In re Arrow Hass, Inc., 51 B.R. 853 (UT, 1985); In re Otero Mills, Inc., 25 B.R. 1018 (NM, 1982).]

reorganization. Typically, *the ground is used mainly by secured creditors seeking to reach their collateral.* There are two elements involved in this ground: **lack of equity in the property** constituting the collateral, and **lack of necessity of the property for effective reorganization.** On the first element, namely, the requirement that it be shown that the debtor has no equity in the property constituting the collateral, the creditor, to be able to make such a showing, will normally accomplish this by showing that the total amount of liens and encumbrances against the property exceeds the value for the property.[*] As is probably to be expected, *the key issue is often that of valuing the property in question. On the debtor's part, to oppose the motion for relief from stay, the debtor will normally attempt to establish a high value for the property; while the creditor seeking the relief, on the other hand, will attempt to establish a lower value.* The court, in the end, must determine the fair market value of the property in the market where the debtor would sell it and it is on the creditor, and not the debtor, that the burden of proof lies to establish the property fair market value to be used for the property evaluation.

Then, on the second element involved in the use of the ground at issues as basis for relief, namely demonstration that the property at issue is necessary for effective reorganization, the burden of proof is on the debtor in possession or the trustee opposing the granting of the relief. To establish to the court's satisfaction that the property is necessary for an effective reorganization, the debtor must show that these two factors apply: a) that there is a reasonable possibility of successful reorganization within a reasonable period (a debtor can demonstrate this, for example, by having timely proposed a realistic plan and met other Chapter 11 deadlines); and b) that the property in question is necessary to effectively reorganize and run the debtor's business, and that it is "essential" and has a "part to play" in the reorganization.[**]

2.   Relief from Stay Based on Cause

With respect to the second ground permissible under the code for which relief from the automatic stay could be granted, namely, *for cause,* true, there are other bases which could be described as qualifying under this category — (e.g., proof that the bankruptcy case was filed by the debtor in bad faith, or the finding of the debtor guilty of misconduct during the case, or the granting of a stay for the purpose of permitting the continuation of a pending personal injury action against the debtor when the debtor is covered by liability insurance,[***] etc. However, *by and large, claims by creditors who contend there's a lack of adequate protection of their interest in the collateral property, is the cause overwhelmingly alleged by creditors in seeking relief from the automatic stay.* And, not surprisingly, such cases involving alleged lack of **'adequate protection'** by creditors constitute probably the most heavily litigated matter in bankruptcy. In practice, this ground for seeking relief is used mostly by secured creditors   and only very occasionally by unsecured creditors having special types of unsecured debts, such as lessors and beneficiaries of property held in trust.[****]

A central question of relevance here is: what is meant by "adequate protection"? To put it very simply, a creditor whose interest in its security (i.e., the collateral property) is

---

[*]See In re Development, Inc., 36 B.R. 998 (HI, 1984).

[**]See In re Koopsman, 22 B.R. 395 (UT, 1982); In re Shriver, 33 B.R. 176 (ND OH, 1983), Mikole Developers, Inc., 14 B.R. 524 (ED PA, 1981), La Jolla Mortgage Fund v. Kanche El Cajon Associates, 18 B.R. (SD CA, 1982) and In re Trina-Dee, Inc., 26 B.R. 152 (ED PA, 1983).

[***]See the following, respectively, Matter of R&M Porter Farms, Inc., 28 B.R. 88 (WD MO, 1984), In re G.Y. Trucking, Inc., 28 B.R. 59 (MD PA, 1982), and Matter of Holtkamp, 669 F.2d 505 (CA 7, 1982).

[****]See In re Attorneys Office Management, Inc., 29 B.R. 96 (CD CA, 1983).

legitimately threatened, is deemed NOT "adequately protected", while a creditor whose interest in its collateral property is not threatened, and who maintains during the course of the case the same (or better) position as it held when the case was filed, is considered "adequately protected." Under Section 361 of the Code, and as interpreted by the courts, the central purpose of the concept of "adequate protection" is to prevent creditor injury, to protect a secured creditor's interest by insuring that a secured creditor receives in value essentially what it bargained for, the underlying policy in bankruptcy being that secured creditors should not be deprived of the benefit of their bargain in a bankruptcy proceeding.

A classic example of a creditor who would be deemed "adequately protected" would be, for example, a secured creditor who is over-secured. This will be considered so because under such a circumstance the amount of the **'equity cushion'** — i.e., the amount by which the value of the collateral exceeds the amount of the creditor's secured claim — if it is at least sizeable, say in the 10 to 20 percent range, is calculated to be sufficient ("adequate protection") to prevent the creditor's interest in the collateral from being threatened.*

As might probably be expected, a major issue in cases applying the equity cushion theory, is that of valuing the collateral. While the secured creditors generally favor valuation (as of the date of the filing of the petition) based on the "liquidation value" of the property, the debtors usually favor a valuation based on the "going concern" value of the property. However, in keeping with the spirit of the Chapter 11 bankruptcy code, which is to rehabilitate and keep the debtor's business alive when at all practicable, the courts tend to favor a going concern value, especially in situations where and when the property in question forms a critical part of the business, where a successful reorganization appears feasible and the debtor seems to have a reasonable chance of remaining in business for a reasonable length of time. At any given time, for the equity cushion to continue to constitute adequate protection for the creditor, the property providing equity cushion may not be allowed to be threatened — a house, for example, must continue to be insured or maintained and kept in good repairs by the debtor in possession, and the real estate taxes on the property paid.

The equity cushion theory does not, of course, apply to partially-secured creditors — that is, creditors whose allowed claim exceeds the value of their collateral (the foreclosure proceeds). A partially secured creditor would generally be entitled to adequate protection (or, in the absence of that, a lifting of the stay), providing a showing can be made to the court that the value of its secured claim is unstable and declining, say, by depreciation in the overall value of the secured property or an increase in the amount of senior liens against the property.**

The motion procedures are rather simple. Only a "party in interest" — i.e., a creditor of the debtor or a legal holder of the right sought to be enforced — may file a motion seeking relief from the automatic stay. The creditor files the motion asking for relief from automatic stay with the court, specifying therein the particular grounds thereof and the reliefs or order sought. (See a sample copy of the motion on p. 168, titled *Motion For Relief From Automatic Stay*). Thereafter, a copy of the motion must be served by the creditor by first class mail or

---

* In determining whether an equity cushion exists, only the lien of the creditor seeking the relief and senior liens against the property are considered, and no junior liens are considered. (See In re Mellor, 734 F.2d 1396 (CA 9, 1984)). For use of the theory of equity cushion in bankruptcy generally, see In re Mallas Enterprises, Inc., 37 B.R. 964 (BAP 9, 1984), In re Mary Harpley Builders, Inc., 44 B.R. 151 (ND OH, 1984), In re Carson, 34 B.R. 502 (KS, 1983), and in re Bramnan, 38 B.R. 459 (NV, 1984).

** See In re Houston, 32 B.R. 584 (SD NY, 1983) and In re Penney, 52 B.R. 816 (ED NC, 1985).

personal service upon the trustee or debtor in possession, and upon such other persons as the court may direct. The case is then set for a hearing before a bankruptcy judge on a designated date, and the "final" hearing on the motion must be commenced within 30 days of the filing of the motion, except that the court may hold a "preliminary" hearing (this hearing does not necessarily have to be evidentiary hearing) during the 30 day period and order the stay continued pending the conclusion of the final hearing.

In general, at such hearings on a motion for relief, except on the sole issue of whether the debtor has an equity in the property in question, which is the only situation when the creditor would be the party having the burden of proof, the burden of proof is on the party opposing the relief (usually the debtor in possession) on all other issues; and *it would be solely the debtor in possession's burden to show the court sufficient reasons and grounds why the relief being sought from the automatic stay should not be granted.* Thus, assuming, for example, that the ground for which the creditor filed the motion, is on the basis of allegation that there is lack of adequate protection of the creditor's interest in property, it would be the task of the debtor in possession (or the trustee, if applicable) to show before the court that the interest of the creditor in the property is, actually, adequately protected.

Upon the court's determination of the motion, if the court rules that the creditor's interest in the collateral is not adequately protect, the court may either require the debtor in possession to adequately protect the interest of the creditor in the property or grant the creditor's request for relief from the stay permitting the creditor to proceed against the property. Generally, though, if it is demonstrated to the court that the property is of such nature that it is necessary for the rehabilitation of the debtor's business, the court will normally permit the debtor in possession to adequately protect the creditor's interest, and would require the debtor in possession (or the trustee) to propose the form and extent of the adequate protection to be provided, as the courts have held that it is the debtor's function, and not the court's, to formulate what would constitute adequate protection in a given case.

Adequate protection may take several different forms. It may be in the form of a single cash payment, or periodic payments, in an amount approximately equal to the periodic decrease in value of the collateral. Or, it may be in the form of providing an additional replacement lien, or permitting the creditor's lien to attach to the proceeds of the sale if it is necessary to sell property constituting a creditor's security, or granting the creditor in question some other relief as will give the creditor the unquestionable equivalent of its interest in the property, or in the form of unconditional, perhaps secured guarantees by third parties with substantial means (e.g., an FHA insurance or VA guarantee on a loan for a loan), or a combination of these.

B. Operation of the Business By the Debtor in Possession

A second major area to be addressed in this chapter relating to the practical issues involved in the exercise by the debtor in possession of the basic duties and responsibilities of the debtor in possession in a Chapter 11 case, is *the operation of the debtor's business.* As previously explained elsewhere in the manual (see, for example, pp.79-80, 82-3)in most Chapter 11 cases the debtor generally acts as the "debtor in possession" during the course of the case, leaving the debtor-turned-debtor-in-possession to remain in control, management and operation of the debtor's business with all the rights, powers and duties attendant thereto.

The Bankruptcy Code Section 1106(a) and 704, which are made applicable to a debtor in possession by Section 1107(a), sets forth the following duties for a Chapter 11 debtor in possession:[*]

(1)   account for and administer all property of the debtor's estate;

(2)   if a purpose would be served, examine proofs of claim and object to the allowance of improper claims;

(3)   unless the court orders otherwise, furnish such information concerning the estate and its administration as may be requested by a party in interest;

(4)   file with the court, the United States trustee, and any appropriate governmental taxing authorities, periodic reports and summaries of the operation of the debtor's business, including a statement of receipts and disbursements, and such other information as the United States trustee or the court may required;

(5)   make a final report and file a final account of the administration fo the estate with the court and with the United States trustee;

(6)   as soon as practicable, either file a plan under 11 U.S.C. 1121, file a report as to why a plan will not be filed, or recommend conversion of the case to Chapter 7 or 13;

(7)   for any year for which the debtor has not filed a tax return required by law, furnish to the taxing authority, without personal liability, any required information that is available;

(8)   after confirmation of a plan, file such reports as are necessary or as the court may order;

(9)   file motion to compel the turnover to the debtor in possession of any money or property of the estate in the hands of a third party which was repossessed, seized or otherwise obtained from the creditor prior to the commencement of the case.[**]

(10)   require an accounting and delivery, or the value thereof, of the property to the debtor in possession, any property that the debtor may need to use, sell, lease or exempt, which is in the possession or control of an entity other than a custodian; and

(11)   Segregate and account for all "cash collateral" that is at any time in the debtor in possession's custody, possession or control [Sec. 363(c)(4) of the Code]

---

[*]11 U.S.C. 1106(a) and 704, which are made applicable to a debtor in possession by 11 U.S. C. 1107(a).

[**]See 11 U.S.C. 542(a) In re California Gulf Partnership, 48 B.R. 959 (ED LA, 1984), In re H. Wolfe Iron & Metal Co., 64 B.R. 754 (WD PA, 1986), and Pied Piper Casuals, Inc., 50 B.R. 549 (SD NY, 1985).

And the Bankruptcy Rules require the following additional duties of a chapter 11 debtor in possession:[*]

(1)   if the court so directs, file with the United States trustee and with the court a complete inventory of the debtor's property within 30 days after entering on its duties, unless such inventory was previously filed;

(2)   keep a record of the receipt and disposition of all money and property received;

(3)   file the reports and summaries required by statute within the times fixed by the court, which, if payments are made to employees, shall include a statement of the amount of deductions for all taxes required to be withheld or paid for on behalf of employees, and the place where these amounts are deposited;

(4)   as soon as practicable after the commencement of the case, give notice of the case to every entity known to be holding money or property subject to withdrawal or order of the debtor, including every bank, financial institution, public utility company, and landlord with whom the debtor has a deposit, and to every insurance company which has issued a policy having a cash surrender value payable to the debtor, except that notice need not be given to any entity who has knowledge of the case or who has been previously notified of the case;

(5)   in every county in which real estate of the debtor is located, file a notice or copy of the petition in the office where transfers of real estate are recorded;

(6)   within 30 days after the date of an order confirming a plan or within such other time as the court may fix, file a report with the court concerning the action taken by the debtor in possession and the progress made in the consummation of the plan and file further reports as the court may direct until the plan has been consummated;

(7)   after consummation of a plan, file an application for a final decree; and

(8)   cooperate with the U.S. trustee by furnishing such information as the U.S. trustee may reasonably require in supervising the administration of the estate, and furnish him or her and file with the clerk regular reports of operations of the debtor's business as such trustee may require.

Promptly after the filing of a Chapter 11 case, certain functions must be performed by or for a debtor in possession in order to comply with the general provisions of the Bankruptcy Code and Rules and with the local rules. These functions include the following:

(1)   open one or more new bank accounts in the name of the debtor in possession (e.g., "JOHN DOE, INC., AS DEBTOR IN POSSESSION IN CASE NO......."), and deposit any funds received after the filing of the case exclusively in such new accounts;

---

[*]See Bankruptcy Rules 2015(a) and X-1007.

(2) amend such items as insurance policies, utility contracts, and agreements with suppliers to show the debtor in possession (as opposed to the debtor) as the insured and responsible party;

(3) make arrangements for the payment of necessary business expenses, including, if necessary, making application to the court for an order authorizing the payment of accrued salaries or wages of the debtor's employees for services performed prior to the commencement of the case; [see sample *Application for Allowance of and Authorization to Pay Claims of Debtor's Employees for Prefiling Wages"* on p.196].

(4) make arrangements for the preparation and filing of any periodic operating or financial reports required by the local office of the United States Trustee or the court, as called for by the local reporting requirements thereof;

(5) make application to the U.S. trustee or the courts for prior approval of any compensation to be paid to officers of the debtor in possession, as may be required by the local district, as your local rules may prohibit compensation of such personnel except upon prior court approval;

(6) make application to the court for approval for the employment and compensation by the debtor in possession of any professionals to be employed in the case, such as an attorney, an accountant or appraiser, etc.

(7) take a complete inventory of the debtor's property if so directed by the court or if required by the local district's rules;

(8) investigate and examine the executory contracts and unexpired lease of the debtor and determine which ones the debtor in possession is to reject, or assume or assign at any time during the course of the case or under a plan.

C. Use, Sale, or Lease of Cash Collaterals by the Debtor in Possession

Another common problem of practical nature often arising in a Chapter 11 case in the administration phase of the case following the initial filing of the petition, has to do with *the use, sale or lease of the so-called 'cash* collaterals' by the debtor in possession.

The question for this discussion is: what are the permissible procedures for using, selling or leasing a cash collateral and how do you practically do this?

To obtain funds to meet its payroll or other regular or day-to-day business expenses, the debtor in possession will usually find it necessary to use (or sell or lease) what is known as "cash collateral", during the course of a Chapter 11 case.

What Constitutes Cash Collateral?

Under the Bankruptcy Code, there are two basic types of collaterals: cash collaterals, and all other collaterals. Cash collaterals are simply the more LIQUID kinds of assets, those which are more readily convertible to cash. They include: cash, negotiable instruments, documents of title, securities, bank deposit accounts, or other cash equivalents in which the debtor estate and another entity have an interest; plus the proceeds, products, offspring, rent, or profits of property, subject to a security interest, if the security agreement so provides.*

Cash collaterals normally arise out of a situation when a secured creditor has a security interest (a lien) in cash or some cash equivalent of the debtor. For example, the creditor may have originally had a lien on the cash collateral itself (say, on a bank account, or on stock or bonds of the debtor), or it may have originally.had a lien on the debtor's property (e.g., its accounts receivable) that is later turned into cash, or it may have had a lien on real or personal property of the debtor that later produces profits, rents or other income.

Cash or other property received by the debtor in possession **after** (as opposed to **before**) the commencement of the Chapter 11 case, may or may not constitute "cash collateral" for a given case depending on the facts of a case. *Here's the simple determining rule:* if a creditor has a "pre-petition" security interest in the property of the debtor estate (i.e., in one existing <u>prior</u> to the filing of the bankruptcy petition), and the tenure of the security agreement creating such security interest so provides that the creditor's security interest shall extend to proceeds, product, offspring, rents or profits of the property, then in that case the creditor's security interest does extend to any such proceeds, product, rent, etc. of the secured property acquired by the estate <u>after</u> the commencement of the Chapter 11 case (unless otherwise ordered or modified by the court), and such "post-petition" proceeds, product, rents, etc., would be deemed to constitute "cash collaterals."**

Making Use of Cash Collateral

What is the precise procedure by which you (i.e., the debtor in possession) actually make use (or sell or lease) the cash collateral at our disposal? Under the Bankruptcy Code [Section 363(c)(2)], the debtor in possession (or the trustee, if applicable) may not use, sell or lease cash collateral unless each entity that has an interest in the cash collateral consents to the act, or unless the court, after notice and a hearing, authorizes such use, sale or lease. In practice, the way it works out is that the debtor in possession (or the trustee) wishing to use a cash collateral would usually seek, first, to obtain the consent of the creditors having valid security interest in the cash collateral in question. And, only if and when such content is not forthcoming from the creditors for the proposed use, would the debtor usually seek authorization from the court.

To seek authorization from the court, the debtor in possession simply files an application ("motion"). for that purpose with the court requesting authority to use specified cash collateral. [See a sample copy of such a motion on p. 174, titled *"Motion for Authority to Use Cash Collateral and Notice of Hearing thereof"*. At the same time, if feasible, while filing the motion, you'll confer with the court clerk and obtain a hearing date at the same time on the motion which will then be entered in the notice of hearing part of the form. Thereafter, copies of the Motion and of the Notice of Hearing will be served, by personal service or first class

---

*See Sections 363(a) and 552(b) of the Code for these definitions.

**·As for income from income-producing real estate or other property that is subject to a mortgage or other security agreement containing an 'assignment of rents' clause, the post-petition income from such property may or may not constitute cash collateral depending on whether the secured creditor's right to such income has been "perfected" (by procedures such as appointment of a receiver or obtaining a court order of sequestration of rents, for example). If an assignment of rents is self-executing under state law, the secured creditor's interest attaches to the rents and the rental income constitutes cash collateral. But if, on the other hand, assignment of rents is not self-executing under the state law, then the rental income does not automatically constitute cash collateral; the secured creditor must take a specific action required under the law to perfect its security interest in the rents before such rental income may constitute cash collateral. [See <u>Butner v. United States</u>, 440 U.S. 48, 99 S.Ct. 914, 59 L. Ed.2d 136 (1979); In re <u>Pine Lake Village Apartment Co.</u>, 17 B.R. 829 (SD NY, 1982); <u>Matter of Village Properties, Ltd.</u>, 723 F.2d 441 (CA 5, 1984).

125

mail, on every party having an interest in the cash collateral in question, and on any creditors' committee appointed in the case or its authorized agent, or, if no committee has been appointed, on the respective creditors listed in the list of 20 largest unsecured creditors filed by the debtor, and on such other parties as the court may direct. If an emergency or immediate need for use of the cash collateral exists, the motion should include a request for *preliminary hearing,* and indicate some specifics about the necessity, such as the possibility that the estate will suffer imminent and irreparable damage unless immediate relief is granted.

The court is required to act promptly on such a motion. The hearing on such a motion must be scheduled in accordance with the needs of the debtor, and if the motion so requests, the court may conduct a preliminary hearing earlier than 15 days after service of the motion, even as early as 72 hours after notice to creditors. The hearing may be *"preliminary" hearing,* or it may be consolidated with a *"final" hearing* on a creditor's request for adequate protection.

At such hearings it is common for creditors secured by the cash collateral to contend that the proposed use or sale of the cash collateral by the debtor would threaten their security and to demand that adequate protection be provided for their interest in the cash collateral, or that they be relieved from the automatic stay in order to reclaim or protect their security. The debtor (or trustee) has the burden of proof on such matters, and *you (the debtor in possession) had better come to the hearing fully prepared to present facts and evidence showing that the creditor will, indeed, be adequately protected.*

D. Use, Sale or Lease of Other Estate Property Other Than Cash Collateral

What if you must, as is often the case in most Chapter 11 cases, use or sell or lease some property of the bankruptcy estate which are not of the "cash collateral" kind — the non-cash collateral property? Under Sections 363(b)(1), and (c)(1) and 1107(a) of the Bankruptcy Code, the non-cash collateral property of the debtor's estate (all other estate property other than cash collateral) are divided into two categories: **(1)** those which generally occur in the ordinary course of business, and **(2)** those which do not occur in the ordinary course of business. For our purposes here, we will simply define the non-cash collateral used in the ordinary course of business as the debtor's business inventory. *With respect to such property (i.e., the non-cash collateral used in the ordinary course of business), the procedure is rather simple: the debtor in possession may generally sell or lease such property (or use them up) in the ordinary course of business, without notice to anyone or a court order.*

And what about non-cash collateral not used in the ordinary course of business? The Bankruptcy Code stipulates (see Sec. 363(b)(1) thereof) that such property may be disposed of (i.e., used, sold or leased) only "after notice and a hearing" to the parties in interest. Under the Code [Sec. 102(1)], though, the phrase "after notice and a hearing" is interpreted as meaning "after notice but without a hearing unless someone asks for one."[*] Consequently, in practice, what it all boils down to is that the debtor needs only usually give a notice of its intention to use or sell or lease such property and then proceed to undertake the transaction. (And if, of course, a creditor or other party in interest should timely ask for a hearing, then [and only then] will a hearing be held to seek determination by the court.)

The procedure is rather simple. Upon filing a notice of such proposed use or sale with the court clerk (see a sample of such notice on p. 185, titled *"Notice of Proposed Sale of Estate Property Not in the Ordinary Course of Business"*), the clerk or some other person as the

---

[*]See also, In re Northern Star Industries, 38 B.R. 1019 (ED NY, 1980) for a parallel judicial interpretation.

court may direct, must give, by first class mail, at least 20 days notice of the proposed use, sale (or lease) of the estate property, to all creditors, the creditors' committees, if any has been appointed in the case, the U.S. trustee, and all known bidders, unless otherwise directed by the court as to the parties to be given notice or the method of giving notice.

On the request of an entity that has an interest in the property in question, the court, with or without a hearing, may prohibit or condition the proposed use, sale or lease as is necessary to provide adequate protection to the interest of such entity in the property. As always, the burden of proof is on the debtor (or trustee) at any such hearing to make a showing that a creditor whose security may be affected by the proposed transaction will be adequately protected, e.g., by providing that the lien of the secured creditor should attach to the proceeds of the proposed sale or lease.

Sale of such property used outside the ordinary course of business are governed by Rule 6004(f). Such sale may be by private or public auction, whatever appears to be more beneficial to the estate, and an itemized statement of the property sold and the receipts thereof filed with the court by the debtor in possession or the auctioneer.

E. Handling Claims and Security Interests by the Debtor in Possession

In order to be able to prepare a realistic Chapter 11 plan that is both feasible for the debtor or the court and acceptable to creditors, it would often be necessary that the accurate status and amount of all the significant claims be determined and fixed. It would be for the debtor in possession (or the trustee or the authorized representative, such as a knowledgeable lawyer or accountant) to determine, for example, the status of those claims that are disputed, contingent, or unliquidated, the **"allowed"** amount of each secured claim, and the status and amount of any priority claims, since such claims must often be paid in full as of the effective date of the plan.

As a rule, it is customary for the debtor against whom the creditors have a claim or interest to inform the creditors of the filing of a bankruptcy petition by the debtor, or at least for the creditors to be otherwise informed of the filing. It is rare, however, for a creditor to be specifically informed of the specific amount of its claim listed in the debtor's bankruptcy petition papers, or whether the claim is listed as "disputed," "contingent," or "unliquidated." Consequently, IT IS USUALLY UP TO THE CREDITOR, HIMSELF RATHER THAN THE DEBTOR, TO ASCERTAIN THE STATUS AND AMOUNT OF ITS CLAIM, AS LISTED IN THE CHAPTER 11 BANKRUPTCY PAPERS FILED BY THE DEBTOR WITH THE COURT, AND TO DETERMINE WHETHER IT IS ACCURATE.

An important rule[*] of great relevance here under the Chapter 11 bankruptcy procedures, is that *so long as a claim or interest is listed in the debtor's petition schedules, the proof of claim or of interest is deemed filed with respect to such claim or interest, unless the claim or interest is listed as "disputed", "contingent", or "unliquidated". And, furthermore, that if a claim or interest is listed on such schedules as "disputed", "contingent", or "unliquidated" (or is not listed at all), then* a Proof of Claim or Interest — i.e., a formal statement of request

---

[*]See especially Bankruptcy Code Sec. 1111(a) and Rule 3003(c)(2).

for allowance of claim or interest against a debtor — must be filed with the court for the claim or interest to be allowable either for voting purposes or for distribution.

*In practice, creditors have found that it is usually less of a hassle for the average creditor to prepare and file a proof of claim or interest than for it to run to the courthouse to examine the filed schedules. Hence, a creditor or equity security holder will, as a rule, usually file a proof of its claim or interest with the debtor on a routine basis. The creditor's **"Proof of Claim"** is simply a written statement setting forth a creditor's claim and the particulars of such claim (see a sample copy of this form on p. 181, titled).*

Under the bankruptcy rules,* the creditor must file such Proof of Claim (and/or Proof of Interests, if applicable) with the clerk of the bankruptcy court within a specified time fixed by the court for filing proofs of claims or interests. The court clerk or some other party as the court may direct, is required to give all creditors by mail at least 20 days notice of the date fixed within which such proofs are to be filed. And, a proof of claim or interest concerning a claim or interest that is not listed in the debtor's schedules, or that is listed but designated as *"disputed", ."contingent", or "unliquidated",* must be filed by the creditor with the clerk by that designated date, or the claim or interest will be barred for purposes of voting or distribution. The debtor in possession or trustee, however, or an entity that is liable to the creditor with the debtor, or that has secured the creditor, may, until 30 days after the designated "bar date", file a claim with the court in the name of the creditor for any creditor who does not file a proof of claim by the first date set for the meeting of creditors.

Duty to Examine Proofs of Claim & File Objections To Improper Claims

One very important responsibility for the debtor in possession (and/or its representatives, such as the designated attorney or accountant), is to scrutinize the statements of claims ("Proofs of Claim") filed by the creditors (and by equity security holders, if applicable), and to be able to file objections contesting allowance of any claims that are improper or inflated.

To begin with, it is important for you to note that, for the creditor, the filing of proof of claim by a creditor constitutes only the aspect that could be called the "easy part" in the process for him. There remains for the creditor the more significant part: to collect on or enforce the claim! For the creditor to be able to do this, the creditor's claim must be **"allowed"** by the court. Under the bankruptcy rules [see Rule 3001(f)], *the principle involved is simple: a properly executed and filed** proof of claim (or proof of interest) automatically constitutes prima facie evidence of the validity and amount of the claim; and a properly filed proof of claim is deemed "allowed" unless a party in interest timely objects to the allowance of the claim.*

To examine a creditor's proof of claims and interests, you (i.e., the debtor in possession or the party acting for you) will usually start out by making a trip to the bankruptcy clerk's office, preferably soon after the **"bar date"** fixed for the filing of proofs of claim by creditors. Then, if you determine that a given claim (or claims) is improper as to the status or amount being claimed, you'll file objection papers with the court to the allowance of the said claim or claims. In practice, most such objections are usually filed <u>after</u> the confirmation of a plan, and hearings on such objections are often consolidated and heard by the court as a single hearing.

Simply, to object, you file with the court a written statement such as the form statement reproduced on p.192 titled ***"Objection to Allowance of Claim and Notice of Hearing Thereof"***.

---

*Rules 3003(c)(2), (3), 20002(a)(8). See also, Rules 3004 & 3005 and Section 1501(b)(c) of the Code.

. **For example, to be properly filed, assuming a claim or interest in the debtor's property which secures the claim is based on a writing, the original copy of the writing (or a duplicate thereof) must be filed with the proof of claim. Proof of claim filed for a security interest in property of debtor must be accompanied by evidence that the security interest has been "perfected" (Bankruptcy Rule 3001).

A copy of the statement of objection, with a notice of the hearing thereof attached to it, must be served by mail or personal delivery on the following parties: the creditor, the debtor, the trustee (if there's any serving in the case), and the United States trustee.

It is on the debtor's party that the burden of proof lies in this matter; it must present credible evidence at such a hearing in proof of the disallowability of the proof of claim in question. The court must determine the amount of a claim in dollars and cents as of the date of the filing of the petition and allow the claim in that amount, to the extent that it is allowable. The general rule is that only claims which actually existed against the debtor (as distinguished from the debtor in possession or trustee) as of the time of the filing of the petition — in short, the "pre-petition" claims — are allowable, and that, with a few exceptions*, allowance of post-petition claims is precluded. Note, however, that this refers only to the post-petition claims against the <u>trustee</u> or <u>debtor</u>; it does not refer to, and hence should not be confused with, the post-petitions against the debtor-in-possession or the trustee — i.e., those arising in the ordinary course of operating the debtor's business <u>after</u> the bankruptcy petition had been filed, since these latter types of claims are, on the other hand, allowable, and are in deed even treated as "priority" type claims under the post-petition administrative expense of the debtor's affairs.

With respect to SECURED claims (as differentiated from unsecured claims), briefly sketched, *the allowability of such claims is dependent on three factors:* the allowability of the underlying claim against the debtor (i.e., does the creditor in fact have an interest in the property?); the validity of the creditor's lien (i.e., does the creditor have a valid lien on the property?); and the value of the collateral or the amount of the setoff (is the claim subject to a setoff?) To sum it up briefly, **first,** the underlying claim must be allowed; **next,** the lien securing the claim must be valid against the avoiding powers of the trustee or debtor in possession under both the bankruptcy and non-bankruptcy law in order for the secured claim to be secured. (Thus, if a secured claim is disallowed for one reason or the other for which a lien securing a disallowed claim is voidable in bankruptcy — say, for example,because a lien or security interest has not been perfected, or because the lien is an invalid statutory lien, or is preferential or fraudulent or the result of an invalid judicial proceeding — the (disallowed) secured claim will become only an **unsecured** claim.) Then **thirdly,** upon the underlying claim being allowed, and upon the lien securing the claim being valid, the third factor in the determination of the allowability of the secured claim then becomes important — namely, the question of the value of the collateral. If the value of the creditor's interest in the collateral (property) securing the claim EQUALS OR EXCEEDS the amount of the claim (and there are no senior liens or surcharges against the property), the claim is deemed fully secured and this type of creditor — the so-called **"fully secured"** creditor — should expect to realize the full value of its claim. But if, on the other hand, the value of the creditor's interest in the collateral that secures the claim is <u>LESS</u> than the amount of its claim (and, assuming that the so-called

---

*Such as claims arising from recovery of money or property by the debtor or trustee, or from rejection by the trustee or debtor of an executory contract or unexpired lease, a tax claim against the debtor arising after the filing of the petition, or claims arising in the ordinary course of the debtor's business during the "gap period" between the filing of the petition and the order of relief or the appointment of a trustee in an involuntary bankruptcy case.

Section 1111(b) election* is not exercised by the creditor), then the creditor's secured claim is allowable only to the extent of the value of its interest in the collateral, and the balance of its claim will become only **unsecured** claim. This latter type of creditor is called **"partially secured"** creditor. Similarly, a creditor having a right of setoff is also partially secured — only to the extent of the value of its setoff.**

Fourthly and finally, the question of the valuation of the creditor's collateral becomes important in the process of determining the amount of the allowed secured claim. As a practical matter, in valuation matters of such kind, the trustee or debtor in possession would normally favor a low valuation for the collateral, while the creditor would normally favor a high valuation for it. For those kinds of collaterals that possess an identifiable market (e.g., real estate, stocks and bonds or automobiles), the court will generally assess the value of such property on the basis of the fair market value or the price the property would command if sold in an orderly commercial manner. For the kinds of secured property having no readily identifiable market, on the other hand, the property is valued in a variety of other methods, including determination of its liquidation value. In any event, whatever method employed, it should be clearly noted and emphasized that the whole issue of valuation is a very subjective matter and, in the final analysis, the court exercises wide discretion on the matter both in terms of the method of valuation to be used and the determination of the value for the claims.* * *

---

*In other words, the partially-secured creditor not exercising the so-called Section 1111(b) election is treated as having two distinct claims for voting and distribution purposes--part secured claim, and part unsecured. If, however, Section 1111(b) election is exercised by the creditor, the claim of a partially-secured creditor is treated as being fully secured, in stead. Basically, there are two types of partially-secured creditors: the so-called "recourse creditors" (ones having the rights of payment of the claims against both the collateral and the debtor), and the "non-recourse creditors" (ones not having rights against the debtor separately, but only against the property). As provided for under Section 1111(b) of the Code, in a Chapter 11 case a non-recourse claim shall be treated as a recourse claim unless EITHER the class of which the claim is a part elects to have a sub-section of the Code, Section 1111(b)(2) thereof, apply to it OR the collateral is sold during the case or under the plan. To put it another way, what this means is that a non-recourse claim will be treated as a recourse claim unless the collateral securing the claim is sold or the class of which it is a part elects to have Section 1111(b)(2) apply. And what would be the benefit to a partially-secured creditor (or claimant) who so elects to have subsection 1111(b)(2) apply? The partially-secured creditor (or claimant) which elects to have the subsection 1111(b)(2) apply, will have its claim treated as being a **fully secured** claim to the extent that the claim is allowed. Thus, by electing under Section 1111(b) of the Code to have the subsection 1111(b)(2) apply, a creditor can get its partially-secured claim to be treated as fully secured for the purposes of distribution and payment under the plan. Note, however, that as alluded to earlier above, the Section 1111(b) election may be exercised only if the collective interests of the class of partially-secured claims in the particular collateral is of substantial value, or if a claim in the class is a recourse claim and the collateral securing the claim is sold during the case or under the plan. Also, to exercise the Section 1110(b) election (to have the subsection 1111(b)(2) apply), the affirmative vote of at least two-thirds in amount and one-half in number of the allowed claims in a class is required.

**The right of setoff, granted under Section 506(1a) of the Code, is a very important one in a Chapter 11 case in that a creditor having a right of setoff has *the same rights and entitlements as a secured creditor*. Basically, a setoff is a right between two parties to net out their respective debts or claims against each other independently arising out of different, unrelated transactions, thereby leaving one party with a net indebtedness to the other. Determining whether a creditor has a right of setoff generally is a matter for state law, and not of the bankruptcy law.

* * * See the following on the general considerations in valuation of collateral and the courts' exercise of discretionary powers thereof: Cohen, 13 B.R. 350 (ED NY, 1981); In re Yoder, 32 B.R. 777 (WD PA, 1983); Matter of Cooper, 7 B.R. 537 (ND GA, 1980), Matter of QPL Components, Inc., 20 B.R. 342 (ED, NY, 1982); and In re Klein, 10 B.R. 657 (ED NY, 1981).

F. Handling Executory Contracts and Unexpired Leases

It may at times be necessary in a Chapter 11 case for a debtor in possession (or trustee) to seek to terminate or renegotiate or modify an executory contract or unexpired lease. The terms of the contract or lease previously signed in the past may have turned out to be so burdensome at this time that any chance of survival of the debtor's business may depend on such contract or lease being terminated or modified. Say, for example, that the debtor had entered into an ill-advised contract to sell property or services at prices which are now so low that the debtor can no longer make profit or still remain in business if it were to comply with the terms of the contract. Or, on the other hand, that the debtor had entered into some lucrative contracts or leases that it wishes to preserve or assign to a third party for profit. *Indeed, some experts maintain that the need to reject or renegotiate such contracts may frequently be a principal reason for filing Chapter 11 bankruptcy in the first place.* One reason this is held to be so is because under the Bankruptcy Code, except for a few limited exceptions, a trustee or debtor in possession may unilaterally assume, reject or assign an executory contract or unexpired lease, often with the approval of the court, but without the need to obtain the consent of the other party.* Further, a trustee or debtor in possession may assume, reject or assign most executory contracts or unexpired leases either by motion made to the court during the course of the Chapter 11 case or under the plan. And if, on the other hand, an executory contract is neither assumed nor rejected or assigned in the course of a Chapter 11 case, such executory contract or unexpired lease would remain in effect and passes with the debtor's property to the reorganized debtor. Furthermore, under the Code [Sec. 365(e)(1)], all so-called *'ipso facto clauses'* contained in an executory contract or unexpired lease — i.e., clauses which basically provide that a contract or lease is automatically terminated if a debtor should file for bankruptcy or become insolvent — are unenforceable and of no legal effect as against a trustee or debtor in possession.

Briefly defined, basically a contract is "EXECUTORY" (or "UNEXPIRED") when there is still a portion of the contract that is still unperformed by one party of the other or both, and the creditor is, in effect, to provide you something in the future in return for some payment on your part. Common examples of executory contracts in business include service contracts, unexpired leases, real estate contracts, license agreements, supply agreements, employment contracts, maintenance agreements, consulting agreements, timeshare contracts or leases, copyright leases, car lease, and collective bargaining agreements.

What is the procedure in a situation where the debtor is already in default on an executory contract or unexpired lease when the bankruptcy petition is filed? In such a situation the ability of the trustee or debtor in possession to **assume** the contract or lease depends on whether the other party has taken steps necessary to terminate the contract prior to the filing of bankruptcy. With respect to the post-petition period (i.e., for the period falling <u>after</u> bankruptcy has been filed), the rule is that the other party to the contract is precluded by the "automatic stay" mechanism and may not therefore take action to terminate such contract or lease. And, with regard to the pre-petition period (i.e., for the period falling <u>before</u> the filing of bankruptcy), the rule is that if, prior to the filing of bankruptcy, the other party to the contract has taken the action necessary to effectively terminate the contract due to the debtor's default, then there is no contract in existence at the time of the commencement of the bankruptcy case, hence no contract can be assumed. But, if, however, the other party has not taken the action necessary to effectively terminate the contract <u>prior</u> to the filing of

---

*See Sections 365(a), (f), 1107(a) and 1123(b)(2) of the Code, as well as <u>Matter of Central Watch, Inc</u>., 22 B.R. 561 (ED WI, 1982).

bankruptcy, only then may the trustee or debtor in possession assume the contract upon taking the proper steps to do so.

An executory contract or unexpired lease for which the debtor defaulted **prior** to the filing of bankruptcy (pre-petition default), or one for which the debtor in possession or trustee defaults after the filing of bankruptcy (post-petition default), **may be ASSUMED only if the following conditions exist at the time of the assumption:**

i) the trustee or debtor in possession cures the default or provides **"adequate assurance"** that the default will be promptly cured;
ii) the trustee or debtor in possession compensate the other party to the contract for any pecuniary loss he incurs as a result of the default, or provides adequate assurance that such compensation will be promptly provided; and
iii) the trustee or debtor in possession provides adequate assurance of future performance under the contract or lease.

And, **to ASSIGN an executory contract or unexpired lease** to a third party, a trustee or debtor in possession must meet the following conditions:

i) he must first "assume" the contract or lease as required above; and
ii) he must then provide adequate assurance of the future performance of the contract or lease by the proposed assignee, regardless of whether there has been a default under the contract or lease or not.

A key issue for the courts in making a determination as to whether the required conditions for assumption of a contract or lease have been met is: what constitutes *"adequate assurance"* of the future performance of a default for a given contract or lease? As interpreted by the courts, the degree of adequate assurance required in a given instance involving a given contract or lease depends greatly on the facts and circumstances of the particular case; it can range from a written or verbal assurance, to the posting of a performance bond, subject to the discretion of the court and the degree to which the assumption is shown to be necessary to the rehabilitation of the debtor's business is frequently a major factor in the making of such determination by the court.[*]

While the trustee or debtor in possession has broad powers to assume (or even to assign) executory contracts and unexpired leases, they have even greater powers to *"reject"* such contracts or leases. A Chapter 11 trustee or debtor in possession may reject virtually any executory contract or unexpired lease of the debtor that has not been previously assumed. To be rejectable, however, a contract must in fact be "executory" — that is, it may not have been substantially performed by one party or the other or both.

It should be noted that, as defined under the Code, *the rejection of an executory contract or unexpired lease by a trustee or debtor in possession does not mean cancellation of the contract or lease, but merely constitutes a "breach" of the contract or lease,* and thereby entitles the other party to the contract to a claim for damages for the breach of contract.[**] And, as a rule, such claim for damages is treated as if it had arisen **prior** to the filing of the bankruptcy petition and most frequently gives the other party (the damaged party) a nonpriority unsecured claim against the debtor's estate, except that in those rare instances when the damaged party is secured by a lien or setoff or a special priority, the claim may become a secured or priority claim, in part or in whole.

---

[*]See In re <u>Bon Ton Restaurant & Pastry Shop, Inc.</u>, 53 B.R. 789 (ND IL, 1985), and <u>Matter of Wesmac Computer Systems, Inc.</u>, 59 B.R. 87 (NJ, 1986).

[**]See Bankruptcy Code Sections 365(g) and 502(g). See also <u>Consolidated Oil and Gas, Inc. v. Sun Oil Co. of Pennsylvania</u>, 16 B.R. 490 (CO, 1981).

The actual court procedures for assumption, rejection or assignment of executory contract or unexpired lease in a Chapter 11 case, is quite simple. Simply put, an executory contract or unexpired lease may be assumed, rejected, or assigned either as part of a Chapter 11 plan, or by motion filed with the court under Bankruptcy Rule 6006. If done as part of a Chapter 11 plan, such matter will usually be handled as part and parcel of the normal procedures in the ordinary course of the plan confirmation process, and there is usually no separate proceeding or hearing for the proposed action. If handled, however, in any other way other than as part of a Chapter 11 plan, then the proceeding is a contested matter governed by Bankruptcy Rule 9014 involving the filing of a motion to assume or reject, and a hearing by the court on notice to the other party to the contract or lease and other parties in interest as the court may direct.* *(See sample copy of "Motion to Assume Executory Contract" on p. 182, and of "Motion to Reject Executory Contract" on p. 180)*.

> Under the applicable rules, the trustee or debtor in possession may unilaterally assume or reject an executory contract or unexpired lease of residential real property (but not of non-residential real property) or personal property of the debtor at any time <u>before</u> confirmation of a plan, and may not be compelled by the other party to the contract to assume or to reject a contract or lease, except that the court may, on a motion formally filed by the other party to a contract, compel the trustee or debtor in possession "to decide" within a specified period whether to assume or reject a contract or lease.

The central "test" applied by the courts in deciding whether to approve a motion to assume or reject an executory contract or unexpired lease, is the so-called *"business judgment rule"*. What this rule says, simply, is that if the trustee or debtor in possession elects to assume or reject a contract or lease, the court will simply respect that wish, and simply deem it a prudent "business judgment" of the trustee or debtor in possession and will approve it, if all necessary legal requirements for assumption or rejection have otherwise been met.** A showing by the trustee or debtor in possession simply that performance of the contract or lease will be advantageous to the debtor's estate and that the trustee or debtor in possession will be able to perform its obligations under the contract or lease, is sufficient proof to satisfy the business judgment standard where a contractual or lease **assumption** is at issue; while a showing only that the proposed rejection is in the best interest of the creditors and the debtor's estate, is sufficient to satisfy the business judgment standard where **rejection** of a contract or lease is at issue, and fairness or injury to the other party to the contract or lease is of no relevance in such a situation.

---

*See also Bankruptcy Rules 6006(b), 6006(c) and 7004.

**See the following: <u>Matter of Minges</u>, 602, F.2d 38 (CA 2, 1979), <u>Global International Airways</u>, 35 B.R. 881 (WD MO, 1983), In re <u>Coast Trading Co., Inc.</u> 26 B.R. 737 (OR, 1982), In re <u>Brada Miller Freight System, Inc.</u>, 702 F.2d 890 (CA 11, 1983), and In re <u>Chi-Feng Huang</u>, 23 B.R. 798 (BAP 9, 1982).

APPENDIX A

SAMPLE FORMS & REPORTS
CITED IN THE MANUAL AND/OR
TYPICALLY USEABLE IN
CHAPTER 11[*]
(Where to Find Them)

Schedule A—Real Property.. 35
Schedule B---Personal Property...35
Schedule C---Property Claimed As Exempt......................................37
Schedule D---Creditors Holding Secured Claims................................39
Schedule E---Creditors Holding Unsecured Priority Claims.....................41
Schedule F---Creditors Holding Unsecured NonPriority Claims..................43
Schedule G--- Executory Contracts & Unexpired Leases.........................45
Schedule H---Co-debtors..47
Schedule I---Current Income of Business Debtors..............................48
Schedule J---Current Expenditures of Business Debtors........................49
Summary of Schedules... 50
Declaration Concerning Debtor's Schedules.................................... 51
Statement of Financial Affairs... 52
List of Creditors Holding 20 Largest Unsecured Claims......................57-8
List of Equity Security Holders..59
Exhibit "A" To Voluntary Petition..60
Notice to Individual Consumers...61
Address Matrix...62
Form 1 –Voluntary Petition...63-4
Debtor's Resolution Authorizing Commencement of Case........................ 65
Request For Order That Creditors' Committee Not Be Appointed................. 66
The Blue Backer/Cover... 67

Appointment of a Creditors' Committee 135
Notice of First Meeting of Creditors & Stockholders 136
Order Directing the Appointment to Trustee 137
Debtor's Application to Terminate Trustee's Appointment 138
Trustee's or Examiner's Report of Investigation (a Model Sample)   139-143
Disclosure Statement (a Model Sample) 144-152
Disclosure Statement — A Model Sample 153-155
Notice of Hearing on Disclosure Statement 156
Plan of Reorganization (Corporate Debtor) — A Model Sample . .   157
Plan of Reorganization (Individual Debtor) — A Model Sample . . 161-166
Debtor's Plan of Reorganization (Corporate Debtor) — A Model Sample 167-169
Notice of Time for Filing Acceptances or rejections of Plan, of Time
  of Hearing on Confirmation, and of Time for Filing Objections
  to Confirmation 170

---

[*]All forms listed under "Initial Chapter 11 Voluntary Case: Debtor's Petition" (pp. 30-61) are reproduced herewith by courtesy of **Julius Blumberg Inc.** of New York. The rest of the forms or documents listed under Appendix A are by courtesy of **Matthew Bender & Company Inc.,** of New York, publishers of "Collier on Bankruptcy" series, and a handful of these forms or documents (some 3 of them), are by courtesy of **Argyle Publishing Co.,** of Lakewood, Colorado, publishers of *The Attorney's Handbook on Chapter 11 Bankruptcy.* Slight modifications have been made by this publisher in some of the forms and reports, in an attempt to obtain better economies or clarity for the purposes of our readers, where deemed necessary.

Ballot for Accepting or Rejecting Plan 171 1

Debtor's Modification of Plan (Before Confirmation) . . . . .172 !

Motion to Object to Confirmation of Plan 173 3

Order Confirming Plan of Reorganization (Corp. Debtor) . . . . .174-5 –5

Order Confirming Plan of Reorganization (Individual Debtor) 176 5

Notice of Order Confirming Plan and Discharge (Individual Debtor) . . .177 7

Motion for Relief from Automatic Stay 178

Trustee's (or Debtor's) Application for Authority to Incur Debt
(Obtained Credit) Secured by Property of Estate 179

Application by Trustee (or Debtor) for Authority to Reject Lease (or
Executory Contract) 180

Order Authorizing Trustee (Debtor in Possession) to Reject Executory
Contract/Lease 181

Application (Motion) for Authority to Assume Executory Contract/Lease 182

Order Authorizing Assumption of Executory Contract/Lease 181

Application (Motion) for Approval of Compensation of Debtor's Officers 183

Application for Authority to Use Cash Collateral 184

Application (*Motion) of the Debtor in Possession [Or Trustee] for
Authority to Employ Attorney for Special Purpose 185

Order Authorizing Employment of Attorney for Special Purpose 186

Application by Debtor in Possession for Authority to Employ Attorney
(Or Accountant, etc.) for General Services 187

Order Authorizing Employment of Attorney for General Service 186

Application (Motion) to Employ Accountants [or Appraisers,
Auctioneers, etc.] 188

Order Authorizing Employment of Accountants, Etc. 188

Application to Modify Account of Deposit With Utility Company . . . 189

Order Modifying Amount of Deposit with Utility Company 190

Proof of Claims 191

Objection to Allowance of Claim & Notice of Hearing Thereof 192

Complaint in Support of Objection to Secured Claim 193

Order Reducing Claim 192

Motion for Authority to Obtain Credit Not In Ordinary Course of Business 194

Notice of Proposed Sale of Estate Property, and of Hearing Thereof . . 195

Motion (Application) for Authority to Pay Claims of Debtor's
Employees for Pre-Filing Wages 196

Motion to Convert Case to Chapter 7 172

Appointment of Creditors' Committee

UNITED STATES BANKRUPTCY COURT
MIDDLE DISTRICT OF *LOUISIANA*

In re

Frederic Motor Company

Debtor

Docket No. . . . .
(Chapter 11)

Appointment of Creditors' Committee

The following persons, selected from unsecured creditors who are willing to serve, hereby are appointed as the creditors' committee in this case:

H.E. Blades, representing *Blades Insurance Agency*

A.T. Whetstone, representing *Ring Piston Company*

D. Givens, representing *Metals, Inc.*

T.E. Goyen, representing *Uncle Billy Rice Co.*

A.H. Stone, representing *First Bank of Madison*

John Wall, representing *Reo Motors, Inc.*

M. Power, representing *Louisiana Parts Company*

Dated: . . . ., 19. . .

. . . .
United States Bankruptcy Judge
Or

. . . .
United States Trustee

COVER LETTER TO TRANSMIT SOLICITATION ACCEPTANCES TO CREDITORS

Hardtimes Supply Company
4455 West 39th Avenue
Gary, Indiana 46404
April 2, 1998

TO: The creditors of Hardtimes Supply Co., Inc.

Subject: Chapter 11 Plan of Reorganization filed by Hardtimes Supply Co., Inc.

Dear Creditor:

As you may be aware, Hardtimes Supply Co., Inc. has filed a proceeding under Chapter 11 of the United States Bankruptcy Code to reorganize the financial aspects of its business under the protection of the bankruptcy court. The recession in the building industry and the financial failure of one of its principal customers are the main reasons that the bankruptcy proceeding was filed.

We are pleased to present for your acceptance and approval a plan for the repayment of as much of our debts as is possible under the circumstances. A copy of our plan is enclosed with this letter. Also enclosed for your information is a copy of a disclosure statement that has been approved by the bankruptcy court and a summary of the court's opinion approving the disclosure statement. The facts and figures supporting our plan are set forth in the disclosure statement. Please take the time to read both the disclosure statement and the plan carefully.

We would like the plan to be accepted by the creditors of every class of impaired claims. A claim that is not paid in full is an impaired claim. To be accepted by a class of claims, the plan must be accepted by more than one-half of the creditors in the class and by creditors holding at least two-thirds of the total dollar amount of claims in the class. Your vote on the acceptance or rejection of our plan is important.

We are enclosing with this letter an official ballot for voting on the acceptance or rejection of our plan. To be counted, this ballot must be properly completed and filed with the clerk of the bankruptcy court, 200 East Court Street, Gary, Indiana, by May 1, 1998. We hope that you will vote to accept our plan.

Once again, please fill out the enclosed ballot and return it to either the undersigned or the clerk of the bankruptcy court in time for the ballot to be counted.

Very truly yours,

Enclosures: Plan of Reorganization dated March 5, 1998
Disclosure Statement dated March 5, 1998
Court Order Conditionally Approving Disclosure Statement and Fixing Times and Dates
Ballot For Accepting or Rejecting Plan

_____
Joseph P. Jones, President,
Hardtimes Supply Co., Inc.

Notice of First Meeting of Creditors and Stock-holders, of Automatic Stay, and Related Matters

UNITED STATES BANKRUPTCY COURT
MIDDLE DISTRICT OF *LOUISIANA*

In re

    Frederic Motor Company,

                Debtor

Docket No..........
(Chapter 11)

Notice of First Meeting of Creditors and Stockholders and of Automatic Stay

TO THE DEBTOR, ITS CREDITORS AND STOCKHOLDERS, AND OTHER PARTIES IN INTEREST:

An order for relief under Chapter 11 of the Bankruptcy Code having been entered on ...., 19... based on a petition filed by [*or* against] *Frederic Motor Company* of *177 Florida Street, Baton Rouge, Louisiana*, notice is hereby given that:

1. The first meeting of creditors and stockholders shall be held at *Room 301, United States Courthouse, Baton Rouge, Louisiana* on ...., 19..., at 10 o'clock a.m.

2. The debtor shall appear by its president or other executive officer [*or, if the debtor is an individual* appear in person, *or if the debtor is a partnership* shall appear by a general partner] at that time and place for the purpose of being examined.

3. The debtor has filed or will file a schedule of debts pursuant to 11 U.S.C. section 521(1). Any scheduled creditor whose claim is not scheduled as disputed, contingent, or unliquidated as to amount, may, but need not, file a proof of claim in this case. Creditors whose claims are not listed, or whose claims are listed as disputed, contingent, or unliquidated as to amount and who desire to participate in the case or share in any distribution, must file their proofs of claim before approval of the debtor's disclosure statement [*or, if appropriate,* on or before a date to be later fixed of which you will be notified]. Any creditor who desires to rely on the list has the responsibility for determining that he is accurately listed.

You are further notified that:

The meeting may be continued or adjourned from time to time by announcement made in open meeting, without further written notice to creditors and stockholders.

At the meeting, the creditors may file their claims, the stockholders may file their proofs of interest, the debtor may be examined as permitted by the presiding officer, and such other business as may properly come before the meeting may be transacted.

The filing of the petition by [*or* against] the debtor operates as a stay of certain acts and proceedings against the debtor and its property as provided in 11 U.S.C. section 362.

[*If appropriate*] Mr./Ms..........., of .... has been appointed trustee of the estate of the above-named debtor.

Dated: ....

                        ....
                        Clerk of the Bankruptcy Court

Order Appointing (Directing the Appointment of)

UNITED STATES BANKRUPTCY COURT **Trustee**
DISTRICT OF *CONNECTICUT*

In re

Roe Hat Manufacturing Co.,
Inc.,
Debtor

Docket No..........
(Chapter 11)

Order Appointing (Directing the Appointment of) Trustee

The application of *John Doe*, an unsecured creditor of the above-named debtor, praying this Court to appoint a trustee having been heard on ...., 19...; due notice of the said hearing having been given earlier by personal service upon the debtor, and upon *George Green*, the attorney for the debtor; and the Court, after hearing the evidence presented and argument of counsel, having filed its findings of fact detailing the reasons for the appointment of a trustee in this case, NOW, in accordance with those findings, it is

ORDERED:

[Use the appropriate one of the following paragraphs]

1. That *George Wilson*, a disinterested person, be, and he hereby is, appointed trustee of the property of *Roe Hat Manufacturing Co., Inc.*, the above-named debtor, and his bond is fixed at *$50,000.*

1. That the United States trustee shall appoint forthwith a disinterested person as trustee of the above-named debtor.

2. *[Include such provisions regarding the operation of the business as the court may direct.]*

Dated: .... 19...

....
United States Bankruptcy Judge

138

Debtor's Application To Terminate Trustee's Appointment

UNITED STATES BANKRUPTCY COURT
DISTRICT OF *CONNECTICUT*

In re

Roe Hat Manufacturing Co., Inc.,

Debtor

Docket No..........
(Chapter 11)

Debtor's Application To Terminate Trustee's Appointment

The Application of *Roe Hat Manufacturing Co., Inc.*, the debtor, respectfully shows the court the following:

1. *George Wilson* was appointed trustee herein by order of the court dated ...., 19....

2. The said trustee has completed his investigation of the debtor and its affairs and has filed with the court and transmitted to the creditors committee and others a report of the results of that investigation.

3. The said trustee's report reflects that there is no evidence of fraud, dishonesty, incompetence, misconduct, mismanagement, or irregularity in the management of the affairs of the debtor, that no causes of action against any officer of the debtor, past or present, exist, and that a general improvement in market conditions has cured the cash flow problem which precipitated the filing of this case.

4. In the circumstances revealed by the trustee's report, there is no need for a continuation of the trustee in office. Such further continuation of his services will result only in a further accumulation of costs to the debtor and its estate, with no commensurate benefit to the debtor, its estate, its creditors, or its equity security holders.

WHEREFORE debtor prays that after notice and a hearing, the court may terminate the trustee's appointment and restore the debtor to possession and management of the property of the estate, and operation of the debtor's business.

Dated: ...., *19....*

(Signed) *Harold Green*
Attorney For The Debtor
2121 Second Avenue
Hartford, Connecticut
Tel. #.......

Report of Trustee's (or Examiner's) Investigation.

UNITED STATES BANKRUPTCY COURT
NORTHERN DISTRICT OF *TEXAS*
DALLAS DIVISION

In re

Allday Aluminum Company,

Debtor

Docket No..........
(Chapter 11)

Report of Trustee's Investigation

Your Trustee, *W.J. Ralph*, has investigated the acts, conduct, properties, liabilities, and financial condition of the Debtor, the operation of its business, and the desirability of the continuance thereof, and other matters relevant to this case and to the formulation of a Plan of Reorganization.

(A) HISTORY OF THIS CASE

This case was instituted by the voluntary petition of the Debtor filed on *September 17, 19....* Your Trustee was appointed and qualified. The first meeting of creditors and stockholders was held on *October 20, 19....*

(B) DEBTOR'S BUSINESS AND PLANT

The Debtor's business is the making of aluminum extrusions. Its facilities consist of 70,000 square feet in rented premises located approximately 20 minutes by auto from downtown *Dallas*.

Its manufacturing facilities include 2 aluminum extrusion presses and ancillary equipment. Maximum scrap utilization is made possible by a gas-fired aluminum remelt furnace of 60,000 pound capacity and a casting unit capable of molding 6 inch and 8 inch logs. This capacity is now being expanded so that Debtor may cast 10 inch logs.

The anodizing plant and finishing plant are well equipped with modern and sophisticated machines. The Debtor also owns a complete die making plant.

The plant presently employs approximately 75 personnel, including 11 office personnel. Prior to the petition, the office personnel consisted of 22 people. The reduction of office personnel has not resulted in any noticeable lack of efficiency.

The Debtor occupies an excellent position as regards the geographic location of competition. Its principal competition, from the standpoint of independent extruder capacity, comes from one plant in *South Texas*, one in *Arkansas*, and one in *Georgia*. Its nearest competition to the west is in *Arizona*.

An analysis of Debtor's customers shows that for a period of the past 5 years the Debtor has served 125 active customers from 10 states, with an average monthly purchase per customer of $1,500. Its customers include manufacturers of outdoor signs, store fronts, lighting fixtures, architectural shapes, boat framework and trim, windows and doors, and truck body manufacturers. During the Trustee's operations for the past 6 months, Debtor has enjoyed sales of approximately $870,000. Of these sales, less than $115,000 was to any one customer. It is apparent, therefore, that the Debtor is not dependent on any one customer or small group of customers, or on any single type of extrusion user.

(C) CORPORATE HISTORY OF THE DEBTOR

The Debtor was incorporated under the laws of the State of *Texas* on *April 13, 19....* Its original capitalization was 500,000 shares of common stock at a par value of $1 per share. The Articles of Incorporation were amended in 19.... to increase the authorized capitalization to 1,000,000 shares at the par value of 50 cents per share. There are now outstanding 585,000 shares of common stock of which 43,000 shares are held as treasury shares. 58,000 shares of preferred stock are outstanding.

In 19.... there was a public issue of 100,000 shares. At the time of the filing of the Chapter 11 petition herein, there were approximately 600 shareholders. No single stockholder owned more than 15% of the outstanding shares.

Some 5 years ago the Debtor commenced an expansion program, purchasing *Morris Plastics Co., Inc.* for 45,000 shares of its common stock and $515,000 cash. This subsidiary company manufactures windshields for boats and uses Debtor's extrusions exclusively. It is operated under the general supervision of the president of the Debtor, and currently shows a small operating profit.

Four years ago the Debtor purchased *Finnegan, Inc.* for 22,500 shares of its common stock, plus the guarantee of a $150,000 note to *Finnegan's* then sole shareholder. *Finnegan* was acquired as a fabricating subsidiary and became Debtor's principal customer for aluminum extrusions. As will be shown later in this report, Debtor's fabrication activity, particularly its curtain-wall business, was, in the opinion of your Trustee, the primary reason for the Debtor's financial difficulties. On the date of the petition in this case, *Finnegan* was indebted to the Debtor for $2,500,000. A decision was made by your Trustee to place *Finnegan* in chapter 7, and it is now being liquidated in this Court.

(D) FINANCIAL HISTORY OF THE DEBTOR

Attached hereto as Exhibits A, B, and C are comparative year-end balance sheets of the Debtor, profit and loss statements, and percentage analyses reflecting the results of Debtor's operations for the past *five* years. A study of these financial statements reveals the not uncommon picture of an overly ambitious company with modest capitalization and grossly inadequate working capital attempting too rapid expansion in a highly competitive industry, frantic borrowing ensuing, resulting in a totally insupportable debt-burden, and inevitable collapse.

Had the Debtor been content to remain in the aluminum extrusion business, it would undoubtedly be successful, just as the Trustee's operation has been successful. Since the extrusion business requires large capital investment in expensive presses and plant facilities, competitors are not numerous. But the fabricating of aluminum extrusions is highly competitive, in that capital investment requirements are not nearly so great.

But if the fabrication business, generally, proved unprofitable, the curtain-wall aspect of the business proved ruinous. It is difficult to break out cost and profit figures for a single phase of the

Debtor's business, but your Trustee is informed that Debtor lost $150,000 on one single curtain-wall job. True, *Finnegan* was the Debtor's principal customer, but when a customer is in chapter 7 and owes you $2,500,000, this is business that you could well have done without.

With the cost of goods sold averaging about 90% of net sales, and with slow payment from customers, especially from subsidiaries, it is apparent that working capital requirements were enormous. This forced the Debtor to go into public offerings, then to bank loans, then to inventory and receivable loans and fixed asset loans, then to financing through a factor, with interest rates nearly 4 points above prime rate. Also, equipment notes were issued to trade creditors. Interest expense during the brief history of the company exceeded $1,000,000.

Other factors contributed to the financial difficulties of the company. It was over-staffed, particularly with expensive executive talent. The pre-petition scrap rate ran as high as 33%, while post-petition scrap rate has been held to well under 25%. Since the filing of the petition, maximum use has been made of the remelt facilities, with resultant savings in the cost of aluminum. This facility was not utilized to the maximum during pre-petition operations.

It is true that under the Trustee's operation the most stringent economics have been effected, and the Trustee has been able to operate without the constantly recurring crises caused by the pre-petition debt-burden. It may not be realistic to expect that future operations can be continued with the favorable percentages recently experienced, but it is obvious that in prior years a "tighter ship" could have been run.

(D) ANALYSIS OF PRE-PETITION DEBT

1) Unsecured Claims:

	0 to $100	$500 to $1,000	$1,000 to $5,000	$5,000 and over
No. of Claims	55	28	36	13
Dollar Amount	$3091	$18,011	$49,844	$1,191,918

Total unsecured claims $1,262,865

These amounts are tentative. Some claims will be reduced by agreement or after contest.

2) Secured Claims:

W.T. Financial Corporation $467,362
Last Bank & Trust Company 50,000
Towne Foundry & Machine 53,797

Total secured claims $521,840

The claim of *W.T. Financial Corp.* has been substantially reduced and will continue to be reduced by post-petition collection of pledged accounts receivable.

The claim of *Last Bank & Trust Co.* has been greatly reduced and should be, shortly, entirely paid by the sale and purchase of inventory collateral.

The claim of *Towne Foundry & Machine* has increased since the petition herein was filed but should be partially self-liquidating.

3) Priority Claims:

Wage claims have been paid. The remaining priority claims total $32,159.

The Trustee expects that the dividend to be received from the *Finnegan* chapter 7 will be sufficient to pay all remaining priority claims in cash and in full, as well as to make substantial reductions in the amounts of the remaining secured claims.

(E) POST-PETITION OPERATIONS

During the 6 months of your Trustee's operation, from *September 20, 19. . . .* through *March 31, 19. . . .* the Debtor realized a profit of $115,000 before interest on pre-petition secured debt, depreciation, and lease payments on the small press. Interest on pre-petition secured debt for the period was $22,700 and lease payments on the small press would have been $25,000. Depreciation at a realistic rate (not necessarily the rate taken for tax purposes) is estimated at $6,000 per month, or approximately $36,000 for the period. Federal income taxes have not been taken into consideration because after the losses sustained by the Debtor during the calendar year preceding the filing of the petition, the Debtor has a net operating loss carry-forward of approximately $1,100,000 as calculated by Debtor's accounting firm. Thus, profit has been shown for this period of slightly more than $31,000 after taking all factors into consideration. This accomplishment, in itself, is remarkable, and the more remarkable because historically, for this Debtor and for the extrusion industry as a whole, the months from *October* through *March*, from the standpoint of sales, are the worst operating months of the year. The best months are *April* through *September*.

One naturally wonders how this profit is possible in view of the staggering loss history of the business. The answer is simple. The Debtor got out of the fabricating business and stuck to the extrusion business. This is all the more proof of your Trustee's conviction that its losses in the fabricating field are the basic reason for the Debtor's present financial difficulties.

Attached as Exhibits D and E are the profit and loss statement for the 6 months of your Trustee's operation, from the date of his appointment to *March 31, 19. . . .*, followed by a detail of plant overhead and operating expense.

During the months of *January* and *February*, maximum usage was made of the remelt facility for scrap, and the Debtor's metal costs were reduced substantially. In the last week of *January*, the Debtor went on a two-shift operation and considerably less overtime was required to be paid. This enabled the Debtor, for these 2 months, to keep its material and direct labor percentages to 55.4% and 57.1% respectively. (Direct labor, in Debtor's present accounting system, includes only the labor working directly on the presses.) This enabled the Debtor, in *January* and *February*, to enjoy a profit percentage, before lease income and interest expense, of 19.0% and 16.6% as opposed to the 6 months' average of 10.5% of net sales. The Debtor's purchasing department has been able to effect savings, on an annual basis, of over $10,000 by more careful shopping for necessary plant overhead items.

The Debtor's current customer relations are excellent. Since the filing of the petition, customer loss has been halted, and many pre-petition customers who had deserted the Debtor have returned and are returning.

At the writing of this report, the Debtor's order backlog is over 1,000,000 pounds. During the month of *March*, the Debtor went on a three-shift operation. This should further reduce the future need for overtime and help hold down direct labor costs. It will further decrease plant overhead and operating expenses as a percentage of net sales.

The comparative balance sheets for the Trustee's operations are attached as Exhibits F and G. These figures vividly demonstrate the ability of the Debtor to generate cash and receivables during the worst operating months of the year.

At the time of the filing of the petition, the only cash available to the Debtor was $26,568.94. Through the cooperation of *W.T. Financial Corp.*, the Trustee has been able to raise operating capital by borrowing up to 90% of his accounts receivable.

The Trustee is on a cash basis with practically all of his suppliers. One supplier of aluminum has given your Trustee 10-day credit terms, but recently two suppliers have agreed to 30-day terms. On other bills, the Trustee pays on receipt of invoice, or, in some cases, pays cash with order or on a sight-draft basis. The Trustee's entire debt to *W.T. Financial Corp.* is self-liquidating. The day by day operating history of your Trustee's operation demonstrates the ability of the Debtor to operate profitably and generate its own working capital when freed from its pre-petition debt burden.

(F) DEBTOR'S KEY PERSONNEL

Some of Debtor's top management had been replaced prior to the filing of the petition at the insistence of its creditors. Since his appointment your Trustee has replaced most of the rest of old management.

The person primarily responsible for the Debtor's success since the filing of the petition is its president, *John J. Drummond. Mr. Drummond* is a graduate of the *University of Illinois* with a degree in electrical engineering. His past experience includes the post of General Manager of a large, nationally known company. He had been director of operations of *Flick Corp.*, and had been a high-placed executive of one of the nation's major aluminum manufacturers. *Mr. Drummond* has served as chief executive officers for your Trustee and also as General Sales Manager.

Mr. Drummond was brought into the Debtor's organization at the instance of its creditors 4 months before the filing of the Chapter 11 petition, and is in no way responsible for the present financial plight of the Debtor.

Charles Willard, an accounting graduate of a major *Texas* university, has been advanced from his pre-petition position of Junior Accountant to Chief Accountant.

Joe Hedge, the Production Superintendent came with the company after college. He came up through the ranks to General Foreman, and since the filing of the petition has been advanced to his present position.

All three of these men have devoted long and tireless hours to the Debtor, and their loyalty has been a key factor in the Debtor's post-petition success.

(G) PROSPECTS FOR THE FUTURE

Your Trustee believes that the Debtor will continue to operate profitably and can discharge its present debt, with interest, within 4 years after confirmation of a Reorganization Plan. This assumes that the economy of the *Southwestern* area of the United States will continue to prosper and that there will be no general recession or depression.

Your Trustee has prepared and attached as Exhibit H his projections for the current year and the ensuing 9 years, and as Exhibit "I" the assumptions on which these projections are based. In making those assumptions your Trustee has endeavored, in every instance, to be conservative. Your Trustee believes his projections are reliable. The Debtor is solvent. If the projections reflected on the attached Exhibits H and I are realized by the Debtor, by *July* of the current year the Debtor will have generated working capital in an amount in excess of $400,000. This working capital should be adequate to support annual net sales of $2,750,000.

(H) REORGANIZATION PLAN

The foregoing projections make an "internal" Plan of Reorganization feasible and should obviate the infusion of additional equity capital for working capital purposes.

The Trustee believes that the dividend from the claim against *Finnegan, Inc.* should be sufficient to retire most, if not all, of the secured indebtedness of the Debtor remaining by the end of the current year. This will leave the unsecured indebtedness in the approximate amount of $1,200,000 and, perhaps, a small amount of secured indebtedness. The projections would justify the belief that this amount can be paid between the second and fourth years after confirmation at the rate of $300,000 per year after the payment of interest at the rate of 5% per annum. By not more than four and one-half years after confirmation, the Debtor will be debt free.

Therefore, the Trustee has filed a proposed Plan of Reorganization which is attached hereto as Exhibit J.

Respectfully submitted,
(Signed) *W.J. Ralph*
Trustee

DISCLOSURE STATEMENT

UNITED STATES BANKRUPTCY COURT
SOUTHERN DISTRICT OF *TEXAS*

In re	
Kenneth Irving Debtor	Docket No. . . . . (Chapter 11)

Disclosure Statement

I. INTRODUCTION

Kenneth Irving, the Debtor, provides this Disclosure Statement to all of his known creditors in order to disclose to all such information as are deemed by the Debtor to be material, important, and necessary for his creditors to arrive at a reasonably informed decision in exercising their right to vote for acceptance of the Plan of Reorganization (hereafter called "the Plan") presently on file with the Bankruptcy Court. A copy of the Plan accompanies this Statement.

The court has set *December 14, 19. . . .*, at 9:30 o'clock A.M. for a hearing on the acceptance of the Plan of Reorganization. Creditors may vote on the Plan by filling out and mailing the accompanying Acceptance Form to the Bankruptcy Court, or may attend such hearing and present the Acceptance in person at that time. As a creditor, your acceptance is important. In order for the Plan to be deemed accepted, creditors that hold at least ⅔ in amount and more than ½ in number of the allowed claims of both Class III and Class IV must vote for the plan.

NO REPRESENTATIONS CONCERNING THE DEBTOR (PARTICULARLY AS TO HIS FUTURE BUSINESS OPERATIONS, VALUE OF PROPERTY, OR THE VALUE OF ANY PROMISSORY NOTES TO BE ISSUED UNDER THE PLAN) ARE AUTHORIZED BY THE DEBTOR OTHER THAN AS SET FORTH IN THIS STATEMENT. ANY REPRESENTATIONS OR INDUCEMENTS MADE TO SECURE YOUR ACCEPTANCE WHICH ARE OTHER THAN AS CONTAINED IN THIS STATEMENT SHOULD NOT BE RELIED UPON BY YOU IN ARRIVING AT YOUR DECISION, AND SUCH ADDITIONAL REPRESENTATIONS AND INDUCEMENTS SHOULD BE REPORTED TO DEBTOR [OR, IF APPLICABLE, TO COUNSEL FOR THE DEBTOR] WHO IN TURN SHALL DELIVER SUCH INFORMATION TO THE BANKRUPTCY COURT FOR SUCH ACTION AS MAY BE DEEMED APPROPRIATE.

THE INFORMATION CONTAINED HEREIN HAS NOT BEEN SUBJECT TO A CERTIFIED AUDIT. THE RECORDS KEPT BY THE DEBTOR ARE DEPENDENT UPON ACCOUNTING PERFORMED BY OTHERS BEYOND THE CONTROL OF *MR. IRVING*. FOR THE FOREGOING REASON, AS WELL AS BECAUSE OF THE GREAT COMPLEXITY OF THE DEBTOR'S FINANCIAL MATTERS, THE DEBTOR IS UNABLE TO WARRANT OR REPRESENT THE INFORMATION CONTAINED HEREIN IS WITHOUT ANY INACCURACY, ALTHOUGH GREAT EFFORT HAS BEEN MADE TO ENSURE ACCURACY.

II. THE PLAN OF REORGANIZATION

The Plan is based upon the Debtor's belief that the present forced liquidation value of his principal assets is so small as to offer the potential of only a minimal recovery to creditors. The Debtor believes that it is possible that some of his properties to be retained pursuant to the Plan will appreciate in value in the future, and debts secured by liens on certain of these properties will be reduced by sales of the properties and future earnings, thus permitting a more substantial recovery to creditors and thus offer the possibility that creditors will receive payment in full by way of extension. Further, certain obligations undertaken by the Debtor in the Plan will be guaranteed by trusts created some years ago for the benefit of his children.

The Plan provides for the division of unsecured creditors into five classes. *Class I and Class II creditors* are those who are entitled to a priority in payment under the provisions of the Bankruptcy Code, and are to be paid in full from cash on hand at the time of the court's confirmation of the plan, except to the extent that these liabilities may be deferred in payment voluntarily.

Class III creditors are those unsecured creditors whose claims are not subordinated and whose claims are not classified in Classes I and II. Each Class III creditor within the time specified in the Plan will receive the Debtor's non-negotiable and non-interest bearing promissory note in an amount equal to the creditor's claim, exclusive of interest accruing subsequent to the filing of the petition in this case ("Class III Note"). These notes will be secured by a lien and security interest on certain of the Debtor's assets set forth in Exhibit "A" to the Plan, and all after-acquired assets (hereinafter "the property"), although the lien and security interest will be subordinate to presently existing liens encumbering the property as well as purchase money security interests as to after acquired assets.

The lien and security interest securing the Class III Notes will be granted in favor of a Custodian who is to perform specific duties outlined in the Plan. The Class III Notes are to be paid in full on the first to occur of (i) a date 3 years from the date of the court's confirmation of the plan, or (ii) a sale of the property to the extent that the net proceeds are sufficient to pay the notes in full.

The Debtor will continue to manage and control the property given as collateral security for the Class III Notes pursuant to his continued ownership thereof, subject, however, to the rights and duties of the Custodian. The Custodian shall have the rights, duties and obligations described in the Plan which include the right to force the sale of all or any part of the property when, in the Custodian's discretion, the net proceeds thereof would be sufficient to pay the Class III Notes, the right to foreclose the liens granted to the Custodian by the Debtor, the right to enforce collection of the guarantees issued by the children's trusts, and the right to accept substitution of all or a part of the property for property bearing a higher value or greater potential for liquidity. If the Class III Notes have not been paid in full at the end of the 3 year period notwithstanding the liquidation of all of the property and attempted enforcement of the guarantees, the Debtor will undertake either a modification of the Plan or a dismissal of the chapter 11 case pursuant to the provisions of the Bankruptcy Code.

Class IV creditors are those creditors who, pursuant to court order or by voluntary agreement, will have their claims subordinated to the payment of the Class III creditors. The Plan sets forth means by which these creditors will be paid from any of the assets set forth in Exhibit "A" to the Plan which may remain after the payment of Class III creditors. The Class IV creditors will receive no payments until Class III creditors are paid in full. Those creditors whose claims are subordinated will be impaired by the Plan.

THE FOREGOING IS A BRIEF SUMMARY OF THE PLAN AND SHOULD NOT BE RELIED ON FOR VOTING PURPOSES. CREDITORS ARE URGED TO READ THE PLAN IN FULL. CREDITORS ARE FURTHER URGED TO CONSULT WITH COUNSEL, OR WITH EACH OTHER, IN ORDER TO FULLY UNDERSTAND THE PLAN AND THE EX-

HIBIT ATTACHED TO IT. THE PLAN IS COMPLEX INASMUCH AS IT REPRESENTS A PROPOSED LEGALLY BINDING AGREEMENT BY THE DEBTOR, AND AN INTELLIGENT JUDGMENT CONCERNING SUCH PLAN CANNOT BE MADE WITHOUT UNDERSTANDING IT.

III. FINANCIAL INFORMATION RESPECTING THE REORGANIZED DEBTOR

The financial information hereinafter presented is to be considered in the context of the Debtor's primary business activity of investments in various business and banking institutions for the purpose of realization of gain and appreciation over a period of time. Such financial data concerns presently existing investments, and promissory notes and other obligations received from the liquidation of investments prior to and during this chapter 11 case. It should be noted that certain property owned by the Debtor is not to be included in the lien granted to the Custodian as security for the Class III Notes. It is felt that the respective present and future fair market values of the properties not included is equal to or less than amounts due and owing to prior secured creditors holding encumbrances on those properties.

However, virtually all of the Debtor's assets are encumbered by holders of prior secured claims, and, accordingly, the amount of both secured claims and unsecured claims is relevant.

A statement of assets and liabilities of the Debtor as of *September 30, 19. . . .*, has been filed with the court and should be inspected by all interested parties. Debtor estimates that the total amount of claims which will qualify for the issuance of Class III Notes approximates $1,850,000. This approximate total excludes claims which the Debtor anticipates will be subordinated as Class IV claims, hereinafter discussed, but includes holders of unsecured promissory notes, trade creditors, secured creditors to the extent that their collateral is insufficient in value to satisfy their entire indebtedness, and contingent claims. As to the latter category, a part of the foregoing total amount of claims includes approximately $276,635 as well as an estimated deficiency to the *Bank of Sark* following consummation of a proposed agreement permitting the Bank to foreclose its security interests securing 3 loans on 25,658 shares of *Fourth Bancorporation*, 1,040 shares of *State Street Bank*, and 1,272 shares of *Dime Box State Bank*. The proposed agreement further provides that the deficiencies will be reduced by the Bank's realization of additional value from the stocks over the next 2 years. The estimated amount of all such claims qualifying for Class III Notes excludes any interest which may have accrued after the filing of the petition in this case.

Schedule A attached hereto sets forth a list of the Debtor's properties, their estimated values, and the prior secured claims thereon, broken down as to principal and interest. An asterisk (*) by the side of a particular property denotes the opinion of the Debtor that there is no equity in the property which can be realized for the Note holders even over a period of time, and hence, these particular properties were not included in Exhibit "A" to the Plan.

With respect to the properties listed on Schedule "A" beside which there are no asterisks, the following facts are deemed relevant:

A. Debtor's major property consists of 185,371 shares of *Laredo Bankshares, Inc.* ("Laredo"), which were received pursuant to a merger consummated on *October 23, 19. . . .*, between *Laredo* and *Fourth Bankshares* ("Fourth"). However, 6,177 shares of *Laredo* received by the Debtor are placed in escrow which has 2 more years to run, to be used in the event that certain anticipated loan losses in *Long Bank* are realized. The debtor believes that the losses on these loans, consisting primarily of his own loans at the Bank, will be minimal since the same are adequately collateralized.

In order to consummate the merger, certain debts of *Fourth* were required to be paid by capital contributions from its stockholders, and the Debtor was required to borrow his pro rata share of these funds to the extent of $3,329,600. This loan, represented by a Series A Promissory Note, is secured by a first lien on all of the Debtor's *Laredo* stock, and it is anticipated that it will be repaid between *December 15, 19...*, and *January 2, 19....*, by the sale of a portion of his *Laredo* stock.

Once the Series A Note has been repaid, the remaining *Laredo* stock, including the Debtor's rights in the escrowed stock, will then be delivered to the creditors listed on Schedule A as holding Series B Notes, to be held by each of these creditors as collateral security for their respective loans represented by the Series B Notes. The liens held by these creditors were required to be subordinated to the Series A Note above mentioned in order to facilitate consummation of the merger. Each of these Series B Notes is for a period of one year, commencing *October 19, 19....*, with interest payable quarterly at the prime rate charged by *Cole National Bank, Houston, Texas*, to its commercial customers. The Series B Notes may be renewed pursuant to certain standards set forth in the Credit Agreement entered into between these creditors and the Debtor and approved by the court, and it is anticipated that these Series B Notes will be serviced by the payment of interest from dividends received on the *Laredo* stock and future earnings of the Debtor.

B. *Fast Serve, Inc.*, is a self service gasoline chain that has been very successful. Although all of the 350 shares of convertible preferred stock are privately held and there is no active trading market, other shareholders have valued the stock at $128.50 a share, for a total value of the Debtor's shares representing a minority interest to be $45,000.

C. A 2.37 percent working interest in the *Del Rio/Atlantic Oil Well*, which has been producing for 11 months and has paid to Debtor's interest an average of $2,000 per month. An expert determination of the fair market value of the Debtor's interest in this oil well as of the date of the filing of the petition in this case, reflects a value of $85,000. A copy of this report will be provided upon request to debtor or counsel for the Debtor.

D. Promissory notes all of which are current as of the date of this report, and not in default, described as follows:

1. A promissory note in the present principal amount of $124,695, made by *Baird Smith, Trustee*, with interest at the rate of 10% per annum. The note is secured by deed of trust lien on certain property located in *Fort Bend County, Texas*.

2. An unsecured promissory note in the principal amount of $127,500 made by *Carl Marks*, with interest at the rate of 9.5%, payable at the rate of $2,500 per month.

3. A promissory note in the principal amount of $50,000 made by *Carl Marks*, with interest at the rate of 9.75%, payable at the rate of $1,850 per month.

4. A promissory note having a principal balance of $10,672 made by *Henry Moore*, payable at the rate of $175 per month.

5. A promissory note having a principal balance of $14,235 made by *Ray Roberts* and secured by a second lien on certain property in *Harris County, Texas*. This note is payable at the rate of $225 per month.

E. *Martin Corporation*, pursuant to a Purchase Agreement concerning Debtor's stock in *Zee International, Inc.*, is obligated to pay to the Debtor within 4 years from closing, the total sum of $125,000, plus interest. However, this amount is subject to reduction by any setoffs that may be claimed by *Martin* resulting from an increase in certain potential liabilities of the corporation and/or for damages resulting from the breach of certain warranties contained in the Agreement.

F. *Candide Paper Company* is a multi-product paper distributor with headquarters in *Houston, Texas*. The stock is traded on the over-the-counter market and during 198.. has had a bid price ranging from $2.25 to $3.25 per share.

G. *Grand Bank* has shown a reasonable growth and is in a desirable location in *Houston,*

Texas. During the past year a majority of the stock was sold to a new control group at approximately $46 per share. At the present time there is no active market in the stock.

H. The Debtor owns an undivided ½ interest in a 109,000 square foot warehouse and manufacturing facility located on the East side of *Houston, Texas.* The present lease at the rate of $11,200 per month has a remaining term of approximately 5 years. The present principal amount owed on the first lien on this property is $725,000, and the rent received has been sufficient to service this debt and to pay operating expenses. After these payments, less than $500 a month is left over.

Although it is anticipated that on the date of the hearing on confirmation of the Debtor's proposed Plan there will be a sizeable amount of cash on hand, it is believed that virtually all of that cash will be required for the deposit for payment of the Class I and Class II claims. However, any unused portion of the cash on hand will be delivered to the Custodian as collateral security for Class III Notes.

IV. FINANCIAL INFORMATION RESPECTING THE *KENNETH IRVING* TRUST OF JUNE 14, 196.., AND THE *ELIZABETH IRVING* TRUST OF JANUARY 2, 197..

The *Kenneth Irving Trust* of *June 14, 196..* ("196.. Trust") and the *Elizabeth Irving Trust* of *January 2, 197..* ("197.. Trust") have each agreed to jointly and severally guarantee payment of the promissory notes to be issued to Class III creditors under the Plan to a total amount of not more than $2,000,000. Current financial statements of the 196.. Trust and the 197.. Trust have been filed with the court and should be inspected by all interested parties.

The primary assets of the 197.. Trust consist of 102,600 shares of the capital common stock of *State Street Bank, Houston, Texas,* and 45,840 shares of *Laredo Bankshares, Inc.,* which are pledged as collateral security for the Trust's promissory notes held by the *Bank of Sark* in the total amount of $2,706,600, including accrued interest. The Bank has declared these notes to be in default and has initiated various proceedings to exercise its remedies, including the filing of a Proof of Claim in the amount of $3,421,700 in Debtor's chapter 11 case. A portion of the amount of this claim is for the foregoing indebtedness of the 197.. Trust pursuant to the Debtor's guarantee thereof. The Debtor has filed an objection to this Proof of Claim, denying a major portion of the liability asserted, and this matter is presently pending before the court.

Ron, Inc., all the stock of which is owned by the 196.. Trust, owns the major assets included in the Trust corpus. Although the basis of these assets is reflected at cost in *Ron's* financial statement, it is believed that the fair market value of some, and in particular that of *Margo Associates, Inc.,* is substantially in excess of cost, although no accurate expression of fair market value can be stated at this time. Virtually all of the assets of the 196.. Trust are encumbered by liens and subject to restrictive agreements with the *Bank of Clear Creek, Houston, Texas,* securing loans in the total approximate principal amount of $1,000,000.

At this time, the 197.. Trust and the 196.. Trust have made a proposal to *Bank of Sark* pursuant to which *Bank of Sark* would finance a purchase by the 196.. Trust of a certain number of shares of the stock of *State Street Bank* owned by the 197.. Trust and other shareholders, and *Bank of Sark* would renew and extend the remaining indebtedness of the 197.. Trust. Although the specific terms of the proposal are subject to further negotiation, the Debtor believes that *Bank of Sark* is favorably disposed to accept the basic concept of the proposal, including providing financing to the 196.. Trust for the proposed purchase of some of the share of *State Street Bank.* Pursuant to the proposal, the new debt of the 196.. Trust, which in effect would reduce the debt of the 197.. Trust, would be secured by a security interest encumbering the major assets of the 196.. Trust, although such lien would be second and subordinate to that held by *Bank of Clear Creek..*

Debtor believes that the consummation of the transactions and loans proposed to *Bank of Sark* will aid in the consummation of the transactions proposed by the Plan. In particular, it is believed that rearrangement of the *Bank of Sark* debt relating to the stock of *State Street Bank* as presently proposed would (i) facilitate a decrease in the amount of *Bank of Sark*'s claims against Debtor's present assets by a total of $4,145,076; (ii) maximize the combined net worth of the 197.. Trust and the 196.. Trust so as to render meaningful their respective guarantees to be issued in connection with Debtor's obligations to Class III creditors; and (iii) reserve the present ownership and control of *State Street Bank* with a view toward a profitable sale or other disposition thereof over a period of time. As to the second objective hoped to be achieved, on payment in full of the debt to *Bank of Clear Creek* and the reduction of the indebtedness to *Bank of Sark* to be undertaken by the 196.. Trust, Debtor believes the guarantees of the 196.. Trust and the 197.. Trust would become more valuable. Although there can be no assurance that the 196.. Trust will continue to reduce the debts owed to *Bank of Clear Creek* and will reduce the proposed indebtedness to *Bank of Sark*, the Debtor has been advised by the Trustees of the Trusts that continuance of the present level of operation of the assets of the 196.. Trust, and in particular that of *Margo Associates, Inc.*, will insure the ultimate orderly payment of the debts owed to *Bank of Clear Creek* and the proposed debts to *Bank of Sark*. Moreover, if such performance continues, a sufficient period of time will be provided to attempt to sell the *State Street Bank* stock at a price sufficient to satisfy in full all claims of *Bank of Sark* relating thereto and thereby eliminate the contingent liabilities of Debtor.

V. SPECIAL RISK FACTORS

Certain substantial risk factors are inherent in most securities issued pursuant to a Plan of Reorganization in a chapter 11 case. If such Plans are accepted it is usually because they represent a greater hope for return than dividends in a liquidating chapter 7 case. ALL OF THE RISK FACTORS INHERENT IN SECURITIES ISSUED PURSUANT TO A PLAN OF REORGANIZATION ARE PRESENT IN THE PROMISSORY NOTES PROPOSED TO BE ISSUED IN THIS CASE. In addition, however, there are certain risk factors peculiar to the instant case which must be set forth in order that creditors who will receive Class III Notes may understand the potential problems associated with either the issuance of such notes pursuant to a confirmed Plan or fulfillment of the promises represented thereby.

1. As indicated previously, the Debtor's major property consisting of 185,371 shares of *Laredo Bankshares* stock, of which 6,177 shares are held in escrow, are encumbered as security for a new loan (Series A Note) in the amount of $3,329,600, plus interest accruing at the rate of 9% per annum, and are further encumbered as security for pre-existing loans (Series B Notes) described as follows:

    a. To *Cole National Bank* in the amount of $2,303,200, with interest accruing at the prime rate.

    b. To *Cole National Bank* in the amount of $15,000 for attorney's fees incurred by the Bank, which is not enforceable against the Debtor or the collateral until the amount of the attorney's fees have been approved by this court.

    c. To *Cole National Bank* in the amount of $268,700, with interest accruing at prime, such note being the primary obligation of *SH Corporation* and co-signed by Debtor.

    d. To *Cole National Bank* in the amount of $5,000 as attorney's fees incurred by the Bank in connection with the *SH Corporation* note, which is not enforceable against Debtor and the collateral until the same has been approved by this court.

    e. To *Sinderson and Polk, Trustees* in the amount of $312,300, with interest accruing at prime.

    f. To *State Street Bank* in the amount of $77,000 with interest accruing at prime.

    g. To *State Street Bank* in the amount of $409,900 bearing no interest and attributable to Debtor's overdraft at the bank, which note is not enforceable against the collateral until an adversary proceeding involving that issue is determined by this court.

    h. To *Express Bank* in the amount of $219,700, with interest accruing at prime.

Eliminating the foregoing Series B Notes which are not enforceable against the collateral until the respective amounts thereof have been approved by this court, the total Series A and Series B debt equals $33.647 per share of *Laredo Bankshares* stock, including that held in escrow. Although a proposal for the purchase of *SH Corporation* is pending pursuant to which the *SH Corporation* debt to *Cole National Bank* would be paid, and the *State Street Bank*'s claim of a security interest in the stock as to the $409,900 overdraft is being contested before the court, if the *SH* note is not paid pursuant to the proposed sale and if all of the Series B Notes subject to court determination are ultimately approved by the court, the total debt would then be increased to $37.413 per share of *Laredo Bankshares* stock.

On the basis of the foregoing, the debt on the *Laredo Bankshares* stock will vary to a maximum of $3.77 per share, depending upon the court's determinations as to some of the Series B Notes, as above indicated, and the consummation of the sale of *SH Corporation* and the assumption by the purchaser of the *SH* debt to *Cole National Bank*. At this time, there can be no assurance that the sale of *SH Corporation* will be consummated or that determinations favorable to Debtor will be made by the court, especially as to the Series B Note held by *State Street Bank* for the overdraft.

At the close of business on Friday preceding the date of this statement, the market value of a share of *Laredo Bankshares* stock on the *New York Stock Exchange* was \$38.25, and total acknowledged debts represented by Series A and B Notes secured by the stock, and which are not subject to contingencies as indicated above, are in the amount of \$6,255,500, plus interest. Accordingly, in order to facilitate payment in full of the anticipated amount of all Class III notes to be issued to creditors, the market price of *Laredo Bankshares* must increase by approximately 10 points, IF NO VALUE IS GIVEN TO DEBTOR'S REMAINING ASSETS. That required increase, however, assumes that the last Friday market price is the same on the date in mid or late *December* when so much of the stock is to be sold to pay the Series A Note, which would leave 98,500 shares being owned by Debtor for future application. Further, the interest expense in excess of anticipated dividends is approximately \$1.00 per share per year, which will be borne by the stock if Debtor has insufficient income in the future to service the debt. There can be no assurance that the market value of the stock will remain the same or that it will increase, and there exists the market risk that its value may be decreased.

2. The total amount of estimated Class III claims that will qualify for the issuance of Class III Notes does not include certain claims asserted by the 197.. Trust, *Margo Associates, Inc.*, and *Ron, Inc.* in the total amount of \$2,325,800, which have been subordinated pursuant to an order of this court approving a settlement agreement between those entities and the Debtor. These entities are classified as Class IV creditors. Further, members of Debtor's family have filed claims in this case totaling \$1,200,000. After the Creditors' Committee filed motions to subordinate those claims to the Class III creditors, consent judgments were entered as to each, and these claimants will participate as Class IV creditors.

3. The total of Class III claims would be substantially and materially increased by the assertion of certain large contingent claims, including that of the *Bank of Sark* above referred to, arising out of Debtor's guarantees and the allowance of those claims by the court over Debtor's objections. It cannot be determined at this time whether such claims will be filed and allowed, although Debtor believes that his potential contingent liabilities are remote in view of the present stability and prior performance of the guaranteed obligations, as well as the possibility of the consummation of new financing arrangements with the *Bank of Sark*.

4. It is expected that no market will exist for the Class III and Class IV Notes issued under the Plan, and realization upon them must await dividend distributions, if any, from the Custodian.

The notes issued under the Plan are exempt from registration under the Securities Act of 1933, and state or local laws, to the extent provided in Section #1145 of the 1978 Bankruptcy Code.*

Dated.......

Signed...........
(Debtor)

* **NOTE:** Under Section 1145 of the Code, securities issued under a plan of reorganization (as well as certain other securities) are exempted from certain provisions of the securities laws. Basically, the Code exempts certain transactions involving securities issued under a plan of reorganization from the registration requirements of the federal Securities Act of 1933 (and of any equivalent law requiring registration for the offer or sale of securities by state or local government)—provided that the securities are not offered or sold by or through an "underwriter." (See Appendix F for definition of underwriter.)
These exempt transactions are the following: (1) The offer or sale of a security under the plan, which is neither an equity security nor convertible into one. (This provision is primarily designed to facilitate the issuance of certificates of indebtedness in a reorganization.) (2) The offer or sale under a plan of a security of the debtor (or his affiliate or successor) "in exchange for a claim against, an interest in, or a claim for an administrative expense in a case" even if some cash or property is received for the security, so long as the security is exchanged principally for a claim against, or interest in, the debtor. (This provision is designed to prevent distribution of securities to other than claim holders or equity security holders of the debtor.) (3) The offer or sale of any security that arises from the exercise of a subscription right or from the exercise of a conversion privilege when such subscription right or conversion privilege was issued under a plan—basically when such right or privilege is offered in the manner specified under item (2) above. (This provision is designed to enhance the marketability of subscription or conversion rights sold under reorganization plans.) (4) The offer or sale of certain portfolio securities of the debtor (i.e., securities owned by the debtor), issued by an issuer other than the debtor or an affiliate of the debtor. And (5) the offer or sale of a security by a stockbroker during the 40 day period after the initial offer of the security under the plan, providing that the stockbroker supplies the kind of disclosure statement required for confirmation of a plan (pp. 81-85 of this manual), and supplemental information if ordered by the court. (This provision is designed to prevent selling into the market "cats and dogs" of a non-reporting company.)

SCHEDULE "A"
(*KENNETH IRVING*, DEBTOR—DISCLOSURE STATEMENT)

	ASSET VALUE	TOTAL LIABILITY
185,531 sh. Laredo Bank shares	$7,096,560.75	$3,329,608.10
		2,303,221.09
		15,000.00**
		312.382.97
		219,701.06
		77,172.65
		409,979.79**
Note Receivable – Carls Marks	127,363.35	118.240.35
*Note Receivable – Vera Marvin	166,145.35	30,659.83
*Note Receivable – G. Grant	50,042.72	80,194.41
*Note Receivable – Wilkerson	16,155.81	
20 sh. Bank of Clear Creek	700.00	14,081.31
*Note Receivable – Michael Dalby	245,623.49	198,131.28
		112,334.71
10,000 sh. The Life Insurance Co.	30,000.00	29,327.75
2,000 sh. Great Bank	80,000.00	97,884.35
Note Receivable – Baird Smith, Trustee	124,694.04	96,313.29
200 sh. Fast Servo, Inc.	25,714.35	26,128.23
150 sh. Fast Servo, Inc.	19,285.65	10.311.78
Escrow Receivable – Martin Corp.	118,120.08	92,100.00**
		216.852.57**
Note Receivable – Carl Marks	50,000.00	
Note Receivable – Henry Moore	10,672.13	
Note Receivable – Ray Roberts	14,232.12	
1 sh. Park Bank	30.00	
1 sh. State Bank	40.00	
180 sh. Grand Bank	7,200.00	
Interest in Del Rio / Atlantic	85,000.00	
Cash – Debtor in Possession Account	127,083.69	
**Certificate of Deposit	264.004.38	
Certificate of Deposit	61.786.12	
211 sh. Candide Paper, Inc.	474.75	

* [Ed. Note. For meaning of * see XI–521, *supra*.]

** Presently disputed as being secured by the collateral indicated.

PRINCIPAL	ACCRUED INTEREST TO 10/1/76***	NOTES PAYABLE
$3,329,608.10	(Series A)	Cole National Bank
2,303,221.09	(Series B)	
15,000.00		
312,382.97	(Series B)	High Nat'l Bank of Denver
219,701.06	(Series B)	Fifth Bank
77,172.65	(Series B)	State Street Bank
118,204.35	—0—	First Bank
30,388.03	271.80	Long National Bank
72,694.06	7,500.35	
13,548.40	532.91	
185,796.57	12,334.71	
100,000.00	12,334.71	
25,595.10	3,732.65	College Bank
85,000.00	12,884.35	College Bank
92,180.64	4,132.65	State Street Bank
20,000.00	6,128.23	Robert Mann, Jr.
8,750.00	1,561.78	Bernard Gray
90,000.00	2,100.00	1st Nat'l Bk.
212,138.41	4,714.16	1st Nat'l Bk.

*** The Series A and Series B Notes secured by Laredo Bankshares stock include interest after 10/1/76.

UNITED STATES BANKRUPTCY COURT
FOR THE NORTHERN DISTRICT OF INDIANA

IN RE The Hardtimes Supply Co., An Illinois Corporation, Employer Identification No. 81-0664332	Case No. 3241-11

DISCLOSURE STATEMENT

The Hardtimes Supply Co., the debtor, submits the following Disclosure Statement pursuant to 11 U.S.C. §1125:

HISTORY AND DESCRIPTION OF BUSINESS

The Hardtimes Supply Co., which will be hereinafter referred to as "Hardtimes," has been engaged in the roofing supply business since 1972, when the business was founded by Arnold A. Smith and Henry S. Smith. The business that is now Hardtimes was originally an informal general partnership, with Arnold A. Smith and Henry S. Smith as general partners. Hardtimes originally had one sales outlet, which was in Gary, Indiana, but as its business prospered during the building boom of the middle and late 1970's, outlets in South Bend, Indiana and Chicago, Illinois were added. In 1982 John J. Jones joined the business and at that time Hardtimes was incorporated under the laws of the State of Illinois.

With the recession in the building industry that started in 1984, Hardtimes' business became less profitable, and in 1986 the outlet in Chicago, Illinois was closed. Hardtimes presently operates from outlets in Gary, Indiana and South Bend, Indiana. Approximately 70 percent of its sales are made through the Gary outlet. Industry figures show that Hardtimes does 26 percent of the roofing supply business in the Gary, Indiana area and 18 percent of the roofing supply business in the South Bend, Indiana area.

In November of 1986 Hardtimes began having difficulty meeting its current obligations. The financial failure of Imperial Builders, Inc. in October, 1986 was a major reason for such difficulties, as Imperial owed Hardtimes the sum of $34,550 when it filed under Chapter 7 of the Bankruptcy Code. To date, Hardtimes has collected nothing on this account. Hardtimes was unable to overcome this loss and continued to have difficulty meeting its current obligations until July 2, 1987 when this Chapter 11 case was filed. It is the opinion of Hardtimes' management that the loss incurred in the Imperial Builders' bankruptcy and the general recession in the building industry are the principal causes of Hardtimes' present financial difficulties.

FINANCIAL INFORMATION

The shares of stock in Hardtimes that are presently issued and outstanding and capitalization of Hardtimes are as follows:

Arnold A. Smith	5,000 shares of common stock at $8.00 per share
Henry S. Smith	3,000 shares of common stock at $8.00 per share
John J. Jones	3,000 shares of common stock at $10.00 per share

The principle tangible assets of Hardtimes are as follows:

A warehouse located at 2020 East 4th Avenue, Gary, Indiana valued by Hardtimes at $200,000.

An office building located at 4422 South Elm Street, Gary, Indiana valued by Hardtimes at $150,000.

Trade accounts receivable presently valued at approximately $80,000 book value and valued by Hardtimes at $40,000.

Inventory on hand valued at $65,600 book value and valued by Hardtimes at $60,000.

The principal liabilities of Hardtimes are as follows:

Note to The First National Bank of Gary in the present amount of $195,000, which is secured by a deed of trust on Hardtimes' warehouse.

Note to The Last National Bank of Gary in the present amount of $155,000 which is secured by a deed of trust on Hardtimes' office building.

Line of credit from Fearless Factors in the present amount of $66,700, which is secured by an assignment of Hardtimes' trade accounts receivable.

Unsecured credit from various trade creditors in the total amount of approximately $155,000.

Taxes due the Internal Revenue Service in the amount of $33,400.

Wages and employee benefits in the amount of $3,600.

The stockholders of Hardtimes are personally liable for the debt to Fearless Factors, for trade debts in the approximate amount of $95,000, and for the taxes owed to the Internal Revenue Service.

PENDING CLAIMS AND LITIGATION

Hardtimes has a claim in the amount of $34,550 pending against Imperial Builders, Inc. in Bankruptcy Case No. 1223 in the Bankruptcy Court for the Northern District of Illinois. It is doubtful that anything will be collected on this claim.

There are three lawsuits presently pending against Hardtimes. All are collection actions by trade creditors whose claims are included in the trade debts listed above in this Disclosure Statement. A judgment has not been entered in any of these cases.

A judgment in the amount of $25,650 in favor of Henry H. High was entered against Hardtimes on June 5, 1987 in the Lake County District Court. The case against Hardtimes was based on a breach of warranty in the sale of roofing supplies.

PRESENT AND PROJECTED EARNINGS

Hardtimes' earnings for the period of July 1, 1986 to July 2, 1987 are shown on the balance sheet and profit and loss statement dated November 2, 1987, copies of which are attached to this Disclosure Statement and marked as Exhibit A and Exhibit B, respectively.

Hardtimes' projected earnings for the two-year period beginning February 1, 1988 is set forth in the projected balance sheet and income statement, copies of which are attached to this Disclosure Statement and marked as Exhibits C and D, respectively.

The balance sheets, profit and loss statement, and income statement described above and attached to this Disclosure Statement were prepared by Edwin Eyestrain, CPA, from information obtained from the books and records of Hardtimes.

It is estimated by Hardtimes' management and its attorney that future expenses in the approximate amount of $2,500 will be incurred in the handling and administration of this Chapter 11 case.

Should Hardtimes file under Chapter 7 of the Bankruptcy Code on the date of this Disclosure Statement, it is estimated that the following assets would be realized by the trustee in the following amounts:

Real Estate	none
Accounts receivable	none
Inventory	$60,000
Other assets	$10,000
Total	$70,000

The expenses of administration in such a Chapter 7 case are estimated to be $5,000, which would leave a balance of $65,000 available for the payment of claims. The estimated total amount of priority claims that would be allowed in the Chapter 7 case is $37,000. This would leave the approximate sum of $28,000 available for the payment of general nonpriority unsecured claims. The total amount of general nonpriority unsecured claims that would be allowed in the Chapter 7 case is estimated to be $187,000. This would permit the payment of a dividend to nonpriority unsecured creditors of approximately 15 cents on the dollar should Hardtimes file a petition under Chapter 7 of the Bankruptcy Code.

MANAGEMENT

The officers, directors, stockholders, insiders, or other persons in control of Hardtimes and their respective annual salaries are as follows:

Arnold A. Smith	President	Director	Stockholder $24,000
Henry S. Smith	Vice President	Director	Stockholder $22,000
John J. Jones	Treasurer	Director	Stockholder $22,000
Mary M. Jones	Secretary		$12,000

The persons listed above will constitute the management of Hardtimes during the period of the proposed Plan. Their salaries will remain as shown above during the period of the Plan.

STATUS OF CASE

This Chapter 11 case was filed by Hardtimes because, in the opinion of Hardtimes' management, it was the only feasible method of dealing with Hardtimes' debt load and remaining in business. In the opinion of Hardtimes' management, most of Hardtimes' creditors will receive considerably more in this Chapter 11 case than they would have received had Hardtimes gone out of business or filed under Chapter 7 of the Bankruptcy Code.

This Chapter 11 case was filed by Hardtimes on July 2, 1987. Since then, under the protection of the bankruptcy court, Hardtimes' business has shown a steady improvement in both total sales and profitability. The financial status of Hardtimes since the filing of this Chapter 11 case is shown on the profit and loss statement dated January 8, 1988, a copy of which is attached to this Disclosure Statement and marked as Exhibit E.

SUMMARY OF PROPOSED PLAN OF REORGANIZATION

The Plan of Reorganization proposed by Hardtimes will pay all secured claims, priority tax claims, priority wage claims, and priority employee benefit claims in full. The plan will pay 80 cents on the dollar on the unsecured claims of Ace Shingle Company, First Bank of Gary, Indiana Asphalt Company, and J & B Roofing Company, and 40 cents on the dollar to the holders of all other unsecured claims in installments totalling $2,000 per month. The funds for implementing and carrying out the Plan will come from the operation of Hardtimes' business and from a $10,000 interest-free loan from Arnold A. Smith. It is estimated that it will take approximately four years for Hardtimes to consummate the proposed Plan. Confirmation of the Plan by the bankruptcy court will serve to release the stockholders of Hardtimes from personal liability for any claim dealt with in the Plan.

Dated and respectfully submitted this 12th day of January, 1988

The Hardtimes Supply Co., (Debtor in possession)

by_____
Arnold A. Smith, President

Notice of Hearing on Disclosure Statement

UNITED STATES BANKRUPTCY COURT
SOUTHERN DISTRICT OF *TEXAS*

In re

Kenneth Irving,
Debtor

Docket No..........
(Chapter 11)

Notice to Holders of Claims and Interests of Hearing
on Approval of Disclosure Statement

To all creditors and other parties in interest:

NOTICE IS HEREBY GIVEN THAT

1. On ...., 19... the debtor in this case filed a proposed Plan of Reorganization and a proposed Disclosure Statement in connection with such plan. A copy of such proposed Plan and a copy of the proposed Disclosure Statement are enclosed herewith.

[If the debtor proposes different disclosure statements for different classes of claims or interests, appropriate additions should be made.]

2. A hearing will be held on ...., 19.... at .... o'clock A.M. in United States Bankruptcy Court, *515 Rusk Avenue, Houston, Texas,* to consider and to rule on the adequacy of the information contained in such proposed Disclosure Statement, and to consider any other matter that may properly come before the court at that time.

3. The hearing may be adjourned from time to time by announcement made in open court without further written notice to parties in interest.

BY ORDER OF THE COURT.

Plan of Reorganization (Corporate Debtor)

UNITED STATES BANKRUPTCY COURT
NORTHERN DISTRICT OF *TEXAS, DALLAS* DIVISION

In re

    Allday Aluminum Company,

                         Debtor

Docket No..........
(Chapter 11)

Plan of Reorganization

Dated: *December* 5, 19.... Filed by *W.J. Ralph*, Trustee.

DEFINITIONS

The following terms, when used in the Plan, shall, unless the context otherwise requires, have the following meanings, respectively:

DEBTOR: *Allday Aluminum Company*, a *Texas* corporation.

CHAPTER 11: Chapter 11 of the Bankruptcy Code.

REORGANIZATION CASE: The case for the reorganization of the Debtor commenced by voluntary petition under chapter 11 on *September* 17, 19..., and now pending in this court and styled "In re *Allday Aluminum Company*, Debtor, No......"

COURT: The United States Bankruptcy Court for the *Northern* District of *Texas, Dallas* Division, acting in this case.

TRUSTEE: *W.J. Ralph*, appointed, qualified, and acting trustee in this case, or his duly appointed successor or successors.

PLAN: This Plan of Reorganization.

BOARD·OF DIRECTORS: The Board of Directors of the reorganized Debtor, to be selected as hereinafter provided.

DEBENTURES: General unsecured obligations of the reorganized Debtor to be issued under date of *January* 1, 19..., to unsecured creditors of the Debtor in Class 3 in payment for the indebtedness owed by the Debtor to such creditors on *September* 17, 19.... The said debentures will bear interest at the rate of 5% per annum from and after *January* 1, 19..., and shall be payable in four equal installments of principal and accrued interest on the unpaid balance, the said installments to be due on *December* 31, 19..., *December* 31, 19..., *December* 31, 19..., and *December* 31, 19..., with the reorganized Debtor retaining the privilege of pre-payment without penalty, and with interest only on the unpaid balance to the date of the final payment. Each creditor in Class 3 shall receive a debenture in a dollar amount equivalent to the dollar amount of the claim of each creditor as finally allowed and approved by the court.

CONFIRMATION OF THE PLAN: The entry by this court of an order confirming the Plan in accordance with chapter 11.

CONSUMMATION OF PLAN: The accomplishment of all things contained or provided for in this Plan, and the entry of an order of consummation finally dismissing this case.

ARTICLE I

CLASSIFICATION OF CLAIMS AND INTERESTS

1. Secured claims as such claims existed on the date of the petition in this case, as finally allowed and approved by the court, and to the extent that such claims are not greater than the value of the Debtor's assets which the court finds are valid security for such debts.

2. Unsecured claims to the extent that such claims are approved and allowed by the court and do not, as finally allowed, exceed $500.

3. Unsecured claims as finally approved and allowed by the court, which claims exceed $500.

4. Interests of the holders of preferred stock of the Debtor.

5. Interests of the holders of common stock of the Debtor.

[*See Item 1, on p.77-78 of this manual, as well as pp.* 199-204 *, for details on classification procedures*]

ARTICLE II

CLAIMS AND INTERESTS NOT IMPAIRED UNDER THE PLAN

Class 2 shall be paid in cash on the effective date of the plan; Classes 1, 4, and 5 shall remain unaltered. These classes are not impaired under the plan.

[*See Item 2 on* p. 86 *of manual, and pp.* 205-6 *, on the concept of impairment*]

ARTICLE III

TREATMENT OF CLASSES THAT ARE IMPAIRED UNDER THE PLAN

The creditors in Class 3 shall receive debentures.

[*See Items 3 & 4 on* p. 86 *of the manual*]

ARTICLE IV

MEANS FOR EXECUTION OF THE PLAN

As soon as feasible after the entry of an order of confirmation herein, the operation of the Debtor shall be and become the general responsibility of the Board of Directors of the reorganized company, who shall, thereafter, have the responsibility for the management, control, and operation of the reorganized Debtor. Such Directors shall have the responsibility for the selection of the officers of the reorganized Debtor and for carrying out the changes necessary in the charter and by-laws of the company to accomplish the requirements of Article V. The said Board of Directors shall also be responsible for the preparation, execution, and issuance of the debentures called for in this Plan. The trustee, until the entry of an order dismissing this case, shall be a member ex-officio of the Board of Directors, without vote, but shall be the representative of the court on the

Board of Directors, and shall report to the court any failure on the part of the Board of Directors or the officers of the reorganized Debtor to carry out the provisions of this Plan. The trustee shall be entitled to receive operating statements and balance sheets of the reorganized Debtor at least monthly, and shall be entitled to attend all meetings of the Board of Directors or any committee or sub-committee of the Board of Directors to which the Board of Directors may delegate authority, responsibility, or duties.

[*See Item 5 on pp. 86-87   of the manual*]

ARTICLE V

PROVISIONS FOR INCLUSION IN THE CHARTER OF THE REORGANIZED DEBTOR AND WITH RESPECT TO SELECTION OF DIRECTORS AND OFFICERS

At the time of the confirmation of the Plan, the Board of Directors of the reorganized Debtor shall consist of 5 members, 3 members of which shall be representatives of creditors, and 2 members shall be representatives of stockholders. So long as any portion of the principal or accumulated interest of the debentures shall remain unpaid, the debenture holders shall be entitled to elect a majority of the Board of Directors. The remaining 2 members of the Board shall be elected by the stockholders.

The initial Board of Directors shall be composed of the following individuals, who shall hold office until the first regular meeting of stockholders is held in the year 19...:

Creditor representatives:

Owen M. Barth, Arthur Crow, and *Sanders Bassett.*

Stockholder representatives:

Dorman McAlister, and *Thomas Johns.*

At said first meeting of the stockholders in 19..., to be held in accordance with the charter and by-laws of the reorganized entity, the stockholders shall elect 2 members of the Board of Directors. The remaining 3 members of the Board of Directors shall be selected by the debenture holders under rules to be promulgated by the court in the order of confirmation. But after the principal and accumulated interest of all debentures have been retired, all debenture representatives on the Board of Directors shall resign and all members of the Board of Directors shall be elected in accordance with the charter and by-laws of the reorganized Debtor.

The initial Board of Directors shall take such action as may be necessary to ensure that the following provisions, which shall be contained in the charter of the reorganized Debtor, shall be realized:

A. Provisions prohibiting the Debtor from issuing non-voting stock, and providing, as to the several classes of securities of the Debtor possessing voting power, for the fair and equitable distribution of such power among such classes, including, in the case of any class of stock having a preference over other stock with respect to dividends, adequate provisions for the election of directors representing such preferred class in the event of default in the payment of such dividends; and

B. (1) Provisions which are fair and equitable and in accordance with sound business and accounting practice, with respect to the terms, position, rights, and privileges of the several class of securities of the Debtor, including, without limiting the generality of the foregoing, provisions with respect to the issuance, acquisition, purchase, and payment of dividends thereon; and (2) provisions with respect to the making, not less than once annually, of periodic reports to security holders which shall include profit and loss statements and balance sheets prepared in accordance with sound business and accounting practice.

[*See Items 6 & 7 on p.* 87 *of the manual*]

ARTICLE VI

PROVISIONS FOR PRIORITY CLAIMS

Each claim of the kind specified in sections 507(a)(1), 507(a)(2), 507(a)(3), 507(a)(4), and 507(a)(5), shall be paid, on the effective date of the plan, cash equal to the allowed amount of such claim. Each claim of the kind specified in section 507(a)(6) shall be paid, in equal monthly installments over a period of *five* years from the date of the assessment of such claim, the value, as of the effective date of the plan, equal to the allowed amount of such claim.

[*See Item 11 on* pp. 103-4 of the manual]

ARTICLE VII

PROVISIONS FOR THE REJECTION
OF EXECUTORY CONTRACTS

A. All valid and existing executory options or rights to acquire the capital stock of the Debtor, if any such valid options or rights exist, shall, upon notice and hearing to any person, firm, or corporation claiming such options or rights, be rejected; and at such hearing on the said rejection, the court shall fix the dollar amount of the damages suffered, if any, by such persons, firms, or corporations on account of the said rejection, and to the extent of such damage found by the court, if any, such persons, firms, or corporations shall become Class 3 creditors and receive debentures in lieu of such money damages.

B. The executory lease contract between the Debtor and *Crow & Company*, shall be renegotiated between the trustee and such company, and to the extent of the damages suffered by such company as the result of such renegotiation, if any, such company shall become a Class 3 creditor and receive debentures for its damages, if any. To the extent that such company is a creditor for rent accruing prior to the filing of the petition herein, such company shall be a Class 3 creditor.

[*See Item 9 on p. 87 of the manual*]

ARTICLE VIII

PROVISIONS FOR THE RETENTION, ENFORCEMENT, SETTLEMENT
OR ADJUSTMENT OF CLAIMS BELONGING TO THE DEBTOR OR
TO THE ESTATE

[*If a cause of action exists against officers or directors of the debtor, or any other cause of action exists which should be retained and enforced by the trustee or the debtor, and if a new corporation is created, and such causes of action have not been settled or adjusted in the plan, adequate provision should be made in the plan for the retention and enforcement of such cause of action for the benefit of the new company by the trustee, (or by an examiner appointed for that purpose, if the debtor has been continued in possession).*]

[*See Item 10 on p. 87 of the manual*]

ARTICLE IX

GENERAL PROVISIONS

Until the case is closed, the court shall retain jurisdiction to insure that the purpose and intent of this Plan are carried out. The court shall retain jurisdiction to hear and determine all claims against the Debtor and to enforce all causes of action which may exist on behalf of the Debtor. Nothing herein contained shall prevent the reorganized Debtor from taking such action as may be necessary in the enforcement of any cause of action which may exist on behalf of the Debtor and which may not have been enforced or prosecuted by the trustee.

[*See "STEP 18," pp. 107-8 of the manual*]

Plan of Reorganization (Individual Debtor)

UNITED STATES BANKRUPTCY COURT
SOUTHERN DISTRICT OF *TEXAS*

In re	
Kenneth Irving,	Docket No..........
Debtor	(Chapter 11)

Plan of Reorganization

Dated: *December 1, 19....*

Filed by *Kenneth Irving,*
Debtor

Kenneth Irving, Debtor, proposes this Plan of Reorganization.

DEFINITIONS

1. "DEBTOR" shall mean *Kenneth Irving.*

2. "CREDITORS" shall mean all creditors of the Debtor holding claims, whether for unsecured debts, liabilities, demands or claims of any character whatsoever.

3. "SECURED CREDITORS" shall mean all creditors who hold a lien, security interest, or other encumbrance which has been properly perfected as required by law with respect to property owned by the Debtor.

4. "PLAN" shall mean this Plan of Reorganization in its present form or as it may be amended or supplemented.

5. "COURT" shall mean the United States Bankruptcy Court for the *Southern* District of *Texas*, including the United States Bankruptcy Judge presiding in the chapter 11 case of the Debtor.

6. "CLAIM" shall mean a duly listed or timely filed claim which is allowed and ordered paid by the court.

7. "SUBORDINATED CREDITORS" shall mean creditors whose claims are subordinated to Class III creditors, and who participate as Class IV creditors.

8. "CUSTODIAN" shall mean that person selected by the Creditors' Committee and approved by the court, who shall perform the duties and have the rights and obligations described in Article IV of this Plan.

9. "CREDITORS' COMMITTEE" shall mean that Creditors' Committee appointed by order of the court dated *October 7, 19....*, the members thereof and any successor members.

10. "EFFECTIVE DATE" shall be that date on which the order confirming the Plan becomes final and nonappealable.

11. "IRVING ENTITIES" shall mean the *Kenneth Irving* Trust of *June 14, 196..*, and the *Elizabeth Irving* Trust of *January 2, 197..*

ARTICLE I

CLASSIFICATION OF CLAIMS

1.1 **Class I**—Costs and expenses of administration as defined in the Bankruptcy Code for which application for or allowance or a claim is filed prior to the effective date, and to the extent, if any, to which they are allowed, approved, and ordered paid by the court.

1.2 **Class II**—Claims entitled to priority under sections 507(a)(3), 509(a)(4), and 507(a)(5) of the Bankruptcy Code, to the extent to which they are allowed, approved, and ordered paid by the court, if any.

1.3 **Class III**—Claims of all creditors of the Debtor, excluding those in Classes I, II, IV, and V, to the extent, if any, to which they are allowed and ordered paid by the court, including, but not limited to creditors whose claims may arise out of the rejection of executory contracts, and secured creditors to the extent that the court finds the same unsecured in whole or in part, or secured creditors who otherwise elect to participate in whole or in part as Class III creditors.

1.4 **Class IV**—Subordinated creditors whose claims are allowed and ordered paid by the court.

1.5 **Class V**—Secured creditors as their claims existed on the date of the petition in this case, as finally allowed and ordered paid by the court, and to the extent that such claims are not greater than the value of Debtor's assets which the court finds are valid security for such claims.

[*See Item 1 on p.85-6 of the manual, and pp.* 199-204 *on classification procedures*]

ARTICLE II

CLAIMS NOT IMPAIRED UNDER THE PLAN

2.1 Class I and Class II creditors shall be paid in cash and in full, as and when their claims are allowed and ordered paid by the court. Class V creditors shall retain unaltered, their legal, equitable, and contractual rights as they existed on the date of the petition in this case. These classes are not impaired under the Plan.

[*See Item 2 on pp.* 86 *; also pp.* 205-206 *on the concept of impairment*]

ARTICLE III

TREATMENT OF CLASSES THAT ARE IMPAIRED UNDER THE PLAN

3.1 Class III creditors shall each receive from the Debtor a non-negotiable, non-interest bearing promissory note (hereinafter called **"Class III Notes"**), dated as of the effective date, in the principal amount of the creditor's claim, excluding interest, if any, accrued thereon subsequent to the filing of the petition in this case. Each Class III Note shall be due and payable as of the first to occur of these: (i) a date 3 years from the date of filing the petition, or (ii) a sale of Debtor's assets, the net proceeds of which are sufficient to pay all Class III Notes in full. The Class III Notes shall be executed and delivered by Debtor within 30 days after the effective date, or with respect to any Class III claim to which an objection is filed, within 12 days following a final and non-appealable order on such objection.

3.2 Class IV creditors shall receive from Debtor a non-negotiable promissory note (hereinafter called "**Class IV Notes**"), dated as of the effective date, in the principal amount of each said creditor's claim, excluding interest accrued subsequent to the filing of the petition in this case. The Class IV Notes shall be due and payable 39 months from the effective date, shall be non-interest bearing, shall be expressly subordinated to the payment of Class III Notes, and shall be paid solely and exclusively from the proceeds of the sale of the assets set forth in Exhibit "A" hereto, to the extent that such assets are not required to be sold to pay Class III Notes or the principal and accrued interest secured by prior encumbrances. If after 3 years from the effective date, any assets listed in Exhibit "A" remain unsold and are not required to be sold to pay Class III Notes, and such Class III Notes have been paid in full, the Custodian shall deliver such remaining assets to Debtor for the benefit of the holders of Class IV Notes. The proceeds from the sale of the said remaining assets, or the said remaining assets in kind, shall be disbursed by the debtor to Class IV creditors. Following the disbursement of the funds, or property in kind, or following the use of all of the assets listed in Exhibit "A" to pay the holders of Class III Notes, whichever first occurs, Debtor shall have no further obligation or liability to Class IV creditors with respect to their respective Class IV Notes.

[See Items 3 & 4 on   p. 86   *of the manual]*

ARTICLE IV

MEANS FOR EXECUTION OF THE PLAN

4.1 As security for payment of the Class III Notes, the Debtor shall, as of the effective date, grant to the Custodian a lien or security interest in all of Debtor's assets more fully set forth in Exhibit "A" attached hereto, and to all assets acquired by Debtor after the effective date, subject to all present liens and security interests encumbering the same, and to purchase money security interests or secured loans whose proceeds are used to acquire after-acquired property. To further assure payment of Class III Notes, the *Irving Entities* shall execute and deliver to the Custodian, for the benefit of all Class III creditors, an agreement guaranteeing the payment of Class III Notes in a total amount of not more than $2,000,000.

4.2 Debtor shall execute and deliver to the Custodian a security agreement encumbering the property. The Custodian shall give written notice to all holders of prior liens and encumbrances on the property regarding such holders' security interest therein. Title to and ownership of the property shall remain vested in Debtor, and nothing contained herein shall constitute a transfer of such title and ownership, or of the rights incidental thereto, to the Custodian. Insofar as each item of the property set forth in Exhibit "A" is encumbered by prior liens or security interests, Debtor agrees to advance such funds as may be required from time to time to keep current the respective prior obligations secured by the property. In the event that the Debtor at any time fails to advance funds required to keep current such respective prior obligations encumbering the property, then and in such event the Custodian may, within his sole and exclusive discretion for that purpose, use funds received on account of the property as rent, royalties, interest and dividends, or cause to be sold so much of the property as may be necessary, all to provide funds to pay so much of such prior obligations as may then be due and owing.

4.3 Notwithstanding anything contained herein to the contrary, the Custodian may, in his sole discretion, at any time subsequent to one year after the effective date, require the Debtor to sell any or all of the property, if by doing so all Class III Notes would be paid in full thereby.

4.4 The Custodian shall approve all sales or other disposition and the Custodian shall approve the Debtor's use of the property as collateral security for any loans hereafter made or the refinancing of existing loans.

4.5 As all or any item of the property is sold, or as funds are collected from loans or the refinancing of loans secured by all or any item of the property, the net proceeds therefrom, after payment of costs of sale and prior obligations encumbering such property, shall be delivered to the Custodian, who, in turn, shall disburse the same to the holders of Class III Notes on a pro rata basis, determined by the amount of all such Notes issued pursuant to Paragraph 3.1 herein; provided, however, that the Custodian may, within his sole and exclusive discretion, withhold the making of a disbursement of all or a part of said net proceeds to the extent that the same may be required to pay obligations to secured creditors holding prior liens and security interests encumbering the remaining property. Further, the Custodian shall have the right, but not the obligation, to do the following: (i) to release from his security interest and lien all or any item of the property (or the net proceeds from their sale or other disposition), upon his receipt from the Debtor of any other property which is then owned by the Debtor and which has a value equal to or exceeding the property to be released from the security interest of the Custodian, (ii) to release from his security interest and lien and any duty with respect thereto, any item of the property which he determines to have a value equal to or less than prior obligations encumbering such item of the property; and (iii) to subordinate his security interest or lien to facilitate new secured financing with respect to the property.

4.6 All disbursements to the holders of Class III Notes shall be made by the Custodian. Reasonable compensation, if any, for the Custodian shall be approved by the Debtor and the Creditors' Committee, upon appointment of the Custodian, and such compensation and all reasonable and necessary out-of-pocket expenses incurred by the Custodian shall be paid from funds received by the Custodian prior to the disbursement of the same to the holders of Class III Notes; provided, however, that no more than one-third (⅓) of the Custodian's total fees shall be paid in any one year unless there are sufficient funds remaining to pay in full all Class III Notes.

4.7 If at the expiration of three (3) years from the date of the issuance of the Class III Notes, sufficient funds have not been received and disbursed to pay such notes in full, then and in such event the Custodian shall immediately cause to be sold, at the highest and best price, so much of the property then remaining in his possession as is necessary to provide net proceeds for disbursement to holders of Class III Notes in an amount sufficient to pay the same in full. If after such sale and liquidation of the property the total amount of Class III Notes has not been fully satisfied, then and in such event the Debtor shall pay to the Custodian for disbursement to holders of Class III Notes, such additional funds as may be required. If the Debtor or the *Irving Entities* pursuant to their guarantees fail to pay such additional funds, the Debtor shall then immediately proceed to file for a modification of the Plan for the purpose of extending the time for payment of the Class III Notes, or for a dismissal of the proceeding, whichever, in the discretion of the Court, is in the best interests of the Estate.

4.8 In the event that prior to or upon the expiration of three (3) years from the date of the issuance of the Class III Notes, funds are disbursed to holders thereof in an amount sufficient to pay the same in full, then any of the property remaining shall be delivered by the Custodian to the Debtor, and the Custodian, as Custodian for the benefit of the Class IV creditors and the security interest therein, shall be released. Other than the delivery of the property remaining, if any, to the Debtor for the benefit of the Class IV creditors, and the release of his security interest, the Custodian shall have no other obligations or duties to the said creditors. On payment in full of all Class III Notes, the Custodian shall be discharged from any and all obligations under this Plan, or otherwise, and upon such payment, all holders of Class III Notes, and each of them, shall indemnify the Custodian and hold him harmless against liability for claims of any character arising out of actions taken by the Custodian in the performance of his obligations under this Plan, subject to the provisions of Section 4.10 hereinbelow.

4.9 Until the first to occur of (i) payment in full of the Class III notes, or (ii) three (3) years from the effective date, the Debtor shall quarter-annually deliver to the Custodian and the Court a written report signed by the Debtor of activities and operations of the Debtor and the *Irving Entities* during such period of time and provide an unaudited balance sheet for each. On receipt of such written report, the Custodian shall forward the same to Class III creditors, together with the Custodian's report reflecting all actions taken with respect to the sale or other disposition of the property and an accounting as to the funds received and disbursed by the Custodian.

4.10 The Custodian shall not be liable for any action or failure to act hereunder in the absence of proof of bad faith or gross negligence.

4.11 If the Custodian shall die or, by refusal, incapacitation or otherwise, shall fail to perform his duties hereunder, the Court, subject to the approval of the Debtor and the Creditors' Committee, shall appoint a successor or replacement Custodian. However, no provision hereof shall be construed to prevent the Creditors' Committee from requesting the Court to appoint a successor or replacement Custodian for any reason at any time, subject to the approval of such successor or replacement Custodian by the Court, with notice of hearing thereon to the Debtor.

4.12 The forms of all documents to be executed by the Debtor in the consummation of this Plan, including the Class III Note, security agreement with respect thereto, and Class IV Note, and all documents to be executed by the Kaplan Entities, including a guaranty agreement, are being filed with the Court contemporaneously with the filing of this Plan, and are available for inspection by interested parties.

[*See Item 5 on pp. 86-7 of the manual, and Item 7 on p. 87*]

ARTICLE V

PROVISIONS FOR REJECTION OF EXECUTORY CONTRACTS

5.1 Except as specified below, all contracts which exist between the Debtor and any individual or entity, whether such contracts be in writing or oral, which have not heretofore been rejected or heretofore been approved by orders of this court, are hereby specifically rejected; provided, however, that this provision is not intended to reject and does not reject any agreement for the renewal or extension of any loan of funds, presently binding and in effect as between the Debtor and any secured creditor.

[*See Item 9 on p. 87 of the manual*]

ARTICLE VI

PROVISIONS FOR PRIORITY CLAIMS

6.1 Each claim of the kind specified in Section 507(a)(6) of the Bankruptcy Code shall be paid in equal *quarterly* installments over a period of 6 years from the date of the assessment of such claim, the value, as of the effective date of the plan, equal to the allowed amount of such claim.

[*See Item 11 on pp. 103-4 of the manual*]

Dated: *December 1, 19....*

(Signed) *Kenneth Irving*
Debtor

166

We, the undersigned consenting parties which are hereby represented to be valid and subsisting trusts under the Laws of the State of *Texas*, do hereby subscribe to the foregoing Plan proposed herein, and, in particular, to the provisions of Section 4.1 thereof, in our capacity so stated, provided that the obligations of each of the consenting parties as set forth herein are conditioned upon the order confirming this Plan of Reorganization becoming final and non-appealable, and the issuance by the Debtor of Class III Notes in a total amount of not more than $2,000,000.

Dated: . . . .

Kenneth Irving Trust of *June 14, 196*. .

By (Signed) *George Irving*
Co-Trustee

By (Signed) *Ruth Jones*
Co-Trustee

Elizabeth Irving Trust of January 2, 197. .

By (Signed) *Ruth Jones*
Co-Trustee

By (Signed) *Sam Wisdom*
Co-Trustee

EXHIBIT "A"

(1) 2180 shares of *Great Bank* stock

(2) 10,000 shares of *The Life Insurance Company* stock

(3) 750 shares of *Fast Serve* common stock

(4) 185,531 shares of *Laredo Bankshares, Inc.* stock

(5) 2.37% of working interest in *Del Rio/Atlantic Oil Well*

(6) 1 share of *Park Bank* stock

(7) 1 share of *State Bank* stock

(8) 211 shares of *Candide Papers, Inc.* stock

(9) Promissory Notes Receivable as follows:

Maker & Terms	*Principal as of 12-1-8*. .
Baird Smith, Trustee, secured by deed of trust; payable 1/7 of principal balance per year	$124,695
Carl Marks, payable $2500 per month	127,500
Carl Marks, payable $1850 per month	50,000
Henry Moore, payable $175 per month	10,672
Ray Roberts, secured by second lien, payable $225 per month	14,235
Martin Corp., pursuant to Purchase Agreement concerning *Zee International, Inc.* (deferred portion of purchase price subject to setoffs)	125,000

(10) All cash remaining in the possession of Debtor in Possession after payment of Class I and Class II creditors.

UNITED STATES BANKRUPTCY COURT
FOR THE NORTHERN DISTRICT OF INDIANA

IN RE   The Hardtimes Supply Co.,   )
        An Illinois Corporation,   )   Case No. 3241-11
        Employer Identification No. 81-0664332   )

DEBTOR'S PLAN OF REORGANIZATION

The Hardtimes Supply Co., an Illinois Corporation, the debtor, proposes the following Plan of Reorganization, which will hereinafter be referred to as the Plan:

CLASSIFICATION OF CLAIMS

The claims to be dealt with under the Plan are classified as follows:

Class 1. The holder of the claim secured by the deed of trust on the debtor's warehouse located at 2020 East 4th Avenue, Gary, Indiana, to the extent that the claim is secured.

Class 2. The holder of the claim secured by the deed of trust on the debtor's office building located at 4422 South Elm Street, Gary, Indiana, to the extent that the claim is secured.

Class 3. The holder of the claim secured by the debtor's accounts receivable, to the extent that the claim is secured.

Class 4. The holder of the judgment against the debtor entered on June 5, 1987 in the Lake County District Court that was recorded in Lake County, Indiana on August 12, 1987, to the extent the judgment is secured.

Class 5. The holders of wage claims against the debtor that are entitled to priority under 11 U.S.C. §507(a)(3).

Class 6. The holders of employee benefit plan claims against the debtor that are entitled to priority under 11 U.S.C. §507(a)(4).

Class 7. The holders of all nonpriority unsecured claims that are less than or reduced to $200, or to an amount approved by the court as reasonable and necessary for administrative convenience.

Class 8. The unsecured claims of Ace Shingle Company, First Bank of Gary, Indiana Asphalt Company, and J & B Roofing Company.

Class 9. All other nonpriority unsecured claims.

CLASSES OF CLAIMS NOT IMPAIRED BY THE PLAN

The following classes of claims are not impaired by the Plan: Class 1, Class 2, Class 5, Class 6, and Class 7. All other classes of claims are impaired by the Plan.

TREATMENT OF NONIMPAIRED CLAIMS

The holder of the secured claim in Class 1 shall be paid the sum of $3,245.80 on the effective date of the Plan to cure all defaults in the debtor's obligation to the holder of the claim. The holder of the secured claim in Class 2 shall be paid the sum of $2,335.70 on the effective date of the Plan to cure all defaults in the debtor's obligation to the holder of the claim. The holders of claims in Class 5 and Class 6 will be paid the full amount of their allowed claims on the effective date of the Plan. The holders of claims in Class 7 will be paid the full amount of their allowed claims on June 1, 1988.

All claims for costs and expenses of administration allowable under 11 U.S.C. §507(a)(1) shall be paid in full upon the approval of such claims by the court. Each allowed tax claim of a governmental unit entitled to priority under 11 U.S.C. §507(a)(7) shall be paid in full in cash over a period not exceeding six years from the date of assessment of such claim. Interest on such claims shall be paid at the rate of 10 per cent per annum.

Author's comment: The special illustrative value and strength of this particular plan (as well as of the related Disclosure Statement for the same debtor), is its brevity, simplicity and clarity, in this author's view, as it concentrates mostly on "facts" rather than "opinions". And readers should take special note of this in formulating their own documents.

*Reproduced by permission, Argyle Publishing Company

The holder of the claim in Class 3 will be permitted to retain its lien and will be paid the allowed amount of its secured claim in 48 equal monthly installments beginning on the first day of the first full month after the effective date of the Plan. Interest on the unpaid portion of the allowed secured claim will be paid at the rate of 10 percent per annum.

The holder of the claim in Class 4 will be paid the sum of $5,000 on the effective date of the Plan, and the sum of $5,000 on January 31, 1989. The lien of the holder of the claim in Class 4 will be extinguished on the effective date of the Plan.

Each holder of a claim in Class 8 will be paid a sum equal to 80 percent of the amount of its allowed claim on June 1, 1988.

Each holder of a claim in Class 9 will be paid a sum equal to 40 percent of the amount of the allowed claim of such holder. Such payments will be in the form of deferred cash payments totalling $2,000 per month beginning June 1, 1988 and continuing until such claims are paid as provided in this paragraph. The $2,000 monthly payments by the debtor shall be divided pro-rata among the holders of allowed claims in the class.

TREATMENT OF INTERESTS

The interests of the stockholders of the debtor shall not be affected by the Plan.

MEANS OF IMPLEMENTING AND CARRYING OUT THE PLAN

The debtor shall retain all of its property and shall operate its roofing supply business during the period of the Plan. The funds for implementing and carrying out the Plan shall be provided by the debtor's business operations, supplemented by a $10,000 unsecured loan to the debtor on the effective date of the plan by Arnold A. Smith, the president and a principal stockholder of the debtor. The loan shall be interest free during the period of the Plan, and shall be repayable during the period of the Plan only as permitted by the bankruptcy court.

AMENDMENT OF DEBTOR'S CHARTER

The debtor shall amend its charter so as to prohibit the issuance of nonvoting stock and to provide, as to the classes of stock possessing voting rights, an appropriate distribution of voting power among such classes, including in the case of preferred stock, if any should exist, adequate provisions for the election of directors representing the preferred stockholders in the event of a default in the payment of dividends to the preferred stockholders.

MANAGEMENT OF DEBTOR'S BUSINESS AND PROPERTY

The debtor's business and property shall be managed during the period of the Plan by the debtor's present management.

REJECTION OF EXECUTORY CONTRACTS

All executory contracts or unexpired leases of the debtor not previously assumed or rejected under 11 U.S.C. §365 are hereby expressly rejected. Claims for damages resulting from such rejection shall be included in Class 9.

HANDLING OF CLAIMS

The debtor shall review all claims filed or deemed filed in this case and all objections to the allowance of such claims shall be filed within 60 days after the effective date of the Plan.

RETENTION OF JURISDICTION

The bankruptcy court shall retain jurisdiction over the parties to and the subject matter of the Plan and all matters related thereto until the Plan has been fully consummated and the case closed, or until the case is dismissed or converted to another chapter. Specifically, the court shall retain jurisdiction to interpret and enforce the provisions of the Plan, determine all disputes or controversies arising under the Plan, enter orders in aid of consummation of the Plan, and determine the allowance of claims or expenses against the debtor or the estate.

MISCELLANEOUS PROVISIONS

The disbursing agent for all payments made under the Plan shall be Betty B. Baker, the controller of the debtor. The disbursing agent shall not be liable for any action or failure to act by the debtor.

All property of the estate not dealt with in the Plan shall be deemed the property of the debtor upon the effective date of the Plan.

The entry of an order confirming the Plan shall serve to release the following stockholders of the debtor from liability for any claim dealt with in the Plan: Arnold A. Smith, Henry S. Smith, and John J. Jones.

The effective date of the Plan shall be the date on which the order confirming the Plan becomes final and can no longer be appealed.

Dated and respectfully submitted this 12th day of January, 1988.

The Hardtimes Supply Co., (Debtor in possession)

by_____
Arnold A. Smith,
President

Notice of Time for Filing Acceptances or Rejections of Plan, of Time of Hearing on Confirmation, and of Time for Filing Objections to Confirmation

UNITED STATES BANKRUPTCY COURT
SOUTHERN DISTRICT OF *TEXAS*

In re *Kenneth Irving,* Debtor	Docket No.......... (Chapter 11)

Notice of Time for Filing Acceptances or Rejections of Plan, of Time of Hearing on Confirmation, and of Time for Filing Objections to Confirmation

To All Creditors and Parties In Interest:

NOTICE IS HEREBY GIVEN THAT

1. On ...., 19.... the court approved a Disclosure Statement in connection with a Plan of Reorganization of *Kenneth Irving*, the above-named debtor.

2. There are transmitted herewith the following:
   a. A copy of the Plan of Reorganization
   b. A copy of the approved Disclosure Statement
   c. Appropriate forms for the acceptance or rejection of the said Plan.

3. *By the said order of the court, acceptances or rejections of the plan may be filed in writing by the holders of all claims and interests impaired by the said plan on or before 3 days prior to the date set for the hearing on confirmation of the Plan.*

4. Appropriate forms for the acceptance or rejection of the Plan are enclosed for the convenience of the holders of claims or interests, if they desire to accept or reject the said Plan. Other forms may be obtained from the undersigned upon request, or from the court.

5. Any holder of a claim or interest whose claim or interest is listed as not disputed, not contingent, or not unliquidated may, but need not, file a proof of claim in order to cast a ballot. Creditors and interest holders whose claims or interests are not listed, or whose claims or interests are listed as disputed, contingent, or unliquidated as to amount and who desire to cast a ballot must file a proof of claim or interest on or before 3 days prior to the date set for the hearing on confirmation of the Plan.

6. Any objection to confirmation of the Plan must be filed on or before 10 days prior to the date of the hearing on confirmation of the Plan.

7. A hearing for consideration of confirmation of the Plan and of such objections as may be made to the confirmation of the Plan will be held on ......, 19...., at 10:00 a.m., in United States Bankruptcy Court, *515 Rusk Avenue, Houston, Texas*.

BY ORDER OF THE COURT.
Dated: ....

Kenneth Irving
Debtor

Ballot for Accepting or Rejecting Plan

UNITED STATES BANKRUPTCY COURT

...... DISTRICT OF ......

In re

....
Debtor

Docket No..........
(Chapter 11)

Ballot for Accepting or Rejecting Plan

The plan referred to in this ballot can be confirmed by the court only if two-thirds in amount and more than one-half in number of creditors in each class and at least two-thirds in amount of each class of interests voting on the plan, accept the plan. This ballot should be returned to:

Name: ....

Address: ....

[*If holder of equity security*] The undersigned, the holder of [*state number*] .... shares of [*describe type*] .... stock of the above-named debtor, represented by Certificate(s) No. ...., registered in the name of ....

[*If bondholder, debenture holder, or other debt security holder*] The undersigned, the holder of [*state unpaid principal amount*] $...... of [*describe security*] ...... of the above-named debtor, due .... [*if applicable*] registered in the name of .... [*if applicable*] bearing serial number(s) ....

[*If holder of general claim*] The undersigned, a holder of a claim against the above-named debtor in the unpaid principal amount of $.........

[*CHECK ONE BOX*]

[   ] ACCEPTS

[   ] REJECTS

the plan of reorganization of the above-named debtor filed by ......, and dated ....

Dated: ....

Print or type name: ....
Signed: ....
[*if appropriate*] By: ....
as: ....
Address: ....

NOTE: The trustee or other person transmitting this ballot to holders of claims and interests should complete the blanks indicating the person filing the plan, the date of the plan, and the person to whom the ballot should be returned.

UNITED STATES BANKRUPTCY COURT
SOUTHERN DISTRICT OF NEW YORK

In re

_____
                                    Debtor

172

DEBTOR'S MODIFICATION OF PLAN
(Before Confirmation)

Case No....
(Chapter 11)

Filed by: *Kenneth Irving,*
Debtor

Debtor hereby modifies the Plan of Reorganization dated ____19__.

1.   Paragraph 3.1 of said Plan shall be modified to read:

Class III creditors shall each receive from the Debtor a non-negotiable promissory note (hereinafter "Class III Notes"), dated as of the effective date, in the principal amount of the creditor's claim, and bearing interest at the rate of _% per annum. Each Class III Note shall be due and payable on the first to occur of (i) a date 3 years from the date thereof, or (ii) a sale of Debtor's assets, the net proceeds of which are sufficient to pay all Class III Notes in full. The Class III Notes shall be executed and delivered by Debtor within 30 days after the effective date, or with respect to any Class III claim to which an objection is filed, within 12 days following a final and non-appealable order on such objection.

2.   This modification does not further impair the Class III claims.

Dated: _____19__

Signed: _____
                                                             (Debtor)

UNITED STATES BANKRUPTCY COURT
SOUTHERN DISTRICT OF NEW YORK

In re

_____
                                    Debtor

Case No....
(Chapter 11)

MOTION TO CONVERT CASE TO CHAPTER 7

The debtor, [or, the Debtor in Possession by its attorney], respectfully represents as follows:

1.   On _____19 _, the debtor filed a voluntary petition for relief under Chapter 11 of the Bankruptcy Code, and is presently a debtor in possession in this case.

2.   The debtor now desires to convert this Chapter 11 case to a case under Chapter 7 of the Bankruptcy Code.

3.   The debtor qualifies as a debtor under Chapter 7 of the Bankruptcy Code, and is entitled to the relief requested under the provisions of 11 U.S.C. §1112(a).

4.   Notice and a hearing are not required for the granting of the relief requested by this motion.

WHEREFORE, the debtor prays for the entry of an order converting this case to a case under Chapter 7 of the Bankruptcy Code.

Dated: _____, 19 _

Signed: _____
Sarah S. Smith, Attorney for Debtor in Possession
                (or, Mr./Mrs. _____, President,
Address: _____
Phone: _____

173

UNITED STATES BANKRUPTCY COURT
FOR THE SOUTHERN DISTRICT OF NEW YORK

IN RE: New Hope, Inc.   )
)   Case No.____
)   Chapter 11
                          Debtor   )

MOTION TO OBJECT TO
CONFIRMATION OF PLAN

COMES NOW the Veterans Bank, a secured and unsecured creditor of the debtor, and by its attorneys, this petitioner objects to confirmation of the Plan dated ____19 _, filed and proposed by New Hope, Inc., the debtor.

1. The Plan does not comply with the provisions of Chapter 11 of the Bankruptcy Code for confirmation on the following grounds:

2. The Plan does not properly classify the secured claim of the Veterans Bank in that while the claim is impaired by the Plan, it is not treated in the Plan as an impaired claim, and the Veterans Bank as the holder of the claim will receive an amount under the plan that is less than what it would receive had the debtor been liquidated under Chapter 7 of the Bankruptcy Code on the effective date of the Plan.

3. The proposed plan is not feasible in that the plan, if confirmed, will still leave the debtor without reasonable prospect of operating at a financial profit or stability, or of meeting the payments under the plan.

4. The plan has not been proposed in good faith by the debtor in that, among other things, the Veterans Bank was not afforded a fair opportunity to vote regarding the plan.

5. The Veterans Bank, a secured creditor, has not accepted the Plan and, to this petitioner's knowledge, at least one other class of secured claims has not accepted the plan.

6. The debtor did not properly solicit acceptances or rejections of competing plans and did not adequately disclose information to Veterans Bank.

WHEREFORE, Veterans Bank objects to confirmation of the said Plan of the debtor and, by this instrument herewith, moves this Honorable Court to deny confirmation of the Plan.

Dated: _____, 19 _   Benson & Benon

                                                 by_____
                                                 David A. Benson
                                                 Attorneys for Veterans Bank
                                                 200 Toledo St.
                                                 New York, N.Y. 10002
                                                 Phone: 447-5000

Order Confirming Plan of Reorganization (Corporate Debtor)

UNITED STATES BANKRUPTCY COURT
. . . . DISTRICT OF . . . .

In re

. . . .
Debtor

Docket No. . . . .
(Chapter 11)

Order Confirming Plan

The plan under chapter 11 of the Bankruptcy Code filed by . . . . . . on . . . . . . [*if appropriate, as modified by modification filed on* . . . . . .], and a copy of the said plan and of the Disclosure Statement(s) approved by the court having been transmitted to the holders of claims and interests; and the court having determined, after notice and a hearing, the following:

1. That the plan complies with the applicable provisions of chapter 11 of the Code;

2. That the proponent of the plan complies with the applicable provisions of the Code;

3. That the plan has been proposed in good faith and not by any means forbidden by law;

4.A. That any payment made or promised by the proponent, by the debtor, or by any person issuing securities or acquiring property under the plan, for services or for costs and expenses in, or in connection with, the case, or in connection with the plan and incident to the case, have been disclosed to the court; and

B. Any such payment made before confirmation of the plan is reasonable; or if such payment is to be fixed after confirmation of the plan, such payment is subject to the approval of the court as reasonable;

5.A. That the proponent of the plan has disclosed the identity and affiliations of any individual proposed to serve, after confirmation of the plan, as a director, officer, or voting trustee of the debtor, or as an affiliate of the debtor participating in a joint plan with the debtor, or a successor to the debtor under the plan; and the appointment to, or continuance in, such office of such individual is consistent with the interests of creditors and equity security holders and with public policy; and

B. The proponent of the plan has disclosed the identity of any insider that will be employed or retained by the reorganized debtor, and the nature of any compensation for such insider;

6. Any regulatory commission with jurisdiction, after confirmation of the plan, over the rates of the debtor has approved any rate change provided for in the plan, or such rate change is expressly conditioned on such approval;

7. That with respect to each class, the following is true: A) each holder of a claim or interest of such class has either accepted the plan; or will, in the alternative, receive or retain under the plan, property of a value, as of the effective date of the plan, that is not less than the amount that such holder would so receive or retain if the debtor were liquidated under chapter 7; or

B) If section 1111(b)(2) of the Code applies to the claims of such class, each holder of a claim of such class will receive or retain under the plan on account of such claim property of a value, as of the effective date of the plan, that is not less than the value of such creditor's interest in the estate's interest in the property that secures such claims;

---

*NOTE that: This format of the Order of Confirmation is for use in a situation when the court directs (or it is otherwise required) that the court's Findings of Fact and Conclusions of Law covering the conditions of the plan's confirmation be included in the order.

8. That with respect to each class, such class has accepted the plan, or, if otherwise, such class is not impaired under the plan;

9. That except to the extent that the holder of a particular claim has agreed to a different treatment of such claim, the plan provides that:

A. with respect to a claim of a kind specified in sections 507(a)(1) or 507(a)(2) of the Code, on the effective date of the plan, the holder of such claim will receive, on account of such claim, cash equal to the allowed amount of such claim;

B. with respect to a class of claims of a kind specified in sections 507(a)(3), 507(a)(4), or 507(a)(5) of the Code, each holder of a claim of such class will receive, if such class has accepted the plan, deferred cash payments of a value, as of the effective date of the plan, equal to the allowed amount of such claim; or, if such class has not accepted the plan, cash on the effective date of the plan equal to the allowed amount of such claim; and

C. with respect to a claim of a kind specified in section 507(a)(6) of the Code, the holder of such claim will receive on account of such claim, deferred cash payments over a period not exceeding 6 years from the date of the assessment of such claim, or a value which, as of the effective date of the plan, is at least equal to the allowed amount of such claim, as allowed;

10. That at least one class of claims has accepted the plan, determined without including any acceptance of the plan by an insider holding a claim of such class;

11. That the plan is feasible; confirmation of the plan is not likely to be followed by the liquidation, or the need for further financial reorganization, of the debtor or any successor to the debtor under the plan, unless such liquidation or reorganization is proposed in the plan.

NOW, WHEREFORE, IT IS ORDERED, that the plan filed by ...... on ...... [*if appropriate*, as modified modification filed on ......], a copy of which plan is attached hereto, is confirmed.

Dated: ....

....
United States Bankruptcy Judge

In re

_____New Hope, Inc._____

                                    Debtor

**ORDER CONFIRMING PLAN OF
REORGANIZATION**
(Individual Debtor)

Case No....
(Chapter 11)

Pursuant to the order of the court dated _____19___, there came on for consideration the confirmation of the Plan of Reorganization filed by ____on ___ 19 _*[if appropriate, as modified by modifications filed ____, 19__]*, and following such hearing the court filed its Findings of Fact and Conclusions of law. In conformity with such Findings and conclusions,

IT IS ORDERED:

1. That the Plan of Reorganization *[if appropriate,* as modified by modifications filed ____, 19 _]*, a copy of which is attached, is confirmed.

2. That the above debtor is released from all dischargeable debts.

3. That the discharge —

(a) voids any judgment at any time obtained, to the extent that such judgment is a determination of the personal liability of the debtor with respect to any debt discharged under 11 U.S.C. §1141, whether or not discharge of such debt is waived;

(b) operates as an injunction against the commencement or continuation of any action, the employment of process, or any act, to collect, recover, or offset any such debt as a personal liability of the debtor, or from property of the debtor, whether or not discharge of such debt has been waived; and

(c) operates as an injunction against the commencement or continuation of an action, the employment of process, or any act, to collect or recover from, or offset against, property of the debtor of the kind specified in section 541(a)(2) of the Bankruptcy Code that is acquired after the commencement of the case, on account of any allowable community claim, except a community claim that is excepted from discharge under section 523 or 1328(c)(1) of the Code, or that would be so excepted, determined in accordance with the provisions of sections 523(c) and 523(d) of the Code, in a case concerning the debtor's spouse commenced on the date of the filing of the petition in a case concerning the debtor, whether or not discharge of the debt based on such community claim is waived.

Dated:_____

_____
United States Bankruptcy Judge

NOTE: The conditions of confirmation are set out in 11 U.S.C. §1129(a). [pp. 93-6 of the manual], and the court may confirm a plan only if all eleven conditions of subsection (a) are met, save only when the "cram down" provisions of subsection (b) are invoked. This form is for use when the court files separate Findings of Fact and Conclusions of Law covering those conditions of confirmation. If the court directs that the findings be included in this order, see the form on p. 164-5 for those that must be included.

UNITED STATES BANKRUPTCY COURT
____DISTRICT OF ____

In re

New Hope, Inc.

Debtor

Case No....
(Chapter 11)

NOTICE OF ORDER CONFIRMING PLAN
AND DISCHARGE
(By Individual Debtor)

To the debtor, his creditors, and other parties in interest:

NOTICE IS HEREBY GIVEN of the entry of an order of this court on ____ 19 _, confirming the Plan of Reorganization filed by _____, on _____19 _ [*if appropriate,* as modified by modification filed on _____ 19__], and providing further that:

A. Except as otherwise provided or permitted by the Plan or such order:

(1) The above-named debtor is released from all dischargeable debts;

(2) The discharge
(a) voids any judgment at any time obtained, to the extent that such judgment is a determination of the personal liability of the debtor with respect to any debt discharged under 11 U.S.C. §1141, whether or not discharge of such debt is waived;

(b) Operates as an injunction against the commencement or continuation of any action, the employment of process, or any act, to collect, recover, or offset any such debt as a personal liability of the debtor, or from property of the debtor, whether or not discharge of such debt has been waived; and

(c) Operates as an injunction against the commencement or continuation of an action, the employment of process, or any act, to collect or recover from, or offset against, property of the debtor of the kind specified in 11 U.S.C. §541(a)(2) that is acquired after the commencement of the case, on account of any allowable community claim, except a community claim that is excepted from discharge under 11 U.S.C. 22523 or 1328(c)(1), or that would be so excepted, determined in accordance with the provisions of 11 U.S.C. §§523(c) and 523(d), in a case concerning the debtor's spouse commenced on the date of the filing of the petition in a case concerning the debtor, whether or not discharge of the debt based on such community claim is waived.

Dated:_____19__

_____
Clerk of the Bankruptcy Court

NOTE: This form, to be signed (and usually prepared) by the Clerk of Court, is to be used to notify creditors of the entry (signing) of the order confirming the plan of reorganization and is to be mailed within 30 days after such entry. See Rule 11-38(e). Additionally, the notice informs the creditors of the discharge provisions of 11 U.S.C. §524, particularly those enjoining suits on discharged debts. Consult local rules for possible additional requirements.

UNITED STATES BANKRUPTCY COURT
SOUTHERN DISTRICT OF NEW YORK   **178**

```
┌─────────────────────────────────┐
  In re:
                                       Case No._____
         New Hope, Inc.,                Chapter 11

                          Debtor
└─────────────────────────────────┘
```

MOTION FOR RELIEF FROM
AUTOMATIC STAY

COMES NOW The Universal Bank, a secured creditor of the above-named debtor, by its attorney and, pursuant to 11 U.S.C. 362(d) and Bankruptcy Rules 4001(a) and 9014, moves this honorable court to grant relief from the automatic stay so as to permit the movant to foreclose on and take possession of the property of the estate described below. In support of this motion the movant represents as follows:

1.   On _____19 _, the above-captioned debtor filed a voluntary petition under Chapter 11 of the Bankruptcy Code, thereupon the automatic stay attaching to the order for relief in the within case has prevented the movant from foreclosing on, obtaining possession of, or otherwise protecting its interest in the property of the estate securing its claim.

2.   The petitioning movant herein holds a valid secured claim against the debtor in the amount of $___, as evidenced by the debtor's promissory note and the security agreement severally dated _____19 _, a copy of which is each attached to this motion and made as part thereof as Exhibits A and B.

3.   The movant has a valid perfected security interest in the property of the debtor's estate, namely the office building located at *[address of the real property]*, as is more specifically described in the said security agreement annexed hereto. The attached security agreement has been duly recorded and otherwise perfected.

4.   Pursuant to Section 362(d) of the Bankruptcy Code, this petitioner is entitled to adequate security and/or adequate protection of its interest in the said property.

5.   The movant does not have and has not been provided adequate protection of its interest in the said property, the said property is deteriorating in value and is not being adequately maintained or protected by the debtor, and thus the value of the movant's secured claim is deteriorating.

6.   As a direct and consummate result of the foregoing, the property securing the movant's claim now has a fair market value appreciably less than the $____amount for the movant's valid secured claim against the debtor. Furthermore, debtor has no equity in the property, and the property is not needed by the debtor for an effective reorganization.

7.   The movant will suffer irreparable damage and loss unless relief from the automatic stay is granted permitting the movant to proceed with foreclosure proceedings.

WHEREFORE, the movant prays for the entry of an order granting relief from the automatic stay and permitting the movant to proceed with foreclosure proceedings on the property described above in this motion.

Dated: _____ 19 ___

                                        Signed: _____
                                                            John A. Josephs
                                                     Attorney for Universal Bank

                                        Address:_____

                                        Phone: _____

Trustee's Application for Authority To Incur Debt Secured by Property of the Estate

UNITED STATES BANKRUPTCY COURT
EASTERN DISTRICT OF *TEXAS*

In re *Phantom Oil Corporation,* Debtor	Docket No........... (Chapter 11)

Trustee's Application for Authority To Incur Debt Secured by Property of the Estate

The application of *Philip Brown*, respectfully represents:

1. Applicant is the duly qualified and acting trustee in this case.

2. In the ordinary course of operating an *oil refinery* it is the accepted practice to assign and pledge accounts receivable evidenced by invoices for the purpose of obtaining current operating funds. In the normal course of such operations, a purchaser of *refinery products* is entitled to a discount of 2 cents per *gallon* of *gasoline* and *propane* if the account is paid within 15 days from the date of the invoice. Most purchasers take advantage of such discount by paying within the 15-day period, but practically all of them do not pay until the 15th day, as a result of which your trustee experiences periodic cash shortages which inhibit optimum operation of the refinery. Your trustee can obtain the necessary immediate funds for continued operation of the business if he is authorized to assign and pledge such invoices.

[If authorization is sought to incur indebtedness secured by a senior or equal lien on property of the estate which is subject to a lien, include the following paragraph 3]

3. Your trustee is required to make modifications in debtor's refinery to reduce its air pollution to come within the standards, for if such standards are not met within 6 months, the refinery will have to cease operations. The cost of such required modification is *$2,250,000*. Your trustee is not able to obtain credit in such amount unless the obligation so incurred is secured by a lien on debtor's refinery which is at least equal to the existing first lien on the plant held by *Third Insurance Company* of *Ashland, Kentucky*. The principal balance now owing on such first lien is *$75,000,000*. The value of debtor's plant presently is *$90,000,000*; when the required modifications have been completed the value will be *$100,000,000*. The equity in such refinery over and above the amount of the first lien affords adequate protection to *Third Insurance Company*, even after imposition of a lien of equal standing in the amount of *$2,250,000*.

4. The debtor is represented in this case by *Henry Taliaferro*, its attorney. The Creditors' Committee herein is represented by *Louis Allen*. *Third Insurance Company* has appeared in the case by *Paul Port*, its attorney.

WHEREFORE, your trustee prays that after notice and a hearing, an order be entered permitting the trustee to assign and pledge accounts receivable evidenced by invoices in order to obtain immediate funds for use in the day to day operations of the business; [*if authority is sought to incur indebtedness secured by a senior or equal lien on property of the estate which is subject to a lien, add this*: that he be authorized to grant a lien equal to the lien of *Third Insurance Company* to secure *$2,250,000*;] and that he have such other and further relief as is just.

Dated: ....

(Signed)   *Stanley Selig*
Attorney for the Trustee
1955 Jefferson Street
Beaumont, Texas
Tel. #.......

Application by Trustee for Authority To Reject Executory Contract

UNITED STATES BANKRUPTCY COURT
THE DISTRICT OF *CONNECTICUT*

In re

Roe Brothers, Inc.,
Debtor

Docket No..........
(Chapter 11)

Application for Authority To Reject Lease

The application of *Charles White* respectfully represents the following:

1. On the *2nd* day of *December, 19....,* your applicant was appointed trustee of *Roe Brothers, Inc.,* the above named **debtor,** and qualified and is now acting as such trustee.

2. On *July 1, 19....,* *Roe Brothers, Inc.,* the said debtor, entered into a certain agreement of lease by which the said debtor **leased** from the *Third Realty Corporation* the basement and the first, second, third and fourth floors of the building, known as *2600 Lexington Avenue, New York City,* for a term of *twenty (20)* years commencing *July 1, 19....,* and terminating *June 30, 19....,* at a rental of *one hundred and fifty-five thousand ($155,000.00)* Dollars per year.

3. Adverse economic conditions, which have affected and are affecting the business of said debtor, have resulted in a marked diminution in the business carried on by the said debtor through the *New York* office, leased as aforesaid, and the said leased space is grossly disproportionate in size to the present and probable future requirements of the said debtor.

4. The geographic center for marketing the type of textile manufactured and sold by the said debtor through its *New York* office is now located further west and somewhat further uptown in the City of *New York* than the premises occupied under the said lease, and the location occupied by the said debtor under the said lease has ceased to be the most desirable location for the debtor's business.

5. The rent reserved in the said lease constitutes a substantial part of the cost of doing business to the said debtor, and also constitutes a large expense which is not warranted by the present volume of business carried on by your applicant through the debtor's *New York* office, nor by the volume of business which may reasonably be anticipated, and the result thereof is that the said lease is a severe drain upon the financial resources of the said debtor.

6. Your applicant has made a careful survey of other more desirable locations for the *New York* office of the said debtor and the probable cost thereof, and your applicant has ascertained that he can obtain other premises which will provide sufficient space at substantially lower rental at a more desirable location than the premises leased from the *Third Realty Corporation,* as aforesaid.

7. The increased business which the said debtor would obtain by the removal of its offices and show-rooms to a more desirable location than the said premises, and the savings in rent which would be effected by such removal, would more than offset the amount which the said landlord could realize from the said debtor as a result of the rejection of the said lease.

8. The said lease with the *Third Realty Corporation* is burdensome to the said debtor and it would be to the best interests of the estate for the said lease to be rejected forthwith.

WHEREFORE your applicant prays that he be permitted to reject the said unexpired lease, dated *July 1, 19....,* between the *Third Realty Corporation,* as landlord, and *Roe Brothers, Inc.,* the said debtor, as tenant, and that your applicant have such other and further relief as is just.

(Signed)

(Address)

Henry Forsyth
Attorney for Trustee
200 Main Street
Hartford, Connecticut
(Tel. No.).......

In re:

Roe Brothers, Inc.,

Debtor

Case No....
(Chapter 11)

Order Authorizing Trustee [Debtor in Possession] To Reject Executory Contract/Lease

The application of *Charles White*, trustee [as President of debtor in possession] of *Roe Brothers, Inc.*, the above named debtor, for authority to reject the unexpired lease between the *Third Realty Corporation*, as landlord, and *Roe Brothers, Inc.*, the said debtor, as tenant, dated *July 1, 19 _*, having been heard on the 2nd day of *January, 19 _*, and notice of said hearing having been given to all the parties to the lease and other parties designated by the court to receive such notice, and after hearing *Henry Forsyth*, and *Hall & Stell*, attorneys for the *Third Realty Corporation*, in opposition to the application, and it appearing that the said lease is burdensome to the estate of said debtor, it is:

ORDERED that *Charles White*, trustee [debtor in possession] of *Roe Brothers, Inc.*, the above named debtor, be, and he hereby is, authorized to reject the unexpired lease between the *Third Realty Corporation*, as landlord, and *Roe brothers, Inc.*, the debtor, as tenant, dated *July 1, 19 _*, and covering premises known as *2600 Lexington Avenue, New York, New York;* and it is further

ORDERED that the entry of this order shall be deemed to constitute a rejection of the lease by the said trustee.

Dated: *January 4, 19 _*

_____
United States Bankruptcy Judge

UNITED STATES BANKRUPTCY COURT
DISTRICT OF CONNECTICUT

In re:

Smith Brothers, Inc.,

Debtor

Case No....
(Chapter 11)

Order Authorizing Assumption of Executory Contract/Lease

The application of the trustee [debtor in possession] for authority to assume the lease of real property referred to in the said application came on for hearing before the court after notice to *Second Avenue Realty Corporation*, the debtor, and the Creditors' Committee. After hearing the evidence and argument of counsel and the parties, the court finds that assumption of such lease will be beneficial to this estate; that the trustee [debtor in possession] is able to cure the debtor's prepetition default, including any actual pecuniary loss which may have been sustained by the lessor; and that the lessor has been furnished adequate assurance of future performance on its lease. It is therefore

ORDERED, ADJUDGED, AND DECREED that *Charles White*, for the trustee [debtor in possession], be, and he hereby is, authorized to assume the debtor's lease with *Second Avenue Realty Corporation* dated ____ 19 __.

Dated: _____19 ____

_____
U.S. Bankruptcy Judge

182

In re:

Smith Brothers, Inc.,

Debtor

Case No....
(Chapter 11)

Application (Motion) for Authority To Assume Executory Contract/Lease

The application of *Charles White* respectfully represents:

1.   Applicant is the duly qualified and acting as trustee [as debtor in possession] in this case.

2.   On _____ 19 __, the debtor entered into a lease by which the debtor leased from *Second Avenue Realty Corporation* the basement, first, and second floors of the building known as *2100 Second Avenue, Hartford, Connecticut,* for a term of 15 years, commencing on the date of said lease and terminating _____ 19 _, at a rental of $125,000 per year.

3.   The rent reserved in said lease is substantially below the present going rate for comparable space in the *City of Hartford*. Your applicant has received a firm offer from a solvent, growing company to sublease the space covered by debtor's lease for the 10 remaining years of the term of said lease at a rental of *$175,000* per year.

4.   Debtor was 3 months delinquent in payment of its rent to *Second Avenue Realty Corporation* at the time of the commencement of this case. Since his appointment and qualification, your applicant has paid all rent as it became due, and is prepared to pay to the lessor the delinquent rent owing to it, and to compensate the lessor for any actual pecuniary loss which may have resulted from debtor's prepetition breach of said lease.

5.   The company to which your applicant proposes to assign the lease is a publicly held corporation of substantial size. Its earnings record over the past 5 years have shown a steady increase, and the prospects are that its growth and stability will continue to rise. The record of this company, and its future prospects as assessed by financial experts, afford to the lessor adequate assurance of future performance under the lease.

WHEREFORE your applicant prays that he be permitted to assume said unexpired lease between the debtor and *Second Avenue Realty Corporation,* and that he have such other and further relief as is just.

Dated: _____ 19 ____

Signed: _____
        For Trustee [Debtor in Possession]

Address: _____
         Hartford, Connecticut, Zip

Phone: _____

NOTICE OF HEARING AND CERTIFICATE OF SERVICE BY MAIL

PLEASE TAKE NOTICE that a hearing on the above Motion for Approval of Assumption of Executory Contract has been scheduled for the _____ day of 19 ____ at ____ A.M./P.M. in Room ___, of the United States Courthouse, at _____ _____, before the Honorable _____ Bankruptcy Judge.

I the undersigned party hereby certify that a true copy of the above Motion and the above Notice of Hearing was mailed, first-class postage prepaid, to Mr._____ _____ to this address: _____ _____, on this _____ day of 19 ___.

Signed: _____
        John A. Johnson (Process serving party)

Address: _____

In re:

Universal Department Stores, Inc.,

Debtor

Case No....
(Chapter 11)

Application (Motion) For Approval of
Compensation of Debtor's Officers

The application of *Universal Department Stores, Inc.*, respectfully represents:

1.   Debtor filed its voluntary petition under Chapter 11 of the Bankruptcy Code on _____19 _ and has continued to operate its business, a department store in *New Orleans, Louisiana.*

2.   During the year preceding the filing of its petition in this case debtor's sales were in excess of *$15,000,000. Joseph Hendon*, the *Vice-President* in charge of operations, has received a monthly salary of *$4,500; Frank Doe*, the *Vice-President* and *General Merchandise Manager*, has received a monthly salary of *$3,000; Arthur Brown*, *Vice-President* and *Advertising Manager*, has received a monthly salary of *$2,500.* These persons have been in debtor's employ for more than 5 years and their services are necessary in the operation of debtor's business and in the maintenance of an efficient working organization.

3.   The said persons are willing to continue in the employ of debtor in possession, from month to month, at the rates of compensation heretofore paid by the debtor, which rates are fair and reasonable. Debtor desires to employ the said persons at the rates indicated, and it is to the best interest of this estate that they be so employed.

4.   *Henry Hackett* is the chairman of the creditors' committee appointed in this case, and *Anthony White* is attorney for said committee.

WHEREFORE debtor prays that the court approve the payment to *Joseph Hendon, Frank Doe,* and *Arthur Brown,* officers of the debtor, of the monthly salaries stated above, and that it have such other and further relief as is just.

Dated: _____19 ____

Signed: _____
Vice-President, Universal Department Stores, Inc.
as Debtor in Possession (or, Attorney for Debtor in Possession)

Address: _____
New Orleans, Louisiana, Zip

Phone: (504)_____

*NOTICE OF HEARING AND CERTIFICATE OF SERVICE BY MAIL**

PLEASE TAKE NOTICE that a hearing on the above Motion For Approval of Compensation of Debtor's Officers has been scheduled for the _____day of 19 _ at _A.M./P.M.** in Room _, of the United States Courthouse, at _____, before the Honorable _____ Bankruptcy Judge.

I the undersigned party hereby certify that a true copy of the above Motion and the above Notice of Hearing was mailed, first-class postage prepaid, to _____ to this address: ._____, on this _____ day of 19 _.

Signed: _____
John A. Johnson (Process serving party)

Address: _____

*NOTE: This application is required to be served in a manner locally provided for service of summons upon the chairman of the creditor's committee, and the creditor's attorney, (if any).

**Cross out one or the other.

UNITED STATES BANKRUPTCY COURT
<u>SOUTHERN</u> DISTRICT OF <u>NEW YORK</u>

In re:

<u>New Hope, Inc.,</u>

Debtor

Case No._____
Chapter 11

MOTION (APPLICATION) FOR
AUTHORITY TO USE CASH COLLATERAL

COMES NOW the debtor in possession who herewith represents as follows:

1. On _____19 _ the debtor filed a voluntary petition under Chapter 11 of the Bankruptcy Code and presently is operating its business as a debtor in possession.

2. The debtor is unable to use cash collateral in the amount of $_____, consisting of funds on deposit in account with the Universal Bank, and said debtor herewith seeks authority to use same.

3. The name and address of each entity having an interest in the cash collateral sought to be used are as follows: The Universal Bank, 20 Broad Street, New York, N.Y.; and the name and address of the party having possession of the said cash collateral is one and the same party above designated.

4. The debtor needs to use the aforesaid cash collateral in order to meet its monthly rents to continue the operation of its business.

5. The debtor has no other funds to meet such expenses and will be unable to continue in business unless the said expenses are timely paid.

6. The debtor proposes to protect the interest of the Universal Bank in the said cash collateral by providing the said bank with a lien on the account owed to the debtor by _____ of _____, which account is in the total amount of $_____payable on _____19 _, and there are no other liens against the account.

7. The debtor hereby requests a preliminary hearing on this motion, to consider granting approval for immediate use of a month's rent in the amount of $____, pending the final hearing on this motion.

WHEREFORE, the debtor prays for the entry of an order authorizing the debtor to use cash collateral as set forth above in this motion and for such other relief as may be just and proper.

Dated: _____ 19 ___

Signed:_____
Edward A. Jones, VP, New Hope, Inc.
Debtor in Possession

Address:_____

Phone: _____

In re:

<u>Richard White, Inc.,</u>

Debtor

Case No....
(Chapter 11)

Application (Motion) of the Debtor In Possession [or Trustee] for Authority To Employ Attorney for Special Purposes

The application of *Walter Horne* respectfully represents:

1.   Your applicant is the President of Richard White, Inc., debtor in possession of the above-named debtor, and has qualified and now is acting as such debtor in possession.

2.   Pursuant to order of this court (and/or rules and procedures of this court thereof), your applicant is now operating the business and managing the property of the debtor.

3.   At the time of the filing of the petition herein there was pending in the *District Court of Bexar County, Texas* a suit brought by the debtor as plaintiff against *William Wells* as defendant to recover the sum of $25,000 for merchandise sold and delivered to the defendant. The defendant interposed a defense of breach of contract and breach of warranty in the said suit. *Thomas Jones,* an attorney duly admitted to practice in the State of *Texas,* represents the debtor in said suit. All discovery has been completed, and the case is specially set for trial in *four weeks.*

4.   Your applicant believes that the debtor has a good and meritorious cause of action in this case. The prosecution of such suit is necessary to preserve the estate of the debtor and to prevent loss thereto. For that reason, applicant has selected *Thomas Jones* as attorney to represent the debtor in the said suit for the reason that he has represented the debtor in said suit since its inception, and is fully familiar with the relevant facts and applicable law, and is well prepared to continue the legal services required in said suit, and your applicant believes that he is well qualified to represent him as debtor in possession in that suit.

5.   The said *Thomas Jones, Esq.,* whose office address is _____ _____, was retained by the debtor in possession to represent him in said suit on a contingency of *40%* of any recovery which might be had against *William Wells.* Said attorney has offered to perform such services as may be required hereafter in said suit in behalf of your applicant for reasonable compensation to be fixed by this court.

6.   To the best of your applicant's knowledge, *Thomas Jones* has no connection with said debtor, the creditors, or any party in interest, or their respective attorneys, except that he has represented the debtor in said suit since its inception.

7.   *Thomas Jones* does not hold or represent any interest adverse to the debtor in possession or the estate in the matters upon which he is to be engaged, and his employment would be in the best interests of this estate.

8.   *Richard White, Inc.,* the debtor, is NOT represented in this case by any attorney and is acting prop se in the said Chapter 11 case. No other party in interest has appeared in this case.

WHEREFORE, your applicant prays that he be authorized to employ the said *Thomas Jones* to represent him as debtor in possession in the prosecution and trial of said suit upon the terms specified herein, and that he have such other and further relief as is just.

Signed: _____

Debtor in Possession
(or Attorney for Debtor in Possession)

Address: _____

Phone: _____

In re:

Richard White, Inc.,

Debtor

Case No....
(Chapter 11)

Order Authorizing Employment of Attorney for Special Purposes

Upon consideration of the application of *Walter Horne,* for debtor in possession herein, seeking authority to employ *Thomas Jones, Esq.* for special purposes, and it appearing that *Thomas Jones* is an attorney duly qualified to practice in the state of *Texas;* that authorization to prosecute said suit is necessary to preserve the estate of the debtor and to prevent loss thereto; and that *Thomas Jones* holds or represents no interest adverse to said debtor or to the estate in matters upon which he is to be engaged; and that his employment is necessary and would be to the best interests of this estate; it is

ORDERED that *Walter Horne,* as said debtor in possession, be, and he hereby is, authorized to employ *Thomas Jones,* as attorney to represent him in the prosecution and trial of the law suit against *William Wells;* and it is further

ORDERED that the compensation of said *Thomas Jones* for his services in behalf of said debtor in possession shall be fixed hereafter by this court.

Dated: _____19 ___

_____
United States Bankruptcy Judge

UNITED STATES BANKRUPTCY COURT
<u>SOUTHERN</u> DISTRICT OF <u>NEW YORK</u>

In re:

Roe Woolen Corporation,

Debtor

Case No....
(Chapter 11)

Order Authorizing Employment of Attorney for General Services

Upon the application of *Roe Woolen Corporation,* the above named debtor, praying for authority to employ and appoint *Arthur Smith, Esq.,* under a general retainer to represent it as debtor in possession herein, and upon the affidavit of said *Arthur Smith,* Esq., and it appearing that said *Arthur Smith* is an attorney duly qualified to practice in this court, and the court being satisfied that *Arthur Smith* represents no interest adverse to said *Roe Woolen Corporation* as debtor in possession herein, or to its estate, in the matters upon which he is to be engaged, that his employment is necessary and would be to the best interests of the estate, and that the case is one justifying a general retainer, it is

ORDERED that *Roe Woolen Corporation,* as debtor in possession herein, be and it hereby is authorized to employ *Arthur Smith,* as attorney to represent it as debtor in possession, under a general retainer, in the within proceeding under Chapter 11 of the Bankruptcy Code.

Dated: _____19 ___

_____
United States Bankruptcy Judge

Application by Debtor in Possession for Authority To Employ Attorney Under General Retainer

UNITED STATES BANKRUPTCY COURT
SOUTHERN DISTRICT OF *NEW YORK*

In re

Roe Woolen Corporation,
Debtor

Docket No..........
(Chapter 11)

Application To Employ Attorney

The application of *Roe Woolen Corporation* respectfully represents the following:

1. On the *17th* day of *October, 19....*, debtor filed a petition herein under Chapter 11 of the Bankruptcy Code.

2. Your applicant has continued in possession of its property, and your applicant as debtor in possession is now operating its business and managing its property.

3. Debtor, as debtor in possession, wishes to employ *Arthur Smith*, an attorney duly admitted to practice in this court.

4. Your applicant has selected *Arthur Smith* for the reason that he has had considerable experience in matters of this character, and believes that *Arthur Smith* is well qualified to represent it as debtor in possession in this proceeding.

5. The professional services the said *Arthur Smith* is to render are:
    (a) to give debtor legal advice with respect to its powers and duties as debtor in possession in the continued operation of its business and management of its property;
    (b) to take necessary action to avoid a lien against debtor's property obtained by attachment by *Doe Supply Company, Inc.*, within 90 days before the filing of said petition, under Chapter 11;
    (c) to represent your applicant as debtor in possession in connection with reclamation proceedings which have been instituted in this court by *White Manufacturing Corporation* and *William Blue*;
    (d) to prepare on behalf of your applicant as debtor in possession necessary applications, answers, orders, reports and other legal papers;
    (e) to perform all other legal services for debtor, as debtor in possession, which may be necessary herein;
[*State in detail any other professional services which the attorney is to render for the debtor in possession; services to be rendered for the debtor as such, as distinguished from the debtor in possession, should not be included.*]
and it is necessary for debtor as debtor in possession to employ an attorney for such professional services.

6. To the best of debtor's knowledge, said *Arthur Smith* has no connection with the creditors, or any other party in interest, or their respective attorneys.

7. Your applicant desires to employ *Arthur Smith* under a general retainer because of the extensive legal services required.

8. *Arthur Smith* represents no interest adverse to debtor as debtor in possession or the estate in the matters upon which he is to be engaged for debtor as debtor in possession, and his employment would be to the best interests of this estate.

WHEREFORE your applicant prays that it be authorized to employ and appoint the said *Arthur Smith* under a general retainer to represent it as debtor in possession in this proceeding under Chapter 11 of said Code, and that it have such other and further relief as is just.

(Signed) By: *Roe Woolen Corporation,*
Charles Roe, Vice-President
Debtor
2000 Broadway
New York, New York

188

Application (Motion) To Employ Accountants [or Appraisers, Auctioneers, etc.]

In re:

Roe Woolen Corporation,

Debtor

Case No....
(Chapter 11)

The application of *Roe Woolen Corporation* respectfully represents:

1.   On _____19 _, debtor filed a petition under Chapter 11 of the Bankruptcy Code and has continued in possession of its property and the operation of its business.

2.   Debtor in possession wishes to employ *Farragut and Associates* as accountants. Your applicants has chosen these accountants for the reason that they are experienced in matters of this character and are well qualified to perform the work required of them in this case.

3.   The professional services *Farragut and Associates are to render are:*

to close out debtor's books as of the date of the filing of this case, and to open new books as of the next day thereafter;

to establish a new bookkeeping system to replace the outmoded system heretofore used by the debtor;

to prepare the periodic statements of the debtor in possession's operations as required by the rules of this court; and

to prepare and file the debtor's income tax return for the fiscal years which ended 3 weeks before the filing of this case.

4.   No trustee has been appointed herein, and no creditors' committee has been designated in this case.

WHEREFORE debtor in possession prays that it be authorized to employ Farragut and Associates as accountants to perform the professional services required by it in and in connection with this case.

Dated: _____19 ____ Signed: _____

Vice-President, Roe Woolen Corporation,
Debtor in Possession

Address: _____

New York, New York, Zip

Phone: _____

UNITED STATES BANKRUPTCY COURT
SOUTHERN DISTRICT OF NEW YORK

In re:

Roe Woolen Corporation,

Debtor

Case No....
(Chapter 11)

Order Authorizing Employment of Accountants

Upon the application of *Roe Woolen Corporation*, the debtor in possession, praying for authority to employ *Farragut and Associates* as accountants, and it appearing that no notice of a hearing on such application need be given, and sufficient cause having been shown therefor, it is

ORDERED that the debtor in possession be, and it hereby is, authorized to employ *Farragut and Associates* as accountants to render professional services to it in this case; and it is further

ORDERED that the compensation of said accountants for their services in behalf of said debtor in possession shall be fixed hereafter by the court.

Dated: _____19 ____

_____
United States Bankruptcy Judge

UNITED STATES BANKRUPTCY COURT
<u>SOUTHERN</u> DISTRICT OF <u>TEXAS</u>

In re:

    <u>Kingsridge Apartments, Ltd.</u>, A
           Limited Partnership

                 Debtor

Case No....
(Chapter 11)

Application To Modify Amount of Deposit With Utility Company

        The application of *Kingsride Apartments, Ltd.*, debtor in possession, respectfully represents:

        1.   Debtor filed a voluntary petition under Chapter 11 of the Bankruptcy Code on _____ 19 _, and continues in possession of its property and is operating its *350 unit* apartment project.

        2.   *Community Electric Company* has demanded from debtor, as a condition for continuation of uninterrupted electric service to the apartment project, a deposit of *$100,000*. Such deposit demanded represents more than 3 times the average monthly electricity bill of debtor during its peak summer months, and more than 5 times the average monthly electricity bill during the more clement winter months.

        3.   The said deposit demanded by *Community Electric Company* clearly is excessive. Debtor is prepared to pay, and will pay, its bills for electricity used since the date of the commencement of this case promptly upon receipt of its bills from the company. Debtor cannot obtain a surety bond in the amount required by the electric company, and if it is required by the company to make a deposit of *$100,000* it cannot continue to operate, and it will be forced to close down its operations, and to convert the case to a case under Chapter 7 of the Code.

        WHEREFORE debtor prays that the deposit for the continuation of electric service be fixed at a reasonable amount, and that it have such other and further relief as is just and equitable.

        Dated: _____ 19 ___

              Signed: _____

                              President, Kingsride Apartments, Ltd.
                                 as Debtor in Possession

              Address: _____

                                    Houston, Texas, Zip

              Phone: (713)   _____

UNITED STATES BANKRUPTCY COURT
SOUTHERN DISTRICT OF TEXAS

In re:

Kingsridge Apartments, Ltd.

Debtor

Case No....
(Chapter 11)

Order Modifying Amount of Deposit With Utility Company

The application of *Kingsride Apartments, Ltd.*, debtor in possession, for modification of the amount of deposit demanded by *Community Electric Company* as a condition to continuation of services to debtor's apartments having been heard on ____ , 19 __, adequate notice of said hearing having been given to *Community Electric Company*, and after hearing the evidence presented and argument of the parties and/or counsel for the parties, the court filed herein its findings of fact. In accordance with such findings, it is

ORDERED, ADJUDGED, AND DECREED:

1. That debtor in possession shall furnish to *Community Electric Company* a surety bond or a cash deposit in the amount of only $25,000 to ensure payment of future billings by such utility company;

2. That in the event debtor in possession decides to make a cash deposit with said utility company in lieu of a surety bond, such deposit shall be paid in 4 monthly installments of $6,250 each, the first of which shall be paid within 10 days after the entry of this order, with the remaining installments to be paid on or before the 15th day of the succeeding 3 months;

3. That the matter of the amount of the deposit by debtor in possession with *Community Electric Company* may be reopened on motion by either party at any time.

Dated: _____ 19 ___

_____
U.S. Bankruptcy Judge

United States Bankruptcy Court

For the ___Southern___ District of ___New York___

In re: _____

_____

Debtor*

BCT 19
(8/83)

Case No. _____

PROOF OF CLAIMS

1. [*If claimant is an individual claiming for himself*] The undersigned, who is the claimant herein, resides at**

[*If claimant is a partnership claiming through a member*] The undersigned, who resides at**

is a member of _____, a partnership,
composed of the undersigned and
of** _____, and
doing business at**
and is authorized to make this proof of claim on behalf of the partnership.

[*If claimant is a corporation claiming through an authorized officer*] The undersigned, who resides at**

is the _____ of
a corporation organized under the laws of
and doing business at**
and is authorized to make this proof of claim on behalf of the corporation.

[*If claim is made by agent*] The undersigned, who resides at** Midland Mortgage Co.
___Oklahoma City, OK 73107___ , is the agent of Victor S & L Assoc. c/o FSl
of** ___Dallas, TX___ , and is
authorized to make this proof of claim on behalf of the claimant.

2. The debtor was, at the time of the filing of the petition initiating this case, and still is indebted [*or liable*] to this claimant, in the sum of
$ 23,859.00

3. The consideration for this debt [*or ground of liability*] is as follows:

4. [*If the claim is founded on a writing*] The writing on which this claim is founded (or a duplicate thereof) is attached hereto [*or cannot be attached for the reason set forth in the statement attached hereto*].

5. [*If appropriate*] This claim is founded on an open account, which became [*or will become*] due on
, as shown by the itemized statement attached hereto.
Unless it is attached hereto or its absence is explained in an attached statement, no note or other negotiable instrument has been received for the account or any part of it.

6. No judgment has been rendered on the claim except

7. The amount of all payments of this claim has been credited and deducted for the purpose of making this proof of claim.

8. This claim is not subject to any setoff or counter-claim except

9. No security interest is held for this claim except

[*If security interest in the property of the debtor is claimed*] The undersigned claims the security interest under the writing referred to in paragraph 4 hereof [*or under a separate writing (or a duplicate of which) is attached hereto, or under a separate writing which cannot be attached hereto for the reason set forth in the statement attached hereto*]. Evidence of perfection of such security interest is also attached hereto.

10. This claim is a general unsecured claim, except to the extent that the security interest, if any, described in paragraph 9 is sufficient to satisfy the claim. [*If priority is claimed, state the amount and basis thereof.*]

$ ___23,859.00/ See Attached___
Total Amount Claimed

Claim Number
(For Office Use Only)

Name of Creditor: Midland Mortgage Co.
(Print or Type Full Name of Creditor)

Dated: ___April   19___   Signed: *Rochelle Gebhardt*, Bankruptcy Administrator

UNITED STATES BANKRUPTCY COURT
NORTHERN DISTRICT OF ILLINOIS

192

Objection to Allowance of Claim & Notice of Hearing Thereof

In re:

Roe Coat Company, Inc.

Debtor

Case No....
(Chapter 11)

Roe Coat Company, Inc., the above named debtor, acting through the undersigned as the debtor in possession herein, objects to the allowance of the claim of *[name of the claimant]* filed herein in the amount of $____, based on the following grounds:

1. The debtor is not justly and truly indebted to said claimant.

2. Said claim was paid by the debtor on or about the _____ day of _ _____19 _.

3. A portion of the said claim is for unmatured interest.

[Separately state and number any other grounds of objections.]

WHEREFORE *Roe Coat Company, Inc.*, *the* said debtor, prays that said claim of *[name of claimant]* be disallowed, and that debtor have such other and further relief as is just.

NOTICE

PLEASE TAKE NOTICE that a hearing on the above Objection will be held before the Honorable _____, Bankruptcy Judge, in Room _ of the United States Courthouse, _____ Street, _____ on the __day of _____ 19 _ at this time _ A.M./P.M.*

Dated: *Chicago, Illinois*

_____, 19 ___

Signed: _____

Debtor in Possession [or Attorney for Debtor]

*Cross out either "A.M." or "P.M.", as necessary.

Address: _____

Phone: _____

CERTIFICATE OF SERVICE BY MAIL

I, the undersigned party, hereby certify that I have on this _____ day of _____, 19 ___, mailed by prepaid first class mail, a copy of the above Objection to Allowance of Claim and Notice of Hearing thereof to the claimant named in the Objection at the address shown in the Objection.

Signed: _____

John A. Johnson (Party Mailing the papers)

Address: _____

UNITED STATES BANKRUPTCY COURT
NORTHERN DISTRICT OF ILLINOIS

In re:

Roe Coat Company, Inc.,

Debtor

Order Reducing Claim

Case No....
(Chapter 11)

The objection of *Roe Coat Company, Inc.*, the above named debtor, to the allowance of the claim of *Robert Blue*, filed herein in the amount of $_____ Dollars, having been heard on the _____ day of _____ 19 _, and due notice of said hearing having been given by mail *[or state any other manner of notice, as the case may be]* to said claimant, *[or, if applicable, state either: (a)* and the debtor and the claimant having consented to the making of this order; *or (b)* and after hearing the debtor, Mr. _____ _____ and/or Mr. _____, attorney for said debtor, in favor of said objection, and said claimant in person, in opposition thereto;*]* it is

ORDERED the said claim of __*[name of the party making the claim]*__, filed herein in the amount of $____ Dollars, be and it hereby is reduced to $_____ Dollars and allowed at said amount.

Dated: _____19 ___

_____
United States Bankruptcy Judge

UNITED STATES BANKRUPTCY COURT
<u>WESTERN</u> DISTRICT OF <u>NEW YORK</u>

In re:

<u>Roe Tire Company, Inc.,</u>
　　　　　　　　Debtor

<u>Roe Tire Company, Inc.,</u>
　　　　　　　　Plaintiff

　　　　　　v.

<u>Henry Brown</u>
　　　　　　　　Debtor

Case No....
(Chapter 11)

Complaint in Support of Objection to Secured Claim

The complaint of *Roe Tire Company, Inc.*, respectfully represents:

1.　　　On _____19 _, debtor filed in this court a voluntary petition under Chapter 11 of the Bankruptcy Code.

2.　　　The plan proposed by debtor provides that its unsecured debts, except such as have priority, be settled and satisfied by payment to the holders thereof of *forty (40%) per cent* of their respective debts, payable *twenty (20%) per cent* cash upon confirmation of the plan, and *twenty (20%) per cent* in *four (4)* monthly installments of *five (5%) per cent* each, commencing *one (1)* month after confirmation.

3.　　　On the _____day of ____ 19 _, debtor executed and delivered to the Defendant herein, *Henry Brown,* a security agreement creating a security interest in debtor's goods and chattels, consisting of machinery, furniture and fixtures contained in premises at this address: _____, to secure the payment of its debt to said *Henry Brown* in the sum of $_____.

4.　　　At the date of the filing of its petition herein, debtor was the owner and in possession of said goods and chattels.

5.　　　*Henry Brown* has filed a proof of claim herein in the sum of *Nine Thousand ($9,000)* Dollars for the unpaid balance of said debt of your applicant.

6.　　　Said proof of claim of *Henry Brown* states that he holds said security interest as security for said debt, that the security has a value of *Seven Thousand ($7,000)* Dollars, and that he is an unsecured creditor of debtor in the sum of *Two Thousand ($2,000)* Dollars.

7.　　　The security interest referred to in paragraph 3 was never perfected in the manner required by the Uniform Commercial Code as enacted in *New York.*

WHEREFORE debtor prays that said security interest be decreed void, that the claim of *Henry Brown* in the sum of *Nine Thousand ($9,000)* Dollars be classified as a wholly unsecured claim, and that it have such other and further relief as is just.

Dated: Buffalo, N.Y.

_____19 ___

Signed: _____
　　　　　　　Debtor or Attorney for Debtor

Address: _____

Phone: _____

In re:	
New Hope, Inc.,	Case No....
	(Chapter 11)
Debtor	

MOTION FOR AUTHORITY TO OBTAIN CREDIT NOT IN THE ORDINARY COURSE OF BUSINESS*

The Debtor in Possession by its attorney (or, Debtor in Possession), represents as follows:

1.   On _____19 _ the debtor filed a voluntary petition for relief under Chapter 11 of the Bankruptcy Code and is now operating its business, which is roofing supplies, as a debtor in possession.

2.   The debtor's business is seasonal and during the months of February and March it is necessary to contract to purchase shingles and other roofing supplies in order to be ready for the busy season that begins in April. It is the practice of manufacturers in the roofing supply business to require a deposit of at least 25 percent on all orders of shingles and other roofing supplies. In order to meet these deposit requirements it will be necessary for the debtor to borrow the sum of $25,000.

3.   The First National Bank of South Bend, Indiana has agreed to lend the sum of $25,000 to the debtor upon the following terms: interest on the unpaid portion of the loan shall be at the rate of one percent per month; the loan shall be repayable at the rate of $5,000 per month beginning on the first day of June, 1988; the loan shall be secured by a senior lien on all accounts payable to the debtor beginning on June 1, 1988; and the loan shall be personally guaranteed by John J. Jones, the president of the debtor. A letter from the First National Bank of South Bend confirming the loan agreement is attached to this motion.

4.   The debtor's accounts receivable are currently subject to a security interest in favor of the Ace Factoring Company of Chicago, Illinois, which security interest the debtor proposes to subordinate to the lien of the First National Bank of South Bend. The debtor proposes to adequately protect the interest of Ace Factoring in the accounts receivable by extending the duration of Ace Factoring's security interest to cover accounts receivable received after August 15, 1988, which is when its present security interest expires.

5.   The debtor in possession is unable to obtain unsecured credit allowable as an administrative expense and is unable to obtain credit other than by granting a senior lien as described above in this motion. The borrowing requested herein is in the best interest of the estate and the debtor expects to be able to repay the borrowed funds as called for in the agreement from the sale of the supplies purchased with the borrowed funds. Unless the debtor is permitted to borrow the funds herein requested, the debtor will be unable to continue in business.

WHEREFORE, the debtor prays for the entry of an order authorizing the debtor to borrow the funds herein requested upon the terms herein set forth.

Dated: _____, 19 _ Signed: _____

                                        Sarah S. Smith
                              Attorney for Debtor in Possession
                                  (or, Mr./Ms. _____, President,
                                Hope, Inc., as Debtor in Possession)
                        Address: _____
                          Phone: _____

*This form, substantially reproduced herein for its illustrative usefulness and value, is from John H. Williamson's *The Attorney's Handbook on Chapter 11 Bankruptcy*, courtesy of Argyle Publishing Co., the publisher to whom the present publisher is greatly indebted.

195

In re:

New Hope, Inc.,

Debtor

Case No....
(Chapter 11)

NOTICE OF PROPOSED SALE OF ESTATE PROPERTY NOT IN ORDINARY COURSE OF BUSINESS, AND OF HEARING

TO: All Creditors and Other Parties in Interest

    1. **NOTICE IS HEREBY GIVEN THAT** the above-named debtor in possession, proposes to sell the property of the estate described in the paragraph below at a public auction on _____19 _ at 10 A.M. thereof at Room _ at this address: ___
_____ .

    2. The property proposed to be sold, is a real property described as follows:

    3. The property is secured by a first and second mortgage by the Universal Bank of New York, New York. The sale is to be free and clear of all liens and encumbrances, with all liens and encumbrances to be transferred and attached to the proceeds of the sale.

    4. No offer may be accepted nor a sale consummated, unless the sale price of the property exceeds the amount of all liens and encumbrances against the property.

    5. Any objections to the proposed sale must be filed with the clerk of the bankruptcy court and served upon the undersigned debtor in possession [upon the attorney for the debtor in possession] NOT LESS THAN five (5) days prior to the date of the proposed sale. If an objection to the proposed sale is filed, a hearing on such objection shall be held before the court on _____19 _ at _ A.M. in Room _ of the above-captioned United States Bankruptcy Court Building at: _____ .

    6. If no objections to the proposed sale are filed and served within the time herein set forth, the sale shall be conducted accordingly as set forth above, unless formally notified otherwise.

Dated: _____ , 19 _

        Signed:_____

            Edward A. Jones, Vice President, New Hope, Inc.

        Address:_____

         Phone:_____

CERTIFICATE OF SERVICE BY MAIL

    I, the undersigned party, hereby certify that I have on this _____day of ___ ____19 _ mailed a copy of the above Notice of Proposed Sale of Estate Property and of Hearing to all creditors, to the United States trustee for the _____District of _____ , and to the Unsecured Creditors' Committee, at the addresses designated by the parties.

        Signed:_____

            John A. Johnson (Process Server)

        Address:_____

UNITED STATES BANKRUPTCY COURT
<u>SOUTHERN</u> DISTRICT OF <u>NEW YORK</u>

In re:

<u>New Hope, Inc.,</u>

_____ Debtor

Case No._____
Chapter 11

APPLICATION FOR AUTHORITY TO PAY CLAIMS OF DEBTOR'S EMPLOYEES FOR PRE-FILING WAGES

The debtor in possession represents as follows:

1. On _____19 _, the debtor filed a voluntary petition under Chapter 11 of the Bankruptcy Code and is presently operating its business as a debtor in possession.

2. The debtor was unable to pay its employees the wages earned by such employees during the 30-day period prior to the commencement of this case. The said employees are still employed by the debtor and are necessary for the continued operation and reorganization of the debtor's business.

3. None of the __ employees for whom payment is sought by this application is an owner, shareholder, director or officer of the debtor, and the claim of each such employee is less than $2,000 and is therefore entitled to priority of payment under 11 U.S.C. 507(a)(3).

4. The debtor's normal practice is to pay its employees on the first and 15th day of each month, the employees are in need of their unpaid wages, and the nonpayment of such wages will result in low morale and a possible disruption in the debtor's business operations.

5. The name and address of each employee for whom payment is sought,a nd the amount of the claim for each employee, is listed on the attached Exhibit A.

6. The debtor has funds available for the payment of such claims and the payment of such claims will not deplete the debtor's estate.

WHEREFORE, the applicant prays for the entry of an order allowing the pre-filing wage claims of the debtor's employees to be paid in the amount and in the manner as set forth in this application and authorizing the debtor in possession to pay said claims.

Dated: _____, 19 _

Signed: _____
Edward A. Jones, Vice-President, New Hope Inc.
Debtor in Possession

Address: _____

Phone: _____

APPENDIX B

THE LEGAL POWERS AND RESPONSIBILITIES OF A TRUSTEE

In any event, if a trustee were, for whatever reason, appointed in your Chapter 11 case, your only real duty would be to step aside while giving him your fullest cooperation in his efforts at the reorganization and management of the company. In general, from the moment the trustee arrives at the company until the case is eventually closed, he is, in a word, the boss—"sifting through your corporate ledgers for a sign of impropriety, stalking every stray creditor's invoice, calculating cash, inventories and accounts receivable to the last digit, and hiring and more often, dismissing employees."* The trustee's powers and duties could often be vast, varied and vitally important to the success or failure of the reorganization effort. That's why a debtor company cannot do any better than to fully cooperate and work with the trustee once one has been appointed.

The legal powers and duties of the trustee may be summarized as follows:

1. The trustee is the official representative of the debtor's estate, and is responsible and accountable for the "property of the estate"—i.e., all property of the estate, including any property turned over to him by the debtor or others or the proceeds of such property. As part of his responsibility to be accountable, he is required to file with the court and with the necessary governmental agencies, periodic reports concerning the operation of the debtor's business and statements of monies paid out, etc. And as a representative of the debtor company's estate, he has the authority to initiate a suit or to defend one, or to intervene to assert a valuable claim in any legal action which adversely affects the debtor's estate.

---

*The rather stark but close description of Alix M. Freedman, in "A Man Who Helps Put Companies Back," *The N.Y. Times*, Sunday, Sept. 12, 1982.

2. The trustee is required to meet with any committee appointed, as soon as practicable after the appointment of such committee, to transact such business as may be necessary and proper; and as the representative of the debtor's estate in any Chapter 11 case, the trustee also has the implied power to settle claims whether with the committee or with other parties in interest.

3. The trustee *may*, where he sees a reasonable prospect of rehabilitation for the business, operate the debtor's business without a court order, unless the court orders otherwise; he may cease operations and ask for direct liquidation where he finds that the business cannot be operated profitably over the long run or that continued operations will deplete the debtor's estate with no reasonable prospects of rehabilitation. (The court can, on its own, direct the trustee to cease operations of certain designated portions of the debtor's business while permitting him to continue operating the balance of such business that shows a reasonable chance of being rehabilitated.)

4. If the business of the debtor is authorized to be operated, the trustee shall file with the court and with any governmental unit responsible for collection or determination of any tax arising out of such operation, periodic reports and summaries of the operations of such business, including statements of receipts and disbursements, and such information as the court requires.

5. The trustee may examine proofs of claims filed with the court, and, when it appears to him that an objection could have a consequence in the administration of the estate, he may file a formal objection with the court against the allowance of any such claims he considers improper.

6. The trustee may furnish information, or respond to reasonable requests of creditors and other parties in interest concerning the estate and its administration.

7. If the debtor should fail to do so within a reasonable length of time, it would be the trustee's responsibility to promptly file the Chapter 11 bankruptcy petition papers (the list of claims and creditors, schedule of debtor's assets and liabilities, statement of his financial affairs, and so on) with the court. The trustee may, except to the extent the court orders otherwise, make an investigation and file with the court a statement of his findings on the conduct of the debtor's (or the management's) affairs, its assets, liabilities and financial condition, the quality and character of its management, and any other matters relative to the case or to the formulation of the reorganization plan. This is to assist the court in forming an informed opinion in matters such as whether a debtor company can realistically be reorganized, the desirability of the continuance of the business, and the soundness and feasibility of proposed reorganization plans.

8. The trustee may bypass the debtor and move directly to file a plan of reorganization, if the debtor has either failed to file a plan of reorganization within 120 days from the date of filing the Chapter 11 petition, or filed one which fails to win the acceptance of the creditors within 180 days. Alternatively, if the trustee should conclude that the debtor's business ought to be liquidated and that the case should not be a Chapter 11 case, he may either recommend to the court that the case be converted to a Chapter 7 or 13 bankruptcy case under the Code, or, in the alternative, that it be dismissed outright.

9. For any year or years for which the debtor has not filed required tax returns, the trustee is required to furnish to the governmental unit with which such return would have been filed, the kind of information which would serve a similar need for the governmental unit.

10. Following the confirmation of a plan of reorganization by the court, the trustee is required to file with the court such final reports as are necessary or ordered by the court—e.g., reports regarding any action taken by the trustee or the progress being made in the consummation of the plan, or regarding an application for a final decree to show that the plan has been consummated, and the like.

APPENDIX C
CLASSIFICATION OF CLAIMS OR INTERESTS

Under the Code, it is the proposed plan of reorganization itself, and not the court, that must classify the claims involved in a case. However, if any party in interest should think that the classifications employed in the plan are improper, he may challenge them by filing a proper complaint with the court.

Classification of claims, and of equity securities, is to be based on "the nature" of the claims or the interests classified—i.e., on whether it is senior or subordinated—and not on the nature or identity of the holder of the claim or interest. The primary rule is that the claims or interests being grouped into a particular class be "substantially similar" to other claims or interests of the class. This does not mean, though, that all claims which are "substantially similar" must necessarily be placed in the same class. Furthermore, a "claim" may not be classified with an "interest" together, since both are inherently different.* As the Tenth Circuit noted in Scherk v. Newton,** "Classification is simply a method of recognizing differences in rights...which call for difference in treatment."

In classifying claims, the general rule followed by the courts is to look at the nature of the claim (i.e., as to whether it is senior or subordinated), and the relationship of the claim to the property of the debtor. For example, claims of the same kind, and the same rank involving the same property may be included within a single class. The holder of a general *unsecured* claim, for example, has a right, which it shares with all other holders of unsecured, non-priority claims, to receive a pro rata share of the debtor's property after payment of secured claims and priority claims and prior to distributions to equity interests. Likewise, holders of *debentures* (bonds) secured by a mortgage on the debtor's plant and equipment should be part of a single class since the claim of each debenture holder is substantially similar and to the extent that the value of the collateral exceeds the

---

*A "claim" has to do primarily with indebtedness, i.e., the right to a payment of any kind, or the right to an equitable remedy for breach of performance if such breach gives rise to payment of any kind in property, money or service. An "interest," on the other hand, has to do with proprietary (ownership) interests—i.e., ownership interests such as the interests, as owners, which the common and preferred shareholders hold in the debtor company, in the case of a corporate debtor, or the interests, as owners, which general and limited partners hold in the debtor company in the case of a partnership debtor, or those held by a proprietor in the case of a proprietorship.

**152 F. 2nd 747 (10th Circuit, 1945).

debtor's aggregate outstanding liability in respect of the debentures, the holder's claims are substantially different from the claims of other creditors of the debtor who do not share the benefits of the lien securing the debenture holders' claims. Although all secured claims are of the same kind and may be of equal rank to the extent that each claim is secured by a first lien on property of the debtor, the fact that the claims are secured by different properties makes the claims substantially dissimilar and thus entitles the holders of such claims to separate classifications.

A separate class could be designated for all unsecured claims which are less than a specified dollar amount, provided that the court approves such classification as being reasonable and necessary for administrative convenience.

A. Classification Categories for Claims

A plan of reorganization must classify "claims" into the following separate classes: non-priority pre-petition unsecured claims, priority claims, secured claims, and subordinated claims.

i) Non-priority, Pre-petition Unsecured Claims

These are all unsecured claims outstanding as of the commencement of the case and claims for damages arising from rejection of executory contracts or unexpired leases. You may classify all such claims together as general unsecured claims, or you may divide them into separate classes if separate classification is reasonable.

If the claims of a group of pre-petition unsecured claims (subordinated creditors) are subordinated under a subordination agreement in favor of other pre-petition unsecured creditors (senior creditors), such creditors may not be treated on a parity one with the other if such classification would result in the senior creditors receiving less than they would receive if the case were being totally liquidated under Chapter 7 of the Code.

ii) Priority Claims

All "priority claim" items which fall under Sections 507(a)(3), (a)(4), and (a)(5) of the Code—i.e., claims for employee wages, for contributions to retirement plans and for debts owed to consumers for monies they had deposited towards the purchase or rental of property or services—must be separately classified. A separate classification of such classes of priority claims is necessary because a plan may propose that these priority claims be paid in full over a period of time, rather than as of the effective date of the plan. (See Item 11 iii) on p. 95 of the manual.)

iii) Secured Claims

In general, except in rare situations, each holder of an allowed claim that is secured by a security interest in specific property of the debtor must be placed in a separate class.

Classification of secured claims may be determined on the following basis: (i) priority (by reference to the state law); (ii) nature of the collateral; and (iii) agreements among creditors (or an order of the court) with respect to subordination [see iv) below].

Priority will be determined by reference to state law. For example, the order of recording of liens on real property will generally determine the priority of creditors whose claims are secured by real property of the debtor with liens of the same priority on the same property being generally classifiable together, while liens of different priority on the same property, liens on different property, or a lien of the same priority on the same property which has been subordinated in favor of the other by a subordination agreement, are all classifiable separately.

iv) Subordinated Claims

In working out the classifications for a plan, you may have to consider the Code's provisions* relative to subordinated claims and the subordination of claims. There are *three* basic kinds of subordination under the Code: i) *"contractual subordination"* (where subordination of a given claim is a result of an agreement); ii) *"equitable subordination,"* by which the court is permitted, after notice and a hearing, to subordinate for purposes of distribution, all or any part of an allowed claim to all or any part of another allowed claim, and by which the court may, at its discretion, also order to have any lien securing a subordinated claim transferred to the estate; and iii) *"statutory subordination,"* by which Section 510(b) of the Code subordinates, for the purpose of distribution and as a matter of law, any claim for recision of a purchase or sale of a security of the debtor to all claims or interests that are senior or equal to the claim or interest represented by such security. (By this rule, for example, a subordinated debenture holder with a right to rescind his purchase of the debenture does not have the right to rescind the subordination of his claim and thereby rank on a parity with those creditors who are beneficiaries of the subordination.)

There are a few general rules regarding the subordination claims: First, the bankruptcy court will generally enforce the terms of subordination agreements in a Chapter 11 case, but will not do so where the senior debt to which the lenders subordinated their claims has accepted the debtor's plan which, in essence, undoes the import of the agreement. Second, the bankruptcy court is authorized, in ordering distribution of assets, to subordinate all or any part of any claim to all or any part of another claims, regardless of the priority ranking of either claim—based on principles of "equitable subordination" which, as generally defined by case law, have generally indicated that a claim (except for tax claims) may normally be subordinated only if its holder is guilty of misconduct.

B. Classification Categories for Interests

Besides classifying claims into various classes, the Chapter 11 plan of reorganization must also classify interests. Follow the following basic principles:

i) In a case involving an individual debtor, the debtor constitutes, of course, a class of the proprietary (ownership) interests.

ii) If a partnership, you may classify the partnership interests together, or you may designate separate classes, one for general partners and another for limited partners.

iii) Where the debtor is a corporation with more than one class of common stock, interests of the same class of common stock should be classified separately. And if the debtor has common and preferred stock outstanding, separately classify the common and preferred shares, and separately classify different series of preferred shares if a distinction could be made between the rights of the holders of the different series.

Principles Governing Classification of Claims & Interests for the Purpose of Treatment Under the Plan

As has been previously explained in another part of this manual (see item 2 on pp. 85-6), under the Code** the classification designated as "claims" has to do primarily with indebtedness —

---

*See Section 510.
** See Section 101(4).

the right to payment or the right to an equitable remedy in lieu of payment; while the classification designated as **"interest"**, on the other hand, refers to the right of shareholders and bondholders as owners having an equity security interest in the debtor.

In preparing a Chapter 11 plan, it may be helpful to you (to the debtor) that you take note of the fact that, except in special circumstances,* as a practical matter, *in most Chapter 11 cases involving small businesses the equity security interests are ordinarily not dealt with in the plan since the parties holding the equity security in most such situations are usually one and the same as the owners of the business;* hence, such plans generally tend to deal exclusively with the creditors and do not usually affect the interests of equity security holders.

Under the bankruptcy rules and procedures, except for three specific types of priority claims which need not be classified — namely, claims for administrative expenses, unsecured gap claims arising in involuntary cases, and unsecured tax claims of governmental units — all other claims of whatever kind must be classified in a Chapter 11 plan, and a plan must separate all **"claims"** and **"interests"** into appropriate classes.

*The basic rule in classification of claims and interests is as expressed by Section 1122(a) of the Code:** a plan may place a claim or interest in a particular class only if the claim or interest is "substantially similar" to the other claims or interests in the class — unless there is a valid reason not to do so.* The one exception to this basic rule requiring a class to consist of substantially similar claims or interests is one holding that, for administrative convenience, a plan may designate a separate class of claims consisting only of every unsecured claim that is less than or reduced to a specified amount set or approved by the court as reasonable and necessary. Typically, small creditors (parties owed about $100 to $200) are offered payment in full to avoid the expense of mailing ballots and a series of small checks to them, while others may be offered the opportunity to reduce their claims to a specified amount approvable by the court and to accept that as payment in full.

By the basic rules of classification requiring claims and interests of *"substantially similar"* nature to be put in the same class, *the following principles follow:* claims of equal rank or priority should ordinarily be placed in the same class; claims of different ranks, or of the same rank but secured by different properties, should not be placed in the same class. Thus, for example, non-priority unsecured claims should not be placed in the same class as either secured claims or priority claims, even if they are receiving identical treatment under the pro-proposed plan; a claim secured by a first mortgage against the estate's property should not be placed in the same class as a claim secured by a second mortgage against the same property; and claims secured by different properties of the estate should be placed in different classes. Each secured claim, therefore, should normally be placed in a separate class.

With respect to nonpriority unsecured claims, some courts seem to require the placement of such claims in a single class; however, most courts allow flexibility on the question and would permit separate classes of substantially similar unsecured claims if there is a valid reason for doing so.*** And, with respect to classifying partially-secured claims, the provisions of Section 1111(b) of the Code [see footnote on p. 129 for an explanatory definition of this provision] permitting the holder of a partially-secured claim to elect to have its claim treated as being fully secured, should be taken into account in undertaking a classification.

---

*E.g., if and when the Plan calls for the debtor's business to be transferred to a new entity, or for additional stock to be issued, or for a buyout or termination of the equity interests of certain owners.

**See, also, In re Pine Lake Village Apartment Co., 19 B.R. 819 (SD NY, 1982)

***See In re Planes, Inc., 48 B.R. 698 (ND GA, 1985), and Barnes v. Whelan, 689 F.2d 193, 201 (CA DC, 1982). On classification principles, generally, see in re Holthoff, 58 B.R. 216 (ED AR, 1985).

All said and done, in practice, however, parties drafting Chapter 11 plans must often place unsecured claims in different classes even though the claims are "substantially similar". This is done principally to enable the plan maker to separate substantially similar claims into different classes and treat the classes differently under the plan. This is permitted since the Code [See Section 1123(a)(4) thereof] requires only that all claims in the same class must be given the same treatment UNLESS the holder of a particular claim agrees to less favorable treatment. Thus, if, for example, unsecured trade creditors are willing to accept, say, 50 cents on the dollar for their claims, while unsecured bank creditors will accept, say 90 cents on the dollar for their claims, it would make sense for the debtor to create separate classes for the claims in order to treat them differently.

PRIORITY OF CLAIMS & INTERESTS

The subject matter addressed in Section E of Chapter 6, pp.124-9, has to do with classification of claims in a Chapter 11 plan *for purposes of setting forth their treatment under the plan.* Here in this section, however, the subject matter to be addressed will be concerned with classification of claims *for purposes of establishing the order of PRIORITY OF* PAYMENT.

It is very important that the two types of classifications be properly distinguished, and that they not be confused with each other. With regard, for example, to the priority of a claim or interest (i.e., the priority of payment to which a claim or interest is entitled), while such matter is an important factor in determining the classification of a claim or interest in a plan, it is not the only factor of importance considered in making such a determination, for, generally, providing there's a valid reason for doing so, a Chapter 11 plan may separate non-priority unsecured claims into different classes and treat the classes differently under the plan. The priority of claims and interests plays an important role from the standpoint of both the administration of a Chapter 11 case and the preparation of a Chapter 11 plan; it is an important factor in determining the classification of a claim or interest in a plan. The priority of a claim or interest also becomes an important consideration in the following situations: if confirmation of a plan is sought under the "cramdown" provisions of the Code (pp. 105-6 of the manual) and the rule of "absolute priority" is to be complied with; if a Chapter 7 plan of liquidation is proposed, or if the Chapter 11 reorganization case is converted to a liquidation case under Chapter 7.

Classification Categories for Claims & Interests

Simply put, the Bankruptcy Code prescribes an absolute priority of claims and interests that must be absolutely complied with, in determining the order of priority in which payments are to be made to qualified claimants under a plan.

Listed below is the order of priority in which claims and interests are entitled to payment under the Code:

(1)   **Secured claims.** Secured claims take priority over unsecured claims of any kind, including priority unsecured claims. [See 11 U.S.C. 506(c)]

(2)   **Superpriority claims.** There are two superpriority claims that must be paid ahead of all other unsecured claims, including expenses of administration; they fall under Sections 507(b) and 324(c)(1) of the Code. They are: the claims created when a secured creditor is granted

adequate protection by the court that later proves to be inadequate (e.g., the claim arising out of an award for damages for lack of adequate protection); and the type of claim created when the court grants such a claim to a person that extends credit to the trustee or debtor in possession in the course of the case.

(3)   **Priority unsecured claims** in the order set forth in 11 U.S.C. 507(a), which is as follows:

First: Expenses of administration
Second: Unsecured gap claims in involuntary cases
Third: Wage claims of employees of up to $2,000 per employee
Fourth: Wage benefit claims of employees up to certain limits
Fifth: Grain producer's and U.S. fisherman's claims
Sixth: Consumer deposit claims of up to $900 each
Seventh: Unsecured tax claims of governmental units

(4)   **Nonpriority unsecured claims,** general unsecured claims having neither security nor priority. As a rule, though, claims falling under this category may be divided into separate classes and treated differently under a plan if a valid reason exists for doing so.

(5)   **Subordinated nonpriority unsecured claims** — claims that have been subordinated to other nonpriority unsecured claims for purposes of distribution by the court under 11 U.S.C. 510.

(6)   **Interests.** The interests of equity security holders have the lowest priority of payment, however dependency on the debtor's charter, the interests of certain interest holders (such as preferred stock holders) may have priority over the interests of other interest holders (such as common stock holders) in a plan.

APPENDIX D

THE CONCEPT OF "IMPAIRMENT" OF CLAIMS OR INTERESTS IN CHAPTER 11 CASES

Under what circumstances is a class of claims or interests in a plan considered to be "impaired"? Basically, a class is impaired if a plan of reorganization "alters the legal, equitable, and contractual rights" to which that class is entitled under the plan.

Under the Code, this interpretation does not differ even if the alteration enhances, rather than reduces, the value of the rights. So long as the rights of a class are altered or modified in one direction or the other, it is an impairment. As in many such matters, there are exceptions, however.

Examples: An alteration or modification of a contract which is as a result of a negotiated agreement with the creditor or other party to the contract and which is then approved by the court prior to the filing of the plan, is not an impairment if a proposed plan adopts the agreement as modified. Likewise, a plan which, for example, provides for the modification of the rights of classes of secured creditors but creates a single class of unsecured creditors whose rights the plan leaves unaltered (say, by providing that unsecured creditors be paid the full amount of their claims) does not impair the rights of the unsecured creditors. A plan which proposes to scale down secured and unsecured claims, and after confirmation creates a positive network for the debtor without issuing any new equity securities would have "altered" the legal, equitable, and contractual rights of the secured and unsecured creditors, *but not* those of the equity security interests in the plan. Hence, the plan shall have impaired the interests of the creditors in this instance, while not impairing those of the equity security holders, inasmuch as their legal rights (i.e., the rights of the equity securities holders) were not altered.

If a holder of a claim or interest has a legal or contractual right to receive an accelerated (or full or immediate) payment of the claim or interest upon the occurrence of a default, the claim is not impaired if the proposed plan proposes to cure the effect of the default by reinstating the original maturity of the claims and interests and paying the amount due on them according to the original terms of the agreement—since such persons shall have been receiving the benefits of its original bargain anyway.

In the final analysis, though, the issue of whether a class is impaired under a given plan could be a complicated and difficult one and must often be determined on the basis of the facts of the particular case. The provisions of the bankruptcy law (esp. Section 1124) as sketched above, as well as of applicable state law concerning the permissible modification of the rights of shareholders in the case of a corporate debtor and the rights of partners in the case of a partnership debtor, should be looked to for guidance.

Why is the Concept of Impairment Important in Chapter 11 Proceedings?

The concept of "impairment" is very important in Chapter 11 reorganization cases. This is so for the following reasons:

i) Whether a class of claims or ownership interests is "impaired," as defined by the Code, determines whether such class is required to vote for or against a plan of reorganization in a Chapter 11 case. If a class is not impaired, it is *deemed* to have accepted the plan and no solicitation of acceptances from such a class would be required. *In other words, under the rules of the Code, only a class which is impaired may reject a proposed plan*; a class which is not impaired may only accept a plan.

ii) Ordinarily, a plan of reorganization may not be "confirmed" by the court (pp. 98-106 of the manual) unless each class of claims and interests either accepts the plan or is impaired under the plan.

iii) The Code does not require that a plan impair all classes of creditors and equity security holders, however. If at least one class is impaired and the requisite majority of the class accepts the plan, the requirement for confirmation is satisfied—providing that the other conditions for confirming a plan (pp. 101-104 of the manual) are met.

iv) An important aspect of the concept of impairment is that it permits the proponents of a proposed plan to limit the scope of the plan and thus reduce the administrative burden of solicitation of consents, while reducing the time and expense associated with valuation hearings in connection with "cram down" under Section 1129(b). While the Code requires that all of the debtor's claims and interests be classified into classes, a plan need not modify the rights of all classes in order to qualify for confirmation by the court. Take, for example, the case of a debtor whose only need is a simple composition or extension of his unsecured claims. Since the Code provides that a class that is not impaired under a given plan "is deemed to have accepted the plan" and requires no solicitation of acceptances from such a class, such a debtor can readily confirm a plan without affecting his secured creditors or equity interests by simply specifying that the legal, equitable, and contractual rights of the holders of the secured claims and equity interests are not impaired, thus greatly simplifying his case.

APPENDIX E

U.S. BANKRUPTCY COURT LOCATIONS IN EACH STATE

NAME OF STATE	COURT DISTRICT	ADDRESS OF COURT
ALABAMA	Northern:	*P. O. Box 3226, 351 Federal Bldg., 1118 24th Ave., **Tuscaloosa,** AL 35401 Phone: 205-752-5966 *P. O. Box 1805, 122 U.S. Courthouse, Anniston, AL 36201. Phone: 205-237-5631 *500 S. 22nd St., Birmingham, AL 35322, Phone: 205-731-1615 :*P.O. Box 1289, 222 Federal Courthouse, **Decatur, AL** 35601. Phone 205-353-2817
	Southern	*P. O. Box 22865, Mobile, AL 36652, Phone 205-694-2390.
	Middle:	*P. O. Box 1248, Suite 127, **Montgomery,** AL 36192, Phone 205-832-7250.
ALASKA	(One District)	*P. O. Box 47, Federal Building, 701 "C" St. **Anchorage,** AK 955133, Phone: 907-271-5232.
ARIZONA	(One District)	*U.S. Courthouse, 230 North First Ave., Phoenix, A Z Phone: 602-261-6965. *2nd Floor, Acapulco Building, 120 W. B'way **Tucson,** AZ 85701: Phone: 602-629-6304.
ARKANSAS	(One District)	*P. O. Drawer 2381, 600 W Capitol, **Little Rock, AR** 72202 Phone: 501-378-6357.
CALIFORNIA	Northern:	*506 Federal building, 34 Civic Center Plaza, Santa Ana, CA 92701. Phone: 714-836-2993 *205 Post Office Building, **Eureka,** CA 95501. Phone: 707-443-3131 *Room 3035, 280 South Fist St., **San Jose,** C.A. 95113. Phone 408-291-7286 *P.O.Box 36053, 450 Golden Gate Ave., **San Francisca,** CA 94612. Phone: 415 – 556-2250. *214 Post Office Bldg., 13th & Alice Streets, **Oakland,** CA 94612. Phone: 415-273-7212 *Room: 200, 699 N. Arrowhead, **San Bernardine,**CA92401.Phone 714-383-5872.

NAME OF STATE	COURT DISTRICT	ADDRESS OF COURT
	Eastern:	*P. O. Box 5276, **Modesto, CA** 95352. Phone: 209-521-5160 *4310 Federal Bldg., 1130 O Street, **Fresco,** CA 93721. Phone: 209-487-5217. *8038 U.S. Courthouse, 650 Capitol Mall, **Sacramento,** CA 95814. Phone 916-551-2662.
	Central:	*Room 906, U.S. Courthouse, 312 N. Spring St., Los Angeles, CA 90012. Phone: 213-894-4696.
	Southern:	*Room 5 – N – 26, U.S. Courthouse, 904 Frost St., **San Diego,** CA 92189. Phone: 619-293-6582
COLORADO	(One District)	*1945 Sherman St., 400 Columbine Bldg., **Denver,CO** 80203. Phone: 303-844-4045.
CONNECTICUT	(One District)	*915 Lafayette Blvd., **Bridgeport,** CT, 096604. Phone: 203-579-5808. *Room 712, U.S. Courthouse, 450 Main St., **Hartford, Ct** 06103. Phone: 203-722-2733
DELAWARE	(One District)	*Lockbox 38, 844 King St., Federal Bldg., **Wilmington, DE** 19801. Phone 302-573-6174.
DISTRICT OF COLUMBIA	(One District)	*Room 1130.U.S. Courthouse, 34d and Connecticut Aves., **NW., Washington DC 2001.** Phone 202-535-7385.
FLORIDA	Northern:	*Room 3120, 227 N. BRONOUGH St., **Tallahassee,** FL 32301. Phone: 904-681-7500 *Room 206A. 299 E. Broward Blvd, Ft. **Lauderdale,** FL 33301. Phone: 305-527-7224
	Middle	*P. O. Box 559, 24 U.S. Post Office & Courthouse, 311 West Monroe St. **Jacksonville,** FL 32201. Phone: 904-791-2852 *598 Federal Courthouse Building, 80 N. Hughey Ave., **Orlando, FL** 32801. Phone 305-648-6365 *Room 708, 700 Twiggs St., **Tampa,** FL 33602. Phone: 813-228-2115 *701 Clanatis St., **West Palm Beach,** FL 33401, Phone 305-€55-6774
	Southern:	*1401 Federal Bldg.., 51 SW First Ave., **Miami,** FL 33130: Phone 305-536-5216
GEORGIA	Northern:	*Room 1340, R.B. Russell Building, 75 Spring St., SW, **Atlanta.** GA 30303, Phone: 404-331-6490 *P. O. Box 2328, **Newnan, GA** 30264. Phone 404-251-5583. *P. O. Box 5231, **Rome GA** 30161. Phone: 404-291-5639.
	Middle:	*P. O. Box 90, 126 U.S. Courthouse, **Macon,** GA 31202. Pone 912-746-2406 *P.O. Box 2147, 233 12th St., 904 Corporate Center, **Columbus,** GA 31902. Phone: 404-527-1556
	Southern:	*P.O. Box 8347, 213 U.S. Courthouse, **Savannah,** GA 31412. Phone: 912-944-4105

209

NAME OF STATE	COURT DISTRICT	ADDRESS OF COURT
HAWAII	**(One District)**	P. O. Box 50121, Federal Building **Honolulu,** HI 96850. Phone: 808-546-2180
IDAHO	**(One District)**	*P. O. Box 2600, 304 N. 18th St., **Boise,** ID 83701. Phone 208-334-1074
ILLINOIS	**(Northern:**	*U.S. courthouse 219 s. Dearborn St. **Chicago,** IL 60604. Phone 312-435-5587 *221 S. Court St., **Rockford,** IL 61101. Phone: 815-987-4202
	Eastern:	*P.O. Box 585, Federal Building 201 N. Vermillion St. **Danville,** IL 61832. Phone: 217-442-0660. *P. O. Box 309, 750 Missouri Ave., 1st floor, **East St. Louis,** IL 62202. Phone: 618-482-9365
	Southern	*Federal Building, 100 NE Monroe St. **Peoria,** IL 61602. Phone: 309-671-7035. *P.O. Box 2438, 327 U.S. Courthouse, 600 E. Monroc St **Springfield,** IL 62705 Phone: 217-492-4550.
Indiana	**Northern**	*222 U.S. Courthouse, 204 S. Main St, **South Bend** IN 46601-2196. Phone: 219-236-8247 *221 Federal Building, 610 Connecticut St., Gary **IN** 46402. Phone: 219-981-3335.
	Southern:	*123 U.S. Courthouse, 46 E. Ohio St., **Indianapolis,** IN 46204. Phone: 317-269-6710 *352 Federal Bldg., **Evansville,** IN 47708. Phone: 812-465-6440.
IOWA	**Northern**	*P. O. Box 4371, Federal Building & U.S. Courthouse, 1st Floor, **Cedar Rapids,** IA 52407. Phone: 319-399-2473.
	Southern:	*3118 U.S. Courthouse, **Des Monies,** IA 50309. Phone: 515-2184-6230
KANSAS	**(One District)**	*155 Federal Building, 812 N 7th St., **Kansas City,** KS 66101. Phone: 816-374-4741 *325 SE Quincy St., **Topeka,** KA 6683. Phone: 913-295-2750, *401 N. Market St. **Wichita,** KS 67202. Phone 316-269-6486
KENTUCKY	**Eastern:**	*P. O. Box 1050, **Lexington,** KY 40588, Phone: 606-233-2608
	Western:	*414 U.S. courthouse, 601 W Broadway, **Louisville,** KY 4020. Phone: 502-582-5145.
LOUISIANA	**Eastern:**	*Room 301, 352 Florida St., **Baton Rouge,** LA 70801. Phone: 504-389-0211 *Room c- 104, 500 Camp St., **New Orleans,** LA 70130. Phone: 504-389-6506.
	Western:	*252 Federal Building, Corner of Union & Vine, **Opelousas,** LA 70570. Phone: 318-948-3451 *4A 18 Federal Building, 500 Fannin St., **Shreveport,** LA 71101. Ph: 318-226-5267
MAINE	**(One District)**	*P. O. Box 1109, 331 U.S. courthouse, 202 Harlow St., **Bangor,** ME 04401. Phone: 318-226-5267 *156 Federal St., U.S. Courthouse, **Portland,** ME 04112. Phone: 207-780-3482

NAME OF STATE	COURT DISTRICT	ADDRESS OF COURT
MARYLAND	**(One District)**	*U.S. Courthouse, 101 W. Lombard St., Baltimore MD 21201. Phone: 301-962-2688 *451 Huntingford Dr., **Rockville,** MD 20850. Phone: 301-442-7010.
MASSACHUSETTS	**(One District)**	*212 John McCormick. Post Office & Courthouse **Boston,** MA 02109. Phone: 617-793-0518.
MICHIGAN	**Eastern:**	*P. O. Box X911, 100 Washington, **Bay City,** MI 48707. Phone: 517-892-1508 *1060 U.S. Courthouse, 231 W. Lafayette, **Detroit,** MI 48226. Phone: 313-226-7064. *102A Federal Building, 600 Church St., **Flint,** MI 48502. Phone: 313-234-5621
	Western:	*P.O. Box 3310, 792 Federal Building, 110 Michigan St., NW **Grand Rapids,** MI 49501. Phone:616-456-2693 *221 W. Washington St., **Marquette,** MI 49855. Phone: 906-226-2117
MINNESOTA	**(One District)**	*416 U.S. Post Office & Courthouse, **Duluth,** MN 55802. Phone: 218-727-6692 *204 U.S. Post Office, 118 s. Mills St., **Fergus Falls,** MN 56537. Phone: 218-739-4871 *600 Galaxy Building, 330 Second Ave. South, **Minneapolis,** MN 55401. Phone: 612-349-5155 *629 Federal Building, 316 N. Robert St., **St. Paul,** MN 55101. Phone: 612-725-7184
MISSISIPPI	**Northern:**	*P.O. Drawe 867, **Arberdeen,** MS 39730-0867. Phone: 601-965-5301
	Southern:	*P. O. Box 1280, 231 Main St., **Biloxi,** MS 39533. Phone: 601-432-5542. *P.O. Drawer 2448, **Jackson,** MS 39205. Phone: 601-965-5301.
MISSOURI	**Eastern:**	*730 U.S. Courthouse, 1114 Market St., **St. Louis,** MO 63101. Phone 314-425-4222
	Western:	*U.S. Courthouse, 811 Grand Ave., **Kansas City,** MO 64106. Phone: 816-374-3321
MONTANA	**(One District)**	*Room 111, Federal Building, 400 N. Main St., **Butte,** MT 59701. Phone: 406 782-3354 *Room 25, Great Falls Post Office Building, 215 First Ave. North, **Great Falls,** MT 59401. Phone: 406-781-3811
NEBRASKA	**(One District)**	*P. O. Box 428 Downtown Sta., 215 N. 17th St., New Federal Building, **Omaha,** NE 68101. Phone: 402-221-4687.
NEVADA	**(One District)**	*Room 300, U.S. Courthouse, 300 Las Vegas Blvd., South, **Las Vegas,** NV 89101. Phone: 702-388-6257. *4050 Federal Building St., **Reno,** NV 89509. Phone: 702-784-5559

NAME OF STATE	COURT DISTRICT	ADDRESS OF COURT
NEW HAMPSHIRE	(One District)	*275 Chestnut St., **Manchester,** NH 03101. Phone: 603-666-7532.
NEW JERSEY	(One District)	*401 Market St., **Camden,** NJ 08191. Phone: 609-757-5023 *970 Broad St., **Newark,** NJ 07102. Phone: 973-645-2630. *U.S. Post Office & Courthouse, 402 E. State St., **Trenton** NJ 08608. Phone: 609-989-2126
NEW MEXICO	(One District)	*P.O. Box 456, 9th floor, 500 gold Ave., **Albuquerque,** MN 87103. Phone: 505-766-2051
NEW YORK	Northern:	*311 U.S. Courthouse, **Utica,** NY 13501. Phone: 315-793-8176 *234 Federal Bldg., **Rochester,** NY 14614. Phone: 716-263-3148 *P. O. Box 398, **Albany,** NY 12201-0398. Phone: 518-472-4226
	Southern	*1 Bowling Green, 6th Floor, **New York,** NY 10004. Phone: 212-791-0143/2247. *P. O. Box 1000, 176 church St., **Poughkeepsie,** NY 12602. Phone: 914-452-4200
	Eastern	*75 Clinton St., **Brooklyn,** NY 11201. Phone: 718-330-2188 *601 Veteran's Highway, **Hauppauge,** NY 12602. Phone: 914-452-4200. *1635 Privado Rd., **Westbury,** NY 11590. Phone: 516-832-8801. *101 E. Post Rd., **White plains,** NY 10601. Phone: 914-683-9755.
	Western	*U.S. courthouse, 68 Court St., Room 310, **Buffalo,** NY 14202. Phone: 716-846-4130
NORTH CAROLINA	Western	*401 W. Trade St., **Charlotte,** NC 28202. Phone: 704-371-6103.
	Middle:	*P. O. Box 26100 **Greensboro** NC 27420-6100. Phone: 919-333-5647.
	Eastern:	*P. O. Box Drear 2807, **Wilson,** NC 27834-2807. Phone: 919-333-5647
NORTH DAKOTA	(One District)	*P. O. Box 1110, **Fargo,** ND 58107. Phone: 701-237-5771.
OHIO	Northern:	*113 U.S. Courthouse, 1716 Spielbusch Ave., **Toledo,** OH 43624. Phone: 419-259-6440. *2 S Main St., **Akron,** OH 44308. Ph: 216-375-5766 *107 F.T. Bow Building. 201 Cleveland Ave., SW, **Canton,** OH 44702. Phone: 216-489-4426 *P. O. Box 147, U.S. Post Office Bldg., **Youngstown,** OH 44501. Phone: 216-746-7702 *Room 427 U. S. Courthouse, Public Square & Superior Ave., **Cleveland,** OH 44114. Phone: 216-522-7555
	Southern:	*124 U.S. Courthouse, 85 Marconi Blvd., Columbus, OH 43215. Phone: 614-469-2087 *705 Federal Building & U.s. Courthouse, 200 W. 2nd St., **Dayton,** OH 45402. Ph: 513-225-2516 *735 U.S. courthouse, 100 E 5th St., **Cincinnati,** OH 45202. Phone: 513-684-2572.

NAME OF STATE	COURT DISTRICT	ADDRESS OF COURT
OKLAHOMA	Northern:	*4-540 U.S. Courthouse, 333 W. 4th St. TULSA. OK 74103. Phone: 918-581-7181
	Western:	*Old Post Office building, 7th Floor. 201 Dean A McGee Ave., **Oklahoma City**, OK 73102. Phone: 405-231-5143.
	Eastern:	*P. O. Box 1347, U. S. post Office & Federal Building, **Okmulgee**, OK 74447. Phone: 918-758-0126
OREGON	(One District)	*P. O. Box 1335, 404 Federal Building, 211 E. 7th St., **Eugene**, OR 97401. Phone: 503-687-6448.
		*900 Orbanco Building, 1001 SW 5th Ave., **Portland**, OR 97204. Phone: 503-221-2231
PENNSYLVANIA	Eastern:	*3726 U. S. Courthouse, 601 Market St., **Philadelphia.** Phone: 215-597-1644.
		*4108 E. Shore Office Building, 45 S. Front St., **Reading**, PA 19602. Phone: 215-375-0930
	Middle:	*217 Federal Building, 197 S. Main St., **Wilkes- Barre**, PA 18701. Phone: 717-826-6450
		*P. O. Box 908 Federal Bldg., 3rd & Walnut Streets, **Harrisburg**, PA 17108. Phone: 717-782-2260
	Western:	* P. O. Box 1755, 314 U.S. Courthouse, Erie, PA 16507. Phone: 814-453-7580
PUERTO RICO	(One District)	*Federal Courthouse, **San Juan**, PR
RHODE ISLAND	(One District)	*308 Westminster Mall, Federal Centre, **Providence**, RI 02903. Phone: 401-528-4477
SOUTH CAROLINA	(One District)	*P. O. Box 1448, **Columbia**, SC 29202. Phone: 803-765-5211
SOUTH DAKOTA	(One District)	*Federal Building & Courthouse, 400 S Phillips Ave **Sioux Falls, SD** 57102. Phone: 605-336-9903
TENNESSEE	Eastern:	* P. O. Box 1189, corner of Martin Luther King Blvd. & Georgia Ave., **Chattanooga**, TN 37401. Phone: 615, 26602126
		*Suite 1501,15th Floor, Plaza Tower, **Knoxville**, TN 37929. Phone: 615-673-4525.
Middle	Middle:	**207 Customs Home, 701 Broadway,** **Nashville**, TN 37203. Phone: 615-736-5590.
	Western:	*P. O. Box 1527, **Jackson**, TN 38302. Phone: 901-424-9751
		*969 Madison Ave., #1200, **Memphis**, TN 38104, Phone: 901-521-3204
TEXAS	Northern:	*C-110 Federal Bldg., 1205 Texas Ave. **Lubbock, TX** 79041. Phone: 806-743-7336.
		*504 U. S. Courthouse, **Forth Worth**, TX 76102. Phone: 817-334-3269.
		*14-A-U.S. Courthouse, 1100 Commerce St., **Dallas**, TX 75242. Phone: 214-767-0814
	Southern:	*U.S. Courthouse, 515 Rusk Ave., **Houston**, TX 77002. Phone: 713-221-9590.
		*521 Starr. Room 101, **Corpus Christi**, TX 78401.. Phone: 512-888-3142
	Eastern:	*211 W. Ferguson St., **Tyler**, TX 75702. Phone: 215-592-1212.

NAME OF STATE	COURT DISTRICT	ADDRESS OF COURT
	Western:	*200 W 8ᵗʰ St., **Austin,** TX 78701. Phone: 512, 482-5237
		*P. O. Box 1349, **Del Rio,** TX 78840. Phone: 512-775-2021
		*511 E. San Antonia St., **El Paso,** TX 79901. Phone: 915-541-7810.
		*P. O. Box 191, **Pecos,** TX 79772. Phone: 915-445-4228
		*P. O. Box 1439, Post Office Building, 1615 E. Houston St., Alamo Plaza. **San Antonlo,** TX 78295. Phone: 512-229-6720
		*P. O. Box 10708. **Midland,** TX 79702. Phone: 915-683-2001.
		*P.O. Box 608, **Waco,** TX 76703. Phone:817-756-0307
UTAH	(One District)	*350 S. Main St., **Salt Lake City,** UT 84101. Phone 801-524-5157.
VERMONT	(One District)	*P. O. Box 865, Opera House, **Ruthland,** VT 05701. Phone: 802-773-0219.
VIRGINIA	Eastern:	*Suite 408 City Bank & Trust Building, 206 N. Washington St., **Alexandria,** VA 22314. Phone: 703-557-1716.
		*P. O. Box 676, 1100 E. Main St., Room 324, **Richmond,** VA 23206. Phone: 804-771-2878.
		*P. O. Box 497, **Newport News,** VA 23607. Phone: 804-247-0196
		*414 U.S. Courthouse, **Norfolk,** VA 23410. Phone: 804-441-6651
	Western:	*P. O. Box 2390, New Federal Building, 2ⁿᵈ St., & Franklin Rd. SW, **Roanoke,** VA 24010. Phone: 703-982-6391
		*205 Federal Bldg., **Lynchburg,** VA 24505. Phone: 703-982-6391
		*P. O. Box 1326, Federal Bldg., **Harrisonburg,** VA 22801. Phone: 703-434-8327
WASHINGTON	Eastern:	*P. O. Box 2164, U.S. Courthouse, Room 321, 904 W. Riverside Ave., **Spokane,** WA 92201 Phone: 509-456-3830.
	Western	*P. O. Box 1797, 224 Post Office Building, **Tacoma,** WA 98402. Phone: 206-593-6310.
		*220 U.S. Courthouse, 1010 5ᵗʰ Av., **Seattle,** WA 98104. Phone: 206-442-2751
WEST VIRGINIA	Northern:	*P. O. Box 70, 12ᵗʰ & Chapline St, **Wheeling,** WV 26003. Phone: 304-233-1655.
	Southern:	*P. O. Box 3924, **Charleston,** WV 25339. Phone: 304-247-5114
WISCONSIN	Eastern:	*216 Federal Bldg., 517 E. Wisconsin Ave., **Milwaukee,** WI 53202. Phone: 414-291-3293
	Western:	* P. O. Box 548, 120 N Henry, **Madison,** WI 53701. Phone: 608-264-5178
		*510 S. Barstow St., **Eauclaire,** WI 54701. Phone: 715 834-3941.
WYOMING	(One District)	*111 S. Wolcott St. Casper, WY 82601. Phone: 307-261-5440.

APPENDIX **F**

GLOSSARY OF TERMS & SOME RELEVANT DEFINITIONS

Acceptor	A person who signs a promise to pay a draft or check to a drawer (the one to whom the check is made out).
Accomodation Paper	A draft or note which the acceptor, drawer, or endorser signs in order to "accomodate" another person who wishes to borrow against the draft or note. An act of trying to help a friend by co-signing his note in a deal with a financial company or bank.
Acknowledgement	A declaration before a person who is legally qualified to administer an oath (such as a notary public), that a document signed by you was actually signed by you voluntarily.
Action	A proceeding or suit in court.
Affiant	The person who makes a sworn (notarized) statement, such as an affidavit.
Affidavit	A statement in writing, sworn to before a person authorized to administer oaths, such as a notary public.

Affirmation	A solemn declaration, made, normally by a person opposed to oath-taking on religious or other grounds.
Agent	A person who is authorized by another to represent him.
Allowed claim or interest	See p. 87 & 113 of the manual.
Amortize	To pay off debt in installments; or gradual recovery of an investment.
Annuity	Money paid annually or periodically.
Appraisal	A valuation of property; the opinion of an expert as to the true value of real or personal property, based upon facts and experience.
Arbitration	A means, often included in a contract and agreed upon by the parties to the contract, to have any disputes between these parties settled by other persons (arbitrators), named by the parties themselves.
Arrangement	A term used in bankruptcy proceedings for reorganization plans, by which the creditors agree to compromise their claims, or to defer their claims.
Assets	The things that a business, person or a bankrupt owns.
Assignment	The transfer of property or rights from one person to another, e.g., a creditor; to endorse over to another, such as promissory note or a lease.
Assignee	The person to whom a property or a right is transferred.
Assignor	The person who assigns (transfers) a property or right to another person.
Attachment	Seizure or taking into custody of property by court order in connection with a pending lawsuit so as to prevent its use or loss by the defendant.
Authorized Capital Stock	The amount of common stock specified in the Articles of Incorporation of a corporation.
Bankrupt	A person who is insolvent; one whose total property is legally declared insufficient to pay his debts.
Bankruptcy	A legal proceeding in a federal court by which a debtor seeks to be relieved or freed from his financial obligations.

Bill of Exchange	A negotiable instrument; an order drawn by one person on another (the drawee) requiring the drawee to pay a certain sum to the order of the person named (e.g., a check, a draft, and a promissory note).
Bills and Notes	Abbreviation for a bill of exchange.
Board of Directors	A group of persons charged with the general responsibility of managing a corporation and setting its policies.
Bond	A written pledge or obligation usually issued by a bonding company, to pay a sum of money in case of failure to fulfill an obligation, or in case of inflicting damage or mishandling funds. (This is different from a corporate note or security evidencing the indebtedness of the corporation).
Book Value	The value of a property as carried on the accounts and books of the owner (usually used in reference to a corporation).
By-Laws	The internal rules of management by which a corporation conducts business.
Capital	The fund of money, assets or property available to an individual or a firm for the conduct of its business.
Capital Gain	Profit from an increase or appreciation in the value of an investment. Under current tax laws, if the property concerned is held for more than 6 months before the profit is realized, the profit becomes taxable at capital tax gain rate, which is a lower rate than ordinary.
Capitalization	The appraisal of the financial worth of a firm or corporation using a pre-determined interest rate and the net earnings of its property as a basis of computing value.
Cashier's Check	A check drawn by a bank on its own account.
Certified Check	A check upon which the bank stamps an indication that money has been set aside from the account of the maker, guaranteeing, in effect, that the money will be there when the check is presented to the bank for payment.
Certified Financial Statement	A statement, listing the assets (what are owned) and liabilities (debts or financial obligations) of a person or firm, and confirmed ("certified") by the person's or firm's accountant to be accurate.
Charter	A certificate issued or approved by a state, giving a corporation the right to exist. Same thing as "Certificate of Incorporation", or "Articles of Incorporation".

Chattel Mortgage	A transfer of legal ownership of personal property to another party, as a security to ensure payment of a debt—e.g., the transfer of a sales contract to purchase an automobile or appliance.
Claim	Any right to payment, whether or not such right is reduced to judgment, or is contingent, disputed, legal, equitable, secured or unsecured.
Collateral Security	Property given as a pledge, to guarantee that a promised obligation or contract will be performed.
Common Stock	A printed certificate that represents ownership of a corporation.
Conglomerate Corporation	A group of corporations merged into a single ownership, normally engaged in different unrelated businesses.
Confirmation (of Bankruptcy Plan)	Special proceedings by which a proposed payment arrangement ("plan") is approved ("confirmed") by a bankruptcy judge before the proposed plan goes into effect.
Contingent (debt)	A debt you may become liable for if a future event happens—e.g., say if a person for whom you are a co-signer or co-maker should die or default on the debt.
Contract	A lawful agreement to do, or not to do certain things.
Convertible Stock	A corporate stock which has the privilege to be changed ("converted") into another class of stock, or into other obligations of the corporation.
Corporation	An artificial person or entity created by law to act with the rights and liabilities of a person.
Co-signer	A person who guarantees the repayment of debt for another person. Same as co-maker.
Creditor	The person to whom money is owed.
Dealer	As defined in Section 2(12) of the Securities Act of 1933, any person who engages either for all or part of his time, directly or indirectly, as agent, broker, or principal, in the business of offering, buying, selling, and generally dealing or trading in securities issued by another person.
Debentures	A note given by a corporation for money it borrowed, which note is not secured with any assets or collateral.
Debt	A legal obligation to pay money.

Debtor-in-possession	A debtor who remains in control ("in possession") of his business and affairs and continues to operate and manage such affairs even as the bankruptcy proceedings run their course.
Director	A person elected by the stockholders of a corporation to manage its affairs in terms of setting policies.
Discharge	The official forgiveness of a debtor's debts by the bankruptcy judge following the order of the court.
Dischargeable Debt	A type of debt which may, under the law, be discharged or forgiven in bankruptcy.
Disinterested person	A person who is *not* a creditor, equity security holder, or insider, and who is not (and has not been) an investment banker of the debtor for any outstanding security of the debtor within 3 years before the date of filing of the petition. (An attorney for such investment banker, or an insider of the debtor or such investment banker, or a person who has an interest materially adverse to the debtor's estate may not qualify as a "disinterested" person, however.)
Dividends	A payment, in money or corporate stock, of a portion of the profits of a corporation to its stockholders, or a like payment by a bank to its depositors as interest on the use of their money.
Dummy Director	A figurehead in the formation of a new corporation who has no duties to perform after its formation.
Equity	The value of a property or company, minus any debts he owes in the property or company.
Equity Security	Ownership share in a corporation, as represented by shares and stock therein; interest of a limited partner in a limited partnership; warrants or rights to subscribe in an equity security.
Execution	The completion of a document, such as a deed, contract, or will, by officially signing it.
Executory Contract	In general, contracts on which performance remains due to some extent, on both sides—e.g., unexpired leases of real property or employment contract.
Executor	The Male person (or corporation) named in a Will to see that the terms of the Will are carried out. If a female, she is called an Executrix.
Exempt Property	The kinds and quantities of property a debtor is allowed to keep after bankruptcy. Under the Federal and State Bankruptcy laws, there are certain specific *personal* property of the debtor (or debt-

ors, if a joint petition), that are designated as "exempt" property—i.e., as property which are exempted from being seized by one's creditors in fulfillment of the debtor's indebtedness, and which may therefore be retained by the debtor even when money is owed on them. A full treatment of the specific exemptions for each state is contained in Appendix D of the sister volume to this manual, "How To File Your Own Personal Bankruptcy Without a Lawyer," by the publisher of the present manual, and such detailed treatment will be too unwieldy to duplicate in this book.

However, for all practical intents and purposes, such exempt property items are nearly always "essential necessity" type of items. They frequently include items such as the following: clothes, household goods, your homestead (the equity in your primary house), cash surrender value of your life insurance, other value of other public benefits (pension, workman or unemployment compensation, public assistance, and the like), automobile (esp. in states where it is a virtual necessity, such as California), tools of one's trade or profession, a certain percentage (or all) of one's wages.

Fidelity Bond	A bond taken out by an employee to ensure the employer that he (the employer) will be protected against the employee's possible embezzlement or mismanagement.
Fiduciary	A general term used to describe a relationship that requires a high trust and confidence. Persons like guardians, trustees, executors, directors of a corporation, or administrators of a dead person's estate, fall under such a category.
File	The process of formally submitting your bankruptcy papers to the court to commence a bankruptcy petition.
Garnishment	Legal notice to someone who holds the property or assets of a debtor asking such person to hold the property or assets pending the settlement of a suit against the debtor.
Gross Income	The total income a business or property earns before the expenses are deducted.
Hardship Discharge	See "Step 11" in Chapter 6 of the Personal Bankruptcy manual.
Holding Company	A corporation which, though it conducts no business operations of its own, is able to own, control and dictate the policies of other corporations because it owns dominant interests in such other corporations.

Homestead	The primary family residence for which a part (or all) of the debtor's equity in it may be exempt.
Impairment	See pp. 195–6 of the manual.
Indemnity	A sum of money, pledge or undertaking given to a person as a guarantee or to protect him against loss or damage.
Indentured Trustee	A trustee under an indenture. (The Code provides, in Sec. 101.22, that "indenture" means "mortgage, deed of trust, or indenture under which there is outstanding a security...constituting a claim against the debtor, a claim secured by a lien on any of the debtor's property, or an equity security of the debtor.")
Insolvent	Inability of a person (or firm) to pay his debts as they fall due; when one's debts (liabilities) are in excess of his assets.
Instrument	A written document which creates or transfers certain rights and obligations in the parties.
Issuer	As substantially defined under Section 2(4) of the Securities Act of 1933 [15 U.S.C. # 776(4)], every person who issues or proposes to issue any security; except that with respect to certificates of deposit, voting-trust certificates, or collateral-trust certificates, certificates of interest or shares in an unincorporated investment trust, the term "issuer" means the person(s) who serve as depositor or manager.
Joint Ownership	A situation where two or more persons (a husband and wife, for example) own or hold property in joint names so that if any of them should die, the entire property goes to the remaining survivors.
Joint Petition	A single petition for bankruptcy filed by the husband and wife together.
Judicial District	An area of a state in which a federal court has jurisdiction.
Legacy	A gift of personal property made to someone by a Will.
Levy	To seize a debtor's property or funds to satisfy a court judgment on a debt.
Lien	A claim put on one's property by a creditor as security against the payment of a debt.
Liabilities	Debts; a listing of what a person or business owes to various creditors.
Limited Liability	A risk of loss limited to the amount of investment made by one in a corporation.

Limited Partnership	(Also known as "special" partnership)—A type of partnership in which one or more partners are relieved from liability beyond a certain amount, in exchange (usually) for limited participation or non-participation by the "limited" partner(s) in the conduct and control of the business.
Liquid Assets	Assets of the type that are easily convertible to cash.
Mechanic's Lien	A legal claim based on labor.
Meeting of Creditors	See pp. 68–70 of the manual.
Modification (of payment plan)	See p. 89 of the manual.
Negotiable Instrument	Instruments (documents or notes) which are easily transferable from one person to another by assignment, endorsement or delivery in the course of trade, such as checks, notes, drafts, bills of exchange, bonds and securities.
Net Income	Remaining income from business or property after proper charges and expenses are deducted.
Net Worth	The difference between the assets of the company (what it owns) and its liabilities (what it owes).
Non-contingent (debt)	A debt that is not dependent on the occurence of any future event to mature.
Nondischargeable (debt)	The types of obligations that cannot be forgiven in bankruptcy under the bankruptcy law.
Nonexempt Property	The types of property that a debtor may not keep in a bankruptcy situation.
Nonpurchase Money-Secured Loan	A debt owed to a creditor who took as security to ensure repayment, property the debtor already owned.
Notary Public	A person authorized, under the laws of a state, to administer oaths and accept acknowledgement of signatures to documents.
Option (Stock)	A written instrument which gives one the right to buy the stock of a corporation at a stated price within a stated time set forth in the instrument.
Paid-Up Capital	The amount of cash with which a new corporation started its business.

Partnership	A business organization among more than one person who join together to pull either property, time and labor in a joint business endeavor and to share the profits and losses in certain proportions.
Par Value	The face (nominal) value placed on a share of corporate stock (normally set by the incorporators).
Petition	A written request to a court for a specific action (such as a bankruptcy petition), as distinct from a suit against another party.
Plaintiff	The one who brings a civil lawsuit against another (the "defendant").
Pledge	A deposit of property to assure payment of a debt or obligation; a promise.
Power of Attorney	An authority given, in writing, by one person to another authorizing the said person to act for the giver in a specified capacity.
Preferred Stock	Shares of stock in a corporation which entitles the owner to some priority over the owners of common stocks in the distribution of profits, dividends, etc.
Principal	1. The one who employs, or in whose employ an agent works 2. The capital of an estate or trust 3. The original fund of money or deposit on which interest is paid
Priority	The state of being first in order of time or importance, e.g., priority debts.
Process	The summons, subpoena, warrant or other legal document used to compel a party or a witness to appear in court.
Promissory Note	A promise, in writing, to pay a certain sum of money to a person at a definite future time.
Pro Se	A person (usually a non-lawyer) who is acting for himself or representing himself in a court case.
Property	Everything a debtor owns, including the right to receive money from someone else.
Property in Trust	One administered for another's benefit.
Proprietorship	A lawful business or calling run by a natural person who does business as the sole owner.
Purchase Money-Secured Loan	A secured debt owed to the seller or lender who loaned the money with which the property itself was bought.

Prospectus	A statement circulated among prospective purchasers of corporate stocks or securities, describing the corporation, its operations and property to generate interest in the purchase of such stocks or securities.
Proxy	The authority to act or vote for another in one's absence.
Quasi-Public Corporation	A corporation which has been granted certain rights and powers usually exercised by governmental bodies, e.g., the public utility companies, the local Port Authority, etc.
Quorum	The number of persons required to be present or represented for a corporate business to be legally transacted.
Registered Agent	A natural person who is a resident of the state and has a business address within the state and is designated by a domestic or foreign corporation to receive process on its behalf and otherwise represent its interests.
Resolution (Corporate)	A written approval of the board of directors of a corporation authorizing certain actions.
Receiver	A person appointed by court to hold property in trust in a bankruptcy or other action.
Remainder	An estate expected but not received.
Replevin	Recovery of goods or property by legal action.
Repossess	The act of a creditor recovering from the debtor possession of property that was unpaid for.
Retained Earnings	That part of the corporation's profits retained by the corporation for business expansion and not distributed as dividend.
Reversion	The return of possession—e.g., return of a car to the seller upon failure to meet payments by a buyer.
Secured Debt	A debt arising out of a written security agreement by which the debtor pledges (puts up) certain property as a kind of "insurance" that he would repay the debt.

Usually, the pledge is in the form of a written agreement (or contract)—a so-called "conditional sales agreement" or "security agreement"—whereby the borrower promises that if he fails to pay as agreed, the creditor could take some particular item the debtor owns—either the same very item the debtor was to purchase, or another separate item the debtor already owned. Examples of transactions which may qualify as secured debts include the following: auto or motor appliance loan, furniture loan, home loan (1st or 2nd mortgage), chattel mortgage loan (loan secured against personal property or household goods), jewelry bills, merchandise loans, encyclopedia credit, etc. |

Under the bankruptcy rules, there are two basic types of secured debt. One type of secured debt (call it *"Type One" secured debt*) is one incurred when the item the creditor may take back ("repossess") in the event the debtor fails to pay, is *the same item* which the creditor sold the debtor or loaned him money to buy. With respect to this kind of secured debts (Type One kinds), the law is that the debtor in bankruptcy must return the secured property to the creditor—or pay for it. And, if he should want to pay the secured creditor for it, he is permitted to pay either the balance due on the debt, or the present fair market value of the property he purchased—whichever is the smaller amount.

The second type of secured debt (call it *"Type Two" secured debt*) is one where the property the debtor pledges to the creditor as "collateral" or "security" is *a separate asset* the debtor already owned. And with respect to this kind of secured debt, the debt would be dischargeable in bankruptcy while the debtor also keeps the property he pledged as collateral, as long as it is classifiable as "exempt" property under the bankruptcy code.

Security	Funds deposited or set aside to assure payment of a debt or the doing of certain act; a person (guarantor) who binds himself to pay a debt if someone else fails to pay it.
Stated Capital	This is calculated as the **sum** of: (1) the par-value of all shares with par value that have been issued, if any; (2) the amount of value received (in money or property) for all shares without par value that have been allocated to surplus in a manner permitted by law; and (3) such amounts as are not included in items (1) and (2) above, and may have otherwise been transferred to stated capital through distribution of shares, etc.
Stock Certificate	A written or printed certificate used as evidence of who owns what number of shares in a corporation.
Stockholder (same as Shareholder)	One who owns any number of shares of stock in a corporation.
Subpoena	A court order requiring a person to appear to give testimony or to produce some documents.
Substantial Consummation (of a bankruptcy Plan)	Defined under Sec. 1101(2) of the 1978 Bankruptcy Code, as meaning: A) transfer of all or substantially all of the property proposed by the reorganization plan to be transferred; B) assumption by the debtor or the successor to the debtor under the plan, of the business or of the management of all or substantially all of the property dealt with by the plan; and C) commencement of distribution under the plan.
Surplus	What is left of the assets of a corporation (if any) after you subtract from it both the liabilities and the "stated capital"

Surety	One who enters into a suretyship agreement with another person to be reponsible for the debt, default or wrong doing of a third party (the principal), if the principal does not perform as agreed.
Trade Name	A name other than one's personal name used by one engaged in business.
Trade Mark	A design, symbol, combination of letter or words identifying a product with its manufacturers.
Treasury Stock	Corporate Stocks of a corporation which have been issued and paid for by someone, but have later been bought back or otherwise reacquired by the corporation.
Trustee	A person who is charged with managing, guiding and supervising a bankruptcy petition through the court process.
Underwriter	As defined in Section 1145(b)(1) of the 1978 Bankruptcy Code, an entity is an "underwriter" if that entity (i) purchases a claim against the debtor or an interest in the debtor with a view to distribution of any security received in exchange for the claim or interest; (ii) offers to sell a security offered or sold under the plan on behalf of the holders of such security; (iii) offers to buy a security offered or sold under a plan for the holder of such security and under an agreement made in connection with the plan, with the consummation of the plan, or with the offer or sale of securities under the plan; or (iv) is an "issuer," as the term is used in Section 2(11) of the Securities Act of 1933.
Unliquidated Claim	A debt in dispute.
Unsecured Debt	A debt that is not secured by any pledge of property. Examples: utility bills, clothing bills, student loans, gas credit cards or bank credit cards, medical, hospital and doctors' bills, attorneys' bills, so-called "signature" loans, grocery bills, etc.
Unissued Stock	Corporate stock that has been authorized to be issued, but has not yet been so issued.
Value	The present, resalable market worth of a property, given its age and present condition.
Verification	Written confirmation of the truth of a document made and sworn to by a person.
Voting Trust	An arrangement to control the management of a corporation by placing in the hands of one person (or a group of persons), the right to vote the stockholders' shares.
Waive	To relinquish or give up a right.
Waiver	The intentional giving up of a right, usually made in writing (or implied from one's conduct).

APPENDIX **G**

SOME BIBLIOGRAPHY

"Americans Confront the Debt the House Built," Iver Peterson, *New York Times*, Sunday, Aug. 11, 1991, Sec. 4, p. 7.

Bankruptcy Code, Rules and Official Forms, ed. Timothy E. Travers. (The Lawyers Cooperative Publishing Co., Rochester, NY: 1991 Edition). Provides a single source of current, up-to-date, bankruptcy-related statutes and rules. Includes the final drafts of the proposed amendments to the Bankruptcy Rules and the Official Forms both of which took effect August 1, 1991.

"Bankruptcy Filings Up 24%," *New York Times*, Dec. 28, 1991.

"Bankruptcies Increase Sharply as the Stigma of Filing Fades," Jay Romano, *The New York Times*, Sunday, Nov. 24, 1991, Sec. 12, p. 1.

"The Banks that Built Connecticut Are Crumbling Under the Recession," Kirk Johnson, *The New York Times*, Sun. Oct. 17, 1991, p. L28.

Caplovitz, D. *Consumers in Trouble: A Study of Debtors in Default.* (New York, 1974). A study of the profile of consumer debtors who defaulted in installment purchases.

"Circle K Plans to Sell or Close 1,500 Stores," *New York Times*, Dec. 6, 1991, p. D4.

Collier on Bankruptcy, 15th ed. (Aug. 1991), Collier Bankruptcy Practice Guide. "Preliminary Draft of Proposed Amendments to the Federal Rules of Bankruptcy Procedure" (Mathew Bender, New York).

Consumer Bankruptcy Law and Practice 3rd ed. (National Consumer Law Center, Boston, MA). Comprehensive discussion of Chapter 7 bankruptcy procedures and the official bankruptcy forms.

Cook, Michael L. *Creative Uses of Chapter 11: Pitfalls and Tactics.* (New York: Practising Law Institute, 1984).

"Court Expands Use of Chapter 11," Linda Greenhouse, *New York Times*, June 14, 1991, p. D1.

Cowans, Daniel R. *Cowans Bankruptcy Law and Practice.* (1989 ed) (West Publishing Co: St. Paul, Minn.) 1991 supplement.

"Daily News Files for Bankruptcy But Seeks to Continue Publishing," Alex C. Jones, *New York Times*, Dec. 6, 1991, pp. A1 & D6.

"Economic Scene: Behind the Gloom of Consumers," Leonard Silk, *New York Times*, Nov. 29, 1991, p. D2.

11 U.S.C. (Title 11 of the United States Code).

Elias, Stephen, et. al. *How to File for Bankruptcy.* (Nolo Press, Berkeley, Ca. 1989).

Girth, Marjorie. *Bankruptcy Options for the Consumer.* (Practising Law Institute: New York, 1991). Discusses the factors that should be evaluated when the consumer is making selection between the two basic options open to debtors under the bankruptcy code — Chapters 7 and 13; the practical issues and questions involved in filing for bankruptcy.

"G.M. Picks 12 Plants to Be Shut As It Reports A Record U.S. Loss," *New York Times,* Feb. 25, 1992, p. 1.

"Grim Monday, General Motors Shutting Down N. Tarrytown Plant. 3,456 Jobs Lost." *New York Daily News,* Feb. 25, 1992, p. 1.

King, Lawrence P., et. al. *Bankruptcy,* 15th ed., Vol. 6 (Nov. 1991), (Mathew Bender, NY, 1991). Adresses cases under Chapters 7 & 13; Vol. 6 addresses cases under Chapter 11.

King, Lawrence P., et. al. *Collier on Bankruptcy,* 15th ed. (Matthew Bender, 1979).

Kosel, Janice. *Bankruptcy: Do It Yourself* (Addison Wesley Publishing Co., 1981).

Kosel, Janice. *Chapter 13: The Federal Plan to Repay Your Debts.* (Nolo Press, Berkeley, Ca., 1982).

"More Assets Shielded by Bankruptcy Ruling," Barry Meier, *New York Times,* June 14, 1991, p. D5.

Nash, Nathaniel. "Do-It-Yourself-Bankruptcy." *New York Times,* June 29, 1976, Sec. 3, p. 9.

New York Daily News, Aug. 26, 1979, p. 5.

New York Times, Dec. 20, 1978, p. C13.

New York Times, Dec. 15, 1979, p. 34.

"On the Rise: A New Breed of Debtors," *New York Times,* April 5, 1979, p. C1.

"Poor Finds Going Broke Is Too Costly," Jason DeParle, *New York Times,* Dec. 11, 1991, p. A24.

"Sons File for Bankruptcy For Private Maxwell Companies," Steven Prokesch, *New York Times,* Dec. 6, 1991, p. D7.

"The Unkindest Cuts of All: How Recession Did a Job on Jobs," *The New York Daily News,* Feb. 25, 1992, p. 45.

Williamson, John H. *The Attorney's Handbook on Small Business Reorganization Under Chapter 11,* Argyle Publishing Co., Lakewood, Co. (1990)

Wilson, Stephen D. *The Bankruptcy of America,* (Ridge Mills Press, Germantown, TN: 1991). Gives economic trends of the past leading to the present proliferation in bankruptcies, pinpointing turning points in the 1980s, such as the origins of the banking troubles, leveraged actions, etc.

Zweibel, Joel B. *Creditors' Rights Handbook Under the Bankruptcy Reform Act of 1978.* (Clark Boardman Co., Ltd., 1980). A comprehensive overview of the law of creditors' rights under the prevailing bankruptcy law. Presents the law in convenient text and outline format; useful for rapid access and ready reference on issues of representation in bankruptcy proceedings, how claims are treated and distribution procedures in Chapter 7 and 11 cases.

APPENDIX

ORDERING YOUR BANKRUPTCY FORMS FOR FILING ◑

The following is a list of bankruptcy forms and related forms or documents obtainable from the Do-It-Yourself Legal Publishers.

- -

(Customers: For your convenience, just make a zerox copy of this page and send it along with your order. All prices quoted here are subject to change without notice.)

TO: **Do-It-Yourself Legal Publishers,** Legal Forms Division
60 Park Place # Suite 1013,
Newark, NJ 07102

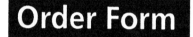

Please send me the initial petition forms for these types of bankruptcy:

	Quantity	Price
Chapter 7 kit, for an individual(s) not engaged in business @ $29 each . . . . •	_____	_____
Chapter 7 kit, for a business person (sole proprietor, partner, corporation) @ $29 each	_____	_____
Chapter 13 kit @ $29.50 each (specify if proprietor or individual).	_____	_____
Chapter 11 (business reorganization) kit @ $49.95 each	_____	_____
Motion Forms (the set) to file for Retention of secured property @ $20 each . . . •	_____	_____

(specify which one: "Reaffirmation", "Redemption", or "Avoidance")

Subtotal · · · · · · · · _____
Postage $5 (each)
Sales Tax . . . . _____
Grand Total . . . . . _____

Enclosed is the sum of $_____ to cover the order, including $$5 per kit for shipping, plus the local sales tax, as applicable.

Send the order to me:

Mr/Mrs/Ms/Dr._____
Address (include Zip Code please):_____
_____Zip_____
Phone No. and area code: (____)_____Job: (____)_____
*New Jersey residents enclose 6% sales tax.

IMPORTANT: Please do NOT rip out the page. Consider others! Just make a photocopy and send.

Appendix I

LIST OF OTHER PUBLICATIONS FROM
DO-IT-YOURSELF LEGAL PUBLISHERS

Please DO NOT tear out this page. Consider others!

The following is a list of books obtainable from the Do-It-Yourself Publishers/Selfhelper Law Press of America.

(Customers: For your convenience, just make a photocopy of this page and send it along with your order. All prices quoted here are subject to change without notice.)

1. How To Draw Up Your Own Friendly Separation/Property Settlement Agreement With Your Spouse
2. Tenant Smart: How To Win Your Tenants' Legal Rights Without A Lawyer (New York Edition)
3. How To Probate & Settle An Estate Yourself Without The Lawyers' Fees ($35)
4. How To Adopt A Child Without A Lawyer
5. How To Form Your Own Profit/Non-Profit Corporation Without A Lawyer
6. How To Plan Your 'Total' Estate With A Will & Living Will, Without a Lawyer
7. How To Declare Your Personal Bankruptcy Without A Lawyer ($29)
8. How To Buy Or Sell Your Own Home Without A Lawyer or Broker ($29)
9. How To File For Chapter 11 Business Bankruptcy Without A Lawyer ($32.95)
10. How To Legally Beat The Traffic Ticket Without A Lawyer (forthcoming)
11. How To Settle Your Own Auto Accident Claims Without A Lawyer ($29)
12. How To Obtain Your U.S. Immigration Visa Without A Lawyer ($28)
13. How To Do Your Own Divorce Without A Lawyer [10 Regional State-Specific Volumes] ($35)
14. How To Legally Change Your Name Without A Lawyer
15. How To Properly Plan Your 'Total' Estate With A Living Trust, Without The Lawyers' Fees ($35)
16. Legally Protect Yourself In A Gay/Lesbian Or Non-Marital Relationship With A Cohabitation Agreement
17. Before You Say 'I do' In Marriage Or Co-Habitation, Here's How To First Protect Yourself Legally
18. The National Home Mortgage reduction Kit (forthcoming) ($26.95)
19. The National Home Mortgage Qualification Kit ($28.95)

Prices: Each book, except for those specifically priced otherwise, costs $26, plus $5 per book for postage and handling. New Jersey residents please add 6% sales tax. **ALL PRICES ARE SUBJECT TO CHANGE WITHOUT NOTICE**

CUSTOMERS: Please make and send a zerox copy of this page with your orders)

ORDER FORM

TO: *Do-It-Yourself Legal Publishers* (Books Division)
60 Park Place # Suite 1013, Newark, NJ 07102

Please send me the following:
1. _____ copies of _____
2. _____ copies of _____
3. _____ copies of _____
4. _____ copies of _____

Enclosed is the sum of $_____ to cover the order. *Mail my order to:*
Mr./Mrs.//Ms/Dr. _____
Address (include Zip Code please): _____
_____
Phone No. and area code: ( ) _____ Job: ( ) _____
*New Jersey residents enclose 6% sales tax.

IMPORTANT: Please do NOT rip out the page. Consider others! Just make a photocopy and send it.

SUBJECT INDEX

Absolute priority rule, defined, 106
Acceptance or rejection of plan:
    acceptance, w hat constitutes, 95-6
    ballot for, 95
    binding, w hat constitutes a, 96
    computing the requisite majorities for, 97
    disclosure hearing in, 89
    disclosure requirements in, 91-3
    eligible parties to cast votes for, 95
    notice of time for filing, 170
    solicitation of, 94-5
    voting requirements for, 95-7
    voting not in good faith in, 97
Adequate assurance, of future performance of contract or lease, 131
Adequate information (in disclosure statement), 90-3
Adequate protection,
    burden of proof, 120
    form of, 120
    w hat constitutes, 83, 118
Administrative convenience, 86, 202
Administrative expenses and claims
    allow ability, 204
    payment of in Plan, 202
    w hat constitutes, 85-6
Allow ance of claims (or interests)
    bar date for filing proof of claim for, 127;
    determination status and amount of disputed, contingent or unliquidated, 126-7;
    duty by debtor in possession (or trustee) to determine accurate status of, 126;
    filing proof of claim in, 126-7;
    objecting to improper, the procedures for, 127-9;
    w hat constitutes, 95-104
Alternatives to Chapter 11, 14-15
Application, see Motion
Assessment, preliminary of the case, 28
Assets, Schedules of, 34-6
Assignment for the benefit of creditors, 53
Assignment of Executory Contract, see Executory contracts
Assumption of executory contract, see Executory contracts
Attorney,
    employment of by debtor, 11, 30, 73, 185-7;
    court approval of, 73;
    role of in putting together a Plan, 88;
    ignorance of the bankruptcy process by the average, v
Automatic stay,
    adequate protection in action for relief from, 70, 118;
    effect of on creditors & collection actions, 15, 117;
    grounds for relief from, 117-9;
    handling motion for relief from, 117-120;
    motion for relief from, the procedures for, 119
Avoidable transfers, 29

Bad faith, filing bankruptcy in, 26
Bankruptcies,
    cases among the top ten in New York, 2;
    causes of the present record filings of, 2, 4;
    tide of, 2, 4;
    unemployment as cause of, 2, 11-12
Bankruptcy Clerk
    filing the petition w ith, 68;
    local court rules or forms and the, 33
Bankruptcy literacy, need to have, iv-v, 5, 6

Bankruptcy mentality, 1
Baptist Medical Center of New York, v
Bar date, fixing of the, 127
Barron's Magazine, 19
    Stan Kulp of, 19, 85
Best interests test, 102
Business,
    operation of by the debtor during case, 79-83, 116-119
    sale of assets of, 123-6
Business failures, 2
    causative factors for, 11-13;
    deterioration in the deby quality as cause of, 13;
    empirical characteristics of firms that failed, 11;
    internal causes of, underlying causes of, 13
Business judgment rule, 132
Byram, Thomas L., v

Cash collateral, 83
    making use of by Debtor-in-Possession, procedures for, 124
        w hat constitutes, 123-4
Chapter 11, see Plan, also
    some major companies w hich survived, 15;
    discharge under, 70, 111;
    disadvantages of filing for, 14;
    how it w orks in a nutshell, 7, 16;
    misconceptions and ignorance about, v;
    nature of the the relief obtainable under, 19;
    should you file for, 13;
    some alternatives to filing, 14;
    stigma about undertaking, 1, 3, 14;
    the most important advantages of for the debtor, 10;
    pre-confirmation of, 111;
    post-confirmation of, 112;
    tide in the filing of, 2, 4;
    w hat is, 9
Chapter 13 bankruptcy
    advantages of, 18; meaning of and differences as against bankruptcy, 13, 17-18
Claims,
    acceptance of in Plan, 95;
    allow ance of, 126-9;
    allow ed, w hat constitutes, 95-6, 127;
    disputed, unliquidated or contingent, 126-8;
    handling of, generally, 126-9;
    impaired, see impaired claims;
    secured, see secured claims;
    supersuperiority, 203
    unsecured, see unsecured claims
Classification of claims in the Plan,
    disputes, handling of, 126-9;
    establishing the order of priority in, 203-4
    impaired claims, 205-6
    priority claims, 200; three specific types not needing classification, 202
    principles governing, 201;
    secured, 200, 203;
    substantially similar claims, 199, 202-3;
    small claims, 202;
    subordination, 200-1, 204;
    treatment of under the plan, 126-9;
    the procedures, generally, 199-200;
    unsecured, 200, 202
Co-debtors, completing the schedule of, 47, 49
Collection actions, stopping of by filing Chapter 11, 10, 9

SUBJECT INDEX

Commission on the Bankruptcy Law s of the United States (1973), 11
   report of the, 14;
   study of business failures by Eric Fredland for, 12
Committee of Creditors
   advisory role of on a Plan, 74-5;
   appointment of, 71;
   composition of, 71-2;
   pow ers and duties of, 72-6
Committee of equity security holders, 72
Committee of unsecured creditors, 71
Commodity broker, 26
Community propert, 34
Conditions precedent to implementation of a Plan, 113
Conference Board, study of corporate debt published by, 13
Confirmation,
   Order of, 111; effects of, 111; pre-confirmation, 111;
   post-confirmation, 111
Confirmation hearing,
   burden of proof on debtor at, 100;
   categories of, 100;
   conduct and procedures of, generally, 98-101;
   matters to establish at, 100-3;
   notice of, 99
Confirmation of Plan
   best interest of creditor test, 102, 111;
   cramdow n standards of, 100-101, 105;
   legal effects of for the debtor, creditor or shareholders, 109-111
   requirements for,
     court approval of payments, 101-2;
     disclosure of management and insiders, 102;
     fairness and equity, 105-6;
     feasibility, 104, 111
     good faith approval, 103
     no unfair discrimination, 105;
     payment of priority claims, 103
   Section 1129(a) standards of, the 13 requirements for, 101-104
Congress, w hy it enacted the bankruptcy law , iii
Consummated Plan, 17, 112, 115
Contractual subordination, 201
Credit Union, 26
Current expenditures of debtor, completing the schedule of, 46, 49

Debt Quality in American Business, 13
Debtor in possession,
   definition of,16;
   duties of, generally, 116-132;
   handling claims dispute by, 126-130;
   handling executory contracts and expired leases by, 130;
   meaning and effect of, 16, 74;
   open new bank account in the name of, 122;
   operation of business by, 120-3;
   rights, pow ers and duties of, 82-3, 116-132;
   w hy most debtors are left in the position of, 77-78;
Declaration concerning debtor's schedules, 51;
Discharge of debtor, the nature of in Chapter 11, 114
Disclosure Statement,
   adequate information in, w hat constitutes, 92-3;
   court's approval of, 91, 93;
   degree of disclosure required, 93;
   filing requirements, 91;
   hearing on, 91;
   importance of, 92;
   notice of hearing on, 156;

   notice requirements, 91;
   objections to, 91;
   preparation of, generally, 92-3;
   requirements of, 92-3;
   w hat is, 16
Discrimination, unfair, w hat constitutes in a Plan, 105-6
Disinterested persons, 83
Dismissal or conversion of case, 17
Disposable income, 18
Docket number, assignment and significance of, 68
Dynamic corporation of America, i, iv

Eligibility requirements for Chapter 11, 26-7
Emergency filing situation, 69
Engagement in business, as no disqualification to file for Chapter 11, 26
Enron, 2, 4
Equitable subordination, 201
Equity cushion, 119
Examination of debtor by creditors, 77
Examiner,
   appointment of, 81;
   conditions for ap;pointment of, 81;
   sample report of investigation of the, 139
Execution of a Plan, 102; adequate means of, 86
Executory contracts and unexpired leases,
   adequate assurance in, 130;
   assignment of, 131;
   assumption of, 87, 131;
   business judgment rule in, 132;
   completing the schedules of, 42, 45;
   handling of, generally, 130-2;
   ipso facto clauses in, 130;
   rejection of, 131;
   w hat constitutes, 130
Exempt property, 37

Failures, causes of business,11, 27
Federal-Mogul Corp, 2
Fees for filing, 10, 69
Fiduciary obligation, of creditors' committee, 83
Filing (Chapter 11 case), step-by-step procedures for, 25-108
Finova Group, 2
First Executive Corp, 2, 4
First meeting of creditors, 67
Fisher, Stanley, 4
Forms,
   official, 33;
   how to fill out the, 31;
   list of sample forms cited in the manual, 133-4;
   local, handling, 33;
   obtaining (ordering) the necessary bankruptcy, 31, 228;
   signing the, 68;
   substantial compliance requirements for, 33
Fredland, Eric Professor., 11
Frozen cold, debt collection actions, 10
Functional equivalence, 6

Gibraltar Financial Corp., 2
Global Crossing, 2, 4
Good faith, plan proposed in, 26, 103
Going concern value of property, 103, 106
Grant, W.T., iv
Great Depression, i, iii

Grounds for relief, from automatic stay, 117-9

Hearing requirements,
   confirmation of plan;
   disclosure statement, 89;
   motion for relief from stay, 120;
   sale of estate property, 124;
   use of cash collateral, 125
Haboian, Tony., 14
HomeFed Corp., 2

I.B.M., 20
Impaired claims
   treatment of in Plan,,, 86;
   w hat constitutes, 205
Imperial Corp, 2
Implementation of plan, 103, 112
Insider, 29, 103
Insurance company, 26
Interests, 204
Internal causes of business failures, 13
International business corporation, 20
Interstate Stoves, i
Involuntary petition, see Petition
Ipso facto clause, 18
Itel Corporation, 19

Judicial, procedure for Chapter 11 bankruptcy, 9

Kellogg Graduate School, see Northw estern University
KMart Corporation, 2, 4
Kulp, Stan, Barron's w riter, 19, 85

Last resort, bankruptcy as, 14
Lees, Francis A., study of corporate debt by, 13
Lerner, Eugene, Professor of Finance, Northw estern Univ., 19
Liabilities, Schedules of, 39-42
Liquidation value of property, 119
List of creditors crditors holding 20 largest unsecured claims, 57-8
Literacy in bankruptcy, iv, v, 5, 6
Little guy, 72
Lloyd's of London, 20, 23
Local rules on forms, 33

Maloon, James H., 20, 22
Manville Corporation, v
MCorp, 2, 4
Meat and beef of the manual, Chapter 3 as the, 5
Meeting of creditors, 76
   conduct of the creditors and debtors at the, 77-8;
   examination of the debtor at, 77;
   purpose of the, 77
Michaels, David P., v
Miller, Harvey R., ii, iv
Miller-Wohl, i
Modification of Plan,
   before confirmation of plan, 97-98, 111
   after confirmation of plan, 97-98, 111, 114-115
Moratorium on payment by the filing of Chapter 11 petition, 16
Motion (Application)
   for appoinment of examiner, 81-3
   for approval of compensation of debtor's officers, 183;
   for authority to assume Executory contract/lease, 182;

for authority to employ attorney for special purposes, 185;
   for authority to emply attorney (or accountant, etc) for general services, 187;
   for authority to use cash collateral, 184;
   for authority to obtain credit, 184;
   for authority to pay claims of debtor's employees, 196;
   for relief from automatic stay, 119, 178
    burden of proof, 120;
    generally, 117-120;
    hearing requirement, 120;
    procedure for, 119;
    sample of, 178
   for conversion to Chapter 7, 172;
   for employment of accountants (or appraisers, auctineers, etc), 188;
   to modify the amount of debt w ith utility company;
   to object to confirmation of plan, 173;
   to terminate appointment of trustee, 138
Murphy, Patrick, iii

New Jersey Psychological Association, 3
New lease on life for a company, Chapter 11 as, i, iii, 11
New popularity of Chapter 11, ii
Non-cash collateral property,
   making use of by the debtor in possession, procedures for, 125
   w hat constitutes a, 125
Northw estern University's Kellogg Graduate School, 19
Notice,
   of first meeting of creditors and stockholders, 126;
   of hearing on disclosure statement, 156;
   of order confirming plan and discharge, 177;
   of proposed sale of estate property and of hearing thereof, 195;
   of time for filing acceptances or rejections of plans, 170-3
Notice of hearing, w hat constitutes under the Code, 125

Objection,
   to allow ance of claims, 127-9, 192;
   to confirmation of plan, 98-100, 173;
   to proposed sale of estate property, 123-6
Ongoing business, being engaged in, 26
Operation of debtor's business, by debtor in possession, 120-127
Order,
   approving disclosure statement, 89-90, 94;
   authorizing assumption of executory contract/lease, 181;
   authorizing employment of accountants, etc., 188;
   authorizing employment of attorney, 186;
   authorizing trustee/debtor-in-possession to reject executory contract or lease;
   for relief from automatic stay, 76;
   directing the appointment of trustee, 137;
   modifying the amount of deposit w ith utility company, 189;
   of confirmation of plan or reorganization, 107, 174, 176;
   reducing claim, 191, ordinary course of business, definition of, 125

Pacific Gas & Electric, 2, 4
Partially secured claims, 38, 129
Party in interest, 72
Penn Central Corporation, i, iv
Penn-Dixie Steel Corp., i, iv
Personal property, 34-5
Petition (for Chapter 11),
   general procedures for filing, 25;
   step-by-step procedures for filing, 25-108;
   w here and how to file, 68;

SUBJECT INDEX

w ho may file, 26
Plan (Chapter 11) Confirmation hearing,
   cramdow n method of, 16;
   regular method, 16
Plan (of Reorganization),
   acceptance or rejection of by creditors, 16
   ballot for accepting or rejecting, 171
   classification of claims and interests in, 85
   conditions precedent for implementation of, 113
   confirmation of, 98
   consummation of, 107, 112-5
   debtor's right to exclusively file a, 84
   execution, adequate means of in a, 86, 101
   fairness and feasibility tests in, 85, 104
   filing of by parties in interest, 84
   formulation principle for, according to Stan Kulp, 85
   fundamental objective of a, 85
   impaired claims, treatment of, 86
   implementation of, 86
   modification of in period of, 114-115
   modification of (sample copy of form), 172
   motion to object to confirmation of (sample form), 173
   notice of order confirming (sample form), 177
   notice of time of hearing on (sample form), 170
   post-confirmation functions to be performed under, 111-112
   putting together of, generally, 88
   requirements, generally, 85-7
   role of creditors in preparation of, 88
   rule of absolute priority in, 106
   section 1111(b) election in, 129
   sample copies of, 157, 161, 167
   substantial consummation of, 115
   time for filing, 84
Post-confirmation, see Plan (of Reorganization)
Practice copies (of Forms), 31
Pre-confirmation, 111, see also Plan (of Reorganization)
Preferential transfers, 29
Priority of claims and interests, order of payment in, 203-4
Proof of claim, 123-4
Psychological disposition, 1
Purifying or cleansing implications of bankruptcy, 19, 20

Real property, 34, 35
Recession, economic recession in the national economy, 1-3, 11-13
Redfield, 21
Reliance Group Hldgs, 2
Relief from automatic stay,
   for cause, 9, 118;
   for lack of debtor's equity in property, 9, 117
Romance, ii
Rule of absolute priority, 106

Schedule of liabilities, 38
Second chance, 80
Section 341(a) Meeting, 76
Section 1111(B0 election, 129
Secured claims
   calculating the market value of, 38-40
   schedule of, 38-40
Sex appeal, ii
Setoff, 129
Signing the forms, 68
Small Business debtor, 30, 33, 71

Southeast Banking Corp, 2
Statement of financial affairs, 52-6
Statutory subordination, 201
Steps, 16 systematic involved in Chapter 11 case, 25
Stigma of bankruptcy, dramatic change in, 1, 3
Street smartness, bankruptcy, iii
St. Johns University, Prof. Francis A. Lee of, 13
Strong-arm pow ers of trustees, 83
Stockholder, eligibility to file for Chapter 11, 12, 26
Substantial consummation, of the Plan, 98, 115
Substantially similar claims, 199, 202-3
Superpriority claims, 203

Texaco, 2, 4
Tide, in bankruptcy filings, 2
Time and notice requirements for Chapter 11, 70
Timidity, attitude of tow ards bankruptcy by business managers, 1
Togut, Segal., 3
Top bankruptcies in U.S. history, 2, 4
Toys 'R' Us, i, iv
Transfers, preferential and fraudulent, 29; avoidable, 29
Trustee,
   appointment of, 85
   debtor's application to terminate appointment of, 138
   order appointing, 137
   sample report of investigation by, 139
   strong-arm pow ers of, 129
   United States, see United States Trusteee

Unemployment, as cause of bankruptcy, 2t
Unimpaired claims under the plan, 86
United Airlines, 4
United States Trustee, appointment of of Creditors
   committee by, 71, 77
University, George Washington, study of business failures by Prof.
   Eric Fredland of, 11
Unsecured gap claims, 202
Unsecured nonpriority claims, completing the schedule of, 42, 43, 44
Unsecured priority claims, completing the schedule of, 40-41

Violation, of court order, 10;
   attempt to collect after the filing of bankruptcy as a, 10

Williamson, John H.,
   on adequacy of disclosure statement, 27, 92-3
   on conduct of the debtor and creditors at meeting of creditors, 78-9
   on the core fundamentals for putting together a good plan, 88
   on the role of creditors' committee in formulation of plan, 75
Williams, Winston., 14